# INTERNATIONAL INTERVENTION

## IN THE

# POST–COLD WAR WORLD

# INTERNATIONAL INTERVENTION

## IN THE

# POST–COLD WAR WORLD

Moral Responsibility
and Power Politics

⁓

EDITORS

Michael C. Davis,
Wolfgang Dietrich,
Bettina Scholdan,
and Dieter Sepp

*M.E.Sharpe*
Armonk, New York
London, England

#51763845

**Library of Congress Cataloging-in-Publication Data**

International intervention in the post–Cold War world : moral responsibility and power
politics / Michael C. Davis, Wolfgang Dietrich, Bettina Scholdan, and Dieter Sepp, editors.
    p. cm.
    Includes bibliographical references and index.
    ISBN 0-7656-1244-5 (cloth : alk. paper)
    1. Humanitarian intervention. 2. World politics—1989– I. Davis, Michael C., 1949–
II. Dietrich, Wolfgang. III. Scholdan, Bettina. IV. Sepp, Dieter.

JZ6369.I58 2004
341.5′84—dc21

2003042791

Printed in the United States of America

# Contents

# About the Editors and Contributors

**Franca D'Agostini**, a native of Turin, Italy, completed her doctorate in philosophy at the University of Turin and teaches contemporary philosophy at the Faculty of Engineering (Politecnico). She is the author of *Analitici e continentali* (1997), *Breve storia della filosofia nel Novecento* (1999), *Logica del nichilismo* (2000), and *Disavventure della verità* (2002) and contributes to the newspapers *la Stampa* and *il Manifesto*.

**Rasheed Akinyemi** is a lecturer in comparative and international politics at the Institute for Political Science, University of Vienna, Austria, where he also received his master's and doctorate in political science. His areas of research include African political systems, Islam and political culture, and civil society and the state in Africa. His recent publications include the book chapters "Zivilgesellschaft als Entwicklungspotenzial in Afrika" (2002) and "Der afrikanische Sozialismus als ein visionäres Modell für die Identität und den Aufbau von Nationen in Afrika"/(2000).

**Peter R. Baehr** is Emeritus professor of human rights. In his academic career, he has served as professor of international relations at the University of Amsterdam; executive secretary and later member of the Scientific Council for Government Policy, The Hague; professor of human rights and foreign policy, Leiden University; and professor of human rights and director, Netherlands Institute of Human Rights, Utrecht University. Recent books in English include *The United Nations at the End of the 1990s*, 3rd ed. (1999), coauthored with Leon Gordenker; *Human Rights: Universality in Practice*, 2nd ed. (2001); and *Human Rights in the Foreign Policy of the Netherlands* (2002), coauthored with Monique Castermans-Holleman and Fred Grunfeld. He studied political science at the University of Amsterdam and Georgetown University.

**Giovanna Bono** is a senior research fellow in European security at the Department of Peace Studies at Bradford University, England. She has a doctorate in international relations from the University of Kent. Her recent publications include the article two book chapters "Implementing the Headline Goals: Institutional Aspects and Consequences," in J. Krause, A. Wenger, and L. Watanbe (eds.), *Unraveling the European Security and Defence Conundrum* (2003), and "Democratic Accountability of Military and Police Ooperation in the EU," in Hans Born and Heiner Hangii (ed.) *Defining the Democratic Deficit* (2003), and the book *NATO's "Peace-Enforcement" Tasks and "Policy Communities," 1990–1999* (2003) and a variety of articles on the European security and defense theme.

**Chris Corrin** is professor of feminist politics at the University of Glasgow, where she teaches feminist theory, politics of protest, and politics of gender in development. She is the convenor of the International Centre for Gender and Women's Studies, and since the 1980s her work with women's groups has supported her research focus on feminist theory and gendered political perspectives, particularly in central and southeastern Europe. Her current research is on women's human rights, violence against women, women's political participation, and gender issues in development studies. Recent publications include *Magyar Women: Hungarian Women's Lives, 1960s–1990s* (1994), *Women in a Violent World: Feminist Analyses and Responses* (1996), *Feminist Perspectives on Politics* (1999), *Gender and Identity in Central and Eastern Europe* (1999), *The Gender Audit of Reconstruction Programmes in South Eastern Europe* (2000), and a variety of articles.

**Robert Cryer** is a lecturer in law at the University of Nottingham, where he teaches criminal law and international law, including international legal theory, international criminal law, and the law of collective security. He received his bachelor of laws at Cardiff University, and his master of laws and doctorate at the University of Nottingham. He was previously a lecturer in law at the University of Manchester. He has published mainly in the area of international law, in particular the law relating to the UN Security Council, international courts, the threat or use of force, and international criminal law. He has also published in the areas of international legal theory and international economic law. He is a book review editor of, and a regular contributor to, the *Journal of Conflict and Security Law.*

**Michael C. Davis** is a professor of law at the Chinese University of Hong Kong. He has served as the Schell Senior Fellow at the Orville Schell Jr. Center for International Human Rights at the Yale Law School, the Frederick K. Cox Visiting Professor of Human Rights Law at Case Western Reserve University Law School, and a visiting scholar at the Harvard Law School. He is the chair of both the Human Rights Research Committee of the International Political Science Association and the Pacific Rim Interest Group of the American Society of International Law and is an editor of the newly established *Journal of Human Rights.* He is author of *Constitutional*

*Confrontation in Hong Kong* (1990) and editor of *Human Rights and Chinese Values* (1995). His publications on such topics as the political economy of human rights, human rights and political culture, humanitarian intervention, constitutionalism, and global order have appeared in a wide range of journals. He has degrees from the Ohio State University, the University of California, and the Yale Law School.

**Wolfgang Dietrich** is a professor of political science at the Institute for Political Sciences, University of Innsbruck, where he has been a member of the faculty since 1986. He has also served on the faculty of the International Center for Peace and Development Studies at the University of Castellón in Spain since 1998. He is the academic director of the Austrian Institute for Latin America and program director of the Master's Program for Peace, Development and International Conflict Transformation at the University of Innsbruck. He is the author of eight books and numerous papers, including *Periphere Integration und Frieden im Weltsystem—Ostafrika, Zentralamerikaund Südostasien im Vergleich* (1998).

**Mark D. Evans** is an analyst with the New Zealand Ministry of Defence. He was previously a lecturer in international relations at the Faculty of International Studies, International Pacific College, Palmerston North, New Zealand, where he chaired the local branch of the New Zealand Institute of International Affairs. His publications to date have focused on China, India, and the English School of International Relations. He received his master's degree from Griffith University, Australia. Under a Claude McCarthy Fellowship and a University of Waikato Postgraduate Scholarship, he completed his doctorate with the University of Waikato in Hamilton, New Zealand. The views expressed in his chapter are his own and do not represent those of the New Zealand Ministry of Defence.

**Victoria Tin-bor Hui** is an assistant professor in political science at the University of Illinois. She has a forthcoming book, *War and State Formation in Ancient China and Early Modern Europe.* After receiving her doctorate with distinction from the political science department at Columbia University, she was a postdoctoral fellow at the Olin Institute for Strategic Studies at Harvard University and at the Center for International Security and Cooperation at Stanford University. In pursuing her graduate studies, she received dissertation fellowships from the Harry Frank Guggenheim Foundation and the Institute for the Study of World Politics.

**Daniela Ingruber** is a freelance researcher in the field of civic education and foreign affairs and works as a researcher in the field of mediation and participation at the Austrian Society for Environment and Technology. Since 2000, she has been teaching at the Institute of Political Science, University of Innsbruck, Austria, and at various universities and academies in the former Soviet Union. Her publications include *Friedensarbeit in El Salvador*

(1999). She has written articles on development cooperation, peace work, civic education in Austria, the Internet and democracy, cryptography, and disinformation.

**Nathalie Karagiannis** has recently completed a doctorate on the articulation of the concepts of responsibility and efficiency in the development discourse of the European Union from the 1970s to the end of the 1990s (forthcoming, 2004, Pluto Press). She currently lives in Zimbabwe.

**Hiroki Kusano** is a doctoral candidate in the international relations program at Sophia University, Japan, where he also received his master's in international relations and bachelor's in journalism. He has published the article "America no Gunji Kainyû no Henyô" ("The Transformation of American Military Intervention") in *The Jouurnal of International Studies*, No. 46, 2000. His doctoral research likewise considers U.S. intervention practice over the past one hundred years.

**Rebecca R. Moore** is a NATO Fellow and an associate professor of political science at Concordia College, Moorhead, Minnesota. She is currently working on a book on the evolution of NATO's political dimension. Her previous research and publications have focused on democracy promotion and U.S. human rights policy.

**Bettina Scholdan** is head of the Austrian Centre for Country of Origin and Asylum Research and Documentation (ACCORD), which is affiliated with the Austrian Red Cross. She has published articles on minority rights jurisprudence and critical race theory, the impact of international administration on postconflict societies, as well as refugee protection and development aid in the European Union, and has conducted human rights research and reporting on sub-Saharan Africa, Afghanistan, and the former Yugoslavia. Since 1999, she has been the coeditor of the ACCORD/UNHCR European Country of Origin Information Seminar Series. In 1997 and 1998, she was a visiting scholar at Columbia Law School. She is currently completing her doctorate in political science at the University of Vienna, exploring the impact of U.S. legal culture on minority politics.

**Dieter Sepp** is a social scientist in Vienna. After concentrating on comparative studies on democratization in Africa and the concept of liberal democracy during his graduate studies at the University of Vienna, as well as during his postgraduate program at the Institute for Advanced Studies in Vienna, he has gradually shifted his interests toward the role of information technology in modern politics and modern society in Europe. He has participated in several research and publication projects at the Institute for Technology Assessment, which is part of the Austrian Academy of Science. After conducting research projects in France and in Africa, he presented a paper on promoting democracy and human rights in Africa at the 1999 Human Rights Research Committee Conference and was instrumental in hosting a workshop for the present project. Currently, he is doing a documentation project with an Austrian software firm specializing in securities trade. He has written several articles on human rights and democratization in Africa.

**Alice Sindzingre** is a senior researcher at the Centre National de la Recherche Scientifique, the national French public agency for research, where she has worked since 1983. She has conducted research on development economics and political economy, mostly in sub-Saharan Africa, has served as a consultant for international organizations and governments, and has been a member of the Core Team of the World Development Report 2000/1 of the World Bank, "Attacking Poverty." She is a member of numerous academic societies in France and abroad, and has published on a large range of topics, including political economy of development, international cooperation, corruption, African politics, poverty, and rural economics. She holds a master's in business science from the University Paris IX-Dauphine and a postgraduate diploma in economics from the National Institute of Statistics and Economic Administration.

**Tania Voon** is a WM Tapp Scholar, an Honorary Cambridge Commonwealth Trust Scholar, and a doctoral candidate in law at Gonville and Caius College, University of Cambridge. She completed her master of laws at Harvard University and her bachelor of laws and bachelor of science at the University of Melbourne. She has practiced both public and private law and is currently a senior fellow of the Asia Pacific Centre for Military Law, University of Melbourne Law School. Her writing on such topics as the law of armed conflict, military justice, international trade, and state sovereignty has appeared in a variety of academic journals and books.

# Acknowledgments

This book grew out of a workshop in Vienna, Austria, in August 2001 held under the auspices of the Human Rights Research Committee of the International Political Science Association. This workshop brought together a diverse group of scholars specifically interested in the relationship between morality and power politics in international intervention actions. We sought to explore often-neglected issues in respect of the growing practice of military intervention for humanitarian purposes. Subsequent collaborative efforts have enabled us to further develop arguments initiated in the Vienna workshop. These ongoing discussions have allowed us to sharpen our arguments to present a challenge to the mainstream discourse and tease out the common theoretical issues and foundations reflected in the chapters of this book. While our views remain diverse, we are hopeful that we have raised some serious challenges in respect of state practices in this area.

At this stage, we would like to thank the sponsors and organizers of our Vienna workshop. At the top of our list in this regard is the Austrian Political Science Association that, with the great efforts of coeditors Wolfgang Dietrich, Bettina Scholdan, and Dieter Sepp, hosted the Vienna workshop. Funding support for the workshop was provided by the Renner-Institut, the Austrian Federal Ministry for Sciences and Art, the Municipality of Vienna, the Chamber of Labour, the British Council, and the Istituto Italiano Cultura di Vienna. As the editor responsible for coordinating the preparation of this book, I would like to thank my two research assistants, Elizabeth Lee and Orianne Dutka, who have assisted at various stages of the editing process. I would especially like to thank the East Asian Legal Studies Program at Harvard University and its director, Professor William Alford, for hosting me for one year at the conceptualization phase of this effort. Finally, we would all like to express our appreciation to the many participants in our original workshop, contributors to various seminars where our ideas have been presented, and the unknown reviewers of our manuscript.

Michael C. Davis, Hong Kong

# INTERNATIONAL INTERVENTION

IN THE

# POST–COLD WAR

## WORLD

# 1

# The Emerging World Order

## State Sovereignty and Humanitarian Intervention

### Michael C. Davis

There have been at least two distinct kinds of war in the post–Cold War period, each of which brings its own set of challenges to human rights and global institutions.[1] The first, humanitarian intervention, came earlier in the form of military responses to humanitarian crises. For these crises, the United Nations' (UN) framework has sometimes proved inadequate. The second, wars primarily based on claims of national defense—evident in Afghanistan, Iraq, and the so-called war on terrorism—has grabbed our attention since September 11, 2001. Such wars, though claimed to be sanctioned by the right of self-defense under UN Charter Article 51, sometimes in combination with a UN Security Council initiative under UN Charter Chapter VII, have spawned expansions of the notion of self-defense in ways that severely challenge the charter regime.[2]

The human rights focus of each of these two types of war is somewhat different. Humanitarian intervention is primarily about protecting entire populations of people against ethnic cleansing and genocide and holding individual elites accountable for such crimes. The current crop of defensive wars and their offshoots have primarily focused human rights attention on the changing character of war, expansive notions of self-defense, the applicability of international standards for belligerents in the fields of battle, and the sources and boundaries of terrorism, though humanitarian concerns are also generally implicated.

In spite of these differences, both cases have common foundations in communal conflicts and both have arisen out of similar circumstances. Among these two pressing areas of human rights concern, this book focuses primarily on the former, though the interconnectedness between the two will sometimes bring our attention back to the latter.

Humanitarian crises of vast proportions, often brought on by communal or ethnic conflicts, have been among the defining events of the post–Cold War world order. The cries of human anguish caused by these events have

3

captured our global media and our political debate. We have, however, inherited an international regime that, in its current state of practice, often appears inadequate to the task of coping with these events. International responses to humanitarian crises are often too late or nonexistent, and when they do occur, they are often inadequate. These kinds of events are sure to repeat themselves. How this debate will shape the instruments of world peace, especially the use of intervention to avert humanitarian crises, is a matter of great concern in the post–Cold War era.

A variety of conceptual questions are involved in the debate over humanitarian intervention, including issues of moral responsibility, strategic concerns, appropriate standards for intervention, the nature of the modern state, and the like.[3] Practical factors that shape global attitudes toward these issues include the prevalence of ethnic domination and the intractability of ethnic disputes, principles respecting self-determination and rights of seceession, classic doctrines of sovereignty and nonintervention, the importance of democracy, individual and collective responsibility in international law, and the global-strategic implications of intervention actions. A compelling concern is that military intervention only be a last resort after a variety of non-military forms of intervention, such as sanctions, humanitarian assistance, legal prosecutions, and so on, have been exhausted. These issues admit no easy answers. It is not surprising that the UN Security Council often cannot agree on an adequate response to such emerging crises. Despite that difficulty, crafting a shared understanding of the appropriate standards for global or regional behavior is vital to alleviating existing humanitarian disasters and averting new ones in the future.

The post–World War II vision of global security was aimed at the prevention of another World War II. The UN Charter thus saw future conflicts as interstate in character, leading to the charter's emphasis on sovereignty and nonintervention. Contrary to the UN Charter vision, in the post–Cold War era, conflicts giving rise to humanitarian crises and questions of intervention often arise out of domestic politics, internal wars, and communal conflicts. The technology of war and global strategic changes in international politics have contributed to the escalation of internal ethnic conflicts and humanitarian disasters in ways that call the classic nonintervention principle into question. In a global age, humanitarian crises almost always have dramatic external effects that countries in the region and beyond ignore at their peril.

At the same time, global strategic political differences have often made cooperation in dealing with humanitarian crises difficult. This has been especially evident in the frequent immobility of the UN Security Council. These debates entangle law and morality and confront a rapidly changing political landscape. So far, the legal side of this equation has generally remained committed, in some formulation, to a principle of nonintervention. But the moral side has presented us with arguments to waive this principle when confronted with humanitarian crises of vast proportions. Efforts to resolve this tension have been encumbered by domestic, international, and global strategic politics. With general inaction against and privileging of great powers and much quicker responses to crises in sensitive areas, geostrategic considerations have further confounded the development of consistent practice.

Much of the literature in this field focuses on important legal issues and historical developments. However, the politics of humanitarian intervention are often neglected. The aim of this book is to capture some of the voices and perspectives that have been sidelined in discussions of humanitarian intervention and in designs of intervention regimes. On the ground, some of these voices are heard only in protests outside various summit meetings. Academically, these voices are on the challenging end of a variety of mainstream and critical schools in intellectual thought in law, international relations, political science, and philosophy. The included contributions are informed by a variety of critical schools, including feminism, critical theory, postmodernism, constructivism, the English School, and development studies.

Critical challenges from legal, political, philosophical, regional, and topical perspectives are addressed in succeeding parts of this book. While the primary focus is on the use of military force in response to humanitarian crises, important nonmilitary interventions and contextual factors are addressed. Part I shapes the broad debate by articulating the legal foundations of humanitarian intervention, including both state action and responsibility and individual action and responsibility. In this part, Peter R. Baehr and Tania Voon set forth the contours of the contemporary legal regime for humanitarian intervention and provide an assessment of practices in Kosovo and East Timor. Baehr, in chapter 2, worries that North Atlantic Treaty Organization (NATO) actions in Kosovo were legally dubious and politically controversial, while Voon, in chapter 3, laments the growing gap between legitimacy and lawfulness in intervention practices. In chapter 4, Robert Cryer closes part I by charting the remarkable recent expansion of the international regime for individual responsibility for crimes against humanity and related crimes, culminating in the International Criminal Court (ICC). Cryer traces the strong pull of international politics in the creation of this legal institution. The succeeding four parts of this book consider the challenges with which the legal discourse must ultimately cope, starting with international politics.

While the growing literature on intervention has offered refined analysis of legal traditions and practices in this area, it has often failed to appreciate the pull of politics in shaping these legal traditions. Victoria Tin-bor Hui, in chapter 5, challenges the common understanding of sovereignty as nonintervention, which necessarily condemns humanitarian intervention as illegal. She advances a more historically fluid concept of "relative sovereignty" that takes into account a state's evolving relations with other states and with societal actors. Mark D. Evans advances this relativity in a different form in his chapter, noting that sovereignty may matter in different ways for weak and strong states. He argues that international authorities could be better served by a "softer" form of intervention, aiming to augment the capacity and willingness of authorities at the national level to protect human rights. In chapter 7, Hiroki Kusano provides a transition argument, contrasting the commands of political calculations with the rich normative tradition in international politics.

Do politics ultimately win out? Part III takes up the philosophical and normative challenges in the preceding two parts. Do we need a philosophical foundation for this debate? Franca D'Agostini's chapter argues that a philosophy that seeks the foundational premises of global responsibility and human rights should be engaged in this debate, rejecting antifoundational debates in the human rights discourse. Nathalie Karagiannis shifts the focus to ethics in chapter 9, insisting that we look more carefully at the notion of responsibility before considering the consequences of global responsibility. She notes that notions of responsibility, autonomy, and knowledge change over time. Finally, this philosophical reflection in part III closes with attention to the contrasting moral concerns of the war on terror. In chapter 10, Daniela Ingruber queries whether the war on terror is an appropriate moral response to the conditions that have spawned terrorism. While that war falls into a different category than humanitarian intervention, Ingruber explores their common foundations, noting in postmodern terms how global discourse shapes our perceptions of both.

In this debate, some regions are superempowered, while others are barely heard. If the UN Charter regime presents political and legal hurdles to humanitarian interventions, will regional institutions be required to take up the slack? In the face of UN immobility, national and regional actors may ultimately shape global practice.

The fourth part of this book addresses the regionalization of this debate through the competing lenses of NATO, Africa, and Asia. A lot of attention has been given to NATO and intervention, but much less to Africa, and almost none to Asia. On NATO, this part of the book enjoys both optimistic and skeptical viewpoints. Rebecca R. Moore argues in her chapter that NATO ultimately has a liberalizing influence and that its expansion has witnessed expansion of a Euro-American community committed to both democracy and liberalization. Moore's analysis leads to the question of whether NATO can provide a foundation for importing democracy and human rights into the intervention norm. In NATO's operations in Kosovo, Giovanna Bono, in chapter 12, sees a policy community committed to a strategy of "diplomacy backed by force" that often sought to renovate NATO's strategic capabilities. She worries that these considerations may have overridden humanitarian concerns. The closing two chapters in part IV consider the role of non-Western countries in shaping our humanitarian intervention practice. Michael C. Davis notes in his chapter that although China is a major power and a permanent member of the UN Security Council, it has followed such a hard-line policy on sovereignty and nonintervention that it has virtually excluded itself from the debate. While most of the contributors to this volume focus on military intervention, Rasheed Akinyemi addresses in chapter 14 "soft" or economic intervention in the form of conditionality and structural adjustments. Using the case of Africa, Akinyemi examines the issue of economic development and institutional responses to it.

Part V takes up two topical issues that reflect sharply on those who are excluded from this debate. As has been teased up in the most recent debate on the war on terror, Alice Sindzingre, in chapter 15, asks whether global poverty and its neglect are the real problems that are responsible for humanitarian disasters in the first place and whether global developmental structures are adequate for this challenge. In chapter 16, Chris Corrin considers how women and their nongovernmental organizations are ultimately the neglected participants in both military intervention and reconstruction. Both chapters remind us that the issues associated with humanitarian intervention neither begin nor end with the question of military intervention.

Various neoliberal and constructivist theories have asserted that domestic institutions and political conditions are constructive of global practices in respect of war and peace.[4] This has implications both for current international proposals and for long-term norm development. We should bear in mind that international norms such as sovereignty and nonintervention are not just constraints on actors with a priori interests, but are also constitutive of the state and other multinational actors that engage this debate.[5] As constructivists in international relations argue, norms and institutions transform actors and actors transform norms and institutions. So, the outcome of this debate is not just about applying moral or legal principles to a given set of facts, but rather will be shaped as circumstances evolve in dynamic processes of change. This outcome will also be shaped in a world where our capacity to do harm is continuously enhanced by the expansion of our technological and political capabilities. A moral antidote for extreme and violent actions against humanity is especially needed in the debate over humanitarian intervention. This debate and its constituents are therefore quite fundamental in efforts to understand the emerging post–Cold War world order. Several later chapters of this book enhance our capacity to sort out these issues by considering their historical and philosophical roots.[6] A brief introductory overview of some of the prime arguments that have animated this debate is therefore a useful starting point for our analysis.

## The Historical Humanitarian Intervention Debate

In practice, in recent years varying perspectives on appropriate responses to humanitarian crises have emerged. Some are impassioned and hopeful about our capacity to devise new mechanisms and institutions to confront the menace of humanitarian crises, while others have despaired at the incapacity of our state system to exceed the narrow interests of its constituent states. The latter realist skepticism has in many ways shaped the current global order and related regimes. Among realists in international relations, the primacy of state sovereignty and nonintervention continues to reign. Realists are skeptical about the plausibility of widely agreed and effective international standards of intervention. This view might permit the most serious humanitarian crises to be dealt with, but only when national interests are satisfied and on an ad hoc basis. Mainstream legal positivist views favor either the realist position or a limited regime of multilateral agreements where countries could consent to future interventions.[7] Contemporary liberal arguments have called for reforms to the UN Charter respecting the UN decision process and international standards for multilateral intervention. Liberals have debated the moral and legal aspects of the use of military force for humanitarian intervention, some harking back to the "just war" tradition and others noting the Kantian quality of peace efforts in the UN regime. Others have focused on the inadequacy of the UN regime to contemporary world issues, noting that its post–World War II design had failed to contemplate the character of modern ethnic conflicts.

The debate over sovereignty and nonintervention has early and variable roots in the liberal philosophical tradition.[8] The hard view equating sovereignty with nonintervention was largely shaped in the eighteenth and nineteenth centuries. John Stuart Mill profoundly shaped the nonintervention principle, arguing that a country could not intervene to impose self-determination on others without defeating such self-determination.[9] Self-help was the essence of self-determination and nonintervention was central to this.

More recently, Michael Walzer notes that this notion of sovereignty allowed exceptions for wars of liberation in states with multiple communal groups and for self-defense in case of invasion.[10] Walzer notes that war is a rule-governed activity with a dual concern with both the reasons for fighting and the means adopted. This was true of the classic statist model as much as it is today. Within the "tyranny of war," Walzer notes, "we have carved out a constitutional regime: even the pawns of war have rights and obligations."[11] Nineteenth-century positivist international legal doctrines on war in many ways track this Mill-Walzer view, though adding their own glaze in respect of principles of neutrality in case of civil war (along with further principles of intervention and counterintervention).[12] Under this positivist legal paradigm, state sovereignty is in many respects the foundation of international law and unilateral intervention is widely disfavored. Going beyond this positivist legal paradigm in the direction of allowing humanitarian intervention, Walzer argues further that an exception to nonintervention should apply in cases where human rights violations are so extreme as to make talk of self-determination irrelevant.[13] This would appear to favor humanitarian intervention in extreme cases of genocide or ethnic violence.

Immanuel Kant goes further, challenging the sufficiency of the positivist legal paradigm by offering a framework to promote a liberal model of perpetual peace built around a federation of republican states.[14] Kant contests the emphasis on exclusive sovereignty of the classic legal positivist model. For Kant, peace, not sovereignty, is the fundamental purpose of international law. Recently, Michael W. Doyle and others have picked up on this Kantian notion of liberal or democratic peace, advancing the argument that democracies will not fight one another.[15] More recent scholarship has even added the notion of a federal democratic peace, noting that the habits of interaction associated with democratic federalism favor peaceful behavior.[16] These various positions may be employed to relate self-determination, and sometimes democratic governance and human rights protection, to full application of the nonintervention principle.

## The Contemporary Regime and the UN Charter

The twentieth century witnessed the evolution of a global treaty regime for peace that in many ways tracks the highest hopes for the institutions reflected in the previous debate. The rights and obligations of those affected by war have been specified in numerous agreements that aim to better achieve a peaceful order. In the mid-twentieth century, the UN Charter appeared to capture both wings of this debate, simultaneously offering a defense of sovereignty and a federation of free states with a human rights commitment.[17] The UN Charter now serves as the basic constitution of this regime, but there is considerable debate surrounding its character and requirements. Many contemporary legal interpretations of the UN Charter appear to track the classic legal positivist view, upholding sovereignty and restricting the use of force to self-defense or actions controlled by the UN Security Council.[18] The current moral debate concerning humanitarian intervention finds this woefully inadequate.

In its dual commitment to international peace and fundamental human rights, the UN Charter appears to reflect a contradictory commitment to the exclusive sovereignty of the state and international protection of human rights. It appears to leave open the question of sovereignty and nonintervention versus human rights, as well as the question of the status of the humanitarian intervention concept. Mainstream legal positivists see maintaining peace under a regime of exclusive state sovereignty and nonintervention as the UN's primary purpose. As discussed later in this book, China, a permanent UN Security Council member, is a prominent proponent of this view, weighing in firmly on the statist side of the debate.[19] On the other hand, liberals have worried that the UN Charter's emphasis on sovereignty is too much a product of the World War II–era belief that future conflicts would continue to be interstate in character. Kofi Annan argues that this has not been the case and pleads for a regime design under the UN Charter that acknowledges the serious threats posed by internal conflicts.[20] For Annan, the UN Charter takes up the Kantian mission of a federation of republics committed to international peace.

The UN Charter regime faces three primary difficulties in responding to humanitarian crises: conceptual, political, and resource-based difficulties. The conceptual difficulties are concerned with whether the many domestically derived military conflicts qualify as threats to international peace to which the charter regime applies.[21] But this difficulty has lately become less pronounced, as the UN Security Council has increasingly characterized internal wars as threats to international peace.[22] The Security Council has come to appreciate that so-called internal conflicts may quickly spill over into surrounding territories and will otherwise produce spillover effects such as refugees. Politically, while the charter provides a formal security regime requiring UN Security Council approval for armed peacekeeping and peace-enforcement missions, the allowance of veto to the five permanent members of the Security Council often renders the charter paradigm unresponsive to humanitarian crises.[23] This shifts the debate down to regional or national actors for whom inaction may not be a sensible option, either morally or politically.[24] This may be the most serious challenge facing the UN Charter regime in respect of humanitarian intervention. The resource difficulty is also quite serious. With countries increasingly unwilling to commit substantial and sustained resources to peacekeeping efforts and with reluctance to risk the lives of their soldiers, the UN faces excessive demands and a confidence crisis in its peace efforts. Actors are then faced with a moral dilemma of the Kosovo variety: inaction is unacceptable and yet high-altitude, low-risk bombing raises further moral issues and risks the loss of international support.

This raises the previously noted option of regional action. Given difficulties in obtaining UN Security Council approval, bypassing the Security Council has become an important component in the evolving humanitarian crisis regime.[25] Unilateral action is suspect. Regional groupings such as NATO, the Organization for African Unity (now the African Union), or the Organization of American States (OAS) may be called on to take military enforcement measures—as occurred in Kosovo—even without the required UN approval.[26] Some regional arrangements in the Americas and Europe appear to take the Kantian thesis even more seriously. The OAS and the European Union/NATO have to a limited extent sought to enforce commitments to democracy.[27] In the long term, will the classic sovereignty regime and the democratic peace be merged in the ways suggested by Annan? If so, participation in global decision processes regarding the use of force and a state's right to resist intervention in respect of a humanitarian crisis could become contingent on its practice of democracy and human rights. This is the move that China and other authoritarian countries have most resisted, both in the humanitarian intervention debate and through other UN human rights channels. This takes place in an environment where there are legitimate questions about the bona fides of intervention actions. Permanent UN Security Council members China, Russia, and the United States have likewise resisted moves to expand individual responsibility for war crimes and genocide under the new ICC, while they have permitted ad hoc tribunals.[28] These battles are sometimes fought over questions of so-called soft or hard interventions short of military force.

The international practice regarding communal conflicts deserves special mention here due to its contribution to humanitarian crises. Numerous recent humanitarian crises have been the outcome of state suppression of communal groups.[29] The international law and practice in this area, in supporting both sovereignty and self-determination, offers a contradiction that tends to encourage the escalation of communal conflicts. International law advances the values of self-determination and related rights, while discouraging the exercise of such rights by communal groups within established states—so sovereignty trumps self-determination and secession is not favored.[30] Classic legal principles regarding intervention on behalf of insurgents in civil wars bear this out, requiring nonintervention until the insurgents have taken substantial territory by armed rebellion and thus acquire belligerent status. Such status affords a right to be treated on more equal terms with the state side of the conflict. Even at such a stage, neutrality would be required unless others intervene, which frequently is the case. These principles appear to signal to resisting communal groups the need to escalate violence to a sufficient level to kick in this international solicitude.[31] Overall, this tends to encourage armed rebellion since peaceful resistance will gain the insurgents little international support. And, at the same time, it may encourage violent state suppression of potential insurgent groups. These twin tendencies have sometimes produced the very conditions that cause humanitarian crises. Contrast Tibet with Kosovo or East Timor. While Tibetan leaders in exile, guided by their own moral compass, have shown little interest in armed rebellion, the message from the current international regime would tend to promise higher international dividends from a more militant approach.[32] Further complicating this problem in strategic terms, Tibet is claimed by a major power that is a permanent member of the UN Security Council.

## Contemporary Solutions and Further Debates

There have been a variety of international proposals in respect to the current intervention regime. Some arguments have favored sticking to a hard sovereign nonintervention principle with informal exceptional case analysis for extreme humanitarian crises.[33] Among leading theorists, Richard Falk notes that "the textual level of analysis, upon which legalists rely, cannot give a satisfactory basis for NATO intervention, nor can it provide a suitable rationale for rejecting the humanitarian imperative to rescue the potential victims of genocidal policies in Kosovo."[34] He appears to favor a nonintervention principle with very limited exceptions. Thomas M. Franck concurs, seeing the NATO action in Kosovo as an exceptional case.[35] W. Michael Reisman argues against this view, noting that the UN Charter is not a "suicide pact."[36]

Some have tried to give further content to such exceptional case analysis, arguing that when human rights abuses persist to the point of massive suffering, the sovereignty of the state and the concomitant right of nonintervention cease to exist.[37] Some in the UN and elsewhere favor a narrow, formal regime for UN crisis avoidance efforts and intervention. Other scholars support suggestions for Kantian-style alliances of democratic states with a regime to restore democracy.[38] The latter might urge that adequate human rights protection and democracy be a condition for sovereign protection from intervention. States should not be free to abuse their local citizens and then hide behind sovereignty. Some advocate that states enter into agreements, perhaps formally supported by communal groups, agreeing to intervention on the collapse of democratic governance.[39] This idea would employ the existing legal positivist sovereignty regime to create an alternative consensual order.

There are a variety of arguments that try to dissolve these competing tensions in the mainstream humanitarian intervention debate. Of these, the most substantial formal effort is the argument for the "responsibility to protect," as articulated in the 2001 report to the UN Security Council submitted by the International Commission on Intervention and State Sovereignty.[40] The move made in this recommendation is to shift the emphasis in the humanitarian intervention debate to the responsibilities that attach to principles of sovereignty and nonintervention under the UN Charter regime. This is done by first emphasizing the responsibility of individual states to protect their own citizens. It is recognized that only when there is a failure in this respect, either by the state harming its own people or failing to protect them from violence perpetrated by others, should the international community become involved in exercising the responsibility to protect. This international collective responsibility is to be exercised where possible by UN institutions in accordance with the UN Charter.

It is felt that by elevating the "responsibility to protect" and de-emphasizing the permissibility of intervention, the objectionable quality of humanitarian intervention may be reduced. But the report does recognize that sometimes the UN Security Council may be immobilized by the veto power of the five permanent members. In such cases, the report recommends that the permanent members establish a convention to not go against a majority decision of the Security Council unless the vital interests of one of the permanent member's are at stake. If this admonition fails to secure an adequate response to a pending humanitarian crisis, the report acknowledges that a regional response may be legitimate, but only after first seeking and failing to get UN Security Council approval. In such regard, the report appears to also open the door to action first and a subsequent request for approval after the regional actor has initially exercised its responsibility to protect through intervention. The report articulates a variety of standards in determining the occasions for such intervention. By shifting the emphasis from intervention to responsibility, the report appears to move the argument forward. It is not clear, however, if this will be enough to satisfy the most ardent objections of countries such as China and Russia, which seek to defend a strong notion of sovereignty and a central role for the UN Security Council in this area.

There are other approaches that focus on the possibility of more proactive regional actions. David Wippman suggests the use of regional treaty-based intervention that would engage domestic communal groups in agreeing on principles for outside intervention.[41] Accepting a largely legal positivist analysis, he stresses the value of the participation of communal groups in making such a commitment binding in international law. I foresee a much larger future role for regional agreements in setting the conditions for intervention and nonintervention. In the absence of agreed international standards to address the full spectrum of intervention concerns, the likely direction appears to be a more proactive engagement of regional states and institutions. States in several regions have increasingly agreed in considerable detail on regional standards of behavior respecting human rights and their enforcement. Such agreements may eventually set up regional standards for intervention that relate intervention to domestic practice, especially the maintenance of democracy and human rights. Soft intervention may more typically be employed, but such agreements may go further, specifying the possibility of military intervention in the face of humanitarian crises. One may characterize this as a constitutive approach that frames the conditions for addressing urgent regional concerns and crises. Such an approach can embody the notion of a "responsibility to protect" and specifically address regional standards for humanitarian intervention when that responsibility is not satisfied. Such intervention standards may increasingly embody requirements respecting democracy and human rights, as these norms are the contemporary embodiment of the more classic notion of self-determination that underlies the noninterventionist principle. Until significant numbers of states are liberal democracies, however, such standards will not achieve significant global endorsement.

In conceptual terms, such a move toward regional alliances in respect to humanitarian intervention would combine the idea of responsibility to protect with precommitment strategies that include democracy and human rights. This combines the Kantian notion of a federation of republics committed to peace and Mill's commitment to self-determination and nonintervention, with certain intervention exceptions that justice and the just war tradition permit. A community of democratic states will be able to limit principles of nonintervention in respect of states that do not maintain basic freedoms and have committed or allowed atrocities. The responsibility to prevent such crises before they occur, as highlighted in the UN report, would certainly be aided by such precommitment strategies. Democracy and human rights can contribute measurably to conflict avoidance and nonviolent means of resolution. At the same time, a democratic state with full protection of rights would be less likely to commit atrocities at home. Local citizens might be deemed to want democracy to be restored if it were lost. Where such a foundation has been laid, members of such democratic regional alliances may be better suited to take such actions against states that do not maintain democracy and slip into humanitarian crises. Under this argument, nonintervention would survive—as would sovereignty—but its full protection within such a community of states would be contingent on requirements of democratic governance and human rights protection.

## Moral Responsibility Versus Power Politics

As reflected in the literature in both international relations and international law, the state has long been thought to be the primary addressee of the modern regime of international human rights. Hidden behind a wall of sovereignty, states are thought to view compliance with human rights obligations as their internal affair, largely barred from outside intervention. Under the onslaughts of an expanding international treaty regime and growing reliance on international institutions and globalization, it is now argued that this has changed, if it ever existed. This assertion of change has gained special currency in the post–Cold War period as the world seeks to deal with an escalating number of humanitarian problems.

Moral and political considerations are now thought to justify and shape interventionist practices. There are certainly a wide range of recent examples on which a discussion about humanitarian intervention can be drawn: Somalia, Rwanda, Bosnia, Kosovo, Chechnya, East Timor, Sri Lanka, Sierra Leone, Liberia, and aspects of the current war on terrorism. With these tragedies in mind, Annan argues that traditional notions of sovereignty and "internal affairs" must give way in the face of human rights disasters. Is the phenomenon of "moral interventionism" a call for the recognition of human rights or is it little more than a new form of power politics?

Geostrategic considerations clearly shape the global picture, reflecting a double standard that is troubling for an evolving regime on humanitarian intervention. Either democracies or great powers appear to be in the best position to resist outside intervention.[42] Great powers are rarely the target of interventionist actions. Compare Chechnya and Tibet with Kosovo and East Timor.[43] They are also frequently, though not always, the intervenor. Unilateral action by great powers may undermine the credibility of their moral position, as they at once challenge extreme or even terrorist action by communal groups while engaging in aggressive and occasionally indiscriminate attacks on their own. Is the moral position of a Kosovo-type bombing campaign further undermined by a political need to engage the enemy from miles up, combined with an unwillingness to take casualties?[44] This hypocritical aspect brings particular resonance to claims that the attempt to override sovereignty is merely Western imperialism.

Overall, the risks of a slippery slope in the humanitarian intervention area are obvious. If self-serving actions are not to be the order of the day, then coherent guidelines are essential to political constraint. In a normative world that depreciates states and advances emerging Kantian global norms, how would such development affect the least powerful states?[45] Would they be left defenseless in the face of international pressure? Should we hold states and whole societies responsible for genocide or ethnic cleansing or should we focus on individual accountability? If both, how should these competing strategies be deployed? Our response to these questions will be shaped not only by strategic concerns or our views of sovereignty and intervention, but also by practical political considerations. It seems apparent that a country resistant to outside intervention will be little attracted to holding leaders individually accountable. The United States, a country that has long supported ad hoc tribunals to hold leaders accountable for humanitarian crimes, has been reluctant to concede criminal accountability of its own officials under the Rome Convention on an ICC. How might the possibility of individual accountability affect state or multilateral intervention strategies?[46]

It is apparent that if the countries of the world are to further develop norms allowing intervention in humanitarian crises, they will do so for a variety of political and moral reasons. Political arguments will consider changing strategic conditions and domestic perceptions. Moral considerations will be grounded in the belief that we live in an evolving world where sovereignty is conceptually changing and where a norm against intervention to prevent humanitarian crises is no longer morally acceptable. Constrained by global strategic considerations and power politics, there has been increasing reluctance to stand by while humanitarian crises ensue. This is a world where shared security concerns such as those revealed in the fight against terrorism are also of increasing significance. The sovereign landscape is, at the same time, being shaped by a greater commitment to free trade, democracy, human rights, and popular sovereign consent. The integrative character of the emerging world may make the sovereign paradigm of nonintervention untenable in the face of humanitarian crises. This may call us to evaluate the values that may animate any alternatives or amendments of the traditional paradigm. Given a growing global consensus around democracy, an attractive way of resolving the tension between sovereignty and intervention may be to increasingly tie the nonintervention principle, in the context of humanitarian crises, to democratic governance in an acceptable form. This may be combined with some mechanism for dealing with extreme crises. As long as numerous countries fall short of democratic standards, however, we may be left in the short run to promoting a democracy-based norm only on a regional level under those conditions where this is feasible.

The Kosovo model of regional response has in many respects already been accepted or at least tolerated. But a variety of constraints still limit our evolving options. Some degree of multilateral response or consensus approving a single-state response appears important (Australia in East Timor).

It is left to determine under what circumstances individual states or regional blocs should be permitted to act and what should be the required content of intervention actions. Kantian-style regional agreements may be the best vehicle to develop standards in this regard. An effective international response to the suppression of domestic communal groups at times short of substantial armed resistance may allow us to head off crises before they ensue. We will also have to consider what should be done to rebuild states and restore communities after interventions have occurred. Our perceptions in this debate are also likely to be shaped by the perceived perils of the aggressive posture respecting the so-called "preemptive self-defense" argued for by the US coalition in the Iraq War. States may ignore emerging geostrategic considerations at their peril. Any regime we devolve must recognize this reality and avoid standards that cannot be sustained or that might otherwise undermine the effectiveness of international regimes. The chapters in this book confront both the possibilities and the challenges of the concerns raised in this debate.

## Notes

1. Both of these types of wars have historical antecedents. See K. J. Holsti, "The Coming Chaos? Armed Conflict in the World's Periphery," in T. V. Paul and John A. Hall, eds., *International Order and the Future of World Politics* (New York: Cambridge University Press, 1999), pp. 283–310, 291, 294. The claim here is merely that they have taken on new characteristics and have become defining phenomena in the current post–Cold War era.

2. Mike Allen and Barton Gellman, "Preemptive Strikes Part of U.S. Strategic Doctrine 'All Options' Open for Countering Unconventional Arms," *Washington Post*, 11 December 2002, p. A1.

3. Jack Donnelly raises a concurring argument regarding the importance of three factors—law, morality, and politics—in respect to the evolving humanitarian intervention norm. See Jack Donnelly, "Genocide and Humanitarian Intervention," *Journal of Human Rights* 1, no. 1 (March 2002): 93–109.

4. Jeffrey T. Checkel, "The Constructivist Turn in International Relations Theory," *World Politics* 50, no. 2 (1998): 324–348; Andrew Moravcsik, "Taking Preferences Seriously: A Liberal Theory of International Politics," *International Organization* 51, no. 4 (Autumn 1997): 513–553; Peter Katzenstein, ed., *The Culture of National Security: Norms and Identity in International Politics* (New York: Columbia University Press, 1996); Michael W. Doyle and G. John Ikenberry, eds., *New Thinking in International Relations Theory* (Boulder, Colo.: Westview, 1997); Alexander Wendt, "Anarchy Is What States Make of It: The Social Construction of Power Politics," *International Organization* 46, no. 2 (Spring 1992): 391–425.

5. Checkel, "Constructivist Turn in International Relations Theory," pp. 324–348; Thomas Risse, "'Let's Argue!': Communicative Action in World Politics," *International Organization* 54, no. 1 (Winter 2000): 1–39.

6. See Victoria Tin-bor Hui, chapter 5, in this volume; Franca D'Agostini, chapter 8, in this volume; Nathalie Karagiannis, chapter 9, in this volume.

7. Editorial Comments, "NATO's Kosovo Intervention, Kosovo and the Law of

'Humanitarian Intervention,'" *American Journal of International Law* 93 (1999): 824–862 (comments are by Louis Henkin, Ruth Wedgwood, Jonathan Charney, Christine Chinkin, Richard Falk, Thomas M. Franck, and W. Michael Reisman), 847–857 (Falk), 857–860 (Franck); David Wippman, "Treaty-Based Intervention: Who Can Say No?" *University of Chicago Law Review* 62 (1995): 607–687.

8. See Hiroki Kusano, chapter 7, in this volume.

9. John Stuart Mill, "A Few Words on Non-Intervention," in John Stuart Mill, *Dissertations and Discussions: Political, Philosophical, and Historical*, vol. 3 (London: Longmans, Green, Reader, and Dyer, 1867), pp. 153–178.

10. Michael Walzer, *Just and Unjust Wars: A Moral Argument with Historical Illustrations* (New York: Basic, 1977), pp. 96–108.

11. Walzer, *Just and Unjust Wars*, p. 40.

12. Walzer, *Just and Unjust Wars*, p. 96.

13. Walzer, *Just and Unjust Wars*, p. 90.

14. Immanuel Kant, *Perpetual Peace and Other Essays* (Indianapolis, Ind.: Hackett, 1983); see also Fernando R. Tesón, "The Kantian Theory of International Law," *Columbia Law Review* 92 (1992): 53.

15. Michael W. Doyle, "Liberalism and World Politics," *American Political Science Review* 80 (December 1986): 1151–1169; Spencer R. Weart, *Never at War: Why Democracies Will Not Fight One Another* (New Haven, Conn.: Yale University Press, 1998); Michael E. Brown, Sean M. Lynn-Jones, and Steven E. Miller, eds., *Debating the Democratic Peace* (Cambridge: Massachusetts Institute of Technology Press, 1996).

16. Scott A. Silverstone, "Federal Democratic Peace: Domestic Institutions, International Conflict, and American Foreign Policy, 1807–1860" (paper presented at the annual meeting of the International Studies Association Chicago, Illinois, February 20–24, 2001).

17. The UN Charter in key clauses reflects a dual commitment to both peace and security and to human rights. For this reason, the charter builds in a dual commitment to state sovereignty and nonintervention and international protection of human rights. The preamble of the charter highlights several commitments to global peace and security and seeks to "reaffirm faith in fundamental human rights." Article 1, paragraph 3 lists among the purposes of the charter, "To achieve international cooperation in solving international problems of an economic, social, cultural, or humanitarian character, and in promoting and encouraging respect for human rights and for fundamental freedoms for all without distinction as to race, sex, language, or religion." Article 2, paragraph 7 highlights the role of the nonintervention principle in the peace and security regime, providing, "Nothing contained in the present Charter shall authorize the United Nations to intervene in matters which are essentially within the domestic jurisdiction of any state or shall require the Members to submit such matters to settlement under the present Charter; but this principle shall not prejudice the application of enforcement measures under Chapter VII." What is "essentially within the domestic jurisdiction" is not made explicit and opens up interpretive room for interventionist arguments, as does the Chapter VII enforcement regime.

18. Richard Falk, "The Complexities of Humanitarian Intervention: A New World Order Challenge," *Michigan Journal of International Law* 17 (1996): 491.

19. See Michael C. Davis, chapter 13, in this volume.

20. Kofi Annan, "Secretary-General Presents His Annual Report to the General Assembly," September 1999. Annan argues that the core challenge is to "forge unity behind the principle that massive and systematic violations of human rights—wherever they may take place—should not be allowed to stand. . . . If states bent on

criminal behavior know that frontiers are not the absolute defense; if they know that the Security Council will take action to halt crimes against humanity, then they will not embark on such a course of action in expectation of sovereign immunity."

21. UN Charter, Articles 33, 39.

22. Note that this does not allow one to get around the problem of providing adequate standards in the *jus in bello* (justice in war) branch of this field as provided in the Geneva Conventions. The higher Geneva Conventions standards regarding the treatment of noncombatants apply only to international armed conflict, though recent war crimes trials do indicate that many of these standards are now thought to apply to internal armed conflict by way of customary international law.

23. UN Charter, Chapters VI, VII. Note that there is an exception allowing use of armed force under the inherent right of individual or collective self-defense under UN Charter, Article 51.

24. UN Charter, Articles 52–54 allow for regional actions, but again explicitly require prior UN Security Council approval. In the face of UN Security Council immobility, this may increasingly be honored in the breach.

25. The UN Charter, Article 53 requirement that the UN Security Council authorize regional enforcement actions may be ignored, as it was in respect to Kosovo.

26. See Rebecca R. Moore, chapter 11, in this volume; Giovanna Bono, chapter 12, in this volume; Rasheed Akinyemi, chapter 14, in this volume. With little development of regional collective actions, Asia has been the weakest actor in respect of regional commitments, though the Association of Southeast Asian Nations may someday join this club of regional actors. See Michael C. Davis, chapter 13 in this volume.

27. See Lori Fisler Damrosch, *Enforcing Restraint: Collective Intervention in Internal Conflicts* (New York: Council on Foreign Relations, 1993). The Organization for Security and Cooperation in Europe (now the Commission on Security and Cooperation in Europe [CSCE]) process has likewise sought to enforce this democracy requirement, declaring democracy and other human dimension concerns to be legitimate matters of international concern, "not belonging too exclusively to the internal affairs of the state concerned." See "Document of the Moscow Meeting of the Conference on the Human Dimension of the CSCE," October 3, 1991, p. 2.

28. See Robert Cryer, chapter 4, in this volume.

29. See David Wippman, ed., *International Law and Ethnic Conflict* (Ithaca, N.Y.: Cornell University Press, 1998).

30. At the same time, on the other side of the equation, there has evolved a degree of international solicitude for rights and sometimes autonomy of such groups, especially for indigenous populations under the rule of dominant groups that control the state. See Daniel Weinstock, "Constitutionalizing the Right to Secede," *Journal of Political Philosophy* 9, no. 2 (2001): 182–203.

31. See Robert H. Jackson, *Quasi-states: Sovereignty, International Relations and the Third World* (Cambridge: Cambridge University Press, 1990), pp. 151–154. Examples where militant resistance pays have been legion, including the creation of Bangladesh, the breakup of key parts of the former Soviet Union, and the breakup of the former Yugoslavia.

32. Michael C. Davis, "The Future of Tibet: A Chinese Dilemma," *Human Rights Review* 2, no. 2 (2001): 7–17.

33. Editorial Comments, "NATO's Kosovo Intervention," pp. 824–862, 847–857 (Falk), 857–860 (Franck).

34. Editorial Comments, "NATO's Kosovo Intervention," p. 853 (Falk).

35. Editorial Comments, "NATO's Kosovo Intervention," p. 859 (Franck).

36. Editorial Comments, "NATO's Kosovo Intervention," p. 862.

37. Falk, "Complexities of Humanitarian Intervention," p. 503; Michael L. Burton, "Legalizing the Sublegal: A Proposal for Codifying a Doctrine of Unilateral Humanitarian Intervention," *Georgetown Law Journal* 85 (1996): 417, 435–436 (offering a moral forfeiture theory).

38. Doyle, "Liberalism and World Politics," pp. 1151–1169; Fernando R. Tesón, *Humanitarian Intervention: An Inquiry into Law and Morality*, 2nd ed. (Irvington-on-Hudson, N.Y.: Transnational, 1997); Louis Fielding, "Taking the Next Step in the Development of New Human Rights: The Emerging Right of Humanitarian Assistance to Restore Democracy," *Duke Journal of Comparative and International Law* 5 (1995): 329; Wippman, "Treaty-Based Intervention," pp. 607–687.

39. Wippman, "Treaty-Based Intervention," pp. 607–687.

40. International Commission on Intervention and State Sovereignty, *The Responsibility to Protect* (Ottawa: International Development Research Centre, 2001); see also Gareth Evans and Mohamed Sahnoun, "The Responsibility to Protect," *Foreign Affairs* 81, no. 6 (2002): 99–110.

41. Wippman, "Treaty-Based Intervention."

42. Mark D. Evans, chapter 6, in this volume; Victoria Tin-bor Hui, chapter 5, in this volume.

43. See Tania Voon, chapter 3, in this volume.

44. See Giovanna Bono, chapter 12, in this volume.

45. See Mark D. Evans, chapter 6; Victoria Tin-bor Hui, chapter 5, in this volume.

46. See Robert Cryer, chapter 4, in this volume.

# Part I

# International Legal Foundations

# 2

# "Humanitarian Intervention"

## A Misnomer?

*Peter R. Baehr*

"[W]hen a state by its behavior so outrages the conscience of mankind, no doctrine can be deployed to defend it against intervention. Thus it might be argued that states had not only a right, but a duty to overrule the principle of non-intervention in order to defend the Jews against Nazi persecution, and a parallel is drawn and similar arguments urged in support of intervention against the institution of apartheid in present-day South Africa."[1]

Are member states obligated to respond positively to a call by the United Nations (UN) to supply armed forces, for instance, in order to terminate gross violations of human rights, as recently happened in Sierra Leone, or to come to the assistance of an attacked state, as in the case of Kuwait? Strictly speaking, that is only the case if the Security Council makes the call, acting under Chapter VII of the UN Charter ("Action with Respect to Threats to the Peace, Breaches of the Peace, and Acts of Aggression"). Gross and systematic violations of human rights may be considered as such a threat. In 1991, the Security Council determined that the consequences of the oppression of the Kurdish population of Iraq threatened international peace and security.[2] The council may respond to such a threat with measures of a nonmilitary nature that may include complete or partial interruption of economic relations and rail, sea, air, postal, telegraphic, radio, and other means of communication, and the severance of diplomatic relations.[3] To provide military means, the members of the UN are obliged to make available to the Security Council, on its call and in accordance with a special agreement or agreements, armed forces, assistance, and facilities, including rights of passage, necessary for the purpose of maintaining international peace and security.[4] No such agreements have, however, ever been reached, and therefore, from a legal point of view, member states are not obliged to provide troops to the UN.

So far, there is thus an absence of a legal obligation. Another matter is, however, whether one can speak of some kind of *moral* obligation. The Dutch constitution contains an article that obliges the government to promote the

23

development of an international legal order.[5] This may be interpreted as a moral obligation to strongly support the activities of the UN, which can be considered the most important initiative toward the institutionalization of an international legal order, even if the UN does not always work in the way one would want.

In common parlance, the term "international community" is often used, which is supposed to request certain actions from the member states. It is, however, unclear what this term exactly means. Sometimes it refers to decisions by the Security Council or the General Assembly of the UN, while at other times (Kosovo) the North Atlantic Treaty Organization (NATO) has been referred to by that term. The use of the term depends entirely on the political situation, and it is often used to legitimize any political decision making, for instance, in the field of collective military action, as occurred in the case of Kosovo. For the time being, at least, the "international community" is nonexistent. Therefore, the term should be banned from official terminology, unless it is given a treaty-based, generally accepted interpretation.

Of interest in this context are the military interventions by countries of the Third World, which at first sight appear to have occurred in reaction to human rights violations. The first of these was the military intervention by India in East Pakistan in 1971, which ended the slaughter of Bengali citizens by the Pakistani army and resulted in the proclamation of the independent state of Bangladesh.[6] The second was the invasion by Tanzania in Uganda in 1979, terminating the murderous rule of dictator Idi Amin.[7] Finally, there was the occupation of Cambodia by Vietnam in 1979, which overthrew the even more murderous rule of Pol Pot's Khmer Rouge. None of the intervening states' actions were motivated by humanitarian or human rights considerations. India justified its attack by alleging that it had first been attacked by Pakistan.[8] Tanzania claimed that its troops had invaded Uganda to punish Amin for an earlier raid into Tanzania—its invasion allegedly coincided with a domestic revolt in Uganda against Amin. Vietnam denied at first that its troops had invaded Cambodia and claimed that Pol Pot had been deposed by the Cambodians themselves.[9] The reason for these denials is obvious: to recognize the legitimacy of humanitarian intervention would have created a precedent that at some other point in time could be turned against the intervening state. Thus, Pakistan might have used it to legitimize attacking India for its treatment of its Muslim subjects or China might invade Vietnam for its treatment of its Chinese minority population.[10]

In articulating the motivation for their actions, the three states—India, Tanzania, and Vietnam—followed customary practice. In the course of history, the principle of nonintervention has been accepted as being in the interest of all states, as it removes a source of possible conflicts and thus contributes to the maintenance of international peace and stability, meaning the maintenance of the territorial status quo. This is also reflected in the UN Charter, which prohibits the use of force by states in their international relations.[11]

The only exception to this rule is the use of force on the demand of the UN Security Council or by way of individual or collective self-defense.[12]

In recent years, the classic situation described earlier has been undergoing important changes. Often, in the case of gross and systematic violations of human rights, a call for "humanitarian intervention" is being heard. This term refers to "coercive action by states involving the use of armed force in another state without the consent of its government, with or without the consent from the United Nations Security Council, for the purpose of putting to a halt gross and massive violations of human rights or international humanitarian law."[13] "Gross and massive violations" are violations, instrumental to the achievement of governmental policies, perpetrated in such a quantity and in such a manner as to create a situation in which the rights to life, to personal integrity, or to personal liberty of the population as a whole or of one or more sectors of the population of a country are continuously infringed on or threatened.[14]

The most important examples of gross and massive violations are crimes against humanity, genocide, and war crimes. These include the following violations as the most important ones: enslavement, arbitrary and summary executions, torture, cruel, inhuman, or degrading treatment or punishment, rape, mass deportations, involuntary disappearances, and ethnic cleansing.[15] In such circumstances, it is often argued that humanitarian intervention by another state or other states is allowed as a last resort, with or even without prior consent of the UN Security Council. In this chapter, this argument is examined and an answer is sought as to whether the term "humanitarian intervention" is properly used or should be rejected as a misnomer.

**Permissibility of Humanitarian Intervention**

In the past in international law, the doctrine of nonintervention was the rule, which was based on the maintenance of stability in international relations and the prevention of states from taking the law into their own hands. When this did happen, nevertheless, it was called "aggression," which under the rules of international law was not permitted (and still is not permitted).[16] The often quoted Article 2, paragraph 7 of the UN Charter reflects this principle, "Nothing contained in the present Charter shall authorize the United Nations to *intervene* in matters which are essentially within the domestic jurisdiction of any state."[17]

Meanwhile, however, the idea has been generally accepted that the promotion and protection of human rights is a matter of concern to all states and that, in reverse, states that violate human rights have no recourse to the doctrine of nonintervention. For instance, the 1993 "Final Declaration of the World Conference on Human Rights in Vienna" states explicitly, "The promotion and protection of all human rights and fundamental freedoms must be considered as a priority objective of the United Nations in accordance with its purposes and principles, in particular the purpose of international cooperation. In the framework of these purposes and principles, the promotion and protection of all human rights is a legitimate concern of the international community."[18]

This may have important consequences. In the case of gross violations of human rights, such as in the past in South Africa, in Rwanda, the former Yugoslavia, or Sierra Leone, one may argue that states are bound by higher obligations than merely refraining from interference in domestic affairs, as the late British professor of international relations R. J. Vincent pointed out more than twenty-five years ago.[19]

There exists a broad consensus that such action should preferably take place under authorization by the UN Security Council, acting under Chapter VII of the UN Charter, this being the proper legal forum, in view of the provisions of Article 2, paragraphs 4 and 7 of the charter. The Security Council has primary responsibility to take as early as possible all necessary measures to prevent or end grave and massive violations of human rights and international humanitarian law that are considered a threat to or a breach of international peace and security.[20]

As is well known, however, the NATO air strikes in Kosovo and Serbia were never discussed in the UN Security Council, as the Western allies were afraid that this would lead to a Russian or Chinese veto.[21] Their rationale was to act outside the UN Security Council rather than act in the face of a negative decision by the council.[22] This has led to an outburst of criticism, not only in political circles, but also in academic arenas. For instance, the Sudanese human rights specialist, Abdullahi A. An-Na'im, who was by no means sympathetic to the Serbian cause, writes, "But this is simply justifying taking the law into one's own hand by imposing one's own remedy to a conflict because the police are expected to be unable or unwilling to enforce it."[23] On the other hand, it would be difficult to think of an effective alternative by way of reaction to the Serbian oppression of ethnic Albanians in Kosovo. As the American human rights expert David P. Forsythe writes, "If ever there were an essentially humanitarian intervention, at least in motivation and intent, this was it."[24]

Nevertheless, action authorized by the UN Security Council should be seen as preferable under all circumstances. If the Security Council is unable to take the necessary action, however, action without Security Council authorization should not be ruled out entirely. Two Dutch advisory councils have advised the minister of foreign affairs that in such a situation, the "next logical step" would be to try to obtain authorization from the General Assembly, for example, on the basis of the resolution "Uniting for Peace."[25] Under the terms of this resolution, which was adopted by the General Assembly in 1950, any seven (later nine) members of the council or a majority of the assembly can summon an emergency special session of the General Assembly, which could meet within twenty-four hours. The procedure makes it possible by a two-thirds majority to label a member state as an aggressor. From there, the assembly can recommend coercive sanctions against that aggressor.[26] The member states that could provide military forces in such circumstances were asked to set them aside for possible UN use. The legal status of that resolution, which at the time had the strong support of the United States and was used against the People's Republic of China in the Korean War, has remained uncertain and controversial and in recent years has only rarely been applied.

The use of violence, if consistent with the purposes of the UN, is not incompatible with Article 2, paragraph 4 of the charter. One of the purposes of the UN is, according to Article 1, paragraph 3 of the charter, "to achieve international cooperation in solving international problems of an economic, social, cultural, or humanitarian character *and in promoting and encouraging respect for human rights and for fundamental freedoms for all without distinction as to race, sex, language, or religion.*"[27] At least state practices of recent years suggest that humanitarian intervention without UN Security Council authorization can be considered morally and politically justifiable in certain cases. This would mean that humanitarian intervention is in a process of becoming part of international customary law.

The international duty to protect and promote the rights of individuals and groups has developed into a universally valid obligation that is incumbent on all states, both individually and collectively. It is desirable that, as part of the doctrine of state responsibility, efforts be made to further develop a justification ground for humanitarian intervention without Security Council authorization. The remainder of this chapter deals with this more difficult subject of intervention without Security Council authorization.

Humanitarian intervention should only be undertaken under exceptional circumstances, if other nonmilitary instruments to improve the situation, such as diplomatic efforts or economic sanctions, are not available or have failed. In the foreseeable future, states will not refrain from such interventions if they are deemed imperative on moral and political grounds. Under these circumstances, it would be helpful if criteria were developed for such intervention in order to help avoid abuse of the concept for purely national ends.

"Humanitarian intervention" may cause the death of armed combatants, but also of innocent civilians. The NATO air strikes during the action on Kosovo in 1999 are a case in point. It should be kept in mind that the crisis was essentially provoked by a pattern of Serbian violations of human rights in Kosovo, including numerous atrocities that can be characterized as crimes against humanity.[28] Bartram S. Brown, quoting an article by Jeremy Rabkin, notes that after the air campaign, Serbian authorities reported at least 2,000 civilian deaths, with thousands more injured.[29] Amnesty International has made the point that "NATO forces did commit serious violations of the laws of war leading in a number of cases to the unlawful killings of civilians."[30] It has criticized more specifically the air strike on April 12, 1999, on the Grdelica railroad bridge, which killed twelve civilians; the attack on April 23, 1999, on the headquarters of Serbian State Television and Radio, causing the death of sixteen civilians; and the missile attack on the Varvarin bridge in May 1999 that killed eleven civilians.[31] Its sister human rights organization, Human Rights Watch, which is based in the United States, also reported a number of civilian deaths and criticized the use of cluster ammunition by NATO, commenting on "weapons that are indiscriminate in effect—the equivalent of using antipersonnel landmines."[32] NATO has responded to such criticisms by referring to unintended but unavoidable "collateral damage" to civilians and the circumstance that the Serbs themselves had inflicted far more damage to civilians.[33]

## Points for Consideration

### Need for Some Manner of Codification

Some kind of guidelines, criteria, or assessment framework would seem to be needed, if only to avoid actions of an arbitrary nature by any state or group of states, whenever it suits its or their purposes. If the necessary international agreement can be reached, it could have the form of legally binding criteria. As the reaching of such agreement may be difficult at this point, however, it may be necessary to settle for (political) guidelines.

The "assessment framework" presented in the report by the Netherlands Advisory Council on International Affairs and the Advisory Committee on Issues of Public International Law (reported in Table 2.1, pg. 10) may provide a useful mechanism in this respect. Such a framework "can clarify the minimum conditions to be satisfied. It can also help to structure deliberations within the UN (Security Council or General Assembly) on specific instances of intervention. At the same time, it can provide the UN community of nations with a basis for assessing instances of unauthorized humanitarian intervention that have already taken place and for tolerating them in appropriate cases."[34]

Such an assessment framework would be useful to answer the following questions:

- Which states should be allowed to engage in humanitarian intervention?
- When should states be allowed to engage in humanitarian intervention?
- What conditions should states satisfy during humanitarian intervention?
- When and in what way should states end their humanitarian intervention?

### Effects of Existing Lack of Codification

A lack of codification carries the danger that military action for humanitarian purposes is performed on an arbitrary basis whenever it suits the foreign policy goals of any particular state or group of states. This may lead to the action itself becoming the object of political controversy, rather than the violation of human rights or international humanitarian law that was the reason for the humanitarian intervention in the first place.

## Danger of Increase in Number of Interventions without Security Council Authorization

There would seem to be no reason to assume that some kind of codification would increase the number of interventions without Security Council authorization, provided that the situation in question is in the first instance submitted to the Security Council for action and provided that the action is fully reported to the council. Such reports should cover both plans for humanitarian intervention and its actual progress. It would also be wise to have more than one state or an international (regional) organization participate in a decision to intervene for humanitarian reasons.[35] This would lessen the chance that the concept would be invoked purely for reasons of national self-interest. However, in the case of the NATO actions in Kosovo, it was clearly the United States and the United Kingdom that dominated the decision making, as they provided the bulk of the aircraft taking part.

## The Need for Codification to Lift a Possible Legal Bar to Such Actions

It is hard to say whether states at present refrain from intervening to prevent humanitarian disasters because there is thought to be a legal bar to such actions. States would rather offer public explanations when they do act than when they do not. In the end, a decision to act or not to act remains the political responsibility of the government(s) concerned. They may decide not to act for a number of reasons, such as uncertainty of international political repercussions, political factors of a domestic nature, lack of available military potential, lack of transport facilities, and so on. Legal arguments are often put forward to cover political considerations.

### Legal or Political Criteria

Newly formulated legal criteria may not be needed.[36] The UN Charter provides such legal criteria, leaving the responsibility to act to the Security Council. What are needed at this point are political guidelines to help governments to make up their minds whether to act or not to act. In the end, decisions on humanitarian intervention will be taken on a case-by-case basis.

Proposing formalized legal criteria may have a counterproductive effect on states that are skeptical of the wisdom of engaging in humanitarian intervention to begin with. Humanitarian intervention in the absence of UN Security Council authorization would be justified on moral and political grounds only, "as an 'emergency exit' from the existing norms of international law."[37]

Table 2.1

**Summary of Main Items of an Assessment Framework**

(1) Which states should be allowed to engage in humanitarian action/intervention?

> (a) The intervening states should not themselves be in any way involved in the grave violations of fundamental human rights or international humanitarian law that the action/intervention is designed to combat.

> (b) For operational reasons, preference should be given to the involvement of the countries in the region.

> (c) Preference should be given to humanitarian action/intervention by a group of states acting under the auspices of an international organization.

(2) When should states be allowed to engage in humanitarian intervention?

> (a) The situation must be one in which fundamental human rights are being or are likely to be seriously violated on a large scale and there is an urgent need for intervention.

> (b) Large-scale violations of fundamental human rights can also be committed by non-state actors and can thus constitute grounds for humanitarian intervention.

> (c) The legitimate, internationallyrecognized government is unable or unwilling to provide the victims with appropriate care.

> (d) Humanitarian intervention may involve either an internal crisis or an essentially humanitarian emergency with international implications.

> (e) The humanitarian emergency can be reversed or contained only by deploying military resources.

> (f) The intervening states have exhausted all appropriate nonmilitary means of action against the state that is violating human rights or international humanitarian law.

There would be a high risk that attempts to modify existing rules would exacerbate differences of view over these highly sensitive matters and have a destructive rather than a constructive impact on the possibility of averting victimization of civilian populations.[38]

*Factors for Consideration before Undertaking*
*a Military Intervention*

The following factors should be considered before a decision to undertake a humanitarian intervention is taken. There should be reliable and objective evidence from different sources of gross and large-scale violations of human rights or the threat of such violations. Such evidence can be supplied by international

(3) What conditions should states satisfy during humanitarian intervention?

(a) Humanitarian intervention must be in proportion to the gravity of the situation.

(b) The humanitarian intervention must not itself constitute an even greater threat to international peace and security than the situation it is meant to prevent or to end.

(c) The impact of the humanitarian intervention must be limited to what is necessary in order to attain the humanitarian objective.

(d) The states engaging in humanitarian intervention must report to the Security Council immediately and in detail with the reason for the operation, its scale, its progress, and its likely duration

(4) When and in what way should states end their humanitarian intervention?

(a) The intervening states must undertake in advance to suspend the humanitarian intervention as soon as the state concerned is willing and able to end the large-scale violations of human rights or international humanitarian law or the Security Council takes the necessary measures for the same humanitarian purposes.

(b) The intervening states must end their intervention when its objective, namely the cessation of violations of human rights or international humanitarian law, has been attained.

(c) The impact of the humanitarian intervention must be limited to what is necessary in order to attain the humanitarian objective.

(d) The states engaging in humanitarian intervention must report to the Security Council immediately and in detail with the reason for the operation, its scale, its progress, and its likely duration.

*Source:* Advisory Council on International Affairs and Advisory Committee on Issues of Public International Law, Humanitarian Intervention (The Hague: Ministry of Foreign Affairs, 2000), p. 26.

organizations such as the UN; regional organizations like the Organization for Security and Cooperation in Europe, the Organization of American States, or the Organization of African Unity; nongovernmental organizations such as Amnesty International or Human Rights Watch; or reliable private sources.

It should be the case that the government of the state concerned is unwilling or unable to take adequate remedial action, or is itself responsible for the violation(s). As in the case of the International Criminal Court, the primary responsibility for the maintenance of human rights and international humanitarian law rests with the state concerned.[39] Only if that state does not meet its responsibilities is external action of a diplomatic, legal, economic, or military nature warranted.[40]

There should be a clear urgency to act. There must be evidence that human lives are at stake or that grave violations of human rights are already taking place or due to take place in the very near future. Gross violations of fundamental human rights include not only extermination by means of summary executions and deliberate armed or police attacks on arbitrary civilian targets, but also torture, the taking of hostages, rape, involuntary disappearances, and other grave infringements of human dignity, such as humiliating treatment.

The use of force should be the last resort. Other means of a nonmilitary kind should be exhausted before military intervention takes place. These include attempts to end the humanitarian crisis with support from civil society in the state concerned, as well as other measures of an international kind. The late Evan Luard, a British diplomat and scholar, has provided by now a classical list of such possibilities.[41] They include the exertion of pressure through diplomatic channels, either bilaterally or in multilateral bodies. The effectiveness of taking economic sanctions has been widely debated.[42] They may be counterproductive or hit the wrong persons or groups. The granting or withholding of development aid as an instrument of human rights policy is also of dubious value. The Dutch government has used this instrument in the case of its former colonies of Suriname and Indonesia, with at best mixed results. Indonesia, for its part, decided to end the development relationship with the Netherlands on its own initiative, rejecting "the reckless use of development assistance as an instrument of intimidation or as a tool for threatening Indonesia."[43] Such nonmilitary measures, however, should be seriously considered before military action is taken.

The primary purpose of the intervention should be to stop the violations. This means, of course, that once the violations have been brought to an end, the intervention should be stopped. The intervening states should suspend their actions as soon as the state concerned is willing and able to end the large-scale violations of human rights by itself or the Security Council or a regional organization acting with Security Council authorization takes enforcement measures involving the use of force for the same humanitarian purposes.

Preferably, the available evidence suggests that those for whom it is intended support the action. This will not always be easy to establish and may involve "public relations wars," as took place during the military operations in Kuwait and the bombing of Iraq by allied forces, and also during the Kosovo air strikes. If the potential or actual victims of the human rights violations do not favor the military action, however, one may well ask what is the point of undertaking it in the first place.[44]

The action has a reasonable chance of success at acceptable costs. These costs pertain both to the affected population and to the intervening forces. "Success" means putting an end to the human rights violations that initiated the military action.

The action must not in itself constitute an even greater threat to international peace and security. This may raise the following dilemma: the use or threat of force must be firm enough to produce the desired effect, but must also be sufficiently controlled to avoid destabilizing conditions in the region, which may result in even greater losses of life than those that led to the actual intervention.

## Guidelines

A number of guidelines should be followed during a military intervention. The purpose of the intervention should be made clear and public from the very beginning. This would help to guarantee that everybody understands the conditions that must be met to bring the action to an end.[45]

The use of force should be limited to what is necessary to attain the stated goals and be proportionate to these goals. This largely concerns the manner in which force is used or threatened. The rules of humanitarian law are applicable here. In this connection, the Geneva Conventions of 1949 must be fully complied with. If the intervention is carried out by a group of states that are not all parties to the Additional Protocols of 1977 and other humanitarian law conventions,[46] the rules of customary law on the subject must be taken into account. States that fail to satisfy the proportionality requirement may find themselves facing unforeseen legal complications.[47]

The effect on the political system of the country should be limited to what is strictly necessary to accomplish the purpose of the intervention. This may, but should not necessarily mean, the replacement of the regime in power. Although this means that the action will be limited to a treatment of the symptoms,[48] this may well be preferable to possible threats to international peace and security as well as internal stability that further-going actions might entail.

There should be full reporting to the Security Council on the reasons for the operation, its scale, and its progress. This may involve, of course, the risk that the Security Council may act to stop the intervention before its objectives have been achieved. Yet, it would be preferable to stick as closely as possible to the regular use of force as permitted by the charter.

## Conclusion

If nonmilitary means to put an end to gross violations of fundamental human rights, such as the mass killings of civilians, torture, ethnic cleansing, genocide, massive rape, and involuntary disappearances in a country, have failed, military intervention remains as a final resort. Such intervention should preferably take place under authorization of the UN Security Council, this being the internationally accepted legal use of force in situations that are beyond the situation of self-defense. As is well known, however, the political situation may be such that the UN Security Council is unable to reach a decision, while grave violations of human rights continue to take place. From a moral— if not legal—point of view, it may then be acceptable to undertake military action without prior Security Council authorization. Although the formulation of legal criteria for such action would be preferable, it may be necessary to settle for political guidelines (e.g., in the form of an "assessment framework") as has been spelled out in this chapter. Once a decision to intervene has been taken, the action itself should be of a limited nature, with the sole objective of ending the violations of human rights that were mentioned.

Although the assessment framework may help to arrive at a somewhat objective basis for action, in the final instance, the decision to intervene by military means is left to the individual governments, which may do so for political reasons that have little or only a partial relationship to the lofty objective of ending human rights violations, while using the term "humanitarian intervention" as the means of justification. This may mean that in certain cases military action will be undertaken, while in other similar cases this will not be done. The reactions to human rights violations in Kosovo, on the one hand, and Chechnya, on the other, bear witness to this—from an ethical point—unpleasant conclusion. The fact that the United States and other Western governments, however, for obvious reasons, have been unwilling to take action in the case of Chechnya should not lead to the conclusion that, for the sake of consistency, nonaction in Kosovo would have been better, as well. In an imperfect world, one must settle for imperfect solutions.[49]

Finally, there is the matter of terminology. The term "humanitarian intervention" wrongly suggests that the intervention will take place using humanitarian means. Nothing, however, is further from the truth. The use of high-flying aircraft that drop bombs on military as well as nonmilitary targets (the often quoted "collateral damage," in the case of Kosovo), is by no means more "humanitarian" than shooting a person at close range or launching a ballistic missile. Strictly speaking, then, it must be concluded that the term "humanitarian intervention" is indeed a misnomer. It would be far better to speak of the use of military force for (allegedly) humanitarian purposes.[50] It is not very likely, though, that governments will be prepared to change their use of terminology. "Humanitarian intervention" has the advantage of sounding nice, while being sufficiently vague so as to leave governments considerable freedom of action—which they like.

In the end, it will be left to one's political judgment, whether one is or is not willing to accept certain military actions for humanitarian purposes. To use military means and to risk causing collateral damage may not accord with high-minded principles of international law or one's personal ethics. But not to respond at all to grave violations of fundamental human rights may be even worse.

## Notes

1. R. J. Vincent, *Non-intervention and International Order* (Princeton, N.J.: Princeton University Press, 1974), p. 346.

2. UN Security Council Resolution (UNSCR) 688.

3. UN Charter, Article 41.

4. UN Charter, Article 43.

5. Constitution of the Netherlands, Article 90.

6. Fernando R. Tesón cites this invasion as a good example of humanitarian intervention. See Fernando R. Tesón, *Humanitarian Intervention: An Inquiry into Law and Morality*, 2nd ed. (Irvington-on-Hudson, N.Y.: Transnational, 1997), p. 208.

7. Bartram S. Brown writes, however, "This invasion markedly improved the human rights situation in Uganda. This was accomplished, however, by completely replacing the unspeakably brutal regime of Idi Amin. This broader political objective would be difficult to justify under a right of humanitarian intervention." See Bartram S. Brown, "Humanitarian Intervention and Kosovo: Humanitarian Intervention at a Crossroads," *William and Mary Law Review* 41 (May 2000): 1704.

8. The Indian representative at the UN initially referred to the Indian move into East Pakistan as an example of humanitarian intervention, but in the final edited version of the debate on the matter in the Security Council this defense had been dropped and it was now claimed to be an act of self-defense since Pakistan had attacked first. See Stephen A. Garrett, *Doing Good and Doing Well: An Examination of Humanitarian Intervention* (New York: Praeger, 1999), p. 63, quoting from Michael Akehurst, "Humanitarian Intervention," in Hedley Bull, ed., *Intervention in World Politics* (Oxford: Clarendon, 1984), pp. 95–99. I thank Hiroki Kusano for providing me with these references.

9. Akehurst, "Humanitarian Intervention," pp. 97–99.

10. Further examples of post–Cold War armed or humanitarian intervention, as mentioned in an Amnesty International internal paper, are the following: (a) Liberia 1990 (not authorized, but endorsed in 1992 by UNSCR 788); (b) Iraq 1991 (authorized under UNSCR 688); (c) Iraq post-1991 (neither authorized nor condemned by the Security Council), (d) former Yugoslavia 1991–1993 (authorized under UNSCR 770, 781, 816); (e) Somalia 1992 (authorized under UNSCR 794); (f) Haiti 1994 (authorized under UNSCR 940), (g) Rwanda 1994 (authorized under UNSCR 929); (h) Kosovo 1999 (no UN authorization); and (i) East Timor 1999 (authorized under UNSCR 1264).

11. "All Members shall refrain in their international relations from the threat or use of force against the territorial integrity or political independence of any state, or in any other manner inconsistent with the Purposes of the United Nations." See UN Charter, Article 2, paragraph 4.

12. UN Charter, Articles 43, 51.

13. Danish Institute of International Relations, *Humanitarian Intervention: Legal and Political Aspects* (Copenhagen: Danish Institute of International Relations, 1999), p. 11. This definition is similar to the one used by Brown, "forcible action by a state on the territory of another to protect individuals from continuing grave violations of fundamental human rights." See Brown, "Humanitarian Intervention and Kosovo," pp. 1686–1687. He quotes the definitions used by Ian Brownlie and Tesón. Brownlie defines humanitarian intervention as a "[t]hreat or use of armed force by a state, a belligerent community, or an international organization, with the object of protecting human rights." See Ian Brownlie, "Humanitarian Intervention," in John Norton Moore, ed., *Law and Civil War in the Modern World* (Baltimore, Md.: Johns Hopkins University Press, 1974), p. 217. Tesón speaks of "the proportionate transboundary help, including forcible help, provided by governments to individuals in another state who are being denied basic human rights and who themselves would be rationally willing

to revolt against their oppressive government." See Tesón, *Humanitarian Interven-tion*, p. 208; see also International Commission on Intervention and State Sovereignty (ICISS), *The Responsibility to Protect: A Report of the International Commission on Intervention and State Sovereignty* (Ottawa: International Commission on Intervention and State Sovereignty, 2001), p. 8. ("The kind of intervention with which we are concerned in this report is action taken against a state or its leaders, without its or their consent, for purposes which are claimed to be humanitarian or protective.")

14. Cecilia Medina Quiroga, *The Battle of Human Rights: Gross, Systematic Violations and the Inter-American System* (Boston: Nijhoff, 1988), p. 16.

15. Peter R. Baehr, *Human Rights: Universality in Practice* (Hampshire, UK: Palgrave, 2001), pp. 20–31.

16. Under Article 5, paragraph 1 of its statute, the International Criminal Court has jurisdiction over (a) the crime of genocide, (b) crimes against humanity, (c) war crimes, and (d) the crime of aggression. Article 5, paragraph 2 says, "The Court shall exercise jurisdiction over the crime of aggression once a provision is adopted . . . defining the crime and setting out the conditions under which the Court shall exercise jurisdiction with respect to the crime. Such a provision shall be consistent with the relevant provisions of the Charter of the United Nations." See UN Doc. A/CONF.183 (1998). Almost needless to say, so far, no agreement has been reached about such a provision.

17. Emphasis added.

18. UN General Assembly, A/CONF.157/23, 12 July 1993, *Vienna Declaration and Programme of Action*, paragraph 4. The term "international community" should be read as "the United Nations." C. Flinterman argues, "The expression of criticism, within the framework of 'quiet diplomacy' or in public, even the taking of diplomatic or economic sanctions in reaction to violations of human rights are, generally speaking, no more considered as unlawful interference." See C. Flinterman, "Soevereiniteit en de Rechten van de Mens" ("Sovereignty and Human Rights") (inaugural address at Utrecht University, January 19, 2001), p. 21, translated from the original Dutch by the author.

19. See Vincent, *Non-intervention and International Order*, for an opposite view, see, for instance, Brownlie, "[A] jurist asserting a right of forcible humanitarian intervention has a very heavy burden of proof. Few writers familiar with the modern materials of state practice and legal opinion on the use of force would support such a view." See Brownlie, "Humanitarian Intervention," p. 218.

20. Peter H. Kooijmans, who is a member of the International Court of Justice, has made the point that, while the Iraqi invasion of Kuwait was termed a "breach of the peace," internal violence in the case of the former Yugoslavia, Somalia, Rwanda, Liberia, and Kosovo was seen as only a "threat to the peace." He wonders how it is possible that the Security Council, while terming the conflict in Rwanda as a "threat to the peace," nevertheless established the Rwanda Tribunal, under Chapter VII of the charter, as a means to the "restoration and maintenance of peace": "How can peace be restored, if it was never breached?" See Peter H. Kooijmans, "De Toekomst van de Vrede" ("The Future of Peace"), *Internationale Spectator* 53 (January 1999): 5, translated from the original Dutch by the author.

21. Brown writes, "Russia opposed any move by the Security Council to intervene militarily. When the Council is paralyzed in this way, it leaves the international community in a difficult position." See Brown, "Humanitarian Intervention and Kosovo," p. 1725. Strictly speaking, however, the Security Council was not "paralyzed"; the issue was never discussed nor put to a vote.

22. Some, including myself, have argued that it would have been better to put the

issue before the UN Security Council, thus forcing Russia and China to take the responsibility of not acting in the face of grave human rights violations that were taking place in Kosovo. For an opposite view, see David P. Forsythe, postscript to David P. Forsythe, ed., *Human Rights and Comparative Foreign Policy* (Tokyo: UN University Press, 2000), p. 339. ("If a resolution authorizing force had been presented and vetoed, although the onus for blocking action would have been on Beijing and/or Moscow, it would have proved more difficult to go ahead with the bombing.")

23. Abdullahi A. An-Na'im, "NATO on Kosovo Is Bad for Human Rights," *Netherlands Quarterly of Human Rights* 17 (September 1999): 230.

24. Forsythe, postscript, p. 338.

25. UN General Assembly Resolution 377 (V), 3 November 1950; see also Advisory Council on International Affairs and Advisory Committee on Issues of Public International Law, *Humanitarian Intervention* (The Hague: Ministry of Foreign Affairs, 2000, official English version), p. 26 (hereafter *Humanitarian Intervention*).

26. The ICISS states that such action will be an additional form of leverage on the Security Council "to encourage it to act decisively and appropriately." See ICISS, *Responsibility to Protect*, p. 53.

27. Emphasis added.

28. Independent International Commission on Kosovo, *The Kosovo Report* (Oxford: Oxford University Press, 2000), p. 164; see also Human Rights Watch, *World Report 1999* (New York: Human Rights Watch, 1999), available at www.hrw.org/wr2k/Eca-26.htm (accessed March 20, 2003); Amnesty International, *Kosovo: A Decade of Unheeded Warnings* (London: Amnesty International, AI Index EUR 70/56/99, 1999); "Indictment of Slobodan Milošević and Others by the Prosecutor of the International Criminal Tribunal for the Former Yugoslavia," available at www.un.org/icty/indictment/english/mil-ii990524e.htm (accessed March 20, 2003).

29. Brown, "Humanitarian Intervention and Kosovo," p. 1733.

30. Amnesty International, *NATO/Federal Republic of Yugoslavia: "Collateral Damage" or Unlawful Killings? Violations of the Laws of War by NATO during Operation Allied Force* (London: Amnesty International, AI Index EUR 70/18/00, 2000), p. 2.

31. Amnesty International, *NATO/Federal Republic of Yugoslavia*, p. 2.

32. General Wesley K. Clark, at a press conference on April 13, 1999, said, "I don't know what the extent of the second strike was, but two bombs were put into that bridge and in both cases there was an effort made to avoid collateral damage. He [the pilot] couldn't, he saw what had happened, it is one of those regrettable things that happen in a campaign like this and we are all very sorry for it, but we are doing the absolute best we can do to avoid collateral damage, I can assure you of that." See "Jaime Shea and General Wesley Clark," *NATO's Role in Kosovo*, April 13, 1999, available at www.nato.int/kosovo/press/p990413a.htm (accessed March 20, 2003).

Shea, a NATO spokesperson, also posited the following, "Two questions on the bombing of the bridge at Varvarin: first of all, can you confirm that the attack took place at 1.00 P.M., or at least in the middle of the day; and second, if it did take place in the middle of the day, how does that square with your repeated assertions, NATO does everything to avoid civilian casualties, since clearly you are going to take more civilian casualties in the middle of the day than you would in the middle of the night?" Colonel Konrad Freytag's response was,

I've got some civilian casualty figures for you this afternoon: 550,000 internally displaced persons in Kosovo; 883,500 refugees in neighboring countries, 75% of which are women and children; 193,845 Kosovar refugees elsewhere in the world from Austria to Australia, spread across the globe. Currently, 1,582,345 displaced persons and refugees resulting from the Serb actions in Kosovo, 93% of the original population of Kosovo; 225,000 men missing, but at least 6,000 killed in summary executions, 10 mass graves. That is, I think, the vital casualty statistics as far as NATO is concerned, and that is the generation of Milosevic's bullets, not NATO's bombs.

See "Jaime Shea and Colonel Konrad Freytag," *NATO Role in Kosovo*, May 31, 1999, available at www.nato.int/kosovo/press/p990531a.htm (accessed March 20, 2003).

33. According to Human Rights Watch, "Although according to the U.S. Defense Department, there were only twenty incidents in which Yugoslav civilians died from bombing," research conducted by Human Rights Watch concluded that "the number of civilian casualties was at least four times higher, although the number of deaths was only a third of the 2,000 casualties reported by the Yugoslav government." See Human Rights Watch, *World Report 1999*; see also Human Rights Watch, "NATO's Use of Cluster Munitions in Yugoslavia," *World Report 1999* (New York: Human Rights Watch, 1999); Human Rights Watch, "NATO's Use of Cluster Bombs Must Stop," Press Release, May 11, 1999, available at www.hrw.org/wr2k/Eca-26.htm (accessed March 20, 2003).

34. *Humanitarian Intervention*, p. 28; see also Barend ter Haar, *Peace or Human Rights? The Dilemma of Humanitarian Intervention* (The Hague: Netherlands Institute of International Relations "Clingendael," 2000). For a summary of its main items, see Table 2.1 page XX).

35. See also ICISS, *Responsibility to Protect*, pp. 53–54.

36. This view is by no means universally shared. Brown, for instance, writes, "Without clear *legal* standards to limit it, the practice of humanitarian intervention threatens to undermine the friendly relations among states and could have an adverse impact upon international peace and security." See Brown, "Humanitarian Intervention and Kosovo," p. 1686, emphasis added.

37. Danish Institute of International Relations, *Humanitarian Intervention*, p. 116.

38. Danish Institute of International Relations, *Humanitarian Intervention*, p. 119.

39. As written in the Statute of the International Criminal Court, "An International Criminal Court . . . is hereby established. It shall be a permanent institution and shall have the power to exercise its jurisdiction over persons for the most serious crimes of international concern, as referred to in this Statute, *and shall be complementary to national criminal jurisdiction*." See Rome Statute of the International Criminal Court, Article 1, emphasis added, available at www.un.org/law/icc/statute/99_corr/1.htm (accessed March 20, 2003).

40. The fact that authorities are willing but unable to uphold the rule of law and thus prevent large-scale violations of human rights has been identified by the UN secretary-general as one of the factors that the Security Council should take into account. See "Recommendations Formulated by the Secretary-General in the Report of the Secretary-General to the Security Council on the Protection of Civilians in Armed Conflict," S/1999/957; see also UNSCR 1265 (1999) of 17 September 1999.

41. Evan Luard, *Human Rights and Foreign Policy* (Oxford: Pergamon, 1981), pp. 26–27.

42. See Katarina Tomaševski, *Between Sanctions and Elections: Aid Donors and Their Human Rights Performance* (London: Pinter, 1997).

43. See Peter R. Baehr, "On an Equal Footing: The Netherlands and Indonesia," in Peter R. Baehr, Monique Castermans-Holleman, and Fred Grünfeld, eds., *Human*

*Rights in the Foreign Policy of the Netherlands* (New York: Intersentia, 2002), pp. 173–194.

44. Similarly, antiapartheid activists in South Africa favored international economic sanctions, even if these would have hurt poor blacks as much as the white racist minority regime.

45. According to the ICISS, "A clear and unambiguous mandate is one of the first and most important requirements of an operation to protect." See ICISS, *Responsibility to Protect*, p. 60.

46. See the Convention for the Protection of Cultural Property in the Event of Armed Conflict (1954) and its protocols; Convention on Prohibitions or Restrictions on the Use of Certain Conventional Weapons Which May be Deemed to Be Excessively Injurious or to Have Indiscriminate Effects (1980) and its protocols; Ottawa Convention Banning Anti-personnel Landmines (1997); the Statute of the International Criminal Court (1998).

47. The advisory committees to the Dutch Ministry of Foreign Affairs make the point that this would allow the state on whose territory the intervention takes place not only to invoke Article 51 of the UN Charter, but also to submit a claim for damages. See *Humanitarian Intervention*, p. 31, n64.

48. "Kurieren am Symptom" is the well-phrased German expression.

49. Or, as another German saying goes, all consistency leads to the Devil ("Jede Konsequenz führt zum Teufel").

50. The ICISS avoids the term "humanitarian" altogether and instead uses "intervention" or "military intervention for humanitarian purposes." See ICISS, *Responsibility to Protect*, p. 9.

# 3

# Legitimacy and Lawfulness of Humanitarian Intervention

*Tania Voon*

The events of 1999 in Kosovo and East Timor provide an important opportunity to reflect on the practice of humanitarian intervention. In 2000, the Independent International Commission on Kosovo (Independent Commission)[1] determined that NATO's war against the Federal Republic of Yugoslavia (FRY) beginning in March 1999 was unlawful because it involved the use of force other than in accordance with the United Nations (UN) Charter and without UN Security Council authorization.[2] The Independent Commission nevertheless considered the intervention to be legitimate for other reasons, and called for reforms to "address the growing gap between legality and legitimacy that always arises in cases of humanitarian intervention."[3] This recommendation highlights the need to examine state practice and public reactions to that practice in order to determine what makes a humanitarian intervention legitimate, even when it is unlawful, and vice versa.[4]

If we accept that in at least some circumstances humanitarian intervention is legitimate, it is possible to propose some criteria of legitimacy by looking at world reactions to the interventions in Kosovo and East Timor. In this chapter, I attempt to draw together the various strands of commentary on these two interventions in order to develop a framework to assess the legitimacy of interventions that are proposed or conducted in the future, and to aid in the reworking of international law to bring lawfulness in line with notions of legitimacy. Due to space limitations, I provide little factual background to the two interventions. Further details may be found elsewhere. A key distinction between the two cases is that the Kosovo intervention was carried out without UN Security authorization, whereas the intervention in East Timor was carried out with such authorization.

I begin by providing a working definition of the term "humanitarian intervention," followed by an explanation of the international legal framework in which humanitarian intervention takes place. The subsequent section examines the gap between lawfulness and legitimacy of humanitarian intervention, as evidenced by the interventions in Kosovo and East Timor. Finally, I consider the various factors that appeared to enhance or diminish the legitimacy of these interventions.

## A Definition of Humanitarian Intervention

The notion of "intervention" discussed in this chapter is limited to actual interference in the territory of another state through the use of military force. While several different bodies may engage in humanitarian intervention or related activities, I focus on intervention by foreign governments through international and regional organizations. A state may have numerous reasons for intervening. In the present discussion, I focus on interventions with the immediate declared goal of alleviating or preventing human rights violations, even though there may be an unrelated, underlying motive for intervening. For the purposes of this chapter, consent is not determinative of whether given actions constitute humanitarian intervention. This is because the complexities in determining sovereignty and the roles played by nongovernmental groups may often mean that a government that purports to consent does not necessarily represent all people in the affected area, or lacks the authority to consent.[5] Moreover, in a "state of complete anarchy," it may be impossible to seek the consent of any authoritative body.[6]

## The International Legal Framework

### Prohibition on the Use of Force

Article 2, paragraph 4 of the UN Charter prohibits members from threatening or using force against the territorial integrity or political independence of any state, or in any other manner inconsistent with the purposes of the UN. According to the International Court of Justice (ICJ), this rule has become a part of customary international law and therefore applies to all states.[7] The principal purpose of the UN is "to maintain international peace and security," such that a breach of the peace through the use of force against another state may itself be contrary to the purposes of the UN. On that view, military intervention constitutes valid conduct under international law only in three circumstances: action taken or authorized by the UN under Articles 39–41, individual or collective self-defense under Article 51, and action of regional organizations authorized by the Security Council under Article 53 of the UN Charter. This prohibition on the use of force reflects the general principle of state sovereignty recognized in Article 2, paragraph 1 of the UN Charter.

### Permissible Use of Force

#### UN Action

Article 2, paragraph 7 of the UN Charter provides that nothing therein authorizes the UN "to intervene in matters which are essentially within the domestic jurisdiction of any state" subject to Chapter VII. Under Article 39, the

Security Council has the role of determining "the existence of any threat to the peace, breach of the peace, or act of aggression" and recommending or deciding measures to be taken to "maintain or restore international peace and security." Where nonforceful means are inadequate, the Security Council may, under Article 42, "take such action by air, sea, or land forces as may be necessary" to achieve that goal, including demonstrations, blockade, and other operations by the forces of UN members. This provision relies on the limited obligations on members under Article 43 to make available their armed forces, assistance, and facilities for the purpose of maintaining international peace and security. Under Article 40, the Security Council may also call on the parties concerned to comply with such provisional measures as it deems necessary or desirable to "prevent an aggravation of the situation" pending decisions or recommendations under Article 39.

The UN's ability to take enforcement action under Chapter VII is limited in several respects. The Security Council is not obliged to use force under Article 42, nor are individual UN members required to assist the Security Council in doing so, unless an agreement has been negotiated between the Security Council and the member to that effect. In addition, in order for the UN to take forceful measures, the situation must constitute a "threat to the peace, breach of the peace, or act of aggression," and the Security Council must determine that the relevant parties cannot peacefully resolve the situation. It is generally assumed that international rather than domestic peace must be threatened or breached.[8]

Since the inception of the UN Charter, the notion of a threat to the peace has broadened. Human rights violations that might once have been regarded as domestic affairs are now more likely to be viewed as a threat to global peace.[9] Anarchy threatening the destruction of a state might itself be said to create a threat to the peace.[10] However, even apart from such transboundary effects, the willingness of the UN to intervene in humanitarian crises primarily to prevent human rights atrocities has grown as a result of the development of human rights law.[11] This change reflects a conception of intervention that focuses not on the international effects of a crisis but on the human rights violations themselves. Such violations will not necessarily be accompanied by the creation of refugees or other destabilizing effects that will enable the crisis to be seen as a threat to international peace. However noble this change may be, an ever-widening gap between the words of Article 39 and Security Council actions may undermine the legitimacy of that body[12] and the UN as a whole.

*Authorized Action by States*

Although the Security Council may not generally order a state to take military action under Article 39 or 42, it may authorize a state to do so. If the Security Council authorizes such action, the target state will be unable to retaliate lawfully in self-defense or claim reparations.[13] Authorization of humanitarian action is subject to the same considerations as UN action as discussed earlier.

## Authorized Action by Regional Organizations

Article 54 of the UN Charter specifically allows for regional arrangements to take enforcement action with Security Council authorization. Such arrangements and agencies are permitted "for dealing with matters relating to the maintenance of international peace and security as are appropriate for regional action," provided that they act consistently with UN purposes.[14] While regional organizations could rely on these articles to justify humanitarian intervention, on a narrow reading, this would only be in circumstances where a humanitarian crisis actually threatened international peace and security. This restricts the ability of regional organizations to engage in humanitarian intervention under the UN Charter in a manner similar to the restrictions on Security Council action. In addition, an originalist view of the UN Charter might suggest that the framers did not intend regional organizations to play a major role in maintaining peace and security, since almost all regional organizations were established after the adoption of the UN Charter.[15]

## Self-Defense

The UN Charter recognizes a specific right of self-defense. Article 51 of the UN Charter preserves the "inherent right of individual or collective self-defense if an armed attack occurs against a Member of the United Nations, until the Security Council has taken the measures necessary to maintain international peace and security." Such measures are subject to certain qualifications: they must be immediately reported to the Security Council, and they do not affect the authority of the Security Council to take such action as it deems necessary to maintain or restore international peace and security. The article also contains implicit restrictions, in that it contemplates action only after an armed attack has actually occurred, and only temporary action pending resolution of the matter by the Security Council. On one view, Article 51 encompasses a right of preventive or anticipatory self-defense, at least where armed attack is imminent and diplomatic channels have failed.[16] Finally, the ICJ has interpreted the right of self-defense as being limited to responses that are immediate, necessary, and proportional to the original attack.[17]

It is unclear from the plain words of Article 51 whether the right of collective self-defense means that a UN member may use force to repel an armed attack against a third member state. Arguably, a right to act in defense of another falls outside the principle of self-defense, or is legitimate only at the request of the attacked state,[18] or at least with that state's consent. Moreover, even assuming that a third-party state could intervene to protect one state from another, the third party might only be able to claim this involved collective self-defense if the second state had staged an armed attack against the first or was about to do so. In other circumstances, in order for humanitarian intervention to be justified under Article 51, the reference to "armed attack" would have to have an extremely broad meaning. For example, grave and widespread human rights violations are arguably analogous to an armed attack in that they threaten international peace and security. However, it is difficult to maintain this broad interpretation without undermining the elementary principles of sovereignty and nonintervention forming the basis of the prohibition in Article 2, paragraph 7.[19]

### A Humanitarian Basis for Unilateral Intervention

On a strict reading, the UN Charter prohibits the use of force against a state other than in the specific circumstances described earlier.[20] Thus, where an individual state or regional organization uses force against another state without Security Council authorization to prevent or halt human rights violations in the target state (rather than in response to a literal armed attack), the action is contrary to international law.[21] However, this is a complex and controversial issue on which views have been developing over time, corresponding with the actual practice of humanitarian intervention. Initially, it should be noted that humanitarian intervention involving the consent of the target state is unlikely to constitute using force in breach of Article 2, paragraph 4, or intervening in breach of Article 2, paragraph 7.[22]

It is possible to argue that intervention in the absence of consent falls outside Article 2, paragraph 4 and therefore need not be justified as self-defense or by UN authorization. The argument would be that humanitarian intervention does not involve the use of force "against the territorial integrity or political_independence" of the target state, but rather to enhance such integrity and independence by ensuring respect for human rights.[23] Such a reading might be buttressed by the reference in the UN's purposes to "promoting and encouraging respect for human rights and . . . fundamental freedoms for all."[24] In addition, several other provisions in the UN Charter require respect for human rights.[25] However, the UN Charter contains no explicit right to enforce its human rights provisions by the use of force. In the face of the prohibitions in Article 2, paragraphs 4 and 7, it is difficult to read this absence as implicitly authorizing such a use of force.[26] Nor can one validly claim that the Security Council provides implicit authorization of humanitarian intervention through silence.[27]

The notion that consensus may be emerging on a norm of justified humanitarian intervention in internal crises, despite the principle of nonintervention enshrined in the UN Charter, is not new.[28] However, a norm of justified humanitarian intervention has recently begun to take clearer shape, particularly due to the increasing recognition in international law of fundamental human rights and individual legal personality and the specific events in Kosovo.[29]

## The Gap between Lawfulness and Legitimacy

### Kosovo

On 24 March 1999, the North Atlantic Treaty Organization (NATO) began its eleven-week bombing campaign against the FRY.[30] Thirteen of NATO's nineteen members participated in the campaign,[31] which was conducted in the name of the alliance as a whole,[32] with the United States supplying most of the intelligence and 65 to 80 percent of the aircraft and precision ordnance.[33] NATO's stated justification for taking such action was to support "the political aims of the international community: a peaceful, multiethnic and democratic Kosovo in which all its people can live in security and enjoy universal human rights and freedoms on an equal basis."[34] In other words, according to certain NATO leaders, it acted primarily to end a humanitarian crisis.[35]

Commentators in academic, popular, and journalistic circles suggest that NATO's use of force against the FRY was contrary to the UN Charter and international law.[36] The ICJ is presently hearing several claims by the FRY against various NATO countries alleging that the resort to force was illegal,[37] although it dismissed the FRY's claim against the U.S. for want of jurisdiction.[38] Other commentators see the NATO intervention as neither clearly legal nor illegal, because of the indeterminate state of the law.[39] Still others suggest that, although the law in this area is uncertain, NATO's conduct may have assisted in the creation of a new right of humanitarian intervention under customary international law,[40] or that it was simply legal.[41] Several commentators, including key international players and analysts, acknowledge the technical illegality of NATO's actions while maintaining that they were nevertheless "legitimate" in some other sense[42] or that there were "mitigating circumstances" that should be taken into account in assessing the actions.[43]

Clearly, no overwhelming consensus emerges as to either the lawfulness or the legitimacy of the NATO bombing. The indeterminacy of the law feeds into the difficulty of assessing the legitimacy of the action. However, it is clear that observers tend to separate the issues of lawfulness and legitimacy. In many cases, the fact that the action can be labeled "unlawful" is a convenient boost for an argument against the action. Conversely, the fact that some doctrinal readings of international law may point to its lawfulness simply provides support for its perceived legitimacy. The notion that the intervention was unlawful but nevertheless legitimate provides the clearest illustration of the gap between lawfulness and legitimacy in this area.

## East Timor

On 5 May 1999, Indonesia and Portugal signed an agreement requesting the UN to conduct a ballot in East Timor enabling the East Timorese to choose between "independence" on the one hand and "autonomy" under Indonesian sovereignty on the other.[44] On 30 August 1999, despite months of violent intimidation, nearly 99 percent of eligible voters cast a vote, and about 78 percent of these people voted for independence. A systematic "scorched earth" campaign by Indonesian military-backed militia groups followed.[45] In September 1999, with the consent of Indonesian president Bacharuddin Jusuf Habibie, the Security Council authorized the deployment of an International Force for East Timor (Interfet), led by Australia, to restore peace and security.[46] The force was deployed on 20 September. The Indonesian troops began to withdraw from East Timor and rarely clashed with Interfet.[47]

At face value, the intervention in East Timor was lawful because the Security Council authorized the establishment of Interfet and Indonesia provided its consent. Media reports often noted that the intervention in East Timor was conducted peacefully and under the auspices of the UN, in contrast to NATO's approach in Kosovo.[48] However, other commentators criticized the UN, Australia, and other members of the international community for failing to intervene earlier—specifically, for failing to insist on providing security in the period leading up to the August 1999 ballot and, more importantly, after the ballot.[49] The devastating aftermath of the ballot was foreseeable, and Western intelligence may well have revealed its likelihood.[50]

Criticism of the intervention in East Timor because it came too late reaffirms the distinction between legitimacy and lawfulness of humanitarian intervention. The lateness of the interventionist response tended to diminish its legitimacy, even though it was widely regarded as legal. The fact that Australia and the UN delayed the intervention until Indonesia consented is also telling on this point. According to the general understanding of the international community, Indonesia had no legal claim to East Timor and therefore no right to authorize intervention. Therefore, the intervention could have proceeded in accordance with international law without Indonesia's consent. Despite this, Australia and the UN evidently regarded Indonesia's sovereignty claim as preventing a legitimate intervention, and so intervened only after obtaining Indonesian consent. In contrast, NATO apparently considered that, despite the FRY's legal claim to sovereignty in Kosovo, it could launch a legitimate intervention.[51] These two examples suggest that the intervening parties themselves regarded lawfulness and legitimacy as two different things.

## Legitimating Factors

Since international law alone does not appear to determine the legitimacy of a particular intervention, it is necessary to examine what other factors might do so. If law remains distanced from legitimacy, this will undermine the authority of the Security Council and the role of the UN in keeping the peace. It will also exacerbate the difficulties of individual states and organizations when asked to intervene. The international community should therefore examine the factors that make an intervention legitimate with a view to articulating them by consensus and incorporating them into international law. In the following sections, I examine various criteria that might bear on the legitimacy of a given intervention at the stage of the original decision to intervene.

## Rights and Lives at Stake

Fernando Tesón premises legitimate intervention on the existence of human rights violations reaching a certain quantitative and qualitative level; specifically, there must be extensive violations of basic civil and political rights.[52] Violations of a *jus cogens* norm are more likely to justify intervention, regardless of whether the target state has accepted the norm.[53] Thus, violations of prohibitions on genocide, torture, and slavery[54] more easily trigger international concerns than do less established human rights norms. Violation of the right of self-determination[55] might also provide a legitimate reason for intervention.[56]

Various commentators alleged that the persecutors were carrying out genocide in East Timor and Kosovo. In East Timor, reports suggested that the Indonesian occupiers committed genocide in contributing to the deaths of at least a third of the population (200,000 people).[57] In contrast, while many media reports on Kosovo used the word "genocide," some critics argue that the Serbian treatment of Kosovar Albanians was nothing of the sort. Although killings occurred, both sides were responsible for the violence, which in any case barely amounted to the status of "atrocity."[58] Before the bombing began, the records showed "only" around 2,000 casualties.[59] Yet, in both cases the public clamored for their governments and the UN to "do something." This may suggest that where oppressors arbitrarily attack ordinary people, the mere quality of the human rights violations will be sufficient to mobilize public support for intervention. This phenomenon is even more likely to arise where the victims include women or children, and where the media captures the violations on film and reports them using words like "genocide" and "ethnic cleansing."

## Identities of Intervenor and Target

### Individual and Collective Intervention

Members of the general public and academic observers are likely to regard the legitimacy of a particular intervention as strengthened where "the decision to intervene stems from a multilateral decision-making process."[60] Although multilateralism does not guarantee that intervention is the right solution, simply obtaining consensus among more participants reduces the chances of intervenors abusing the power of humanitarian intervention. One difficulty with relying too heavily on Security Council authorization for humanitarian intervention is that some states may exercise veto rights so as to defeat the intervention simply in order to avoid establishing "an institutional precedent that could be used against them . . . at some future point in time."[61] In addition, if victims can rely only on the Security Council, they may find themselves without assistance at a crucial time or without assistance soon enough.[62] Regional organizations may provide a welcome compromise between the well-resourced but reluctant U.S. and the under-resourced but willing UN acting as global police officers. If such organizations or groups of states have the blessing of the Security Council before acting, this will lend legitimacy both to the intervention and to the Security Council itself.[63]

The legitimacy of NATO's intervention in Kosovo was increased by its multilateralist backing, but decreased by its failure to engage the UN early on and by the leadership role played by the U.S. The exclusion of the UN probably caused concern more because it reflected poorly on the lawfulness of the operation than because it evidenced a lack of multilateralism. Similarly, the perceived dominance of the U.S. within NATO caused difficulties because of the particular nature and history of the U.S. within the global system, rather than because it suggested that one state alone was calling the shots. In East Timor, since the intervention was conducted with the explicit authority of the Security Council and with UN support, commentators complained not about a lack of multilateralism but about other factors discussed in this chapter. Thus, from these two cases it seems that the unilateral or multilateral nature of the intervenor or intervenors may matter less in determining the legitimacy of an intervention than other factors, such as the rights and lives at stake. This conclusion might differ, of course, if the intervention were conducted purely by a single state, rather than under the auspices of a regional organization or the UN.

*Relationship between Intervenor and Target*

Australia has had a long and complex relationship with East Timor and Indonesia. The many facets of the relationship are too extensive to cover here. In December 1975, the Indonesian army invaded East Timor, and in July 1976, Indonesia purported to incorporate the territory as an Indonesian province. Indonesia continued to occupy East Timor for twenty-five years,[64] with escalating violence by the Indonesian military against the East Timorese people.[65] The UN never recognized Indonesian sovereignty over East Timor,[66] and Australia was the only Western democracy to offer de jure recognition of Indonesian sovereignty.[67] Australia's recognition of Indonesian sovereignty over East Timor formed the basis of its entry into the Timor Gap Treaty with

Indonesia in 1991,[68] which provided for joint exploration and exploitation of the oil and gas resources in the waters between Australia and East Timor.[69] The Australian position was widely condemned.[70]

For many years, the Australian government was involved in a constant balancing act between appeasing Indonesia and satisfying public opinion at home,[71] often failing in both respects.[72] In September 1999, Australia's leadership of Interfet[73] finally seemed to tip the balance of Australian policy on East Timor in favor of complying with the demands of the Australian public. Support throughout Australia for the intervention in East Timor enabled the Australian government to meet most of the costs of the international mission by imposing a levy on the Australian public.[74] Before the August 1999 vote, a television poll showed 83 percent of Australians supporting the East Timorese right of self-determination.[75] Public protests and trade union actions in Australia against Indonesia also evidenced the extent of public support.[76] However, Australia's high profile in the election and intervention process "led to some doubts of Australia's good faith" given its long recognition of Indonesian sovereignty.[77]

While some media reports outside Indonesia labeled Australia's intervention "ironic" or "hypocritical" given its prior relations with Indonesia and East Timor,[78] others suggested that Australia had a moral responsibility to intervene[79] and that it had done a good job of remedying past errors.[80] UN members and others have praised Australia for its role in East Timor,[81] particularly in showing conviction to act in the face of U.S. indecisiveness.[82] The largely positive response to Australia's role suggests that potential intervenors need not be overly concerned about losing face should they decide to take action to reverse a human rights situation in which they were previously accomplices. On the contrary, one of the few ways for a state to begin to make amends for such conduct is by taking a lead role in a legitimate and genuinely humanitarian intervention.

*Western Hegemony*

The fact that NATO conducted the bombing campaign against the FRY should not mask the fact that the public tended to view the campaign as primarily a U.S. operation.[83] Christine Chinkin was particularly concerned by the fact that the leading nation in the campaign was the U.S., revealing the "new world order" as a "Western hegemon."[84] Other commentators also described the U.S. involvement as evidencing "a new form of colonialism."[85] A distinct fear of U.S. imperialism characterized the response of many nations to the commencement of NATO bombing.[86]

The same resentment of imperialism, colonialism, and Western superiority characterized some reactions to Australia's intervention in East Timor: "For all its kow-towing to Indonesia, Jakarta considers Australia to be a meddling busybody—too white, too Western, and too Christian by half."[87] Asian nations in particular were insulted and wary about Australia's self-appointment as the regional deputy to the "U.S. global policeman."[88] Australian prime minister John Howard claimed not to have used any such words himself. However, Howard was severely criticized (particularly within Australia and in Asian countries) for failing to dispel media suggestions that this was the role Australia intended to play, and for expounding what came to be known as the "Howard doctrine" of foreign affairs.[89]

These reactions to intervention by the U.S. and Australia highlight how important it is for Western intervenors to be sensitive to their targets and neighboring countries. Australia went too far with its long courtship with Indonesia and its policy of associating Asian violations of human rights with Asian values. Nevertheless, particularly where the intervenor is a developed country and the target a developing country, the intervenor must keep in mind the tensions created by the development gap and fears of cultural and even military imperialism. Where the intervenor is the U.S., these tensions are multiplied. This means not only that the intervenor should handle with care any media representations or negotiations with the target, but also that it should scrutinize its own motivations and actions before intervening.

*Nonhumanitarian Interests*

A purist might argue that a state or organization should undertake humanitarian intervention only where its motivations are wholly humanitarian. This rule would be extremely difficult to enforce. More problematically, it would risk chilling genuine desires to assist persecuted groups because of the near impossibility of excluding "strategic policy considerations."[90] A rule that humanitarian intervention was only lawful or legitimate where unclouded by any interests beyond a desire to protect human rights would also fail to protect those rights. It could mean, for example, that the existence of natural resources of interest to the intervenor would render invalid an otherwise valid intervention, even though the impact on the persecuted individuals would be identical regardless of the existence of such an interest.[91] Accordingly, Kurt Mills suggests that as long as the intervenor's primary interests in intervention are humanitarian, the existence of other interests does not detract from the legitimacy of the intervention.[92] Similarly, Tesón suggests that nonhumanitarian motives will not necessarily destroy the humanitarian nature of the intervention, provided that they do not "impair or reduce the first paramount human rights objective."[93]

Reactions to the interventions in East Timor and Kosovo tend to suggest that an intervenor need not have a seamless commitment to human rights in its own or other territories in order to claim a humanitarian basis for a given intervention. Critics will generally view such claims with a realistic eye—resigned to the fact that extraneous interests will undoubtedly affect the decision to intervene—provided that real concerns of a humanitarian nature demand intervention. Nevertheless, observers tend to remain wary of any subsequent conduct of the intervenor that suggests such extraneous interests may be playing a leading role.

## Last Resort

Richard Falk has criticized both NATO's resort to force in Kosovo and the conduct of the intervention: "it was justifiable to act, but not in the manner undertaken."[94] He argued that the lead up to the military intervention was impaired by a failure to engage in flexible diplomacy, for example, by excluding Russia and China from attempts to negotiate with the FRY.[95] Thus, force was used in defiance of the "legal, moral and political commitment to make recourse to war a *last resort.*"[96] Other commentators have also suggested that NATO failed to explore fully the possibility of reaching a resolution at the initial negotiation stage.[97]

These criticisms emphasize the importance of the would-be intervenor making genuine attempts to reach a peaceful resolution to the conflict before launching a military intervention. However, in the context of diplomatic negotiations, different stakeholders will always hold differing views as to who blocked the resolution. If the intervenor does not explore diplomacy at all, observers are likely to doubt the intervention's legitimacy, even if it ultimately works out well. If it does not work out well, the failure to exhaust other options will likely increase in significance. Thus, in the case of Kosovo, the prolonged bombing and civilian casualties tended to support arguments that NATO moved too hastily and without adequate preparation. On the other hand, where, as in East Timor, the intervention seems to have worked smoothly, with few casualties on either side, commentators may tend to suggest in retrospect that it should have taken place more quickly.

In some circumstances, diplomacy cannot resolve a humanitarian crisis. In the case of East Timor, without minimal U.S. support, Australia and the UN would have had little bargaining power with Indonesia. Ironically, despite Australia's decades of attempting to appease Indonesia and strengthen cultural and trade ties with that country, it had little diplomatic influence when it came to dealing with sensitive issues like East Timor.[98] In these circumstances, the would-be intervenor must strike a balance between intervening quickly to save the lives of the persecuted and waiting for a diplomatic breakthrough to prevent an unnecessary war. Clearly, in the final result, the intervention is likely to be judged not on how this decision is made but on its outcome.

## Consistency

Consistency is a key determinant of legitimacy in the context of humanitarian intervention.[99] The coin of consistency has two sides: ensuring that intervention takes place in every case where it is justified and ensuring that it does not take place in cases where it is not justified. If states have a right rather than a duty to intervene, they have discretion in determining whether or not to intervene in a particular case. If it is not only a moral but also a legal duty, then a state or organization that fails to intervene in a case worthy of intervention impairs consistency and violates international law.[100] Moreover, in comparing treatment by a state or regional organization of various cases of humanitarian crisis, it is necessary to consider not only whether the state or organization itself intervenes with military force, but also whether it arms either side in the conflict or provides aid to the victims.[101]

Economic or political interests could create a danger of unjustified intervention[102] but, in practice, states and the international community have more often failed to intervene in humanitarian crises at all, or until it is too late.[103] Uncertainty exacerbates this tendency.[104] In these circumstances, an insistence on consistency risks creating a consistent platform of nonintervention— a state can then justify its failure to intervene in one worthy case by its failure to intervene in another such case. Surely an erratic response by the international community to domestic human rights violations is preferable to no response at all. The international community should therefore focus not on ensuring consistency per se, but on encouraging intervention in appropriate cases and being attentive to the emergence of humanitarian crises. Nevertheless, when states exhibit a discernible pattern of selectivity, such as a greater willingness to intervene when the victims are European rather than African, the international community should carefully scrutinize such conduct.[105]

The issue of consistency arose specifically in the context of Kosovo and East Timor. Several U.S. media commentators highlighted the dramatic difference in the U.S. response to the two cases, despite the similar nature of the human rights at stake[106] and the fact that the violations in East Timor appeared to be on a far greater scale, at least before NATO began bombing. Nevertheless, particularly within the U.S., it is generally recognized that a state cannot stand up for human rights throughout the world, particularly where this requires military intervention. Inconsistency is therefore likely to reduce the legitimacy of a humanitarian intervention significantly only where it confirms existing suspicions about illegitimate motives of the intervenor to an extent that overrides the positive humanitarian effects of the intervention. Furthermore, where the intervenor is a state or states lacking overwhelming power or resources (for example, Australia), the bite of inconsistency will not be as harsh, particularly where the target country is geographically or historically related to the intervenor. Thus, critics rarely target Australia for inconsistency in failing to lead interventions to address human rights violations in countries outside East Timor.

## Conclusion

NATO's intervention in Kosovo was illegal, at least according to a purely textual reading of the UN Charter, yet many saw the decision to intervene as legitimate. In contrast, the Australian-led force did not intervene in East Timor until the Security Council had authorized and Indonesia had consented to the intervention, yet some aspects of the intervention are questioned on other grounds. Clearly, there is a gap between the legitimacy and lawfulness of humanitarian intervention. The most important factor determining legitimacy at the stage of deciding to intervene appears to be the rights and lives at stake. If basic human rights are being violated, particularly if they involve the persecution of a particular ethnic or religious group and may be classified as genocide, the public is likely to make a strong demand for action, typically translating into intervention. Moreover, if media reports of the violations are widespread and graphic, this will fuel the demand for intervention. In those circumstances, the actual number of victims involved may make little difference.[107]

If the rights and lives at stake are sufficiently compelling, certain other factors will assist in validating the intervention. These include multilateralism, UN support, and prior attempts at reaching a peaceful resolution. The existence of certain other "negative" factors will not necessarily preclude a legitimate intervention. For example, if the intervenor has a history of a contradictory relationship with the target through supporting the current persecutors, this may justify, rather than preclude, intervention on humanitarian grounds. Similarly, if the would-be intervenor has nonhumanitarian reasons for intervening or an inconsistent pattern of intervention in the past, this will not necessarily render its intervention illegitimate.

Two contrasting proposals to close the gap between legitimacy and lawfulness would be to codify the norms of intervention in an international treaty or to allow the jurisprudence surrounding the UN Charter in connection with "threats to the peace" to develop without amendment to the text.[108] The better view is that the law should be reformed to ensure a clear and consistent response to humanitarian crises according to agreed principles. This would diminish present uncertainties about the lawfulness of humanitarian intervention, bring the law closer in line with accepted factors of legitimacy, and restore integrity to the text of the UN Charter and the UN itself. A parallel development could be the creation of a standing UN force to act where the interests of other states and organizations are insufficient to mount an intervention despite the compelling need for one.[109] Until reforms of this kind are effected, states or organizations considering intervening in another state on humanitarian grounds should act quickly but forcefully, taking into account the factors described here, in addition to the precise doctrines of international law.

## Notes

This chapter derives from a longer article that was originally published in *UCLA Journal of International Law and Foreign Affairs* 7 (2002): 31. I wrote that article as part of my Master of Laws studies, in which I was generously supported by the Australian Federation of University Women (Queensland and Victorian branches), the Foundation for Young Australians, the International Chapter PEO Sisterhood, and Mallesons Stephen Jaques.

1. The Independent Commission was initiated by the prime minister of Sweden and endorsed by the UN secretary-general. Members of the Independent Commission were appointed on the basis of their expertise and participated "solely in their personal capacities." See Independent International Commission on Kosovo, introduction to *The Kosovo Report* (New York: Oxford University Press, 2000).

2. Independent Commission, *Kosovo Report*, p. 290.

3. Independent Commission, *Kosovo Report*, p. 290.

4. See Dino Kritsiotis, "Reappraising Policy Objections to Humanitarian Intervention," *Michigan Journal of International Law* 19 (1998): 1005, 1049.

5. Rein Müllerson and David J. Scheffer, "Legal Regulation of the Use of Force," in Lori Fisler Damrosch et al., eds., *Beyond Confrontation: International Law for the Post–Cold War Era* (Boulder, Colo.: Westview, 1995), pp. 93, 115.

6. Steven R. Ratner, "The United Nations in Cambodia: A Model for Resolution of Internal Conflicts?" in Lori Fisler Damrosch, ed., *Enforcing Restraint: Collective Intervention in Internal Conflicts* (New York: Council on Foreign Relations Press, 1993), pp. 241, 265–266.

7. "Military and Paramilitary Activities (Nicar. v. US)," International Court of Justice, 27 June 1986, pp. 14, 98–101.

8. Sean Murphy, *Humanitarian Intervention: The United Nations in an Evolving World Order* (Philadelphia: University of Pennsylvania Press, 1996), p. 78.

9. Jane E. Stromseth, "Iraq's Repression of Its Civilian Population: Collective Responses and Continuing Challenges," in Damrosch, ed., *Enforcing Restraint*, pp. 77, 79, 87.

10. Ratner, *United Nations in Cambodia*, p. 266.

11. UN SCOR, 47th sess., 3046 mtg. p. 143, UN Doc. S/PV.3046 (1992); "An Agenda for Peace: Preventative Diplomacy, Peacemaking and Peace-Keeping," UN GAOR, 47th sess., Agenda Item 10, paragraph 13, UN Doc. A/47/277, S/24111 (1992); Murphy, *Humanitarian Intervention*, pp. 285–288.

12. Murphy, *Humanitarian Intervention*, pp. 297–304.

13. Peter Malanczuk, *Akehurst's Modern Introduction to International Law*, 7th ed. (New York: Routledge, 1997), p. 390.

14. UN Charter, Article 52.

15. Tom Farer, "A Paradigm of Legitimate Intervention," in Damrosch, ed., *Enforcing Restraint*, pp. 316, 318.

16. Malanczuk, *Akehurst's Modern Introduction to International Law*, p. 314.

17. "Military and Paramilitary Activities (Nicar. v. US)," pp. 94, 122–123; "Legality of the Threat or Use of Nuclear Weapons," *International Legal Materials* 35 (1996): 809, 822.

18. "Military and Paramilitary Activities (Nicar. v. US)," pp. 98–101.

19. Murphy, *Humanitarian Intervention*, p. 75.

20. See Richard A. Falk, "NATO's Kosovo Intervention: Kosovo, World Order, and the Future of International Law," *American Journal of International Law* 93 (1999): 847–848.

21. "Declaration on Principles of International Law Concerning Friendly Relations and Co-operation among States in Accordance with the Charter of the United Nations," General Assembly Resolution 2625 (XXV), UN GAOR, Supp. no. 28, UN Doc. A/5217 (1970); see also, "Corfu Channel (UK v. Alb.)," International Court of Justice, 9 April 1949, pp. 4, 35.

22. Compare Jeffrey Clark, "Debacle in Somalia: Failure of the Collective Response," in Damrosch, ed., *Enforcing Restraint*, pp. 205, 332.

23. Murphy, *Humanitarian Intervention*, p. 71.

24. UN Charter, Article 1, paragraph 3.

25. For example, see UN Charter, Articles 55–56, 62, 68, 76.

26. Lori Fisler Damrosch, "Changing Conceptions of Intervention in International Law," in Laura W. Reed and Carl Kaysen, eds., *Emerging Norms of Justified Intervention* (Cambridge, Mass.: Committee on International Security Studies, American Academy of Arts and Sciences, 1993), pp. 91, 96, citing Farer, "Paradigm of Legitimate Intervention," p. 316.

27. Christine M. Chinkin, "NATO's Kosovo Intervention: A 'Good' or 'Bad' War?" *American Journal of International Law* 93 (1999): 841–843.

28. See generally, Richard B. Lillich, ed., *Humanitarian Intervention and the United Nations* (Charlottesville: University Press of Virginia, 1973); Reed and Kaysen, eds., *Emerging Norms of Justified Intervention*; Murphy, *Humanitarian Intervention*; Fernando R. Tesón, *Humanitarian Intervention: An Inquiry into Law and Morality*, 2nd ed. (Irvington-on-Hudson, N.Y.: Transnational, 1997).

29. Kurt Mills, *Human Rights in the Emerging Global Order: A New Sovereignty?* (New York: St. Martin's, 1998), p. 130.

30. "Final Report to the Prosecutor by the Committee Established to Review the NATO Bombing Campaign against the Federal Republic of Yugoslavia," paragraph 1, PR/P.I.S./510–E, 13 June 2000.

31. Sean D. Murphy, ed., "Contemporary Practice of the United States Relating to International Law," *American Journal of International Law* 93 (1999): 628, 632.

32. Amnesty International, *NATO/Federal Republic of Yugoslavia: "Collateral Damage" or Unlawful Killings? Violations of the Laws of War by NATO during Operation Allied Force* (London: Amnesty International, AI Index EUR 70/18/00, 2000), chapter 2.4.

33. Amnesty International, *NATO/Federal Republic of Yugoslavia*, chapter 3.1; Michael Ignatieff, "The Virtual Commander: How NATO Invented a New Kind of War," *New Yorker*, 2 August 1999, p. 30.

34. Lord Robertson of Port Ellen, *Kosovo One Year On: Achievement and Challenge* (2000), p. 11.

35. Javier Solana, "Fresh Cause for Hope at the Opening of the New Century," in William Joseph Buckley, ed., *Kosovo: Contending Voices on Balkan Interventions* (Grand Rapids, Mich.: Eerdmans, 2000), pp. 217–218; Wesley K. Clark, "The Strength of an Alliance," in Buckley, ed., Kosovo: *Contending Voices* (2000), p. 253.

36. For example, see Jonathan Charney, "Anticipatory Humanitarian Intervention in Kosovo," *American Journal of International Law* 93 (1999): 834; "Law and Right: When They Don't Fit Together," *Economist*, 1 April 1999; Michael Ignatieff, *Virtual War: Kosovo and Beyond* (New York: Metropolitan, 2000), p. 182.

37. International Court of Justice, "Yugoslavia Institutes Proceedings against Ten States for Violation of the Obligation Not to Use Force against Another State and Requests the Court to Order That the Use of Force Cease Immediately," Press Communiqué 99/17, 29 April 1999.

38. "Legality of the Use of Force (Yugo. v. US)," International Court of Justice, 2 June 1999, p. 1.

39. Bartram S. Brown, "Humanitarian Intervention and Kosovo: Humanitarian Intervention at a Crossroads," *William and Mary Law Review* 41 (2000): 1683, 1740.

40. See Louis Henkin, "Kosovo and the Law of 'Humanitarian Intervention'," *American Journal of International Law* 93 (1999): 824, 828; Frances Horsburgh, "Campbell Insists Action Is Legally Justified," *Herald* (Glasgow), 24 April 1999, p. 9; "At Least It's an Altruistic War," *Canberra Times*, 19 April 1999, p. A9.

41. Walter Gary Sharp Sr., "Operation Allied Force: Reviewing the Lawfulness of NATO's Use of Military Force to Defend Kosovo," *Maryland Journal of International Law and Trade* 23 (1999): 295, 324–325.

42. For example, see *Independent Commission, Kosovo Report*; Kofi Annan, "The Effectiveness of the International Rule of Law in Maintaining International Peace and Security," in Buckley, ed., *Kosovo: Contending Voices* (Grand Rapids, Mich.: Eerdmans, 2000), pp. 221–222.

43. Thomas M. Franck, "Lessons of Kosovo," *American Journal of International Law* 93 (1999): 857, 859.

44. See generally "Agreement between Indonesia and Portugal on the Question of East Timor," UN SCOR, 53rd sess., Annex I, p. 4, UN Doc. S/1999/513 (1999); "Agreement between the United Nations and the Governments of Indonesia and Portugal Regarding the Modalities for the Popular Consultation through a Direct Ballot," UN SCOR 53rd sess., Annex II, p. 24, UN Doc. S/1999/513 (1999); "Agreement between the United Nations and the Governments of Indonesia and Portugal Regarding Security Arrangements," UN SCOR, 53rd sess., Annex III, p. 29, UN Doc. S/1999/513 (1999).

45. UN High Commissioner for Human Rights, "Report of the International Commission of Inquiry on East Timor to the Secretary General," 54th sess., Agenda Item 96, paragraphs 93, 127, 129–130, 132, UN Doc. S/2000/59 (2000); see generally Human Rights Watch, *Forced Expulsions to West Timor and the Refugee Crisis* (1999); "Report of the High Commissioner for Human Rights on the Human Rights Situation in East Timor," UN ESCOR, 4th special sess., paragraphs 14–46, UN Doc. E/CN.4/S-4/CRP.1 (1999).

46. UN Security Council Resolution 1264, UN SCOR, 4045th mtg., UN Doc. S/RES/1264 (1999).

47. Damien Kingsbury, conclusion to Damien Kingsbury, ed., *Guns and Ballot Boxes: East Timor's Vote for Independence* (Clayton, Australia: Monash Asia Institute, 2000), p. 185.

48. For example, see "NATO's Decision Is Drastic and Flawed," *Bangkok Post*, 27 March 1999.

49. Scott Burchill, "East Timor, Australia and Indonesia," in Kingsbury, ed., *Guns and Ballot Boxes* (2000); see also Rupert Cornwell, "It Is We Who Are to Blame for the UN Failure in East Timor," *Independent* (London), 7 September 1999, p. 4; Robert Manne, "Howard's Real Failure on Timor," *Sydney Morning Herald*, 11 October 1999, p. 17; Karen Middleton, "Troops Pay for PM's Judgment," *West Australian*, 17 September 1999, p. 16.

50. Noam Chomsky, *A New Generation Draws the Line: Kosovo, East Timor and the Standards of the West* (London: Verso, 2000), pp. 73–74.

51. Burchill, "East Timor, Australia and Indonesia," p. 180.

52. Tesón, *Humanitarian Intervention*, p. 123.

53. See Jonathan I. Charney and Gennady M. Danilenko, "Consent and the Creation of International Law," in Damrosch et al., eds., *Beyond Confrontation*, pp. 23, 46–50.

54. Mills, *Human Rights in the Emerging Global Order*, p. 40.

55. *International Covenant on Civil and Political Rights*, opened for signature 19 December 1966, 999 UNTS 171; Article 1; *International Covenant on Economic*,

*Social, and Cultural Rights*, opened for signature 16 December 1966, 993 UNTS 3 Article 1; UN Charter, Articles 1, 55, 73, 76.

56. Mills, *Human Rights in the Emerging Global Order*, pp. 159–160.

57. John Pilger, foreword to Paul Hainsworth and Stephen McCloskey, eds., *The East Timor Question: The Struggle for Independence from Indonesia* (London: Tauris, 2000), p. ix.

58. Doug Bandow, "NATO's Hypocritical Humanitarianism," in Ted Galen Carpenter, ed., *NATO's Empty Victory: A Postmortem on the Balkan War* (Washington, D.C.: Cato Institute, 2000), pp. 31, 33–34.

59. James Galbraith, "Intervention in Kosovo Unjustified," *Dallas Morning News*, 17 April 1999, p. 31A.

60. David Wippman, "Enforcing the Peace: ECOWAS and the Liberian Civil War," in Damrosch, ed., *Enforcing Restraint*, pp. 157, 193.

61. Kritsiotis, "Reappraising Policy Objections to Humanitarian Intervention," p. 1032; see also Michael C. Davis, chapter 13, in this volume.

62. Kritsiotis, "Reappraising Policy Objections to Humanitarian Intervention," p. 1034.

63. See Michael Hirsh, "Calling All Regio-Cops: Peacekeeping's Hybrid Future," *Foreign Affairs* (November–December 2000): 2.

64. See generally John Taylor, *The Indonesian Occupation of East Timor 1974–1989: A Chronology* (London: Catholic Institute for International Relations, 1990).

65. Stephen McCloskey, "Introduction: East Timor—From European to Third World Colonialism," in Hainsworth and McCloskey, eds., *The East Timor Question*, pp. 1, 7.

66. For example, see Security Council Resolution 389, UN SCOR, 31st sess., paragraph 2, UN Doc. S/RES/389 (1976); General Assembly Resolution 36/50, UN GAOR, 36th sess., paragraphs 3, 5, UN Doc. A/RES/36/50 (1981).

67. Jim Aubrey, "Canberra: Jakarta's Trojan Horse in East Timor," in Paul Hainsworth and Stephen McCloskey, eds., *The East Timor Question: The Struggle for Independence from Indonesia* (London: Tauris, 2000), pp. 133, 142; see also Department of Foreign Affairs (Australia), Press Release, 20 January 1978.

68. "Treaty between Australia and the Republic of Indonesia on the Zone of Cooperation in an Area between the Indonesian Province of East Timor and Northern Australia, December 11, 1989," *Australian Treaty Series*, no. 9 (1991); "Case Concerning East Timor (Port. v. Austrl.)," International Court of Justice, 30 June 1995, p. 90 (Weeramantry J, dissenting).

69. Michael Shane French-Merrill, "The Role of the United Nations and Recognition in Sovereignty Determinations: How Australia Breached Its International Obligations in Ratifying the Timor Gap Treaty," *Cardozo Journal of International and Comparative Law* 8 (2000): 285, 288–289.

70. For example, see French-Merrill, "Role of the United Nations," pp. 288–289.

71. Geoffrey C. Gunn, *East Timor and the United Nations: The Case for Intervention* (Lawrenceville, N.J.: Red Sea, 1997), pp. 63–68.

72. Burchill, "East Timor, Australia and Indonesia," p. 170.

73. See A. W. Grazebrook, "East Timor: A Balanced Force at Work," *Asia-Pacific Defence Reporter* (December 1999): 9 (describing the makeup of the Australian component of Interfet).

74. Treasury (Australia), "Defence–East Timor Levy," Press Release, no. 078, 23 November 1999.

75. "Sunday" (Channel 9 Network television broadcast, Australia, 19 July 1998), cited in Aubrey, "Canberra: Jakarta's Trojan Horse in East Timor," p. 145.

76. Andrea Carson and Richard Baker, "Bans and Boycotts: A Nation Acts," *The Age* (Melbourne), 9 September 1999, p. 7.

77. James Cotton, "East Timor and Australia—Twenty-Five Years of the Policy Debate," in James Cotton, ed., *East Timor and Australia* (Canberra: Australian Defence Studies Centre, Australian Defence Force Academy, 1999), pp. 1, 16.

78. K. P. Waran, "Australia Insensitive to Asia in Wanting to Be Mata-Mata," *New Straits Times* (Malaysia), 26 September 1999, p. 2; William Keeling, "Letters to the Editor: Abhorrent Siblings," *Financial Times*, 22 September 1999, p. 22.

79. For example, see "An Asian Kosovo," *Le Monde*, 7 September 1999, p. 18; Gary Klintworth, "International Community Has a Right and Duty to Intervene," *Straits Times* (Singapore), 8 September 1999, p. 42.

80. Thomas O'Dwyer, "Distress Down Under," *Jerusalem Post*, 15 September 1999, p. 6.

81. "Security Council Briefed on East Timor by Assistant Secretary-General for Peacekeeping," Press Release, 22 December 1999, UN Doc. SC/6776; Felix Soh, "A Salute to East Timor's Good Guys," *Straits Times* (Singapore), 15 October 1999, p. 72.

82. Stephen Morris, "Australia Stands Tall While US Drifts in a Vacuum," *Australian Financial Review*, 30 September 1999, p. 23.

83. Alan Stephens, "Operation Allied Force," *Asia-Pacific Defence Reporter* (August–September 1999): 20–21.

84. Chinkin, "NATO's Kosovo Intervention," p. 843.

85. Fatos Lubonja, "Reinventing Skenderbeg: Albanian Nationalism and NATO Neocolonialism," in William Joseph Buckley, ed., *Kosovo: Contending Voices*, pp. 101, 107.

86. See Stanley Kober, "Setting Dangerous International Precedents," in Carpenter, ed., *NATO's Empty Victory*, pp. 107, 114–115.

87. O'Dwyer, "Distress Down Under," p. 6.

88. For example, see Sangwon Suh, "Unease over East Timor," *Asiaweek*, 15 October 1999, p. 28.

89. Tony Wright, "The Sheriff Rides Out," *The Age* (Melbourne), 2 October 1999, p. 3.

90. Frederick J. Petersen, "The Facade of Humanitarian Intervention for Human Rights in a Community of Sovereign Nations," *Arizona Journal of International and Comparative Law* 15 (1998): 871, 885.

91. See Kritsiotis, "Reappraising Policy Objections to Humanitarian Intervention," p. 1038.

92. Mills, *Human Rights in the Emerging Global Order*, p. 162.

93. Tesón, *Humanitarian Intervention*, p. 121.

94. Falk, "NATO's Kosovo Intervention," p. 854.

95. Falk, "NATO's Kosovo Intervention," pp. 854–855.

96. Falk, "NATO's Kosovo Intervention," p. 855.

97. Chomsky, *New Generation Draws the Line*, pp. 124–126.

98. Bob Lowry, "Australia's Dilemma in East Timor," *Asia-Pacific Defence Reporter* (June–July 1999): 4–5.

99. Lori Fisler Damrosch, "Concluding Reflections," in Damrosch, ed., *Enforcing Restraint*, pp. 348, 361.

100. See Kritsiotis, "Reappraising Policy Objections to Humanitarian Intervention," p. 1027.

101. See Chomsky, *New Generation Draws the Line*, pp. 9–10.

102. Brown, "Humanitarian Intervention and Kosovo," pp. 1710, 1728.

103. Chinkin, "NATO's Kosovo Intervention," p. 847.

104. Petersen, "Facade of Humanitarian Intervention for Human Rights," p. 881.

105. Chinkin, "NATO's Kosovo Intervention," p. 847.

106. For example, see Charles Trueheart, "Mission Implausible: Putting a Doctrine to the Test," *Washington Post*, 19 September 1999, p. B4.

107. On the role of the media in promoting sentiments for intervention, see Daniela Ingruber, chapter 10, in this volume.

108. Damrosch, "Concluding Reflections," pp. 358–360.

109. Damrosch, "Concluding Reflections," pp. 361–362; Mills, *Human Rights in the Emerging Global Order*, p. 145.

# 4

# Human Rights and the Question of International Criminal Courts and Tribunals

*Robert Cryer*

International criminal law is often seen as a means of enforcing human rights,[1] although the law of human rights and international criminal law are conceptually distinct. Any single abuse of any human right during peacetime is a violation of the relevant treaty and may be the subject of international adjudication.[2] It is, however, unlikely to be an international crime, let alone the subject of an international prosecution. Crimes against humanity, the most relevant international crime for human rights abuses, are required[3] to be committed as part of a widespread or systematic attack against a civilian population. This excludes isolated violations of human rights. It may be possible, in theory, to construct a scenario where a single, isolated act could amount to genocide.[4] Even so, single acts are to all intents and purposes excluded from the jurisdiction of the International Criminal Court (ICC). The only possible single violation of internationally protected human rights that is arguably an international crime is a single act of torture, which is thought by some to amount to an international crime.[5] This appears unlikely. There is nothing in the 1984 Torture Convention[6] to suggest that it creates an international crime in the strict sense, that is, a crime for which international law directly provides for criminality, rather than creating a duty on states party to that convention to make torture a crime under their domestic law. The attempt by the House of Lords in *ex parte Pinochet (No. 3)*[7] to conflate international crimes in the stricter sense with the offense created under the Torture Convention led to a great deal of incoherence in the opinions.

Human rights groups have, perhaps understandably, begun to use international criminal law in their work. This may be related to the recent upswing in enforcement possibilities for such law, which give it a concrete applicability that has been lacking in human rights law, at least in the past. Nevertheless, international criminal law, in particular war crimes law, is unlikely to become a panacea for human rights groups. Its concepts, tests, and underlying assumptions do not dovetail with the aspirations of human rights activists, as the debate over the North Atlantic Treaty Organization bombing of Kosovo showed.[8] We must also be careful not to expect criminal enforcement to solve all of the world's ills. Intervention by means of criminal prosecution,[9] either by other states, on the basis of universal jurisdiction,[10] or by the "international community" in the form of international tribunals, is both controversial and limited.[11] Court cases do not bring victims back to life or erase scars. As David P. Forsythe states, "[Apartheid] in South Africa was not ended by a court case. . . . Torture was not ended in the Shah's Iran by a court case. Death squads were not suppressed in El Salvador by a court case."[12] Fortunately, prosecution is only one mechanism of enforcement; moral, diplomatic, economic, and other sanctions remain as relevant as they were prior to the move to criminalization.[13]

Despite those caveats, the adoption of international criminal law into the lexicon of international relations is to be welcomed, as is the increased profile international criminal law has enjoyed in the past decade among the nongovernmental organization (NGO) community. The input of human rights NGOs into the Rome Statute of the ICC (hereafter Rome Statute) was, for the most part, well thought out and positive.[14] Aside from any deterrent effect it may have, the use of international criminal law as a mechanism for dealing with large-scale human rights violations allows guilt to be personalized, preventing those responsible for the most serious abuses of fundamental human rights from hiding behind the veil of state sovereignty and also keeping perceptions of collective guilt arising for what are often, in essence, individual acts. The comment of the Nuremberg International Military Tribunal (IMT) remains as relevant today as it was at the time of its utterance, "[C]rimes against international law are committed by men, not abstract entities, and only by punishing individuals who commit such crimes can the provisions of international law be enforced."[15] In addition, a factual record that has withstood the rigors of the courtroom contest and prepared by (it is to be hoped) impartial judges may be an important legacy of legal proceedings. Such a factual record can stimulate reconciliation.[16]

This chapter concentrates on international criminal law and international criminal tribunals. Notwithstanding the loopholes and lacunas in substantive international criminal law,[17] it remains one of the most useful tools available with which to respond to egregious violations of fundamental standards of humanity. Taking as its theme "from power politics to global responsibility," this chapter will attempt to show that there has, in the past decade, been a swing toward prosecution of international crimes, which had its genesis in the creation of the International Criminal Tribunal for Former Yugoslavia (ICTY) in 1993. Nonetheless, this trend of prosecution is by no means irreversible, and it is clear that despite substantial legalization of the response to international crimes, power politics remains influential in prosecutorial efforts. The delivery of Slobodan Milosevic to the ICTY for prosecution was an effect of his fall from power and external pressure. Although he remained influential, prosecution of Milosevic was, at best, a remote possibility. Nevertheless, it is also fair to say that his indictment served to delegitimize him in the eyes of those who originally saw him either as a strong local leader or a necessary part of the peace process in former Yugoslavia.[18]

It in no way reduces the appalling nature of the acts that are laid at the feet of alleged international criminals to note that the accused are most commonly drawn from defeated regimes. Nonetheless, the view is often still expressed that war crimes trials are little more than "retributory theater"[19] in which those who have fallen from power and are without influential friends are ritually vilified. In other words, prosecution for international crimes is, like war, the continuation of politics by other means. Although the criticism is overstated, indictments or allegations of international crimes against those associated with powerful states remain, for the most part, the prerogative of NGOs, "people's tribunals,"[20] and authors.[21] Actual court proceedings are thin on the ground. Considerations of high politics remain an integral aspect of prosecution for international crimes, as they do for most areas of international law. This should come as no surprise. There has been, however, a notable move to using the law—rather than purely political means—as a mechanism for dealing with the acts that are criminalized under international law. Despite its links to politics, law remains, to a considerable extent, an autonomous discipline, and a turn to the law may involve a greater cession of political power to (legal) procedure and its concomitant ideals than those who invoke it may realize.[22] This chapter will attempt to appraise this move to law utilizing a short case study on amnesties.

**The Prosecution Option**

In a statement released just after the Rome Conference, which adopted the statute for the ICC, Amnesty International claimed:

> [The] true significance of the adoption of the statute may well lie, not in the actual institution itself in its early years, which will face enormous obstacles, but in the revolution in legal and moral attitudes towards the worst crimes in the world. No longer will these crimes be simply political events to be addressed by diplomacy at the international level, but crimes which all states have a duty to punish themselves, or, if they fail to fulfill this duty, by the international community in accordance with the rule of law.[23]

A little hyperbolic perhaps, but, flourishes aside, there is a good deal of truth in this. About a decade ago, one of the most respected textbooks on international law stated that "in spite of extensive consideration of the problem in committees of the General Assembly, the likelihood of setting up an international criminal court is very remote."[24] Soon after, *Oppenheim's International Law*, the grandfather of international law treatises, was, if anything, less optimistic.[25] Yet, here we are, a decade on, with two functioning international criminal tribunals (the ICTY and its African sibling, the International Criminal Tribunal for Rwanda [ICTR]), a "special court" for Sierra Leone and, of course, the ICC preparing for action. What road did we take to get this far? Perhaps more importantly, what was the force driving this extraordinary progress?

## The Modern History of International Criminal Courts

The modern project for an international criminal court is little more than ten years old. In 1989, a group of Latin American counties suggested the revival of consideration of an international criminal court by the United Nations (UN).[26] Notably, their reasons for suggesting this act of near necromancy was not the protection of human rights, but to create a collaborative measure for enforcing national laws based on the 1988 Vienna Convention against the Illicit Trafficking in Narcotic Drugs and Psychotropic Substances.[27] Countries whose judicial systems were unable to cope with the power and influence of drug barons might pursue prosecution in an independent forum, less subject to the pressures that could be brought to bear on national politicians, judges, and prosecutors. The project took an interesting turn between 1993 and 1994, away from this conception of the court as one to deal with drug suppliers. Between the 1993 and 1994, International Law Commission (ILC) reports focused on the ILC Draft Statute[28] for an international criminal court shift from treaty crimes to international crimes in the narrow sense.[29]

The biggest boost to international criminal law enforcement in decades came about almost entirely by accident. This was the creation of the ICTY in 1993. Prior to 1993, there had been some support for an international criminal court,[30] but the only body with the authority to set up a tribunal with the power to issue binding orders, the Security Council, began very cautiously in Yugoslavia by condemning violations of humanitarian law,[31] calling for states to submit evidence,[32] and then setting up a Commission of Experts to investigate atrocities.[33] None of these actions were particularly successful, and there was immense clamor for "something to be done." There were three such "somethings": military action to forcibly bring a halt to "ethnic cleansing"; a nonforcible response, which although possibly less effective, would be less costly in terms of "blood and treasure";[34] or do nothing, which would have serious negative public relations implications, particularly in the Western democracies. The creation of an international court was seen as the easiest option, one that was unlikely to be particularly effective,[35] but that would nonetheless give at least the appearance of making an effort to bring an end to the Yugoslav wars of dissolution.[36]

The ICTR may be another example of an accident. In 1994, when the world stood by and allowed genocide to occur, there was again a sense that something should be done. Unlike those arguing for an international tribunal

in 1992–1993, what those arguing in favor of a tribunal now had was a recent precedent. Of course, the Nuremberg and Tokyo IMTs could be said to
be precedents for the ICTY, but they were considerably further away, and
none of the numerous conflicts between 1945 and 1993 had produced an
international tribunal. International criminal law has universal applicability,
and this gave proponents of another tribunal a strong argument, as the
Rwandan government both publicly and rhetorically asked, "[I]s it because
we are Africans that a court has not been set up?"[37]

The big breakthrough came in 1998. After a politically sensitive and difficult set of negotiations, the Rome Statute was promulgated, which drew
and built on the statutes and case law of the ICTY and ICTR. There is also a
fair argument that the creation of those two tribunals was one of the major
catalysts for the acceptance of an international criminal court at all. As Ian
Brownlie said in 1998, "[Unease] in the face of the creation of ad hoc tribunals has given impetus to the creation of an international criminal court."[38]
The specter of selectivity in the application of the law may well have been
one of the reasons for the creation of a more broadly based court. Forsythe
eloquently sums up this position, "[What] started out in 1993 as mostly a
public relations ploy, namely to create an ad hoc tribunal to appear to be
doing something about human rights violations in Bosnia without major risk,
by 1998 had become an important global movement for international criminal justice."[39]

The Rome Statute was not the end of the line for the creation of international criminal courts. More recently, the UN secretary-general has, with the
blessing of the Security Council, created a "special court" for Sierra Leone.[40]
There have also been very tentative steps toward prosecution of Khmer Rouge
leaders. The Sierra Leone Special Court and the proposed trials of Khmer
Rouge leaders are of particular interest. When the Sierra Leonean conflict
began in 1991, the idea that there would be an international criminal court to
deal with offenders was not even mooted[41] and the Cambodian Peace Agreements appeared to preempt accountability.[42] It would appear that the tendency to consider prosecution is now reaching into situations for which
prosecution had not previously been considered as a viable option.[43] The
same might be said for the domestic prosecutions in Spain and Chile of General Augusto Pinochet, which, despite being brought to an end by the general's
ill health, were unthinkable even recently.

## Ideas, People, and Institutions

The developments canvassed earlier represent a pronounced turn to law
in the treatment of international crimes in the past decade. The beginning
of the move is readily explainable in realist terms of rational self-interest.
Yet, the developments over the past decade must also be explained within
the realm of ideas, people, and institutions.[44] The various factors are

interlinked. Institutions are repositories of values and ideas, and it is people who create, staff, support, and comment on such institutions.

Criminal law is a potent form of discourse, inevitably involving, as it does, issues of censure and condemnation.[45] This applies a fortiori to international criminal law, which is in a number of ways highly symbolic.[46] The word "genocide," for example, has been appropriated for its rhetorical value by a number of different causes, and there has been a trend to call any form of mass killing or tragedy a genocide.[47]

The universalist rhetoric of international criminal law and its institutions is highly pertinent. Jurisdiction over international crimes is said to be universal. Criminal law is traditionally territorial or nationality based.[48] States are thought to have an interest in prosecuting acts that occur in their territory or by their nationals. It is considered part of a state's national interest. Universal jurisdiction, by contrast, is thought to be in the common interest that those who commit international crimes be punished, so any state can prosecute such crimes no matter where they occur and by whom they are committed.[49] The corollary is that international criminal law is intended to apply universally, to all people, powerful and weak, rich and poor. It is the allegations of selective prosecution that are thought to undermine some of the legitimacy of international criminal law. As Herbert L. A. Hart makes clear, it is part of the concept of law that "in any large group general rules . . . must be the main standard of social control, and not particular directions given to each individual separately."[50] The universalist rhetoric and formal applicability of international criminal law explains why accusations of selective application seem to cut more deeply into the legitimacy of international criminal law than they do in national law.

This universal applicability and the interest in maintaining the legitimacy of the ICTY may explain the decision to create the ICTR. Remember the powerful rhetorical tool used by the Rwandan delegate, who asked for equal applicability and enforcement of the law in Africa as well as in Europe. This, of course, is nothing new. It was the failure to apply the same standards to the Allies as to the Japanese that provoked the famous and furious dissent of Mr. Justice Pal at the Tokyo International Military Tribunal.[51] In the interim period between 1945 and 1993, however, there was no institution charged with the actual concrete enforcement of international criminal law, and thus no single totem that could be invoked as a modern precedent for application of international criminal law. The Nuremberg and Tokyo IMTs were disappearing fast into the haze of history, and their universalist legacy was undermined by fairly understandable allegations of victor's justice. Those two tribunals were seen as contingent on the total military defeat of the Axis, rather than the vindication of law. The ICTY, however, was not created by the winners in a war, and indeed was created by the UN, a body that certainly has at least the self-image of the voice (and possibly the conscience) of the "international community," if such a thing exists. Therefore, although the actual reasons for the creation of the ICTY may not have been as honorable, the notional reason was that enforcement of the law by a neutral third party would assist in the restoration of international peace and security.[52] Hence, the enforcement of international criminal law was in everyone's interest. This provided fertile ground for the Rwandan claim to equal treatment. In order to vindicate the legitimacy of the ICTY, the UN could not be seen itself to be engaging in selective justice, with courts just for Europe.

Perhaps one of the most important things the ICTY did was show that, when the mood takes it, the "international community" can create an operational international criminal tribunal in a remarkably short time. The secretary-general's legal staff drafted a report and a statute for the ICTY in under sixty days. It made the years of largely fruitless negotiations about an international criminal court in the UN seem pedestrian. The legal problems many had considered insoluble were not so intractable when the will to create a tribunal was there. The statute drafted by the Office of Legal Affairs was passed unaltered and provided the blueprint for the ILC's draft statute. This shows another example of how the creation of the ICTY fed into the process of creating an international criminal court. The decisions taken in a hurry by the Office of Legal Affairs were seen to be workable.

In addition, by the time of the 1998 Rome Conference for the ICC, the ICTY had found some innovative answers to procedural and legal questions and was operating relatively well. Many of the decisions of the ICTY assisted the delegates at Rome on difficult issues by providing detailed and referenced legal suggestions. A number of the ICTY's definitions and solutions were taken up in the Rome Statute. An example of this was the definition of armed conflicts. The precise definition of international and noninternational armed conflicts was always going to be difficult. In the end, the Rome Statute adopted, almost verbatim, the definition created by the ICTY in the *Tadic* decision.[53] By having (probably self-consciously) set about attempting to clarify the law in its decisions (particularly at the appellate level), the ICTY made the legal problems easier to solve at Rome. Institutional influence can have ripple effects, both at the symbolic and practical levels. The significance of showing that international criminal justice could be done and how it could proceed was certainly a factor in the creation of the ICC.

Having two bodies that were actually, although in the beginning haltingly, vindicating the law through prosecutions promoted interest in these tribunals and in the law they applied from transnational actors, including the NGO community and international lawyers.[54] Most are broadly supportive of the tribunals. The role of NGOs in ensuring that the experience of these tribunals fed into the process of the creation of the international criminal court was clearly a factor. Amnesty International, in particular, tried to draw in the experiences of the tribunals in formulating policy positions for the ICC.[55] It also engaged in vigorous lobbying. Other NGOs, working under the "no peace without justice" label, offered legal assistance to states at Rome whose delegations were small or inexpert. The quid pro quo, of course, was that the NGO lawyers enjoyed greater access to the negotiating process by being members of delegations.

This is, of course, not to say that there has been an irreversible shift toward international criminal tribunals or one that has been shared by all states. A number of large, important states, such as China, India, and, of course, the United States, have, working on rather traditional realist principles, rejected the international criminal court for various reasons. The underlying theme of many of these arguments is the possibility that an international court could assert jurisdiction over their nationals, which these states simply are not prepared to accept.[56]

## Investigating the Change: A Tentative Framework

This chapter will now attempt to explain some of the developments discussed earlier by reference to international relations (IR) theory. This chapter is eclectic in its selection of those IR theories that will be used. As theories of this nature have an important heuristic value, it seems useful to draw on the theory that best explains any particular development.[57] Nonetheless, it must be said at the outset that this chapter takes no position on the predictive nature or policy choices that some of these theories espouse.

Liberal IR scholars have recently begun to identify a trend toward the use of the law in international politics, at least in some areas, a movement that they term "legalization."[58] The central tenet of this version of liberal theory is a three-dimensional appraisal of institutions.[59] These three dimensions, which are considered continua, are obligation, precision, and delegation. The first, obligation, is pretty clear: it is the legal obligation to do, or refrain from doing, something.[60] In relation to international criminal law, at least for the "core crimes," it is evident that this criterion is present. International criminal law is mainly based on customary international law and thus binds every state (and every person within a state).[61] Precision is a feature of the rules themselves, and they are relatively clear and determinate. The rules of international criminal law are possibly more problematic on this count. The third aspect is delegation, which "means that third parties have been granted authority to implement, interpret, and apply the rules; to resolve disputes; and (possibly) make further rules."[62] As will be seen, international criminal tribunals have been entrusted with differing levels of delegated authority.

Some uses of liberal theory are problematic. For example, liberalism cannot be an exclusive explanation of increased international cooperation and development;[63] it has a tendency to have a pro-Western bias[64] and can at times reveal a decidedly intolerant side.[65] Nonetheless, legalization is a useful lens through which we can investigate the intersection of law, politics, and power in international criminal tribunals. This chapter is concerned with bodies that are created specifically to enforce and apply international law, to which theories of legalization seem particularly apposite. Realism and critical approaches tend to marginalize such institutions or downplay the role of law by treating it as merely epiphenomenal. That is not to say that these theories are irrelevant; indeed, this chapter will also refer to aspects of international criminal law and its institutions that are perhaps most readily explainable in a realist framework. Liberal theories of legalization, however, will form the starting point. As mentioned earlier, though, the use of liberal theory here is as an explanatory tool, rather than a normative framework from which to make policy recommendations. When liberal theory is used in this latter sense, many of the previously mentioned problems arise.

## The Three Aspects of Legalization

Legal obligations are already in existence. This section will therefore compare the various international criminal tribunals with reference to the two other factors. Although the ICC is a step forward in many ways, there are also certain retrograde steps. This is no surprise. As Kenneth W. Abbott and Duncan Snidal observe, legalization is not always a forward journey, and sovereignty remains a large part of international politics and relations.[66]

### Precision

The rules of international criminal law, particularly in relation to the "general principles" of criminal liability, such as the law relating to accomplices and defenses, were not particularly well defined prior to the 1990s. The Nuremberg and Tokyo IMTs, along with a number of national trials, notionally working on international law principles gave some help, but there were a number of conflicting cases relating to, for example, whether or not superior orders could be a defense. When the ICTY was created, there was not that much to go on. Antonio Cassese states that "it is well known that the current rules on individual criminal responsibility make up a body of law that is still fairly rudimentary and unsophisticated."[67] This means that prior to the creation of the ICTY there was only a low level of precision in this area. As a result, authority was granted to the ICTY to determine these issues. The ICTY Statute itself is, to say the least, brief. It merely includes a provision rejecting the defenses of superior orders and official position and lists, rather than defines, the principles of liability (Article 7). The secretary-general expressly mentions the grant of authority to the ICTY in his report that accompanied the statute, "[The] International Tribunal will have to decide on various personal defenses which may relieve a person of individual criminal responsibility, such as minimum age or mental incapacity."[68] This grant of authority to develop the law does not necessarily contradict Article 7 of the European Convention of Human Rights, as the European Court of Human Rights has specifically found that the development of criminal law by courts is acceptable within certain limits.[69]

Nor is this grant necessarily inconsistent with precision. Although the literature on legalization appears to take it that determinacy comes from detailed rules set down in written form, determinacy can be seen not only as a characteristic of the rules themselves, but also of the process of their interpretation. Thomas M. Franck argues that although written determinacy is preferable, there is another form of determinacy, "judicially supplied process determinacy."[70] Although the rules or their applicability may not be especially clear, legitimacy may inhere in such rules if there is a body ascribed to the function of authoritatively determining their content and applicability. Abbott et al. mention that in domestic legal systems, standards like "due care" are acceptable since there are courts who are entitled to determine the content.[71] But they appear to conceptualize this as an aspect of delegation of authority to interpret, rather than a contribution to precision of the rules.[72]

When the Rome Statute was drafted, the states creating the ICC were well aware of the fact that it could exercise jurisdiction over their own nationals, as well as those of other states. Previous international criminal tribunals, by contrast, were created primarily for the prosecution of people not linked to the governments that supported their creation. In these new circumstances, states wished to create far more detailed rules. As a result, the Rome Statute has lengthy and detailed provisions of principles of liability and defenses,[73] which ensure that there are clearer and more detailed regulations and a greater degree of precision. The case law of the ICTY and ICTR, however, was also beginning to work itself into a precise set of principles. But this is not a simple, linear story of increased legalization and progress, from vagueness, to process determinacy, to determinate statutory provisions. It appears that in a number of areas, in particular on superior orders and the responsibility of commanders, the Rome Statute represents a retrenchment compared to the emergent jurisprudence of the ICTY and ICTR.[74]

*Delegation*

Delegation involves a number of aspects, but two particularly fall under consideration here: the authority to interpret and apply rules, and the authority to initiate cases.[75] The first, as alluded to earlier, is present in the ICTY and ICTR to a considerable degree. Those tribunals were given a very broad mandate to interpret and apply the law relating to genocide, crimes against humanity, and war crimes. The ICTY has made quite daring interpretations of its statute and customary international law in cases like *Tadic*.[76]

For the ICTY, though, there was one notable omission. There was no authority to apply the law prohibiting aggression (crimes against peace). It is likely that had that authority been mooted, one of the permanent five (P5) members of the Security Council would have vetoed the decision to create the court. It has to be remembered that the statute was passed unamended. Permitting alterations to the statute would open a Pandora's box of amendments.

There was, thus, a tacit agreement between the P5 not to permit debate on what the statute contained. The secretary-general's legal team probably knew that although a certain amount of delegation was acceptable, jurisdiction over crimes against peace would have prevented the statute from being passed at all.

The initiation of individual cases is a decision for the prosecutor, and the ICTY and ICTR have been careful to defer to policy decisions of the prosecutor on that front.[77] But there was no real thought of delegation of authority over which situations the prosecutor could investigate. Both the ICTY and ICTR are tribunals of limited jurisdiction. The ICTR is limited to Rwandans and those in Rwanda in 1994,[78] and the ICTY to the territory of former Yugoslavia and events since 1991.[79] The fact that the latter tribunal has jurisdiction over the Kosovo affair and the conflict in the former Yugoslav Republic of Macedonia must be regarded as fortuitous. It is notable that the ICTY prosecutor was unwilling to consider crimes in Kosovo until the Security Council implied that she may do so.[80] Therefore, the delegation of authority to decide whom to prosecute is actually rather limited.

The ICC is to have jurisdiction over the four "core crimes": war crimes, crimes against humanity, genocide, and aggression. It might be thought then that there has been a considerable degree of delegation. In some ways, that is the case, although there are significant claw-backs. The first is Article 124. This provision allows a state, when accepting the Rome Statute, to "opt out" of the jurisdiction of the ICC over war crimes for the first seven years of the functioning of the ICC. This is a dilution of delegation, and at least one state (France) has exercised its option to withdraw jurisdiction under Article 124. Second, as mentioned earlier, the rules are framed in a far more detailed way in the statute and also in the "Elements of Crimes."[81] Thus, less authority to interpret international criminal law has been delegated to the ICC than was passed to the ICTY and ICTR.[82] In addition, unlike the ICTY Statute, the list of war crimes in the Rome Statute (Article 8) is exhaustive rather than illustrative. Therefore, there is no opportunity for the ICC to rely on customary international law to bring other war crimes under its jurisdiction as the ICTY has done. The list is also incomplete.

Aggression has caused further problems. There is, as of yet, still no widely accepted definition of the crime of aggression, and unless and until such a definition is adopted by the states party to the statute, the ICC is not to prosecute it.[83] A definition is unlikely to be rapidly forthcoming, and it is likely to require at least a decision by the UN Security Council to trigger possible prosecution. In other words, the P5, in particular, have tried to ensure that delegation of this type of authority over aggression does not preempt their vetoes in the Security Council.

In terms of jurisdiction *ratione personae*, the ICC has a broader mandate than the two ad hoc tribunals. The ICC's jurisdiction is exclusively prospective,[84] but it will have jurisdiction over offenses committed by nationals of states parties to the treaty and those committed on their territory.[85] Leaving aside the unlikely event of the Security Council referring a matter to the ICC, there is a two-track system for commencing such prosecutions. First, a state party to the Rome Statute can request the prosecutor to begin investigations.[86] This is a moderate delegation, as only one state has to bring such a request for the affair to be investigated. A far broader and more controversial form of delegation is the power the prosecutor has, acting on his or her own motion, to begin an investigation.[87] This is a large delegation of authority to an independent international body, which is entitled to receive information and so on from NGOs and other bodies. Although it falls short of allowing individuals to directly begin prosecutions before the ICC, which would have been impracticable, this represents a huge step forward for international criminal justice.

Nevertheless, the Security Council still has a role. Acting under Article 16 of the statute, the Security Council can issue a binding "request" that the prosecutor defer investigation for twelve months, and it may repeat this "request" as often as it can to gain the relevant majority in the council (including the permanent members). So, although there has been some delegation, the most powerful states have retained a level of control over prosecutions. This control was controversially asserted by the Security Council in July 2002 in Resolution 1422.[88] This resolution, which is probably ultra vires, sought to exempt from the ICC's jurisdiction all nationals of nonparties to the Rome Statute engaged on UN-authorized missions. It also showed that powerful states, in particular the United States, seek to use the power granted to them by the Rome Statute to its maximum effect.

**Evaluating the Evidence**

By applying the tools of legalization, we can see that in a number of ways the ICTY and ICTR represent at least a similar level of legalization to the ICC, which is more commonly seen as the millennial project par excellence. The Security Council, traditionally seen as the home of old-fashioned power politics, has retained a role for itself in overseeing the prosecution of international crimes in the ICC, especially when the offense charged is not the mistreatment of people, but the sovereign act of beginning a war. In addition, when setting up tribunals with jurisdiction over them, states may not only wish to limit the delegation of judicial authority to interpret the rules, but may also narrow the substantive coverage of those rules. Nevertheless, a clear trend can be identified in which there has been a replacement of certain political prerogatives of states in relation to the prosecution of international crimes with either clearly enunciated law, or the delegation of the authority to decide whether to proceed in an independent, international prosecution. This thesis can be further illustrated by the changing viability of amnesties for international crimes.

*Amnesties*

Amnesties, which prevented the prosecution of offenses in the past, have been a feature of peace agreements since the inception of the modern system of states. The Treaty of Utrecht, which brought about the Peace of Westphalia (1648), contained an amnesty for all signatories. The legal position of amnesties and the international response to them provide a useful example of the increàsing resort to law where violations of human rights have reached a scale that engages international criminal law. Given their prevalence throughout history, it might be thought that amnesties would remain central to the resolution of conflicts. In the last decade, however, the status of amnesties has gone from an important, necessary (or perhaps expedient) political tool, to one whose status and use is now openly questioned as a matter of both law and politics. Again, we can see a swing toward the implementation of international criminal law in preference to a purely political approach to persuading those involved in atrocities to lay down their arms and, sometimes, to relinquish their positions as high-ranking government officials. Traditionally, it was thought more important to ensure peace, in the sense of absence of armed confrontation, than to require the prosecution of perpetrators of international crimes. More recently, this has been queried, particularly by the NGOs working under the banner of "no peace without justice," who argue that a long lasting peace cannot be based on impunity.

The use of amnesties has been quite frequent in the recent past, in particular for civil wars. At times, the UN has supported amnesty provisions. An example was the amnesty in Haiti in 1994.[89] Although there were clear examples of abusive use of amnesties, such as the self-granted amnesty of the Pinochet regime, the South African case may represent a more nuanced approach to the use of such provisions. It is notable that the South African approach has not attracted such condemnation as the self-serving amnesties of Latin American military regimes in the 1970s and 1980s. Although there have been certain court decisions, in particular of the Inter-American Court of Human Rights, that imply that amnesties may amount to a violation of human rights, at least as they are protected in the Americas,[90] the legality of amnesty provisions is still controversial.[91] This fact notwithstanding, the unmistakable trend is moving away from the negotiated, political disposition of offenses through amnesties, toward a legal regime where the prosecution option is seriously considered for international crimes and, at the very least, subject to scrutiny by international legal professionals. Illustrations can be found in the Sierra Leone Special Court and the Rome Statute.

### The Sierra Leone Special Court

One of the obstacles facing the secretary-general when creating the statute for the Sierra Leone Special Court was the Lomé Peace Accord, signed in 1999. Article 9 of this accord, signed by the parties to the Sierra Leonean conflict and the secretary-general's representative; offered an amnesty to all parties for actions in that conflict. The secretary-general's representative appended a disclaimer, noting that in his view, the amnesty did not apply to international crimes. Subsequently, the secretary-general's report totally rejected the legality of any amnesty for international crimes. The report asserted that not only was the amnesty inapplicable to international crimes, but *pro tanto* illegal under international law.[92] The legality of amnesties under international law remains moot, but the action of the secretary-general, through his representative, represents a significant change in opinion from previous holders of that post, who have accepted such deals. For example, the UN supported the agreement in Haiti that prevented prosecution of the military regime that ousted Jean-Bertrand Aristide. Given the secretary-general's action and the strong statement of opposition to amnesties contained in his report on the creation of the Sierra Leone Special Court, it now appears that an exclusively political disposition of international crimes may be unacceptable. The possibility of legal process has, at the very least, to be left open.

### The Rome Statute

The preamble to the Rome Statute affirms "that the most serious crimes of concern to the international community as a whole must not go unpunished [and that states are] . . . determined to put an end to impunity for the perpetrators of these crimes."[93] Nonetheless, there is still a possibility that amnesties may, in certain circumstances, be acceptable.[94] This relies on the prosecutor deciding, as he or she may have the right to do, that a democratically accepted, openly negotiated amnesty provides "substantial reasons to believe that an investigation would not be in the interests of justice."[95] This decision is reviewable by the ICC under Article 53, paragraph 3. Henceforth, even if the Rome Statute allows amnesties, which is by no means certain, their propriety is subject to review and possible reversal by the prosecutor or the court itself. This is a considerable example of the "legalization" of what has, at least until recently, been considered a domestic matter for states. The transfer of authority from states party, to the Rome Statute, to the prosecutor and court regarding the acceptability of domestic amnesties is quite remarkable. The prosecutor may adopt the position recently taken by the secretary-general and deny the legality of any form of amnesty. Even if he or she does not, by deferring to legal authorities such as the prosecutor and court, states that ratify the Rome Statute have narrowed the political options open to them when deciding what provisions to include in a peace agreement.

### Conclusion

The rise in interest in, and enforcement of, international criminal law is nothing short of phenomenal. It is all the more so as the beginnings of the change were, to put the best face on the evidence, fortuitous. The momentum, however, that attached to the two ad hoc tribunals served to rekindle the flame of international justice and fed in to the process of the creation of a permanent international criminal court. That permanent court, although welcome in many ways, displays some interesting delegations of authority and refusals to delegate authority. There are striking differences between the authority of the ICC to create and interpret rules of international law and the corresponding jurisdiction of the ICTY and ICTR. It also cannot be ignored that the Security Council (or, to be more accurate, the P5) maintains a notable political role in the operation of the ICC, as do the states who, for example, set its budget and appoint its personnel, in particular the prosecutor and the judges.

These criticisms should not be overstated. In less than a decade, the project for an international criminal court has come down from the clouds over Utopia and been grounded in international law. The ICC came into existence in 2002, less than ten years after the creation of the ICTY. The turn to law involved in the formation of the ICTY proved to be the catalyst that transformed international criminal law from an arcane discipline of mainly historical interest into a prominent aspect of contemporary conflict management. It is too early to determine whether or not this move toward international criminal courts as a viable mechanism for enforcing international criminal law will last. It is possible that continued opposition from a number of powerful states, such as the United States, China, and India, will lead to an emaciated regime of prosecution or even an abandonment of international criminal law similar to that which characterized the post-Nuremberg Cold War period.

Yet, there are grounds for hope. The past decade has seen a radical transformation in international society and the most optimistic international criminal lawyer would not have foreseen the level of support that now exists for the ICC. Ten years on, the use of international tribunals is considered an appropriate and feasible policy option for responding to large-scale violations of the law. Numerous suggestions for an international court to prosecute members of the al Qaeda group in the aftermath of the September 11, 2001, attacks are only the latest manifestation of this trend.[96] Returning to the ICC, even states that are uncomfortable do not (publicly) denounce the idea of an international criminal court, although they may criticize the ICC. Once an institution actually exists, half the battle is won. It is far more difficult to demolish an institution than it is to prevent it from coming into being. In addition, international criminal tribunals have, in the past, slowly but surely gathered support from states who were initially, at best, lukewarm about the idea of their creation. The experiences of the ICTY and ICTR are instructive on this point. Outside of international criminal law, the same can be said for the European Court of Human Rights.

Many states have provided financial, logistical, and political support to the ICTY and ICTR. This includes the United Kingdom, which the ICTY now counts among its staunchest supporters. The United Kingdom was initially unconvinced of the wisdom of creating the ICTY and gave little assistance in its formative period. Though some states, such as Russia, have occasionally adopted an antipathetic stance toward the ICTY, the degree of support for the ICTY has gradually but perceptibly grown. Witness, for example, the central role accorded to the ICTY in the Kosovo conflict, compared to its marginalization in the Dayton negotiations. The evidence is inconclusive, since there were political reasons for supporting the ICTY during the Kosovo conflict. Nevertheless, the extent to which states have accepted the ICTY and come to support it is sufficient to give hope that the creation of the ICC may, at least in the medium to long term, become an established part of the international architecture. This hope must, of course, be tempered with the knowledge that the United States is arguably acting with the intention of undermining the ICC.

Still, the impact of the ICC is not, as many believe, to be measured in completed trials. It is unlikely that the ICC will try large numbers of alleged international criminals, nor is it intended to. One of the major purposes of the ICC will be to encourage national courts, which have the resources of domestic enforcement mechanisms, such as the police, to prosecute suspects. The court is structured with this in mind.[97] Another, perhaps even more important, feature of the ICC will be its symbolic role as a visible reminder and repository of the values protected by international criminal law. Even the most litigious lawyers will concede that the power of law does not reside primarily in coercive enforcement, but in generating and reinforcing customs and traditions of respect for the law. The ICC may well help cement such traditions.[98] Adequate state support for, or tolerance of, the ICC may already be present, not only to usher in a new era of enforcement of international criminal law against the grossest human rights abuses, but also to promote that law and make such abuses less likely in the future.

## Notes

I would like to thank Nigel White and Paul Roberts for their comments on an earlier draft, and the British Council for its support.

1. David J. Harris, *Cases and Materials on International Law* (London: Sweet and Maxwell, 1998), pp. 738–764.

2. For example, see the European system contained in the 1950 European Convention on Human Rights, 213 UNTS 221 (as amended).

3. 1998 Rome Statute for the International Criminal Court (hereafter Rome Statute) A/Conf.183/9, Article 7, paragraph 1.

4. Even if this is the case under customary international law, prosecution before the ICC would probably fall foul of the "Elements of Crimes," which require that "the conduct took place in the context of a manifest pattern of similar conduct." See PNICC/20000.INF/3/Add.2, Article 6, paragraph a.

5. For example, see Steven R. Ratner and Jason Abrams, *Accountability for Human Rights Atrocities in International Law: Beyond the Nuremberg Legacy* (Oxford: Oxford University Press, 2001), p. 118.

6. Misc. 12 (1985) Cmnd. 9593.

7. *R v Bow Street Stipendiary Magistrate ex parte Pinochet Ugarte (Amnesty International and Others Intervening)* [No. 3] (1999), 2 All ER 97; see Neil Boister and Richard Burchill, "The Pinochet Precedent: Don't Leave Home without It," *Criminal Law Forum* 10 (1999): 405–442.

8. According to the "Final Report to the Prosecutor by the Committee Established to Review the NATO Bombing Campaign against the Federal Republic of Yugoslavia," "[it] is unlikely that a human rights lawyer and an experienced combat commander would assign the same relative values to military advantage and to injury to noncombatants." See "Final Report to the Prosecutor by the Committee Established to Review the NATO Bombing Campaign against the Federal Republic of Yugoslavia," June 8, 1999, paragraph 50. For criticism of the report, see Paulo Benvenuti, "The ICTY Prosecutor and the Review of the NATO Bombing Campaign against the Federal Republic of Yugoslavia," *European Journal of International Law* 12 (2001): 503–530.

9. See David J. Scheffer, "International Judicial Intervention," *Foreign Policy* 102 (1999): 34–51.

10. Universal jurisdiction is the principle by which any state can try an international crime, no matter where it was committed.

11. Although prosecution is intervention, in many ways, that is not to say that such intervention is illegal.

12. David P. Forsythe, *Human Rights in International Relations* (Cambridge: Cambridge University Press, 2000), p. 13. For passionate advocacy of forgiveness as a response to human rights violations, see Archbishop Desmond Tutu, *No Future without Forgiveness* (London: Routledge, 2000).

13. Alfred P. Rubin, *Ethics and Authority in International Law* (Cambridge: Cambridge University Press, 1997).

14. William Pace and Mark Thieroff, "Participation of Non-governmental Organizations," in Roy S. Lee, ed., *The International Criminal Court: The Making of the Rome Statute, Issues, Negotiations, Results* (The Hague: Kluwer, 1999), pp. 391–398.

15. "Nuremberg International Military Tribunal: Judgment and Sentence," reprinted in *American Journal of International Law* 41 (1947): 172–333. Questions could be raised about the term "only."

16. See Mark J. Osiel, *Mass Atrocity, Collective Memory and the Law* (New Brunswick, N.J.: Transaction, 1998).

17. Steven R. Ratner, "The Schizophrenias of International Criminal Law," *Texas International Law Journal* 33 (1998): 237–256.

18. See generally P. Williams and M. P. Scharf, *Peace and Justice: War Crimes and Accountability in Former Yugoslavia* (London: Rowman and Littlefield, 2002).

19. Edward Morgan, "Retributory Theater," *American University Journal of International Law and Policy* 3 (1988): 1–64.

20. Such as the Russell Tribunal, convened by Earl Russell to appraise the U.S. involvement in the Vietnam War.

21. For example, see Christopher Hitchens, *The Trial of Henry Kissinger* (London: Verso, 2001).

22. This, although in a very different context, is the theme of Edward P. Thompson, *Whigs and Hunters* (Harmondsworth, UK: Penguin, 1990).

23. Quoted in Pace and Thieroff, "Participation of Non-governmental Organizations," p. 396.

24. Ian Brownlie, *Principles of Public International Law* (Oxford: Clarendon, 1990), pp. 563–564.

25. Robert Y. Jennings and Arthur Watts, eds., *Oppenheim's International Law* (London: Longmans, 1992), p. 998.

26. General Assembly Resolution 44/39, UN Doc. A/RES/44/39.

27. 1019 UNTS 175.

28. An interesting semantic point is that unlike the ILC's work, which was for an international criminal court, the Rome Statute is for the ICC.

29. Although their inclusion or otherwise in the Rome Statute arose again in Rome itself, and has not been ruled out, see the "Final Act" of the Rome Conference, A/ Conf.183/10. On the shift, compare James Crawford, "The ILC's Draft Statute for an International Criminal Tribunal," *American Journal of International Law* 88 (1994): 140–152, with James Crawford, "The ILC Adopts a Statute for an International Criminal Court," *American Journal of International Law* 89 (1995): 404–416. Interestingly, the terrorist attacks on the United States on September 11, 2001, have led to a revival of calls for the ICC to deal with terrorist crimes.

30. Payam Akhavan, "Prosecuting War Crimes in Former Yugoslavia: A Critical Juncture for the New World Order," *Human Rights Quarterly* 15 (1993): 262–289.

31. UN Security Council Resolution (UNSCR) 764, UN Doc. S/RES/764.

32. UNSCR 771, UN Doc. S/RES/771.

33. UNSCR 780, UN Doc. S/RES/780.

34. Forsythe, *Human Rights*, p. 94.

35. There were grave doubts expressed about it even by the drafters of the statute of the ICTY. See Ralph Zacklin, "Bosnia and Beyond," *Virginia Journal of International Law* 34 (1994): 277–281.

36. Forsythe, *Human Rights*, p. 94.

37. Virginia Morris and Michael P. Scharf, *The International Criminal Tribunal for Rwanda* (New York: Transnational, 1998), p. 62.

38. Ian Brownlie, *Principles of International Law* (Oxford: Clarendon, 1998), p. 568.

39. Forsythe, *Human Rights*, p. 221.

40. Robert Cryer, "A Special Court for Sierra Leone?" *International and Comparative Law Quarterly* 50 (2000): 435–446.

41. Cryer, "Special Court for Sierra Leone," p. 435.

42. Steven R. Ratner, "The Cambodia Settlement Agreements," *American Journal of International Law* 87 (1993): 1–41.

43. The prosecutions in Sierra Leone will relate only to post-1996, although this is purely for pragmatic/financial reasons. See Cryer, "Special Court for Sierra Leone," p. 442.

44. This is not to ignore the other aspects, positive and negative. See Gary J. Bass, *Stay the Hand of Vengeance: The Politics of War Crimes Tribunals* (Princeton, N.J.: Princeton University Press, 2000).

45. A. P. Simester and G. R. Sullivan, *Criminal Law: Theory and Doctrine* (Oxford: Hart, 2000), chapter 1.

46. Some say that it will remain symbolic alone, such as Eugene Davidson, *The Nuremberg Fallacy: Wars and War Crimes since World War II* (New York: Macmillan, 1973).

47. William A. Schabas, *Genocide in International Law* (Cambridge: Cambridge University Press, 2000), pp. 9–10.

48. Michael Akehurst, "Jurisdiction in International Law," *British Yearbook of International Law* 46 (1972–1973): 145–257.

49. Rosalyn Higgins, *Problems and Process: International Law and How We Use It* (Oxford: Oxford University Press, 1994), pp. 58–59.

50. Herbert L. A. Hart, *The Concept of Law* (Oxford: Clarendon, 1994), p. 125.

51. R. John Pritchard and Sonia M. Zaide, *The Tokyo War Crimes*, Vol. 22, *Separate Opinions* (New York: Garland, 1981) (dissenting opinion of Mr. Justice Pal, member for India).

52. As expressed in UNSCRs 808 and 827, UN Docs. S/RES/808, S/RES/827.

53. *Prosecutor v. Tadic*, Decision on the Interlocutory Appeal on Jurisdiction, 2 October 1995, IT-94-1-AR72, paragraph 70, and Rome Statute, Article 8(2)(f).

54. International criminal law has almost singly been rehabilitated as an academic discipline by the creation of the ICTY, the ICTR, and now the ICC.

55. Amnesty International, *The International Criminal Court: Making the Right Choices Parts I-V* (London: Amnesty International, 1995–1998).

56. The United States signed the Rome Statute but has formally declared that it will not ratify it.

57. See Nigel D. White, *The Law of International Organizations* (Manchester: Manchester University Press, 1996).

58. Judith L. Goldstein et al., eds., *Legalization and World Politics* (London: Massachusetts Institute of Technology Press, 2001).

59. Kenneth W. Abbott et al., "The Concept of Legalization," in Judith L. Goldstein et al., eds., *Legalization and World Politics* (London: Massachusetts Institute of Technology Press, 2001), pp. 17–35.

60. Abbott et al., "Concept of Legalization," p. 17.

61. This includes heads of state. See Rome Statute, Article 27.

62. Abbott et al., "Concept of Legalization," p. 17.

63. José Alvarez, "Do Liberal States Behave Better? A Critique of Slaughter's Liberal Theory," *European Journal of International Law* 12 (2001): 183–246.

64. Martti Koskenniemi, *The Gentle Civilizer of Nations* (Cambridge: Cambridge University Press, 2001), chapter 6.

65. Gerry Simpson, "Two Liberalisms," *European Journal of International Law* 12 (2001): 537–572.

66. Kenneth W. Abbott and Duncan Snidal, "Hard and Soft Law in International Governance," in Judith L. Goldstein et al., eds., *Legalization and World Politics* (London: Massachusetts Institute of Technology Press, 2001), pp. 37–72.

67. Antonio Cassese, "The Rome Statute of the International Criminal Court: Some Preliminary Reflections," *European Journal of International Law* 10 (1999): 144–171.

68. "Report of the Secretary-General Pursuant to Paragraph 2 of Security Council Resolution 808," UN Doc. S/25704, paragraph 58. The ICTR provisions are, to all intents and purposes, identical.

69. *SW v. UK*, 27 November 1995, ECHR Reports Series A, vol. 335–B.

70. Thomas M. Franck, *The Power of Legitimacy among Nations* (Oxford: Oxford University Press, 1990), p. 64.

71. Abbott et al., "Concept of Legalization," p. 31.

72. Abbott et al. note the level of detail in the Rome Statute was because of a wish to limit the delegation of authority in their section on determinacy. This shows that the categories are not entirely stable. See Abbott et al., "Concept of Legalization," p. 31

73. Rome Statute, Articles 25, 27, 28, 30, 31, 32, 33.

74. Robert Cryer, "The Boundaries of Liability in International Criminal Law, or 'Selectivity by Stealth,'" *Journal of Conflict and Security Law* 6 (2001): 3–31.

75. Abbott et al., "Concept of Legalization," p. 32.

76. Colin Warbrick and Peter Rowe, "The International Criminal Tribunal for Yugoslavia: The Decision of the Appeals Chamber on the Interlocutory Appeal on Jurisdiction in the *Tadic* Case," *International and Comparative Law Quarterly* 45 (1996): 691–701.

77. *Prosecutor v. Ntuyuhaga*, Decision on the Prosecutor's Motion to Withdraw the Indictment, March 19, 1999, ICTR-98-40.

78. ICTR Statute, Article 7.

79. ICTY Statute, Articles 1, 8.

80. Williams and Scharf, *Peace and Justice*, chapter 10.

81. PNICC/2000/INF/3/Add.2.

82. This has been noted by Abbott et al., "Concept of Legalization," p. 31.

83. Rome Statute, Article 5, paragraph 2.

84. Rome Statute, Article 24.

85. Rome Statute, Article 12.

86. Rome Statute, Article 14.

87. Rome Statute, Article 15, paragraph 1.

88. UN Doc. S/RES/1422.

89. Michael P. Scharf, "Swapping Amnesty for Peace: Was There a Duty to Prosecute International Crimes in Haiti?" *Texas International Law Journal* 31 (1999): 1–41.

90. *Velasquez-Rodriguez v. Honduras*, Judgment of July 29, 1988, Inter-American Court of Human Rights, Inter-American Court of Human Rights, Reports of Judgments Series C no. 4.

91. John Dugard, "Dealing with Crimes of a Past Regime: Is Amnesty Still an Option?" *Leiden Journal of International Law* 12 (1999): 1001–1015, contra Diane F. Orientlicher, "Settling Accounts: The Duty to Prosecute Human Rights Violations of a Former Regime," *Yale Law Journal* 100 (1991): 2357–2415.

92. "Report of the Secretary-General on the Establishment of a Special Court for Sierra Leone," UN Doc. S/2000/915, paragraph 24.

93. Rome Statute, preambular paragraphs 4–5.

94. Michael P. Scharf, "The Amnesty Exception to the Jurisdiction of the International Criminal Court," *Cornell International Law Journal* 32 (1999): 507–527.

95. Mahnoush Arsanjani, "The Rome Statute of the International Criminal Court," *American Journal of International Law* 93 (1999): 22–42; Gerhard Hafner et al., "A Response to the American View As Presented by Ruth Wedgwood," *European Journal of International Law* 10 (1999): 108–123.

96. Anne-Marie Slaughter, "Al Qaeda Should Be Tried before the World," *New York Times*, 17 November 2001, available at www.nytimes.com/2001/11/17/opinion/17SLAU.html?todaysheadlines (accessed March 21, 2003).

97. Jonathan Charney, "International Criminal Law and the Role of Domestic Courts," *American Journal of International Law* 95 (2001): 120–124.

98. Traditions need not be long established to qualify as such or be considered natural. See Eric Hobsbawn and Terence Ranger, *The Invention of Tradition* (Cambridge: Canto, 1983).

# Part II

## The International Politics of Intervention

# 5

## Problematizing Sovereignty

### Relative Sovereignty in the Historical Transformation of Interstate and State-Society Relations

*Victoria Tin-bor Hui*

It is often argued that humanitarian interventions in the post–Cold War era present a new challenge to state sovereignty. In this debate, sovereignty is typically understood to mean nonintervention, so that humanitarian interventions necessarily violate sovereignty. This chapter attempts to address the issue by tracing the genealogy of sovereignty and intervention. Although most studies of interventions focus on the 1990s, more and more historically grounded analysts point out that interventions have always been routine and sovereignty has been porous throughout the history of the modern state system. If the phenomenon of intervention is as old as the history of international politics, then we would be mistaken to treat sovereignty as an absolute concept and intervention as its necessary negation. We may consider the possibility that it is rather the concept of sovereignty that has been historically problematic. In this chapter, I problematize sovereignty by, first, treating it as a *composite concept* that entails a state's relations with other states and with its society, and, second, examining it as a *historical variable* rather than a constant. Borrowing the concept of relative capabilities from theories of international politics and that of relative autonomy from theories of the state, I argue that a state's degree of autonomy from external actors is relative to both interstate and state-society relations.

Sovereignty is relative to interstate relations as it involves mutual recognition and relative capabilities. In the current debate, attention is focused on mutual recognition or juridical sovereignty. For most of world history, however, there was no de facto sovereign equality between the strong and the weak. In fact, weaker states frequently fell prey to encroachment by their more powerful neighbors. Sovereignty is also relative to state-society relations as it involves control and authority over not just territories, but also populations. If the ruled have motivations and capabilities to resist their rulers, then even militarily powerful states may not be able to prevent internal conflicts from becoming internationalized. In early efforts at establishing sovereignty, "civil" conflicts and "international" wars were inextricably intertwined. Indeed, it was in response to prevalent interventions that the principle of nonintervention emerged in the late eighteenth century. But it was not until the nineteenth century that elite members of the international system simultaneously achieved military prowess, acquired the capacity to pacify their populations, and enjoyed the consent of the governed. For states that achieved high degrees of relative sovereignty, the major venue left for international intervention was mutual recognition. Although the two world wars reversed this trend for losers, Western powers gradually established even higher levels of relative sovereignty in the postwar period.

Decolonization at the end of World War II gave birth to new states that had to face the same challenge of establishing relative sovereignty. At the height of the Cold War, many strategically located developing countries suffered from overt and covert interventions by the two superpowers. After the Cold War, such centuries-old coercive interventions have subsided. But the explosion of humanitarian crises have called for a different type of intervention. While Western countries proceeded on all dimensions of relative sovereignty over several centuries, decolonized countries were expected to attain juridical sovereignty overnight without having established internal authority and control. At the end of the Cold War, various Third World countries that had not effectively developed internal sovereignty in the postwar period witnessed state collapse on a massive scale. While the phenomenon of international intervention is not at all new, that of *humanitarian* intervention—military action to protect people in another country from suffering grave harm—is doubtless new.[1] In debating whether this type of intervention undermines sovereignty, it is important not to forget that various Western powers that lead humanitarian interventions now were once subject to coercive interventions to an even larger extent. Moreover, in debating whether humanitarian interventions since 1989 have been driven by moral responsibility or power politics, it is important not to forget that interventions were motivated by the shameless pursuit of territorial, political, or economic gains for most of international history. The bigger challenge now is not that great powers are too interventionist in the name of moral responsibility, but that they are unwilling to intervene in parts of the world that present few geostrategic or economic stakes.

The dilemma between sovereignty and intervention is reflected in the United Nations (UN) Charter, which contains "two principles that at times, and perhaps increasingly, conflict."[2] The charter simultaneously prohibits "intervention into matters that are within the domestic jurisdiction of any state"[3] and enshrines "respect for human rights and for fundamental freedoms."[4] This "incoherence"[5] of the charter would be less puzzling if sovereignty is seen as relative to state-society relations as well as to interstate relations. From this perspective, it also makes better sense why Emmerich de Vattel, who in the late eighteenth century, was one of the first to articulate the principle of nonintervention also argued that "if the unjust rule of a sovereign led to internal revolt, external powers would have the right to intervene on the side of the just party when disorder reached the stage of civil war."[6] If intervention is as old as international politics and sovereignty is a *variable* rather than a constant, then it is not very instructive to compile a list of violations of sovereignty. Rather, the more interesting agenda is to examine how states have struggled to establish relative sovereignty—both in the West and in "the Rest," both then and now. UN secretary-general Kofi Annan argues that the charter is "a living document" whose interpretation and implementation should change with the times.[7] By the same token, relative sovereignty is a living concept that has evolved with transformation in interstate and state-society relations. This chapter will address the state of the debate, introduce the concept of relative sovereignty, trace the historical transformation of relative sovereignty, and examine what this reconceptualization means in the new wave of humanitarian interventions in the post–Cold War era.[8]

**The State of the Debate: Intervention As Violation
of Sovereignty**

The concept of sovereignty lies at the heart of theories of international politics. However, for most of the post–World War II era, sovereignty was so taken for granted that it was rarely discussed in the international relations literature. Since humanitarian interventions became an issue in the 1990s, an interest in this concept has been rekindled. In this debate, it is often argued that "the stronghold of sovereignty [has been] cracked and supplanted by a general concern for human rights."[9] A survey of the emerging literature shows that sovereignty is typically defined as "internal supremacy and external independence,"[10] "exclusion of external actors from domestic authority configurations,"[11] "exclusive authority over a fixed territorial space,"[12] "constitutional independence of other states,"[13] "jurisdictional exclusivity within . . . borders,"[14] and the like. All these definitions can be traced to Christian Freiherr von Wolff, who wrote in the 1760s that "[t]o interfere in the government of another, in whatever way indeed that may be done, is opposed to the natural liberty of nations, by virtue of which one is altogether independent of the will of other nations in its action."[15] This view essentially treats sovereignty and nonintervention as forming "two sides of the same coin,"[16] thus relegating intervention as its "conceptual opposite."[17] As R. J. Vincent most explicitly proclaims, "if sovereignty, then nonintervention."[18] If sovereignty is seen in absolute and exclusive terms so that intervention by external actors necessarily contradicts state sovereignty, then it follows that "a state can do as it pleases in its own jurisdiction,"[19] "pursue whatever policies it deems wise," and "decree whatever laws it deems necessary."[20] No matter what this state does within its territorial jurisdiction, no other states have the right to interfere.

It is noteworthy that this view of sovereignty is held by not just opponents to intervention, but also advocates of intervention. Indeed, the latter have treated humanitarian interventions as driven by a set of values, most notably, human rights, in opposition to state sovereignty. Stephan Krasner, for example, argues that individual and minority rights are "alternative principles" to and therefore "inconsistent with" state sovereignty.[21] To justify humanitarian interventions, advocates have generally resorted to the argument that morality should trump legality—that protection of citizens' rights entails a more fundamental value and so violation of state sovereignty is from time to time justifiable.[22] Liberal interventionists from John Stuart Mill[23] to Michael Walzer[24] devote immense efforts at compiling lists of human rights that should be defended beyond borders. However, by accepting that intervention represents an exception to the norm, this conceptualization of sovereignty imposes serious limits on the room for humanitarian interventions. Moreover, by emphasizing that "human rights are intended to curb sovereignty rights,"[25] this conceptualization inevitably invites rejection by authoritarian rulers who can easily claim that imposition of liberal values on non-Western cultures is another form of imperialism.

It is my contention that a genealogy of sovereignty and intervention may provide a better solution to the seeming contradiction between intervention and sovereignty.[26] In the early stage of the debate, the concept of state sovereignty is often attributed to the Peace of Westphalia in 1648. International relations scholars generally followed Leo Gross's view that Westphalia marked "the end of an epoch and the opening of another."[27] More specifically, Westphalia is taken to signify "man's abandonment of the idea of a hierarchical structure of society and his option for a new system characterized by the coexistence of a multiplicity of states, each sovereign within its territory, equal to one another, and free from any external earthly authority."[28] From Westphalia on, it is argued that sovereign states "came to espouse nonintervention as a cornerstone of international diplomacy."[29]

Nevertheless, more careful historical research shows that the majesty of Westphalia—along with the sanctity of nonintervention—is merely a "founding myth."[30] Even the very term "Westphalian sovereignty" is "historically inaccurate."[31] As Andreas Osiander points out, the primary goal of the treaties of Münster and Osnabrück, which ended the Thirty Years' War, was to restore order within the Holy Roman Empire—a political entity that was supposed to become illegitimate and even extinct in the Westphalian order of sovereign territorial states.[32] Moreover, the peace settlements were "silent on the issue of sovereignty or . . . any corollary of sovereignty . . . such as nonintervention."[33] In fact, the principle of nonintervention was not to be articulated until the second half of the eighteenth century. The treaty terms included extensive provisions that fixed the religious affiliations of principalities as they were on January 1, 1624, irrespective of the changing preferences of princes.[34] The settlements even stipulated basic constitutional relations between the Holy Roman emperor and various principalities—and such "internal" matters were guaranteed by the victorious powers France and Sweden. Not surprisingly, then, even Gross has to acknowledge that the Peace of Westphalia "may fairly be described as an international constitution which gave to all its adherents the right of intervention to enforce its engagements."[35]

Such formal endorsement of the "right of intervention" was repeated in subsequent peace settlements. As Krasner highlights, "Every major peace treaty from Westphalia to Helsinki has included provisions that contradict the Westphalian model: religious toleration in Westphalia, succession rights in Utrecht, minority rights and issues of legitimate order in Vienna, minority rights in the 1878 Treaty of Berlin, minority rights in Versailles, and human rights in Helsinki."[36] Similarly, the very constitutional order of a polity has always been subject to international intervention, "whether this involved the formation of Protestant polities in the sixteenth century, of absolute monarchies in the seventeenth century, of republics in the nineteenth century, or of fascist, communist, and now democratic states in the twentieth century."[37] In addition to these legitimate forms of intervention sanctioned by international treaties, there are other more sinister forms—assassinations, subversions, subsidies, briberies, and other covert interventions—that fill volumes of historical records. Far from being exceptions to the norm, therefore, "[i]nternational interventions are in many ways ordinary topics in international relations."[38] As Daniel Philpott, a champion of the Westphalian order, summarizes the critical view, "It is not that sovereignty no longer is; it is that it never quite was."[39]

## Problematizing Sovereignty: *Relative* Sovereignty

A genealogy of sovereignty thus shows that it is sovereignty, rather than intervention, that has always been problematic in international history. Krasner not only demystifies the so-called Westphalian order, but also problematizes sovereignty.[40] While most analysts treat sovereignty in a single dimension, he introduces a composite concept with four dimensions. The typical dimension, or "Westphalian sovereignty," refers to the exclusion of external authority. (Krasner uses this "historically inaccurate" term because it "has so much entered into common usage."[41]) The second dimension, "international legal sovereignty," refers to "the mutual recognition of states or other entities."[42] The third dimension, "domestic sovereignty," refers to "the formal organization of political authority within the state and the ability of public authorities to exercise effective control within the borders of their own polity."[43] And the fourth dimension, "interdependence sovereignty," refers to "the ability of public authorities to control transborder movements."[44] With a multidimensional conceptualization of sovereignty, Krasner comes to the important insight that intervention is not necessarily the negation of sovereignty: while humanitarian interventions violate Westphalian sovereignty, voluntary participation in international human rights regimes can strengthen a state's "international legal sovereignty."[45]

Nevertheless, Krasner does not go far enough in problematizing sovereignty. First, he still views Westphalian sovereignty as nonintervention and intervention as its negation. This is evident in his efforts at compiling instances of its violations in the history of the modern states system. Second, Krasner focuses his attention on Westphalian sovereignty and international legal sovereignty but brackets domestic sovereignty and interdependence sovereignty. The rationale is that "the organization of authority within a state and the level of control enjoyed by the state are not necessarily related to international legal or Westphalian sovereignty."[46] In doing so, Krasner tacitly follows the assumption among mainstream international relations scholars that there is little value-added from looking inside states. While this position may be justifiable in some issue areas of international politics, an analysis of sovereignty is not one of them.[47] The very distinction between the "international" and the "domestic" realms is an anachronistic conceptualization that did not originally exist in history. After all, the doctrine of sovereignty as originally formulated by Jean Bodin and Thomas Hobbes was "directed above all against forces threatening the state from within."[48] In short, Krasner takes an important first step at making sovereignty a problematic concept, but comes significantly short in this effort.

To further problematize sovereignty, I treat sovereignty as, first, a composite concept that entails state-society as well as interstate relations and, second, a historical *variable* that evolves over time.[49] I also borrow the concept of "relative capabilities" from theories of international relations[50] and the concept of "relative autonomy" from theories of state-society relations.[51] As such, sovereignty may be seen as *relative* to interstate and state-society relations. While Krasner's four dimensions of sovereignty are "not logically coupled,"[52] I see interstate and state-society relations as inextricably intertwined. If sovereignty involves relations with different actors—both other states and societal actors—then exclusion of external actors should be seen as a difficult goal that states cannot take for granted. If sovereignty involves relations with societal actors, then state sovereignty and citizens' rights are not necessarily in opposition to each other. If sovereignty does not mean nonintervention, then it is not very useful to compile a list of instances of violation in international history. If sovereignty is a historical variable, then the more interesting agenda is to examine how *relative* sovereignty has evolved through transformations in interstate and state-society relations.

### Relative Sovereignty in Interstate Relations

Sovereignty is relative to interstate relations as it involves mutual recognition with other states and distribution of relative capabilities. The first point is generally taken for granted in the literature on sovereignty: A state does not have "international-legal" or juridical sovereignty unless it is recognized by other states. Moreover, the delineation of territorial sovereignty also involves recognition, either as informal understandings or in formal treaties. John G. Ruggie points out that "any mode of differentiation inherently entails a corresponding form of sociality."[53] If sovereignty refers to exclusive authority over demarcated territory, then the territorial space within which a state can exercise supreme authority has to be first demarcated. The act of mutual recognition, of course, involves inclusion rather than exclusion of external actors.

Sovereignty is also a function of relative capabilities.[54] Vattel argues in *Le droit de gens* that all states, weak and strong, are entitled to the principle of juridical equality.[55] However, as Mill observes, "Power . . . is wont to encroach upon the weak."[56] Indeed, weak states have been subject to all forms of intervention from blatant conquest to covert subversion throughout international history. It is noteworthy that, in the practice of realpolitik, Europe was in fact substantially modern long before the Peace of Westphalia. As Jack Levy observes, "By the middle of the fifteenth century several territorial states were well on their way toward consolidation into centralized organizations with stable frontiers. These new territorial states had become virtually independent of the authority of both the pope and the emperor."[57] Such emergent great powers soon sought to dominate their weaker neighbors. Italian city-states, with their "combination of military weakness and enormous wealth," became "irresistible prey."[58] From the Italian wars on, European states were connected by massive armies in wartime and diplomatic exchanges in peacetime. Hence, Europeanists generally view the French invasion of Italy at the end of 1494, rather than the Peace of Westphalia in 1648, as a marker for the onset of the modern international system.[59]

With intensification of international competition, the principle of *raison d'état*—that international relations should be dictated by the calculation of national interests rather than by religious or other moral concerns—was first alluded to by Niccolò Machiavelli in 1513 and then formally articulated in the late sixteenth century. In the ensuing "age of reason," sovereignty was understood "as a principle that permit[ed] state rulers to do anything in their own self-interest, including attacking the territory of a neighboring state."[60] Territorial expansion would be "justified simply by its success,"[61] and success would be rewarded by mutual recognition. William Coplin notes that "the legal concept of boundaries provided a means through which the expansion and contraction of power in the form of territory could be measured."[62] International treaties thus "reinforced the idea that the struggle for power was an essential and accepted part of international politics."[63] Although European statesmen frequently spoke of preserving the independence of states in order to maintain the balance of power, they referred only to great powers and would not hesitate to partition weak states. At the height of territorial competition in the late eighteenth century, the "sickman of Europe"—Poland— was partitioned. At the Congress of Vienna, which settled the Napoleonic Wars, victorious powers redrew the European map but had little interest in restoring Poland's independence. The great powers only requested that Prussia, Russia, and Austria respect the minority rights of Poles so as to prevent Polish resistance. In ensuing decades, territorial competition on the European continent was tamed by widespread weariness of war.[64] However, in the late nineteenth and early twentieth centuries, "the anarchic view of sovereignty" resurged with "the convergence of nationalism, positivism, and Darwinism."[65]

The ravage of the two world wars, in turn, transformed sovereignty from a principle legitimizing territorial conquest into one "limiting the right of states to pursue territorial claims."[66] The territorial integrity norm, or "the proscription that force should not be used to alter interstate boundaries,"[67] began to gain momentum around World War I. But it was only after World War II that territorial boundaries "became sacrosanct."[68] The territorial integrity norm was extended not just from great powers to weak states in Europe, but also from the Western world to former colonies in other parts of the world.[69] Nevertheless, short of territorial conquest, other less blatant forms of intervention were available. Most notably, "forcible domestic regime promotion," which had a long history from the Reformation and Counter-Reformation through the revolutionary and counterrevolutionary eras, was widely practiced by both the United States and the Soviet Union in their respective spheres of influence.[70] At the height of the Cold War, the two superpowers also fought proxy wars on the soils of weak states.

For most of international history, therefore, sovereignty was a function of relative capabilities. The nonintervention principle articulated by Wolff, Vattel, and Mill was largely meaningless for weak states. Weak states would think themselves exceptionally fortunate if neighboring great powers only sought to dictate their foreign policies. From this macrohistorical perspective, humanitarian interventions at the end of the Cold War merely followed a long trend in international politics. If anything has changed, it is that the character of interventions has in fact become less coercive in the post–Cold War era: from the old repertoire of outright conquest, regime imposition, and covert subversion, to the new formula of humanitarian assistance and democracy promotion.

### Relative Sovereignty in State-Society Relations

Sovereignty is also relative to state-society relations because it involves authority and control over populations as well as territories. As reflected in such labels as "territorial sovereignty" and "the sovereign, territorial state," the literature typically equates sovereignty with territoriality. As sovereignty is seen in territorial terms, it is also taken to be analogous to private property rights. Drawing from Hugo Grotius, Ruggie observes that "the rediscovery from Roman law of the concept of absolute private property" coincided with the emergence of "mutually exclusive territorial state formations, which stood in relation to one another much as owners of private estates do."[71] Louis XIV's famous remark *"L'Etat, c'est moi"* connoted sovereignty as the private property of the king. Like an owner of a piece of property who could do whatever he pleased with his possession, the king should have absolute control and authority over all matters within his territorial boundaries—at least until the property changes hands. While it is reasonable enough to treat territory as private property, it would be far more problematic to do so with people.

Unlike inanimate real properties, human beings may have motivations and capabilities to resist rulers' sovereign claims over them. Potential tensions between rulers and the ruled can be safely ignored only in two extreme scenarios: either when the ruler achieves total domination over the subjects so that they are incapable of resistance, or when the ruler commands consent from the citizens so that they have no motivation for resistance. In early modern Europe, kings and princes typically tried to establish absolute domination over their subjects, but no European rulers could be "truly inwardly sovereign *de facto.*"[72] As Immanuel Wallerstein puts it, "The doctrine of the absolute right of monarchs" was no more than "a theoretical claim of weak rulers for a far-off utopia they hoped to establish."[73] As sizable sectors among subject populations across Europe had both the motivations and the resources to resist, even the most militarily powerful states—for example, France, Spain, and England in the sixteenth and seventeenth centuries—could not escape "internationalization" of "internal" conflicts.

The three main categories of "civil" problems that frequently became "internationalized" were succession struggles, religious dissent, and ethnic conflicts. As dynastic families intermarried one another, succession disputes frequently touched off intrigues, subversions, assassinations, and even outright wars of succession.[74] But such conflicts were limited to the ruling class. Religious and ethnic conflicts, on the other hand, were resistance movements by the ruled against their rulers. In the early modern period, resistance was widespread because rulers had relatively low state capacity and did not yet monopolize the means of coercion. State capacity refers to "the degree of control state agents exercise over persons, activities, and resources within their government's territorial jurisdiction."[75] Rulers and ruling apparatuses acquired capacity "through four often complementary processes: replacement of indirect by direct rule; penetration by central states of geographic peripheries; standardization of state practices and identities; and instrumentation—growth in the means of carrying out intended policies."[76] It is noteworthy that, while early modern Europe was decidedly modern in the practice of realpolitik, it was also persistently medieval in the development of state capacity. For most of the early modern period, various European states "had small and ineffective bureaucracies, armed forces they did not control very well, and all sorts of strong local authorities and overlapping jurisdictions."[77] With low state capacity, European kings generally had to rule through intermediaries, such as clerics, landlords, urban oligarchs, and independent professional warriors. Indirect rule was a relatively convenient form of government, but it also left ruling courts with no effective control over either territories or populations. As Charles Tilly points out, indirect rule not only "set serious limits on the quantity of resources rulers could extract from the ambient economy," but also made it possible for intermediate power holders to ally with local populations in their resistance to central demands.[78]

During the Reformation, religious resistance was inseparable from central-local conflicts and interstate rivalries. Suppressed by Catholic rulers, Calvinists and Huguenots developed the right of resistance.[79] When quasi-independent power holders became sympathetic to their cause, Protestants were able to form their own armies and divert state revenues for their own use. In the struggle between Huguenots and the Catholic League in 1578–1579, both sides controlled provinces and were practically independent of French kings. Even more ominously, when Protestants sought assistance from outside sympathetic rulers to help fight their Catholic rulers, they found many princes who were eager to use such opportunities to expand their own power. As Machiavelli warned in *The Prince* a century earlier, "[I]f . . . your subjects hate you . . . , once they have risen in arms, [they] will never be short of foreign allies who will come to their support."[80] Even Bodin, who first articulated the principle of absolute sovereignty in relations between kings and subjects, argued that it would be "a most beautiful and magnificent thing for a [foreign] prince to take up arms in order to avenge an entire people unjustly oppressed by a tyrant's cruelty."[81] Hence, by the end of the Thirty Years' War, Catholic rulers came to recognize that "they were more likely to keep their crowns, and their heads, if they acquiesced to religious differences rather than suppressing them."[82]

Although religious toleration was upheld at the Peace of Westphalia (and in all major peace settlements afterward), state-society and interstate struggles continued to be hopelessly interwoven. In an age when territorial expansion was sanctioned by an anarchic view of sovereignty, there was little regard for ethnic composition in conquered territories. Ethnic minorities might then have incentives to resist alien rulers and invite co-ethnics in neighboring countries to help. However, ethnic resistance faced a different scenario than religious resistance. During the Reformation, Catholic rulers had extremely weak state capacity vis-à-vis Protestant dissenters. However, in the century after the Peace of Westphalia, European kings gradually established standing armies and used them to subjugate unwieldy regional power holders and local populations. European states not only built up "fearsome coercive means of their own," but also "deprived civilian populations of access to those means."[83] As states gradually monopolized the means of coercion, it became increasingly "impossible for a dissident faction to seize power . . . without the active collaboration of some segments of the state's own armed forces."[84] With a very different balance in coercive capabilities, therefore, ethnic minorities were far less successful than religious minorities in gaining concessions from rulers.

The reversal in relative capabilities between rulers and the ruled reached a new height when direct rule was introduced in the revolutionary era. After overthrowing the old regime, French revolutionaries "recast the French map into a nested system of departments, districts, cantons, and communes," thus establishing a hierarchy of administration linking the central government to local villages.[85] The capacity for direct rule significantly altered the character of state-society struggles, because this development allowed European rulers to shift from "reactive to proactive repression."[86] As Tilly elaborates, "With the installation of direct rule came the creation of systems of surveillance and reporting that made local and regional administrators responsible for the prediction and prevention of [resistance] movements."[87] In the subsequent nineteenth and twentieth centuries, the state's coercive power grew exponentially. Developments in administrative technology, industrial capability, and military weapons facilitated large-scale genocide and ethnic cleansing, culminating in the "systematized, routinized, and industrialized conveyor belt killings" of Jews in the Holocaust.[88]

If we take at face value the mainstream view of sovereignty as "internal supremacy and external independence," then an analysis of the historical transformation of relative sovereignty in state-society relations would be an account of increased state power and heightened repression. This image no doubt accounts for the formation of the totalitarian state in Prussia/Germany. Fortunately, in other cases success at realpolitik international competition in the international realm "demanded a closer partnership" between rulers and the ruled in the domestic realm.[89] This is because European rulers who wanted to build larger armies and raise higher revenues had to bargain with resource holders in society. Bargaining, in turn, allowed subjects to make "enforceable claims on the state so extensive [that] we can begin to speak of citizenship rights."[90]

Hence, at the same time that the French Revolution introduced direct rule and proactive repression, it also swept away the divine right of kings to rule and the tendency of kings to treat sovereignty as private property. As Paul Schroeder observes, "After 1815, the legitimacy of states, especially new ones, rested not on patrimonial divine right, but on the treaty system, backed by the consent of Europe. The state itself had now become the subject of sovereignty, a kind of moral person, and its prince had become essentially the executive organ of that sovereignty."[91] It was remarkably progressive for great powers in the Concert of Europe to transform monarchical sovereignty from the private realm into the public realm. However, the same great powers also used military force to suppress revolutionary movements and restore monarchical rule across Europe, thus preventing monarchical sovereignty from further descent into popular sovereignty. Such reactionary interventions were deplored as "unjust" by classical liberals of the time. As Mill laments, "A government which needs foreign support to enforce obedience from its own citizens is one which ought not to exist."[92]

Although the revolutionary movements did not overthrow kings and queens, they did compel the lingering monarchs to introduce limited political and welfare reforms to placate the restive populations. The subsequent introduction of elections—no matter how narrowly confined they were— paved the way for the final devolution of sovereignty. State rulers across the Western world gradually commanded the consent of the ruled—along with the capacity to pacify them. Thus, "Max Weber's historically contestable definition of the state [as] a human community that (successfully) claims the monopoly of the legitimate use of physical force within a given territory finally began to make sense for European states."[93] The transitions from monarchical sovereignty to popular sovereignty suffered further reversals and setbacks in subsequent decades. But the franchise was eventually expanded to cover all adult males, then women, and then eighteen-year-old youths in the twentieth century. In the postwar era, even authoritarian rulers had to pay lip service to the idea of popular sovereignty by claiming that they were servants, rather than masters, of the people.

In short, sovereignty has been relative to interstate and state-society relations. If a state exercises effective control within its territorial boundaries and enjoys the consent of the governed, then there is little room for internal dissent and international interference. If such a state also commands power and wealth, then the opportunity for intervention is further reduced to mutual recognition. It was not until the nineteenth century that elite members of the international system began to attain such a high degree of relative sovereignty. For lesser members of the Western world, this achievement occurred only as recently as the postwar era.

### Intervention from the West to the Rest

In the years following World War II, Western powers achieved not just relative sovereignty, but also relative peace. Unfortunately, although interstate wars have subsided in the postwar era, many parts of the newly independent world have descended into "zones of turmoil."[94] Civil wars, ethnic violence, religious conflicts, secessionist wars, and state breakups have occurred on massive scales in the Third World, culminating in grave humanitarian crises in the post–Cold War era.[95] What lessons can we draw from international interventions in the Western world on the new wave of humanitarian interventions in the Third World? As Mohammed Ayoob argues, the proliferation of internal conflicts in the Third World should be understood in terms of "sovereign state-making—including both domestic authority and external recognition over clearly demarcated territorial domains."[96] It may be argued that Western experiences have little relevance to the rest of the world. It would probably be unfair to judge the Third World by Western standards achieved in the postwar period. However, the challenge of state making is comparable if we examine the West in the early modern period and the Rest in the contemporary period. Thus, although Ayoob criticizes mainstream international relations theories for focusing on Western powers and ignoring Third World states, his "subaltern realism" is in fact a call to return to "the classical propounders of realism—Machiavelli and Hobbes."[97] As he elaborates, various developing countries "are currently at the same stage of historical development in terms of consolidation and legitimation of state power as Florence . . . in the fifteenth century or England in the seventeenth century."[98]

There is a growing consensus that the root cause of most problems in the Third World may be found in the disjuncture of international and domestic sovereignty. Following independence, various Third World countries acquired juridical sovereignty or international recognition almost overnight. However, this international dimension of sovereignty was truncated from the domestic dimension. Robert H. Jackson uses the term "quasi-states" to refer to states that have juridical sovereignty but no empirical sovereignty.[99] In developing their state institutions, quasi-states copy the shells of the modern state but leave out the substance. They establish bureaucratic offices without centralization and meritocracy. They form treasury and inland revenues departments without nationalization of taxation and centralization of finance. They build up the army, navy, air force, and police without centralization of command and monopolization of the means of coercion. Not surprisingly, then, such Third World states have had little capacity to exercise effective control over their demarcated territories and populations.

Nor have quasi-states earned the consent of the governed. States in sub-Sahara Africa fail to deliver "even such fundamental public goods as property rights, roads, and basic health and education."[100] Worse, many rulers "act as if sovereignty is their license to exploit people."[101] In different parts of the Third World, there is little more than the pretense of public interest. In the worst cases, the state—if the term still applies at all—is merely a network of private business arrangements and personal loyalties that focuses on trading natural resources for weapons and mercenaries.[102] Moreover, as rulers can treat whole pieces of territory—along with populations and resources—as private property, there are plenty of contenders who are tempted to capture the grand prize. With multiple predators preying on the most helpless, human rights violations can easily escalate to humanitarian crises.

It is often presumed that the problem of state failure is a legacy of colonialism and unique only to the Third World.[103] However, as analyzed earlier, various European states were rather medieval in their development of state capacity and legitimacy until the revolutionary and reform eras. The old regimes of France and Spain, in particular, witnessed "state *de*formation," being hierarchical but rotten from within, autonomous but incapable, and despotic but ineffective.[104] Like predators of quasi-states, absolutist rulers of old regimes also tried to dominate their subjects and treated sovereignty as private property. For instance, the English state during the reign of Charles I was "a kind of parasite, extracting resources from the productive sectors of the nation and redistributing them among a small political class with access to power, offices, and contracts."[105] Tilly even argues that European state makers resembled "racketeers" who "constitute[d] the largest current threats" to their people.[106] The major difference between European states and Third World states is that the latter do not face life-and-death struggles in interstate relations.[107] Unlike Italian city-states or Poland in the early modern period, the juridical independence of militarily weak states is more or less guaranteed by the territorial integrity norm now. Relative peace in interstate relations, unfortunately, "undermines if it does not eliminate altogether [rulers'] incentive to improve the domestic conditions of their states in order to elicit taxation, conscription, and other forms of legitimacy and support from their populations."[108] As David Wootton observes, even Machiavelli's prince "must serve the interests of his subjects . . . in order to maximize his own power."[109] Similarly, for Hobbes, "[t]he office of the sovereign consisteth in the end, for which he was trusted with the sovereign power, namely the procuration of the safety of the people."[110] As the relative absence of the threat of survival stacks the odds "in favor of sovereigns against citizens more than it was in the past,"[111] the racketeers of quasi-states are far worse than those of old regimes.

It is also argued that the horrendous ethnic conflicts in Africa are unique to the postcolonial world. There is no doubt that "colonially crafted boundaries of most Third World states paid little attention to the populations' precolonial affinities and shared myths and loyalties."[112] As newly independent countries inherited the borders of their European masters, they often look "far more like internal empires than nation-states," with civil discords along ethnic-religious lines lying not far beneath the surface.[113] However, it is simply not true that "European state-makers found themselves confronting relatively homogeneous societies . . . whereas postcolonial state elites faced societies that were heterogeneous."[114] In fact, Europe was long dominated by multiethnic empires that drew and redrew boundaries with little regard for ethnic composition. There is no doubt that European societies are relatively homogeneous now, but this is the product rather than the cause of successful state making. No nation-states are mature at birth with populations sharing a single identity.[115] It was only through the process of state-building that heterogeneous populations in Europe came to believe "the claim that a given state's citizenry constituted a homogeneous community of common origin."[116]

From a macrohistorical perspective, then, there are striking similarities in the difficulties of state making in both the West and the Rest. If the Weberian state with both capacity and legitimacy forms the basis for the high degree of relative sovereignty for Western powers, it may also provide the solution to the problem of state collapse in the Third World. It may be countered that, just as Western states had to build the Weberian state on their own, so Third

World states should be left alone to solve the same problems. However, the fact that the poor in the early modern period received no social welfare does not mean that the underprivileged in the twenty-first century should be left on their own.

Although the *nature* of the challenge of state-building has remained the same, the *seriousness* of the challenge is significantly higher for Third World states now than for Western states then. First, while European states had four or five centuries to achieve the current high levels of relative sovereignty, Third World states have had only four to five decades to do the same tasks.[117] Second, the territorial integrity norm established in the postwar era has deprived Third World states of the most crucial mechanism that compelled successful state-building in earlier eras.[118] Furthermore, the standards of civility and humanity have changed—although the "civilized" world largely closed its eyes to mass killings that preceded the breakup of the Ottoman Empire, the same acts are viewed as far more repugnant now.[119] Hence, great powers should engage in humanitarian interventions to stop civil conflicts and to alleviate human sufferings.

If state failure is the problem and state-building is the solution, then humanitarian interventions should not stop at making peace and delivering humanitarian aid. History shows that the Weberian state with both legitimacy and capacity has contributed to not just relative sovereignty, but also relative peace. Therefore, the international community should help to establish in "zones of turmoil" the rule of law, a free and fair political system with safeguards for minorities, a civil society, a functioning economy, public confidence in the police and the courts, and so on.[120] The UN's second-generation peacekeeping operations have indeed engaged in "facilitating the transition from civil war to civil society, from 'failed state' to a state able to govern itself, by investing it with popular legitimacy and democratic forms of rule."[121] It may be said that peacekeeping, state-building, and democracy promotion are acts of paternalism and neocolonialism. However, state capacity and state legitimacy—whether we use the label "Weberian" or something else—are basic constitutive elements for any healthy political community.[122] Moreover, intervention is not just something the neoimperial West has done to the neocolonial Rest. In fact, the more powerful among Third World states have engaged in military interventions in their weaker neighbors: Syria in Lebanon (1949, 1976), Egypt in North Yemen (1962–1967), North Vietnam in Laos (1964–1973), South Yemen in Oman (1968–1975), India in Pakistan (1971), South Africa in Angola (1975–1988), Cuba in Angola (1975–1991), Tanzania in Uganda (1979), Chinese-backed Khmers Rouges in Cambodia and Vietnam in Cambodia (1979), and so on.[123]

Viewed in this light, the issue whether humanitarian interventions are motivated by power politics or moral responsibility should not be seen as an either-or matter, but as a historical process. Critics of intervention have focused on instances of humanitarian intervention where strategic or economic interests are involved. However, advocates for humanitarian interventions highlight that the more vexing problem is the lack of political will to intervene in parts of the world where geopolitical or business interests are not at stake. UN secretary-general Annan has been admonishing member states that "the collective interest is the national interest."[124] The threat of global terrorism shows unequivocally that state-building, national security, and international security are highly interconnected. It is unfortunate that the world's superpower remains averse to the notion of state-building—even in the case of Afghanistan. Apparently, although sovereignty has evolved from the right of territorial conquest to the norm of territorial integrity, its further transformation into the norm of humanitarian intervention still has a long way to go.

## Notes

I would like to thank the Center for International Security and Cooperation at Stanford University for sponsoring the initial research and writing of this chapter. I also want to express my gratitude for faculty members of the Department of Politics and Public Administration at the Hong Kong University for their helpful comments.

1. Humanitarian *justifications* for forcible interventions are not new. See Martha Finnemore, "Constructing Norms of Humanitarian Intervention," in Peter J. Katzenstein, ed., *The Culture of National Security: Norms and Identity in World Politics* (New York: Columbia University Press, 1996), pp. 153–185. However, "the idea that complex humanitarian disasters of the type experienced by Somalia and Liberia must . . . be the responsibility of the international community is a new phenomenon in international relations." See Jeffrey Herbst, "Responding to State Failure in Africa," *International Security* 21, no. 3 (Winter 1996–1997): 144.

2. Finnemore, "Constructing Norms of Humanitarian Intervention," p. 181.

3. UN Charter, Article 2.

4. UN Charter, Article 1.

5. Robert H. Jackson, *Quasi-States: Sovereignty, International Relations and the Third World* (New York: Cambridge University Press, 1990), p. 180.

6. Emmerich de Vattel, *The Law of Nations*, trans. and ed. Joseph Chitty, bk. 2 (Philadelphia: Johnson, Law, 1852), chapter 4, section 56.

7. According to Annan, "The Charter is a living document. . . . [I]t is not the deficiencies of the Charter which have brought us to this juncture, but our difficulties in applying its principles to a new era, an era when strictly traditional notions of sovereignty can no longer do justice to the aspirations of peoples everywhere to attain their fundamental freedoms." See Kofi Annan, "Secretary-General Presents His Annual Report to General Assembly," Press Release, SG/SM/7136 GA/9596, September 20, 1996, available at www.un.org/News/Press/docs/1999/19990920.sgsm7136.html (accessed March 21, 2003).

8. The International Commission on Intervention and State Sovereignty recently recommended that "the issue must be reframed not as an argument about the 'right to intervene' but about the 'responsibility to protect.'" See Gareth Evans and Mohamed Sahnoun, "The Responsibility to Protect," *Foreign Affairs* 81, no. 6 (November–December 2002): 101. This reconceptualization of "intervention" as "responsibility" represents an ingenious move forward. Nevertheless, this report is silent on the traditional notion of sovereignty in terms of states' right to nonintervention. Hence, it does not resolve the presumed dilemma between "responsibility" and sovereignty.

9. Frederick J. Petersen, "The Façade of Humanitarian Intervention for Human Rights in a Community of Sovereign Nations," *Arizona Journal of International and Comparative Law* 15 (1998): 903.

10. Daniel Philpott, "Usurping the Sovereignty of Sovereignty?" *World Politics* 53 (January 2001): 316.

11. Stephen Krasner, *Sovereignty: Organized Hypocrisy* (Princeton, N.J.: Princeton University Press, 1999), p. 9.

12. Hendrik Spruyt, *The Sovereign State and Its Competitors* (Princeton, N.J.: Princeton University Press, 1994), p. 34.

13. Jackson, *Quasi-States*, p. 32.

14. Bruce W. Jentleson, *Coercive Prevention: Normative, Political, and Policy Dilemmas*, Peaceworks Series, no. 35 (Washington, D.C.: U.S. Institute of Peace, 2000), p. 18.

15. Quoted in Krasner, *Sovereignty*, p. 21.

16. Jackson, *Quasi-States*, p. 27.

17. Cynthia Weber, *Simulating Sovereignty: Intervention, the State, and Symbolic Exchange* (New York: Cambridge University Press, 1995), p. 21.

18. R. J. Vincent, *Human Rights and International Relations* (New York: Cambridge University Press, 1986), p. 113.

19. David P. Forsythe, *Human Rights and World Politics* (Lincoln: University of Nebraska Press, 1983), p. 4.

20. Immanuel Wallerstein, "States? Sovereignty? The Dilemmas of Capitalists in an Age of Transition," in David A. Smith, Dorothy J. Solinger, and Steven C. Topik, eds., *States and Sovereignty in the Global Economy* (New York: Routledge, 1999), p. 22.

21. Krasner, *Sovereignty*, pp. 183, 237, 238, 125.

22. Fernando R. Tesón, *Humanitarian Intervention: An Inquiry into Law and Morality* (Dobbs Ferry, N.Y.: Transnational, 1988); Tania Voon, "Legitimacy and Lawfulness of Humanitarian Intervention," chapter 3, in this volume.

23. John Stuart Mill, "A Few Words on Non-Intervention," *Dissertations and Discussions: Political, Philosophical, and Historical*, vol. 3 (London: Longmans, Green, Reader, and Dyer, 1867), pp. 153–178.

24. Michael Walzer, *Just and Unjust Wars: A Moral Argument with Historical Illustrations* (New York: Basic, 1977).

25. Jackson, *Quasi-States*, p. 44.

26. There is a growing trend among constructivists to study sovereignty from the Nietzschean perspective of genealogy, which takes the view that concepts acquire different meanings in the course of history. For example, see Jens Bartelson, *A Genealogy of Sovereignty* (New York: Cambridge University Press, 1995); Thomas J. Biersteker and Cynthia Weber, eds., *State Sovereignty As Social Construct* (Cambridge: Cambridge University Press, 1996); Weber, *Simulating Sovereignty*.

27. Leo Gross, "The Peace of Westphalia, 1648–1948," in Richard Falk and Wolfram Hanrieder, eds., *International Law and Organization* (New York: Lippincott, 1968), p. 50.

28. Gross, "Peace of Westphalia," pp. 54–55.

29. Philpott, "Usurping the Sovereignty of Sovereignty?" p. 213.

30. Andreas Osiander, "Sovereignty, International Relations, and the Westphalian Myth," *International Organization* 55, no. 2 (Spring 2001): 266.

31. Krasner, *Sovereignty*, p. 20.

32. Osiander, "Sovereignty, International Relations, and the Westphalian Myth," p. 269.

33. Osiander, "Sovereignty, International Relations, and the Westphalian Myth," p. 266.

34. Krasner, *Sovereignty*, pp. 79–81.

35. Gross, "Peace of Westphalia," p. 50.

36. Krasner, *Sovereignty*, pp. 68–69.

37. Krasner, *Sovereignty*, p. 42.

38. Michael W. Doyle, *Ways of War and Peace: Realism, Liberalism, and Socialism* (New York: Norton, 1997), p. 422.

39. Philpott, "Usurping the Sovereignty of Sovereignty?" p. 298.

40. Although Krasner is not a constructivist, he consciously adopts the constructivist term "problematizing" to emphasize that sovereignty is "problematic and contested," and that it is "constantly being constructed and deconstructed through interactions among agents and between agents and structures." See Krasner, *Sovereignty*, p. 49.

41. Krasner, *Sovereignty*, p. 20.

42. Krasner, *Sovereignty*, p. 9.

43. Krasner, *Sovereignty*, p. 4.

44. Krasner, *Sovereignty*, p. 9.

45. Krasner, *Sovereignty*, pp. 4, 9.

46. Krasner, *Sovereignty*, p. 12.

47. As will be discussed later, the literature on humanitarian crises in Africa has highlighted the disjuncture between international and domestic sovereignty as the root problem. It is thus surprising that scholars of sovereignty have continued to ignore the domestic dimensions of sovereignty.

48. William Ebenstein, *Great Political Thinkers: Plato to the Present*, 4th ed. (New York: Holt, Rinehart and Winston, 1969), p. 351.

49. My reconceptualization of sovereignty as a variable parallels similar efforts to problematize state strength and international anarchy in both theories of state-society relations and theories of international relations. See J. P. Nettl, "The State As a Conceptual Variable," *World Politics* 20 (July 1968): 559–592; Alexander Wendt, "Anarchy Is What States Make of It: The Social Construction of Power Politics," *International Organization* 46, no. 2 (Spring 1992): 391–425.

50. Kenneth Waltz, *Theory of International Politics* (Reading, Mass.: Addison-Wesley, 1979).

51. For example, see Ira I. Katznelson, "The State to the Rescue? Political Science and History Reconnect," *Social Research* 59, no. 4 (Winter 1992): 719–737.

52. Krasner, *Sovereignty*, p. 9.

53. John G. Ruggie, "Continuity and Transformation in the World Polity: Toward a Neorealist Synthesis," in Robert Keohane, ed., *Neorealism and Its Critics* (New York: Columbia University Press, 1986), p. 145.

54. Although Krasner discusses power asymmetries, he does not take the next step of arguing that sovereignty is relative to distribution of relative capabilities.

55. Cited in Krasner, *Sovereignty*, p. 14.

56. Mill, "Few Words on Non-Intervention," p. 153.

57. Jack Levy, *War in the Modern Great Power System, 1495–1975* (Lexington: University Press of Kentucky, 1983), p. 21.

58. Quentin Skinner, *The Foundations of Modern Political Thought*, vol. 1 (New York: Cambridge University Press, 1978), pp. 149–150. The Dutch republic, which was much stronger than Italian city-states, was also victimized by Habsburg Spain and Bourbon France.

59. Levy, *War in the Modern Great Power System*, p. 22.

60. Alexander B. Murphy, "The Sovereign State System As Political-Territorial Ideal: Historical and Contemporary Considerations," in Thomas J. Biersteker and Cynthia Weber, eds., *State Sovereignty As Social Construct* (Cambridge: Cambridge University Press, 1996), p. 87.

61. David Kaiser, *Politics and War: European Conflict from Philip II to Hitler* (Cambridge, Mass.: Harvard University Press, 1990), p. 264.

62. William Coplin, "International Law and Assumptions about the State System," in Richard Falk and Wolfram Hanrieder, eds., *International Law and Organization* (New York: Lippincott, 1968), p. 21.

63. Coplin, "International Law and Assumptions about the State System," p. 21.

64. Robert Jervis, "Security Regimes," *International Organization* 36, no. 2 (Spring 1982): 364.

65. Murphy, "Sovereign State System As Political-Territorial Ideal," p. 98.

66. Murphy, "Sovereign State System As Political-Territorial Ideal," p. 87.

67. Mark W. Zacher, "The Territorial Integrity Norm: International Boundaries and the Use of Force," *International Organization* 55, no. 2 (Spring 2001): 215.

68. J. Samuel Barkin, "The Evolution of the Constitution of Sovereignty and the Emergence of Human Rights Norms," *Millennium* 27, no. 2 (1998): 244.

69. Note that classical liberals in the nineteenth century did not believe that "uncivilized" populations in the colonies were qualified for self-determination.

70. Forcible domestic institutional promotion is "any effort by state A to create, preserve, or alter the political institutions within state B." See John M. Owen, "The Foreign Imposition of Domestic Institutions," *International Organization* 56, no. 2 (Spring 2002): 377.

71. Ruggie, "Continuity and Transformation," p. 144.

72. Wallerstein, "States? Sovereignty?" p. 22.

73. Wallerstein, "States? Sovereignty?" p. 23.

74. Wars of succession in the modern period include the War of the Spanish Succession (1701–1713), the War of the Polish Succession (1733–1738), the War of the Austrian Succession (1739–1748), and the War of the Bavarian Succession (1778–1779).

75. Doug McAdam, Sidney Tarrow, and Charles Tilly, *Dynamics of Contention* (New York: Cambridge University Press, 2001), p. 78. Note that Krasner's domestic sovereignty is quite similar to the concept of state capacity.

76. McAdam, Tarrow, and Tilly, *Dynamics of Contention*, p. 78.

77. Wallerstein, "States? Sovereignty?" p. 23.

78. Charles Tilly, *Coercion, Capital, and European States*, A.D. 900–1992 (Cambridge, Mass.: Blackwell, 1992), p. 104.

79. Vincent, *Human Rights and International Relations*, pp. 24–25.

80. Niccolò Machiavelli, *The Prince*, cited in David Wootton, trans. and ed., *Selected Political Writings: The Prince, Selections from the Discourses, Letter to Vettori* (Cambridge: Hackett, 1994), chapter 20.

81. However, Bodin believed that a subject could not lawfully take up arms against his own prince. See Jean Bodin, *On Sovereignty*, ed. Julian H. Franklin, bk. 2 (New York: Cambridge University Press, 1992), p. 113.

82. Krasner, *Sovereignty*, p. 76.

83. Tilly, *Coercion, Capital, and European States*, p. 68.

84. Tilly, *Coercion, Capital, and European States*, p. 70.

85. Tilly, *Coercion, Capital, and European States*, p. 109.

86. Tilly, *Coercion, Capital, and European States*, p. 115.

87. Tilly, *Coercion, Capital, and European States*, p. 115.

88. Mark Levene, "Why Is the Twentieth Century the Century of Genocide?" *Journal of World History* 11, no. 2 (Fall 2000): 307. Similarly, the Rwandan population registration facilitated the systematic singling out of Tutsis for ethnic cleansing.

89. Roberto M. Unger, *Plasticity into Power: Comparative-Historical Studies on the Institutional Conditions of Economic and Military Success* (New York: Cambridge University Press, 1987), p. 170.

90. Charles Tilly, "Futures of European states," *Social Research* 59, no. 4 (Winter 1992): 708.

91. Paul Schroeder, *The Transformation of European Politics, 1763–1848* (New York: Oxford University Press, 1994), pp. 578–579.

92. Mill, "Few Words on Non-Intervention," p. 172.

93. Tilly, *Coercion, Capital, and European States*, p. 70.

94. Max Singer and Aaron Wildavsky, *The Real World Order: Zones of Peace/Zones of Turmoil* (Chatham, N.J.: Chatham House, 1993).

95. According to Kalevi J. Holsti, "of the approximately forty million deaths by armed conflict since 1945, more than 99 percent have been suffered in the 'zone of turmoil.' . . . Of the 164 wars between 1945 and 1995 (excluding wars of "national liberation"), 77 percent were domestic." See Kalevi J. Holsti, "The Coming Chaos? Armed Conflict in the World's Periphery," in T. V. Paul and John A. Hall, eds., *International Order and the Future of World Politics* (New York: Cambridge University Press, 1999), pp. 293–294.

96. Mohammed Ayoob, "Subaltern Realism: International Relations Theory Meets the Third World," in Stephanies G. Neuman, ed., *International Relations Theory and the Third World* (New York: St. Martin's, 1998), p. 41; see also David Holloway and Stephen John Stedman, "Civil Wars and State-Building in Africa and Eurasia," in Mark R. Beissinger and Crawford Young, eds., *Beyond State Crisis?* (Washington, D.C.: Woodrow Wilson Center, 2002), pp. 161–188.

97. Ayoob, "Subaltern Realism," p. 39.

98. Ayoob, "Subaltern Realism," p. 41.

99. Jackson, *Quasi-States.*

100. Cited in Krasner, *Sovereignty*, p. 145.

101. Jackson, *Quasi-States*, p. 140.

102. Holsti, "Coming Chaos?" pp. 303–304.

103. See, most notably, Kalevi J. Holsti, *The State, War, and the State of War* (Cambridge: Cambridge University Press, 1996).

104. For "state *de*formation" in early modern Europe, see Victoria Tin-bor Hui, *War and State Formation in Ancient China and Early Modern Europe* (New York: Cambridge University Press, forthcoming), chapter 5.

105. Thomas Ertman, *Birth of the Leviathan: Building States and Regimes in Medieval and Early Modern Europe* (New York: Cambridge University Press, 1997), p. 184.

106. Charles Tilly, "War Making and State Making As Organized Crime," in Peter Evans, Dietrich Rueschemeyer, and Theda Skocopol, eds., *Bringing the State Back In* (New York: Cambridge University Press, 1985), p. 171.

107. Jackson, *Quasi-States*, p. 167.

108. Jackson, *Quasi-States*, p. 187.

109. Wootton, *Selected Political Writings*, p. xxxvi.

110. Thomas Hobbes, *Leviathan*, in Michael Morgan, ed., *Classics of Moral and Political Theory* (Hackett Publishing Company, 1992), part 2, chapter 30.

111. Jackson, *Quasi-states*, p. 187.

112. Ayoob, "Subaltern Realism," p. 42.

113. Jackson, *Quasi-States*, p. 162.

114. Karen Barkey and Sunita Parikh, "Comparative Perspectives on the State," *Annual Review of Sociology* 17 (1991): 531.

115. Jeffrey Herbst, "War and the State in Africa," *International Security* 14, no. 4 (Spring 1990): 131.

116. Tilly, "Futures of European States," p. 710. Although the terms "states" and "nation-states" are often used interchangeably, most states are not nation-states. Only "a state whose people share a strong linguistic, religious, and symbolic identity" is a "nation-state." Others are "national states" with "relatively centralized, differentiated, and autonomous organizations successfully claiming priority in the use of force within large, contiguous, and clearly bounded territories." See Tilly, *Coercion, Capital, and European States*, pp. 3, 43.

117. Ayoob, "Subaltern Realism," p. 44.

118. Herbst, "War and the State in Africa."

119. Finnemore, "Constructing Norms of Humanitarian Intervention."

120. Paddy Ashdown, "What I Learned in Bosnia," *New York Times*, 28 October 2002, p. A25. Herbst argues that the worst cases of failed states cannot be rebuilt. He believes that the UN should have taken over Somalia as a protectorate and decertified Zaire. At the same time, the international community should more readily confer sovereign status on substate actors that have managed to establish empirical sovereignty, such as Somaliland. See Herbst, "Responding to State Failure in Africa."

121. Michael N. Barnett "Bringing in the New World Order: Liberalism, Legitimacy, and the United Nations," *World Politics* 49, no. 4 (July 1997): 547.

122. It is noteworthy that not all African states have witnessed collapse. For example, Benin, Malawi, and Zambia rode the third wave of democratization in the 1990s and have been better off than their neighbors. See Holloway and Stedman, "Civil Wars and State-Building in Africa and Eurasia," p. 176; see also Herbst, "Responding to State Failure in Africa," p. 125.

123. Owen, "Foreign Imposition of Domestic Institutions," p. 389, table 3.

124. Annan, "Secretary-General Presents His Annual Report to General Assembly."

# 6

# Weak States, State Making, and Humanitarian Intervention

## With a View from the People's Republic of China

*Mark D. Evans*

It is generally accepted that human rights are matters of international law. The dilemma of national sovereignty versus international responsibility, therefore, is frequently addressed in terms of the legal legitimacy of outside intervention in the event of human rights abuses. External intervention tends to be directed against the authority in control of the country in question.[1] This chapter questions the comprehensiveness of a debate on humanitarian intervention that mainly focuses on the extent to which international actors can intervene contrary to traditional domestic jurisdiction principles. It suggests that, rather than focusing on the legality of directing punitive intervention measures against incumbent authorities during or after humanitarian crises, international authorities could be better served by a form of intervention or involvement that taps into the resources states possess at the national level. This form of intervention would focus on augmenting the capacity and willingness of national-level authorities to protect human rights. This may allow for avoidance of the more intractable jurisdiction problems and would be a "precrisis" and longer-term preventative approach to human rights abuses based on an in-depth understanding of the state-making security needs of the target state.

Holding the view that the state remains the principal instrument presently available to organize politically the vast majority of humanity, this chapter addresses the international intervention topic in a state-centric manner. However, it attempts to shift the focus of the debate toward the national level of analysis. Due to continuing international concern over human rights issues in the People's Republic of China (PRC), and its relative impunity to intervention based solely on force, the PRC is an ideal case study for such an approach.

This chapter initially outlines weak-state security theory and the related state-making process in a post–Cold War context. It then assesses the relationship of these areas to the general international intervention and global responsibility debate. This relationship is assessed in order to make clear the potential for a long-term preventative intervention based on weak-state security analysis of the state(s) involved. Finally, this chapter applies this analysis to the PRC as a means of examining whether such an approach is capable of initiating a realistic agenda for containing potential human rights abuses in theoretically weak states. Conterminous with this analysis are the perspectives of a non-Western state with regard to the question of humanitarian intervention.

## Weak States and State Making in the Post–Cold War World

The end of the Cold War was initially welcomed as a "New World Order" in which the two big post–World War II issues of spreading communism and decolonization were largely resolved. A United Nations (UN) backed international coalition of forces had, at least in early appearances, thoroughly dealt with Iraq and its invasion of Kuwait. This "New Order" enthusiasm was dampened by the bloodshed in the former Yugoslavia, which was a typical example of a long-term trend in warfare that continues to issue new challenges to international society in the post–Cold War era.[2]

This section outlines what is meant by the aforementioned trend in warfare and the impact that such a change has had on international society. These issues are addressed by explaining intrastate war in relation to the state-making process and related security issues.

War, according to Kalevi J. Holsti, can take three forms. The first form is institutionalized or "Clausewitzian-type" war, namely "the continuation of politics by other means," having both the purpose of furthering the interests of the state and government and of resolving disputes between rulers of the state when diplomacy has failed. The second form is "total war," involving the mobilization of the resources of the entire nation and state with the purpose of elimination of the enemy's society. This second form of war is beyond professional war between state rulers as it involves struggles between nations as well as states, and the line between combatant and noncombatant becomes quite blurred. The third form is "wars of the third kind" or "people's wars." This kind of war involves resistance and guerrilla movements, secession, and ideological warfare. It is without organized fronts or declarations of war. Wars of this kind are prestate wars; that is, their aim is state creation. In this last category, there is almost no distinction between combatant and noncombatant.[3]

According to Holsti, wars of the third kind have been the most numerous since 1945 and weak states are the primary location of wars currently in progress. As Holsti points out, "strong states are an essential ingredient to peace within and between societies,"[4] therefore, order in international society is necessarily affected by the internal security problems of member states. These aspects are also closely linked to the Third World security predicament and have become problems of international politics that are attracting considerable attention in the post–Cold War environment.[5] "Students of the Cold War, most of whom had been bedazzled by the intricacies of deterrence theory, deployment doctrines, and the introduction of new technologies capable of incinerating millions, discovered that wars of the third kind were ubiquitous in certain areas of the world and that the intellectual tools of the Cold War era strategic studies were not particularly relevant to understanding them."[6]

To a certain extent, the post–Cold War era is about rethinking or refocusing attention from a superpower bipolar conflict to a kind of conflict that had been growing in frequency within the states system well before the actual end of the Cold War. The low level of awareness of this change is indicated by a further comment by Holsti. "The end of the Cold War has not fundamentally changed either practitioner's or academic's views about war." This suggests that war is still often considered as a problem of war and peace *between* states.[7]

An essential element of Holsti's argument is that the shift to wars of the third kind should not be understood simply either as an increase in ethnic rivalry or as a result of the end of superpower suppression of Third World conflicts (via their support of weak Third World regimes in an effort to maintain Cold War strategic alliances). As Holsti argues, "The enduring contest between the forces of state unification and group-sponsored fragmentation transcends both the beginning and the end of the Cold War. Whatever the collaboration between the great powers after 1989, nothing they have done or can do puts an end to the paradoxes of state-making and community survival. . . . Some states . . . are on the trajectory of increased strength. Others are moving toward the 'failed state' end of the strength-weakness continuum."[8] In this manner, Holsti argues that wars of the third kind are best understood by a focus on state making, the security predicament, and the consequential dilemmas these processes create.

### Security and State Making

Security is defined briefly as "the interplay between threats and vulnerabilities and the attempts by a variety of actors to position themselves in this interplay to their best advantage given the circumstances in which they find themselves."[9] Security analysis helps to highlight the effect that the growing trend toward wars of the third kind has on the states of international society. This section demonstrates that international security concerns have changed as a consequence of the increase in wars of the third kind and that these trends have varied effects on international society as a result of a core-periphery structure.

Acknowledgement of this structure enables better comprehension of the viewpoints of non-Western states.

Barry Buzan explains that contemporary international society is a hybrid of gesellschaft- (functional and contractual) and gemeinschaft- (cultural and evolutionary) type international societies. Because a gemeinschaft-type international society evolves within a common culture, it maintains interaction through a wider range of rules and institutions. Furthermore, much more so than those that feature in a gesellschaft-type society, these are underpinned by shared cultural norms and values. (The evolution of these is closely tied in both types of international society to modernity—an important underlying process that frames both the norms and values mentioned and, indeed, this chapter as a whole. This is a topic that is not, however, pursued here.)[10]

A gemeinschaft-type society has come to form the core of international society with the majority of the membership of this core being Western states. Lacking a common culture and the depth of interaction that accompanies it, the functionally included gesellschaft members of the contemporary global international society tend to be pushed into the periphery—their interaction with the core is based largely on relatively tenuous institutional links. A single definitive line drawn between core and periphery is unable to display the variety of possibilities, so Buzan describes a spectrum of possible relative distances from the core, captured by his concept of concentric circles of commitment.[11] Most wars of the third kind occur in the periphery, where the power-security dilemma exerts a greater influence than it does in the core.[12] Thus, the core of international society is usually only indirectly affected by wars of the third kind. This has ramifications for how the various states of international society choose to deal with the trend toward intrastate warfare. The problems created by the differing perspectives and security requirements of states in the periphery, in comparison to those of states in the core, challenge the very integrity of the wider and fragile gesellschaft international society. Often, these differing security perspectives are imprecisely perceived as East-West cultural differences.

Mohammed Ayoob explains that to understand why wars of the third kind predominantly occur in the periphery, the problem should be viewed as one of internal dimensions. He argues that conventional, principally system-level, security analysis, as it reigned before and during the Cold War, does not isolate the true nature of the security predicament in the Third World. The security predicament in the Third World stems from the need for the ruling regime to maintain and build its position of authority, and it is the result of a state-making process, which includes a number of aspects:

1. The expansion and consolidation of the territorial and demographic domain under a political authority, including the imposition of order on contested territorial and demographic space (war)

2.  The maintenance of order in the territory where, and over the popu-
    lation on whom, such order has already been imposed (policing)
3.  The extraction of resources from the territory and the population
    under the control of the state essential to support not only the war-
    making and policing activities undertaken by the state but also the
    maintenance of apparatuses of state necessary to carry on routine
    administration, deepen the state's penetration of society, and serve
    symbolic purposes (taxation)[13]

A weak state, or a state that lacks "unconditional legitimacy for its state
structures and governing regimes,"[14] faces the dilemma of how to enforce
and maintain its integrity without alienating its citizens—an increasingly difficult task, as the demands of its citizens often reflect unrealistic expectations of higher living standards such as those that already exist in the
developed world. The ruling elites in weak states tend to support the status
quo international order because it helps them to maintain the legitimacy of
their domestic rule. Well-established international laws, which protect existing state boundaries, such as the principle of nonintervention, bolster elites'
hold on contested territory in weak states.[15] Buzan expands on Ayoob's weak-
state definition by analyzing the component parts of a state along a weak
state–strong state continuum. The three component parts of the state, according to Buzan, are the idea of the state, the physical base of the state, and
the institutional expression of the state. Weakness in any of these components may result in security problems, increasing the likelihood of political
violence and secessionist movements.[16]

The link between the state-strength dilemma, the Third World security
predicament, the shift to wars of the third kind, and the core-periphery structure of contemporary international society is important for understanding
present-day security concerns. This linkage compels consideration of two
main aspects of security as they relate to contemporary international society.
The first aspect exists because the power-security dilemma is relatively un-
controlled between states in the periphery. The states in the core have es-
caped from, or have largely mitigated the effects of, the security dilemma by
transparency in activity designed to decrease mutually perceived threats. They
may operate, therefore, within a security community,[17] which is more readily
achievable in a gemeinschaft-type international society.[18] Both the power-
security dilemma and the security predicament, as described by Ayoob, prevail in the periphery to various degrees. The essence of this is that security
problems in the periphery of international society will arise more frequently
than in the core, especially in relation to the security predicament.

The second related security problem highlighted by the previous linkages
is a consequence of the core-periphery structure itself and also involves the
threat of intervention. Buzan also describes the core and periphery in the
terms of a spectrum from absolute insiders to absolute outsiders with relative

Table 6.1

**Possibilities for Development in International Society by Sector**

| Levels of development | Sociopolitical sector | Military sector | Economic sector |
|---|---|---|---|
| Maximal | Security Confederation Political | Economic Community Security | Union Common |
| Middling | Union | Regimes | Market |
| Minimal | Mutual diplomatic recognition | Mutual diplomatic recognition | MFN agreements |

Table 6.2

**Insiders and Outsiders in International Society**

| | Position in International Society | |
|---|---|---|
| Absolute insiders | Absolute outsiders | |
| Inner circles (core) | Outer circles (periphery) | Nonmembers |
| | | Members of other international societies |
| | Relative insiders or outsiders | |

*Source:* Barry Buzan, "International Society and International Security," in Rick Fawn and Jeremy Larkins, eds., *International Society after the Cold War: Anarchy and Order Reconsidered* (London: Macmillan, 1996), pp. 270–271, tables 11.1, 11.2.

insiders and relative outsiders in between.[19] "International society generally exacerbates the security problems of outsiders by confronting them with the risk that outside values will be imposed upon them. Absolute outsiders are at serious risk across the board when international society is powerful. Even relative insiders, who are outsiders for specific regimes, face the risk of intervention from the core."[20]

The powerful societal force of homogenization not only threatens the periphery through the possibility of intervention, but may also, through a desire for conformity, threaten the distinctiveness of even insiders "where the growth of internationalism undermines the ability of local cultures to maintain and reproduce themselves."[21] Tables 6.1 and 6.2 seek to provide a diagrammatic depiction of what has been discussed in the previous paragraphs. Note that Table 6.1 should be viewed keeping in mind that a gemeinschaft-type international society is most likely to reach the maximal level of development, provided it also features advanced gesellschaft- or functional-type institutions.

Security analysis in the form outlined reveals that the shift toward wars of the third kind is a consequence of factors related to, particularly the modern, state-making process. It highlights the problems of an international society whose institutions have been and are still being created by way of both gemeinschaft and gesellschaft processes and suggests why non-Western states, often in the periphery, may perceive international security and law in a different manner from the core states of international society. How does this influence such states' views on humanitarian intervention?

### Humanitarian Intervention, Global Responsibility, and Weak States

The question to be addressed is: How does adoption of a weak-state analytical framework impact on consideration of newly promoted norms for humanitarian intervention and ideas of a global responsibility to uphold them? Before answering this question, humanitarian intervention needs to be defined to alleviate uncertainty and ambiguity. It may be defined as:

1. "[U]nsolicited military intervention in another state's internal affairs with the primary intention of alleviating the suffering of some or all within its borders."[22]
2. "[H]umanitarian intervention aims to stop the gross and widespread violation of human rights occurring within a state; and for that reason it has traditionally been directed against the authority in control of the country in question."[23]

Intervention itself may be defined in more general terms. "Intervention, quasi-intervention, and positive non-intervention define a continuum of behavior that seeks to influence or interfere in the internal affairs of another state, ranging from invasion to overthrow a government to quiet diplomacy."[24] Where along this continuum of behavior "intervention" becomes simply "involvement" is a matter of debate. However, the crucial factor of definition is whether the intervention is coercive or not. If not coercive, then the term "intervention" is probably inappropriate. Certainly, the term "soft intervention" pushes the definitional boundaries.

A rash of humanitarian crises in the 1990s (such as the ethnic violence in Somalia, Rwanda, and the former Yugoslavia) contributed to ideas advocating interventionist action to uphold humanitarian norms. More generally, this involved the notion that the principle protecting the absolute sovereignty of the state was outdated and that in the modern world a "permeable" sovereignty better reflected modern problems. At the extreme of these views is the idea that the state itself has ceased to be the most effective means of organizing politically the vast bulk of humanity. A world society or global civil society based around rights of the individual is considered to construct the new international political order.

However, "part of the persistence of the norm of non-intervention rests on the fact that it continues to correspond to the true level of development of the international community. For better or worse, states remain the terminal locus of the political loyalties for most people."[25] In addition, the state "continues to perform an important historical role, as it alone is currently able to provide a stable and democratic structure of authority, to establish the rule of law, to maintain order, to ensure social justice, to manage conflict and to give its citizens a collective sense of agency."[26]

The state, therefore, remains an indispensable instrument for international political order and the state system provides the "stable" political framework for a world society to develop. A notion of global responsibility need acknowledge that this is the case and that, "[h]istorically, states practice has given little support to the legitimacy of such action [humanitarian intervention], [however] at the end of the Cold War, some commentators argue that recent cases demonstrate a new-found acceptance of the concept, and argue furthermore that such a development is to be welcomed on the grounds that it strengthens the normative value of the society of states."[27]

In sum, state sovereignty is crucial to international order. Nascent norms of global responsibility for the protection of human rights do not at present make it otherwise. Nonetheless, the notion of global responsibility does dictate the need for new criteria for intervention within the state sovereignty framework.

On what basis could this "new interventionism" in an era of global responsibility take place? Are democratic criteria a way of recognizing secessionist and self-determination movements within the bounds of the existing international order based on absolute state sovereignty? This is an option further considered by Michael C. Davis in chapter 1. However, according to Rick Fawn and James Mayall, "the prospects of conditioning the future democratic character of new polities, through the 'conditioning' of international institutions, weighs lightly in considerations of recognition." In other words, strategic reasons, national interests, and pragmatism have been more likely to govern the decision of existing states to recognize new states.[28] This point is relevant because it indicates that power political factors remain dominant over self-determination principles, which include the notion of global responsibility to human rights norms, such as the right to political representation. The bottom line in terms of power versus principle is as Ivor Jennings states with regard to decolonization. "On the surface it seemed reasonable: let the people decide. It was in fact ridiculous because the people cannot decide until someone decides who are the people."[29]

This is not intended to argue that new norms for humanitarian intervention are meaningless in the face of the entrenched principle of absolute state sovereignty and the imperatives of power politics. Rather, it seeks to emphasize the following point:

The causes of human rights violations are largely national (especially where governments do not owe their power to external intervention). The solutions must also be largely national. . . . External actors often do not have the capability, through humanitarian intervention, to remove an offending regime from power. . . . Multilateral (and bilateral) actions can provide transitional assistance and continuing financial and political support. . . . If they are vigilant and respond with firm measures of positive non-intervention whenever backsliding appears, they may have a very important humanitarian impact. But these efforts are supplemental to national efforts. And they point to a humanitarian politics that places minimal reliance on intervention.[30]

This is particularly the case with regard to the PRC, which is a great power and holds veto rights in the UN Security Council—making external (by definition coercive) intervention in the name of humanitarian intervention unlikely. If democratic criteria for intervention are limited by power political concerns, as argued earlier, and the solutions to human rights violations are national, then intervention criteria need to be set in respect of the internal circumstances of the target state. Such internal circumstances are wide and varied and, as noted, in the case of the PRC intervention measures to protect human rights would necessarily have limits. It would, therefore, seem reasonable to argue that such criteria would be more effective if they were supplemental to national efforts and included a clear perception of national interests and security concerns. In the light of this statement, it is pertinent to review how the question of humanitarian intervention is approached in the PRC.

**Humanitarian Intervention and the PRC**

Literature on the subject of humanitarian intervention in the PRC is predominantly found within the following interwoven categories: "new interventionism" and North Atlantic Treaty Organization (NATO) expansionism; American (and Western) hegemony; human rights, U.S.-PRC relations, and intervention; and a small amount within international relations theoretical literature.

*New Interventionism and NATO Expansionism*

Even prior to the 1999 bombing of the Chinese embassy in Belgrade, a large amount of literature was published in Chinese that interpreted NATO's activities in the former Yugoslavia as an example of aggressive power politics. The humanitarian intervention argument was and still is perceived as sophistry and nothing more than a mask for NATO's territorial aggrandizement. Furthermore, many authors in the PRC think that the United States has been utilizing NATO as a tool to gain hegemonic control over the international system.[31] The United States' forthright claims of being a world leader are not considered a benign fact by many commentators in the PRC.[32]

Such articles refuse to perceive the idea of absolute state sovereignty as having limits in the face of humanitarian crises. Western ideas about creating norms for humanitarian intervention or the new interventionism are considered contrary to well-established noninterventionist international law. The war in Kosovo is cited as further evidence of NATO's and especially America's plan to extend control over Europe and is thought of as nothing more than power politics in disguise.[33]

However, there is evidence that this intransigent position on sovereignty is undergoing some modification, especially with regard to the realities of economic interdependence. "[S]overeignty is not synonymous with national interests anymore, rather it should be subject to overall national interests, not protected at all costs."[34]

### American (and Western) Hegemony

In a similar vein to the previous discussion, the United States' leadership in NATO is viewed by many commentators in China in very realist terms. There is a substantial body of literature that deals with the "problem" of U.S. hegemony in its own right, and these views are easily carried over to analysis of U.S. aims in respect of humanitarian intervention cases.[35]

International intervention is dependent on already existing structures—collective security's inherent defects have caused international intervention to be controlled by large powers and provided an excuse for large powers to interfere with the internal politics of other countries. Current Western "new interventionism" is the misuse of Western states' power in the post–Cold War era and in essence is no more than hegemony in another guise.[36]

The Eastern expansion of NATO, especially the United States' world hegemon strategy, necessarily contravenes existing international law.[37]

Again, NATO's interventionist actions in the Balkans have been interpreted by Chinese commentators as further evidence of U.S. and Western use of power politics to obtain hegemonic control over world affairs.

### Human Rights, U.S.-PRC Relations, and Intervention

The debate over human rights is a source of significant differences between the United States and China. A large amount is written on this topic in contemporary Chinese publications. Events in the former Yugoslavia and the humanitarian justification for intervention are frequently perceived as possible precedents and therefore considered relevant to U.S.-PRC relations. Is there real concern in the PRC that human rights abuses could be used as justification for the United States and the West to intervene in PRC affairs?

As mentioned earlier, the PRC has veto rights in the UN Security Council and is a great power by both military and economic measures. These facts alone make intervention in the PRC's sovereign affairs an unlikely possibility. This is especially the case if it came to conflict in China's interior territories, that is, Tibet or Xinjiang. However, there are those in China who consider the U.S.-Japanese alliance as an "Asian NATO," which could circumvent Security Council approval (as was done in the Balkans) in order to intervene militarily in, particularly, a PRC-Taiwan crisis.[38]

The overwhelming view in China, among both academics with a stake in the establishment and "common" citizens, is that human rights have become a tool of the West and especially the United States for manipulating China's internal affairs. The PRC is perceived by its own citizens as a weak but rising state. External criticism is increasingly seen as endangering the PRC's somewhat fragile system. This is in keeping with PRC justification of its resistance to humanitarian intervention "with the argument that such interventions might foster domestic turbulence, civil wars, and even regional conflict."[39]

Human rights criticism is, therefore, to some extent missing the mark. Rather than encouraging adoption of human rights standards, such criticism is giving credence to the hawks and hard-liners who resent intervention of any kind, particularly that stemming from the United States. Nationalistic sentiment and pride is the common response to external human rights criticism. Presently, national unity appears to be a more powerful force than any domestic concerns over human rights abuses, although it is admitted quietly by more moderate voices that human rights pressure from the United States has been thankfully partly responsible for the more tolerant Chinese society presently enjoyed.[40]

*International Relations Theoretical Literature*

It does appear that a great majority of literature regarding humanitarian intervention takes the defensive line outlined in the previous paragraphs. However, in the largely academic world of international relations theory there are also publications that offer a more dispassionate analysis.[41] It is noticeable that many such articles contain frequent references to literature outside of the Chinese-speaking world.

**An Explanation of the PRC's Attitude to Humanitarian Intervention: State Making and Weak-State Analysis**

Chris Brown argues that, while rights associated with positive law are not technically *human* rights, citizens must commonly turn to the legal rights upheld by positive law for confirmation of the rights that they hold. Unfortunately,

Brown argues, it is in the states where the rule of law is weak that human rights abuses most commonly take place. Human rights are a product, not a cause, of a civilized and secure society. "China continues to argue that human rights are the internal affairs of a sovereign state . . . [other states'] interference is in contradiction of the principle of non-intervention in international relations. China also insists that its cultural tradition and economic conditions predetermine its human rights."[42]

The view that some "basic" human rights have priority over others while economic development takes place is certainly widely shared in the PRC, especially by those with a stake in the establishment.[43] These opinions are linked to a single general approach, that is, that the lack of resources or capacity determines a state's ability to maintain human rights. If this is truly the case, then outside exhortations to uphold human rights, while maybe setting guidelines, will not materially remedy the situation. The need to trade off human rights in favor of economic development is a common and powerful argument. Rapid social transformation associated with modernization inevitably involves repression of existing and entrenched interests among the population, making repression in some instances unavoidable, but not necessarily a matter of course—a subtle but important distinction.[44] It is clear that the state plays an important role in the developmental process and that while historically some repression has almost always been the case during such a process there is scope to minimize it.

The repression of civil and political rights for the purposes of development is much more likely in the earlier stages of transition to a modern economic and social system (be it a capitalist or a mixed economy). This is because existing structures are more entrenched at this point. As a society reaches more advanced stages of development, the repressive measures taken in the name of development become more difficult to justify. This may result in a crisis of legitimacy and reverse cycles of conservative repression and liberalization.[45] Such a cycle would especially be the case if a more liberal government was unable to achieve the levels of economic growth expected of it after it replaced a previously more authoritarian regime.

In the PRC, the civil and political rights trade-off is proffered with the addition of the almost pathological emphasis in Chinese culture on the need for social and political stability. Repression of some political rights provides social stability, and social stability provides the conditions for economic development, and, predictably, it is then argued that achievement of social stability requires the existing regime to remain in power. Such ideas can be assessed further by utilizing the weak-state framework outlined earlier.

If the state ideology is suffering a legitimacy crisis, then the idea of the state is likely to be weak. Moreover, if a regime's legitimacy were to become based purely on successful economic growth, then this would indicate that the institutional base of the state is also inadequately formed.[46] What then is the PRC's status with regard to these theoretical considerations? Is the PRC a weak state? If so, has the result of this led to cycles of human rights repression and liberalization? And finally, are such actions taking place with any consideration of the threat of external intervention?

It appears uncontroversial to define the PRC as a weak state. Especially after mention of possible democratization, it is common for analysts in the PRC to point to the logistical and possibly destabilizing problems that would most probably arise in the event of attempting to gauge popular support for government decisions from a vast democratically illiterate population. This view, while possibly simply blatant paternalism, is evidence that the institutional base and the idea of the state in the PRC is considered inadequate at present to allow for democratic legitimization of the government to take place. The Chinese Communist Party (CCP), therefore, to a large extent relies on economic growth and general nationalistic sentiment for legitimization of its rule. This view is supported by David Shambaugh, who categories China as being in a position of "stable unrest," and furthermore:

> Weaknesses of the institutional mechanisms for dealing with popular grievances and mobilized discontent are likely to produce crude and coercive regime responses in some instances, leading to continuing human rights abuses . . . [w]hile we [the United States] have a strong interest in China's stability, the ways in which this stability is maintained are likely to include measures we find highly unpalatable. Although we may be able to provide for some forms of assistance that will lessen the chances of social instability—such as through fostering continued legal reform and further development of institutional mechanisms for expressing and resolving grievances.[47]

Shambaugh continues these thoughts with some disparagement of how effective these latter measures can prove to be and asks the question of whether such support is made in exchange for the continued existence of a regime that provides stability but represents a "failed social movement of an earlier era."[48]

The answer to this question must surely be a utilitarian one. If this "outmoded regime" is allowed or pushed toward collapse, there is a high probability that the ensuing chaos will result in an even greater humanitarian crisis. There is historical evidence that demonstrates that the PRC administration is gradually moving in the right direction and coming to pay more respect to humanitarian norms.[49] Careful assistance made in consideration of the PRC's weak-state status, in the form suggested earlier by Shambaugh, may promote more gradual and less risky developments at the national level. Such development may lead toward greater respect for human rights norms and, in the long term, avoid international military humanitarian intervention. This point is made with a long-term preventative approach in mind, that is, such a view would be difficult to maintain after a humanitarian crisis situation has arisen and, therefore, the approach would require a case-by-case assessment. As Shambaugh comments, this gradual path may well involve reluctant toleration of unpalatable measures.

Further to this case is the fact that the PRC's post–Cold War position and present circumstances critically influence its ability to precipitate changes domestically and internationally. A security analysis based on the weak-strong state continuum allows for calculation of domestic influences on PRC behavior as well as further understanding of its international stance.

> China occupies an uneasy position in post–Cold War international society. It is neither completely in nor entirely out. It is now the target of international efforts not only to promote harmonization of international economic practices but also to facilitate political changes and democratization. Further integration of China into international society therefore contests its multiple identities: as a non-European culture, as a civilizational-state, as a Communist regime, as a dynamic economy, as a developing nation and as a rising power.[50]

The PRC is either an Absolute Insider, but still positioned in the outer circles or periphery of the core of international society, or a Relative Insider.[51] China is in the awkward position of being expected to conform to core member levels of organization and commitment, while in several respects it is still faced with the type of security problems more commonly associated with peripheral and outsider states. This directly influences the way that China is able to utilize the institutions of order in international society. The PRC, for example, is unable to enjoy the benefits of a decreased power-security dilemma, which is enjoyed by core members operating inside a security community, and instead must contend with the basic balance of a power system that tends to exist in the periphery. Moreover, the PRC is plagued by problems stemming from its weak territorial base, such as separatist movements (e.g., the Tibetans in Tibet and the Uighurs in Xinjiang[52]) and relatively low-level territorial disputes (e.g., the Diaoyu and Spratly Island groups and the ongoing border dispute with India), which are far less common among core states.

In several ways, China's peripheral position in international society has been made more intractable by the end of the Cold War, which has seen the status quo great powers coalesce or bandwagon around liberal beliefs and practices generally supported by Western capitalist democracies, creating a "grand confederation" of Western democracies.[53] The PRC's identity as a communist, non-Western state tends to exclude it from this exclusive great power society. This, in turn and to a large extent, affects its influence in the great power cooperation institution and limits its ability to integrate in a gemeinschaft manner.

Changes in international society then, highlighted and encouraged by the end of the Cold War, have revealed limitations to the PRC's gesellschaft-type integration into global international society. As core states have increasingly sought to reinterpret the principles of the society of states in accordance with their own common values, the gemeinschaft-gesellschaft split has become more significant. The PRC has found itself more isolated in its views on how international society should be ordered. These factors expose the limitations of gesellschaft development in China's regard, unless, in the long term, this contractual-style entry into international society continues to stimulate the development of common values.[54] The theoretical explanations of gemeinschaft development would suggest that the PRC is likely to acquire the most successful patterns of behavior through interaction with other states of international society. If this is the case, then some change in the PRC's internal structure and identity as a state is, albeit slowly, likely to occur. Such changes would include attitudes toward the multilateral use of force and values that drive calls for humanitarian intervention.

**Conclusion**

This chapter has sought to argue that the minimization of human rights abuses needs to take the developmental processes of weak states into consideration. This is particularly so in a post–Cold War era in which wars of the third kind are generating many international security issues. Moreover, the core-periphery structure of international society has become more pronounced. Regime maintenance in weak states will inevitably result in repression, but international organizations may be able to mitigate this with targeted assistance that shores up weak-state security concerns.

As a weak state and a great power, criteria for humanitarian intervention in the case of the PRC need to consider associated internal security–state-making concerns, compelling a long-term preventative approach. Such an approach may avoid the need for more confrontational or coercive measures, which tend to give more credence to belligerent nationalistic voices in the PRC—voices that tend to work contrary to a more open, less repressive, and interactive society. It is already apparent that the bulk of the literature in the PRC concerning humanitarian intervention is unconstructively defensive in nature. This chapter has suggested that, especially in the case of the PRC, greater consideration of the chief and vital role that national-level efforts play in the maintenance of human rights is needed. It was argued that weak-state security concerns define the PRC's uneasy position in the post–Cold War society of states, yet, at a minimum theoretically, it is possible that the PRC will increasingly concur with the views or values of other powerful states that encourage international intervention when a state fails to meet its humanitarian obligations. This is the case even while those weak-state security concerns help to explain the PRC's present conservatism vis-à-vis humanitarian intervention. In short, it is not only international power politics that may compete with states' sense of global moral responsibility, but also the power political demands made on regimes that preside over weak states.

# Notes

1. Danesh Sarooshi, *Humanitarian Intervention and International Humanitarian Assistance: Law and Practice*, Wilton Park Paper, no. 86 (London: HMSO, 1994), p. 1.
2. The idea of states forming a society is commonly associated with the English or British School of international relations. As the concept will be used extensively in this chapter, the following is an often cited definition of international society as given by Hedley Bull, a leading author of the English School:

> A system of states (or international system) is formed when two or more states have sufficient contact between them, and have sufficient impact on one another's decisions, to cause them to behave—at least in some measure—as parts of a whole. . . . A society of states (or international society) exists when a group of states, conscious of certain common interests and common values, form a society in the sense that they conceive themselves to be bound by a common set of rules in their relations with one another, and share in the working of common institutions.

The institutions of order in international society are commonly listed as the balance of power, diplomacy, international law, great power cooperation, and war. See Hedley Bull, *The Anarchical Society: A Study of Order in World Politics*, 2nd ed. (London: Macmillan, 1995), especially pp. 9, 13.
3. Kalevi J. Holsti, *The State, War, and the State of War* (Cambridge: Cambridge University Press, 1996), pp. 28–40.
4. Holsti, *State, War, and the State of War*, p. xiii. Weak statehood should not be confused with power. It is possible for a militarily and economically large and powerful state to also be a weak state.
5. The "security predicament" is a term utilized by Mohammed Ayoob to explain Third World security problems as stemming chiefly from inside the state. His views are considered with greater depth in due course. See Mohammed Ayoob, *The Third World Security Predicament: State Making, Regional Conflict and the International System* (Boulder, Colo.: Rienner, 1995).
6. Holsti, *State, War, and the State of War*, p. 123.
7. Holsti, *State, War, and the State of War*, p. 6.
8. Holsti, *State, War, and the State of War*, p. 126.
9. Barry Buzan, "International Society and International Security," in Rick Fawn and Jeremy Larkins, eds., *International Society after the Cold War: Anarchy and Order Reconsidered* (London: Macmillan, 1996), p. 261.
10. See Ralph Pettman, *World Politics: Rationalism and Beyond* (Hampshire, UK: Palgrave, 2001); Ralph Pettman, "Making Sense of International Relations Theory: The Metaphysics of World Affairs" (unpublished manuscript), appendix 1.
11. See Barry Buzan, "From International System to International Society: Structural Realism and Regime Theory Meet the English School," *International Organisation* 47, no. 3 (Summer 1993): 347. In fact, the topic under discussion is dealt with comprehensively by a combination of both the article just cited and by Buzan, "International Society and International Security," pp. 261–287.
12. The power-security dilemma is a theoretical explanation of a dynamic that occurs among states in an anarchical environment. It is initiated by the buildup of military capability in state A, which stimulates state B to increase its armaments— state B is in a dilemma as it is unsure whether state A's motives are offensive or defensive. State B's military buildup in turn threatens state A, and a cycle of insecu-

rity and miscommunication is created. See Barry Buzan, *People, States and Fear: An Agenda for International Security Studies in the Post–Cold War Era*, 2nd ed. (New York: Harvester Wheatsheaf, 1991), chapter 8.

13. Ayoob, *Third World Security Predicament*, pp. 22–23.

14. Ayoob, *Third World Security Predicament*, p. 74.

15. Ayoob, *Third World Security Predicament*, p. 74.

16. Buzan, *People, States and Fear*, pp. 65–111.

17. Ole Waever, paraphrased by Buzan, *People, States and Fear*, p. 218, suggests a spectrum ranging between chaos and security community in any given security complex. Briefly, in chaos, relations are defined by enmity. In a security community, none of the members fears, nor prepares for, military attack by others.

18. Buzan, "International Society and International Security," p. 278.

19. Buzan, "International Society and International Security," p. 271.

20. Buzan, "International Society and International Security," p. 285.

21. Buzan, "International Society and International Security," p. 285.

22. Nicholas J. Wheeler and Justin Morris, "Humanitarian Intervention and State Practice at the End of the Cold War," in Rick Fawn and Jeremy Larkins, eds., *International Society after the Cold War: Anarchy and Order Reconsidered* (London: Macmillan, 1996), pp. 135–136.

23. Sarooshi, *Humanitarian Intervention*, p. 1.

24. Jack Donnelly, "Human Rights, Humanitarian Crises and Humanitarian Intervention," *International Journal* 15, no. 2 (Autumn 1993): 610–611.

25. Donnelly, "Human Rights," p. 638.

26. Bhikhu Parekh, *Rethinking Multiculturalism: Cultural Diversity and Political Theory* (New York: Macmillan, 2000).

27. Wheeler and Morris, "Humanitarian Intervention," p. 136.

28. Rick Fawn and James Mayall, "Recognition, Self-Determination and Secession in Post Cold War International Society," in Rick Fawn and Jeremy Larkins, eds., *International Society after the Cold War: Anarchy and Order Reconsidered* (London: Macmillan, 1996), pp. 194–195.

29. Ivor Jennings in James Mayall, *Nationalism in International Society* (Cambridge: Cambridge University Press, 1990), p. 40.

30. Donnelly, "Human Rights," p. 640.

31. Indeed, recent calls for U.S. European allies to contribute more militarily to the ability of NATO to project force outside of Europe could be interpreted as evidence of just such a strategy, depending on one's perspective. (Examples of such authors are cited later on.)

32. As is commented in a recent *International Herald Tribune* article, "Americans have become used to running the world." This bald statement makes some smile with the audacity of it. The smiles are not likely to be so wide in China. See Thomas E. Ricks, "U.S. Urged to Embrace an 'Imperialist' Role," *International Herald Tribune*, 22 August 2001.

33. See Zaibang Wang, "Guanyu beiyue xin zhanlue yu kongxi nanlianmeng wenti de sikao" ("Pondering the Problems of NATO's New Strategy and Its Air Attacks on the Serbian Federation"), *Shijie jingji yu zhengzhi* (World Economics and Politics) 6 (1999): 21–25; Ping Pu, "Guoji ganyu yu xin ganshe zhuyi" ("International Intervention and New Interventionism"), *Jiaoyu yu yanjiu* (Education and Research) 5 (2000): 38–42.

34. Xuetong Yan quoted in Bates Gill and James Reilly, "Sovereignty, Intervention and Peacekeeping: The View from Beijing," *Survival* 42, no. 3 (Autumn 2000): 43.

35. The word "hegemony" in Chinese (*ba quan*) has very negative connotations and is associated with arrogant, aggressive, and unreasonable behavior. This is not necessarily the case in English. The word "leadership" also appears to be understood differently. When statements are made from the United States about leading the world, they appear to be frequently interpreted by Chinese authors as an indication of the United States' desire to rule the world. See Jisi Wang and Shaojun Li, "Baquan yu fan baquan" ("Hegemony and Opposing Hegemony"), in Wei An and Dongyan Li, *Shi zi lukou shang de shijie* (A World at the Crossroads) (Beijing: Zhongguo Renmin Daxue Chubanshe [The People's University of China Press], 2000), pp. 76–80.

36. Ping Pu, "International Intervention and New Interventionism," p. 38, translated from the original Chinese by the author.

37. Nanlai Liu, "Yi Meiguo wei shou de beiyue cubao jianta guoji fa" ("U.S. Led NATO Crudely Violates International Law"), *Shijie jingji yu zhengzhi* (World Economics and Politics) 6 (1999): 26, translated from the original Chinese by the author.

38. Academics and bureaucrats stated such views to me during interviews held in the PRC over March 2001.

39. Gill and Reilly, "Sovereignty, Intervention and Peacekeeping," p. 46.

40. These views were stated during interviews held in the PRC over March 2001.

41. The following article is a good example of this genre of literature, Chun Zhang and Yaling Pan, "Youguan rendaozhuyi ganshe de sikao" ("Thoughts Regarding Humanitarian Intervention"), *Shijie Jingji yu Zhengzhi* (World Economics and Politics) 7 (2000): 71–75.

42. Chris Brown, "Universal Human Rights: A Critique," in Tim Dunne and Nicholas Wheeler, eds., *Human Rights in Global Politics* (Cambridge: Cambridge University Press, 1999), pp. 107–120.

43. This viewpoint was frequently expressed to me while I was in the PRC during March 2001.

44. Jack Donnelly, *Universal Human Rights in Theory and Practice* (Ithaca, N.Y.: Cornell University Press, 1989), pp. 187–188.

45. The repeated change between autocratic military rule and democratic rule through the later part of the twentieth century in Thailand could serve as an example of such a cycle.

46. Admittedly, most modern types of states to some extent base their legitimacy to rule on economic prosperity. A poorly performing democratic state and government are likely to lose legitimacy due to economic crisis. Nevertheless, states that have democratic or strong ideological legitimacy to rule (an example of the latter would be CCP and Maoist rule for a period after 1949) would not be as vulnerable to crisis as those that rely solely on the development trade-off.

47. David Shambaugh, ed., *Is China Unstable?* (Armonk, NY: Sharpe, 2000), pp. 160–161.

48. Shambaugh, *Is China Unstable?*, pp. 160–161.

49. For ample evidence of this trend, see Yongjin Zhang, *China in International Society since 1949: Alienation and Beyond* (London: Macmillan, 1998).

50. Zhang, *China in International Society since 1949*, p. 250.

51. As depicted in the preceding quotation and by Buzan in table 6.2.

52. The PRC's support of the U.S.-led "war on terrorism" is in some measure stimulated by the potential need for reciprocal support with reference to the PRC's internal territorial issues, particularly in Xinjiang. Such action also provides opportunity for the PRC to cooperate with the "grand federation" of Western democracies.

53. Lewis Fretz, "Bill Clinton's New World Order Takes Shape," *New Zealand International Review* 22, no. 6 (November–December 1997): 16–21.

54. As mentioned by Michael C. Davis, chapter 13, in this volume, there are those who argue that China's economic integration is "neomercantilist," suggesting that PRC foreign policy may attempt to intentionally limit gemeinschaft integration and instead seek to benefit only from gesellschaft integration. (China's behavior after entry into the World Trade Organization may provide an interesting study of these processes.)

# 7

# Humanitarian Intervention
## The Interplay of Norms and Politics

### Hiroki Kusano

During the Cold War, debates over humanitarian intervention often seemed detached from reality. Some moralists and jurists argued over the desirability or legitimacy of humanitarian intervention in international politics. But under the overwhelming influence of the Cold War, it seemed that an ideal or model intervention could rarely be realized. States that intervened almost always pursued other goals, often more vital, in the name of humanitarianism.[1] And so the arguments of proponents of humanitarian intervention were criticized as too groundless or idealistic, and the issue was only on the fringe of the field of international politics. However, immediately after the end of the Cold War, the trend of academic debates regarding humanitarian intervention drastically began to change. In particular, the consequences of the Persian Gulf War in 1991, including the humanitarian disaster of Kurds scattered throughout the mountains of northern Iraq, urged the United Nations (UN) Security Council to pass Resolution 688. In doing so, the Security Council recognized that the gross violation of the Kurds' human rights constituted a "threat to the international peace and security," and, at the same time, it authorized their humanitarian protection. This action brought a new urgency to the debate about military intervention in the service of humanitarianism.

Any effort to evaluate or validate one's own position on humanitarian intervention encounters various, in some cases irreconcilable, counterarguments or viewpoints. The principle of nonintervention or the prohibition of threat or use of force seems to provide a degree of stability to state-to-state relations. In dealing with humanitarian intervention, we are forced to weigh state sovereignty against individual human rights, or, in other words, international order against universal justice. Therefore, it is not easy to synthesize various opinions or combine various academic perspectives on the issue of humanitarian intervention, much less conceive of its underlying logic.

In this chapter, I propose an analytical framework for this intrinsically knotty and complicated issue and attempt to make the logic intelligible. I believe that this requires simplifying the various approaches or factors included in humanitarian intervention according to the logics of both norms and politics. The former is related to "guidance devices" that give meaning, roles, and context to an actor conducting humanitarian intervention, which approximate a "logic of appropriateness." The latter refers to the political-rational calculations of an actor engaged in humanitarian intervention, which corresponds to a "logic of consequences."[2] Controversies over humanitarian intervention may result from a mixture of these perspectives.[3] Analytically, distinguishing these two logics and explicating their interplay may contribute to a greater understanding of humanitarian intervention.

In the first section, I trace the historical evolution of norms that direct state behavior regarding humanitarian intervention through a study of "just war" concepts, liberal thought, and legal arguments. This analysis aims at reaffirming which actions can be appropriate in the name of humanitarian intervention and coming up with a model of humanitarian intervention as an ideal type. In the second section, I consider the politics of intervention, arguing that states often do not feel bound to implement contemporary norms and that decision makers are rational egoistic calculators. This will shed light on the political processes, which may impede or promote the realization of the ideal model defined in the first section. Finally, based on this analysis, I draw a conclusion as to where the global responsibility for humanitarian intervention is located in the contemporary international society.

## Humanitarian Intervention and Norms

Recent research has shed new light on the extent to which norms work in international relations and how they affect governmental decision making. Constructivism, in particular, assumes a model of human and state behavior where rule-governed action and the logic of appropriateness prevail.[4] Using this kind of framework, Martha Finnemore examines the role of humanitarian norms in shaping patterns of humanitarian military intervention over the last 150 years. Through case analysis, she shows that shifts in intervention behavior corresponded with changes in normative standards articulated by states concerning appropriate ends and means.[5]

My stance in this section is partly similar to that of the constructivist approach, in that I think it is necessary to take into account the normative context in which humanitarian intervention occurs and to conceptualize it. But, in other aspects, I am quite doubtful about the constructivists' perspective. I proceed in two steps. In this section, I offer a normative analysis of humanitarian intervention and do not consider the political logic with which it must deal. Such political logic will be examined in the second section. In this chapter as a whole, state interests and preferences are assumed to be rationally fixed and rooted, not in altruism but in egoism, which might be antithetical to constructivism. Put differently, as the implementation of humanitarian intervention in accordance with the norm is identified as an action of providing "international public goods," states are not assumed to behave generously enough to fulfill the *obligations* of international society. What I attempt to do here is to explicate the extent to which we can capture the existence of the norm and trace its development.

## Just War and Humanitarian Intervention

Let me begin a brief review of the normative history of humanitarian intervention by examining the just war tradition. Such tradition historically provided moral and legal scholars certain analytical roots, and even today remains influential.[6] The notion of a just war is found in Christian political theology, notably that of St. Augustine. Augustine's writings have implications for humanitarian intervention in respect of the reasons for using force and the proportionality of the force used.[7] His most explicit just causes include defense against unprovoked threats to the safety, independence, or integrity of the nation. This may seem at first sight to accord with contemporary realist international relations theory, whose view says that states form military alliances with other states as a way of securing or maximizing their own security. However, the action cited in the just war theory is far from the Waltzian state assumption of a relative gain seeker motivated by the principle of self-help.[8] In the just war thinking, since war includes killing other people, as dictated by the Christian command of love, "government or its agents may kill without sinning if they are motivated by love, *not* of themselves or of their own self-preservation, but of the *others* in the community *and* if they possess no hatred for the criminal enemy."[9] This other-regarding consideration in the use of military force can be seen in the reasons for using arms for humanitarian intervention today. This norm presupposes "the logic of community" that cannot be reduced to individualistic self-aggrandizements.

About one millennium later, St. Thomas Aquinas developed a more systematic and detailed formulation of Augustine's ideas and reinforced this logic. The medieval Europe of Aquinas constituted a more universal society and made possible a unified discourse for evaluating and justifying the use of force. Under this system, "every prince is somehow responsible for the welfare of the total Respublica as well as his own specifically defined territory. Consequently, he may be called upon to resist aggression or unjust treatment of subjects any place in the Respublica Christiana."[10] As Hersch Lauterpacht argues, Aquinas provided a doctrine for challenging a sovereign ruler's maltreatment of his subjects, offering justification for "service to the individual; a King who is unfaithful to his duty forfeits his claim to obedience."[11] It may seem inappropriate to derive a justification for humanitarian intervention only from the dictates of a ruler's responsibility for the protection of his subjects. But the important thing is that the theologians articulated a responsibility of rulers "in the community" to respect human dignity and even a duty to take certain military measures when this duty was violated. As the political fabric of Christendom collapsed in the sixteenth and seventeenth centuries, European thinkers such as Francisco de Vitoria and Hugo Grotius, who were strongly influenced by the ideas of the just war, began to discuss related legal issues.[12] We had to await the emergence of nonintervention as a norm in the eighteenth and nineteenth centuries before the concept of intervention gained a substantive legal meaning.[13] Even so, the theme or principle of having something to do with the use of force that these great European ethical thinkers suggested indicates that the just war theory is an original source for normative thinking on humanitarian intervention.

If we examine the just war theory, it can be determined that the use of military force toward another country is deemed legitimate or ethical in order to redress the sufferings of fellow human beings from a brutal ruler in that country. What is more, pursuing that policy is formulated as a responsibility of statesmen in the community. This ideal also dictates the principle of how to undertake a "humane" military mission, that is, it demands that states keep the rule of proportionality.

### Liberal Thinking and Humanitarian Intervention

Liberalism has also had a significant effect on the contemporary norm of humanitarian intervention. As some realists critically argue, humanitarian intervention in U.S. foreign policy after the Cold War may be seen as a manifestation of liberalism or Wilsonianism again on the march.[14] Apart from realist grumbling, it seems appropriate to argue that liberal thought has influenced state leaders seeking to justify ideationally oriented humanitarian intervention. As Stanley Hoffmann notes, in its various philosophical guises, liberalism has been strongly opposed to authoritarian regimes. It has advanced the main theme of freeing individuals from tyranny by providing them with the right to consent to their government and its policies, and a set of freedoms to protect them from governmental abuses.[15] However, particularly after the establishment of the principle of nonintervention in the works of Christian Freiherr von Wolff and Emmerich de Vattel, the issue over how to weigh state sovereignty against individual rights in order to achieve justice and other liberal goods came to the fore. One of the most crucial debates is about "whether such liberal goods as self-government and self-determination—two forms of emancipation from autocracy and arbitrariness—are to be exported, especially by force."[16] Liberal thinkers like John Stuart Mill and Michael Walzer attempt to find a middle ground. As it is beyond the scope of this chapter to cover completely these arguments, I focus mainly on the perspectives of these two thinkers.

Mill is basically a proponent of nonintervention, a view he derives from his objection to paternalism. As mentioned earlier, even before Mill's era, it was long recognized that there were brutal oppressors who violated the liberty of people. However repulsive this situation was, Mill thought that it should be eliminated not by outside assistance, but by the struggle of people for their own liberty. To a cynical mind, the people always get the government they deserve, and so some grave humanitarian disasters must be tolerated until the voluntary establishment of eternal liberty, for which achievement the grievances and sufferings of people are costs to be paid. As some liberals assert, Mill seems to underestimate the value of human rights.[17] But he does indicate support for intervention for assisting secessionist movements, which is demonstrated in his comment on the Hungarian Revolution in 1848. In this case Walzer explains that the Austrian emperor asked for Russian intervention in order to crush the Hungarian revolt, and Russia invaded Hungary. Mill says that in some sense the Austrian government was a foreign yoke. As Walzer argues, if it is recognizable that a community actually exists and that its members are committed to independence and ready and able to determine their own existence, military action against the former ruler, who probably becomes a foreign yoke the moment the resistance movement begins, would be justified.[18] Some contemporary ethnic conflicts, such as Bosnia and Kosovo, share the character of this classic case. It might be said that Mill's argument, regardless of his intention, partially laid the moral groundwork for humanitarian intervention, especially in terms of a secessionist conflict.

Walzer is more explicit and definite than Mill in defending humanitarian intervention; he abhors wholesale massacres of individuals. He first distinguishes aggression from intervention and regards the latter not as a criminal activity, but as sometimes justifiable, in spite of the threat it might pose to the independence of the targeted state. Through a study of Mill's work, Walzer categorizes three types of permissible intervention.[19] In particular, he declares that "humanitarian intervention is justified when it is a response (with reasonable expectations of success) to acts that 'shock the moral conscience of mankind.'"[20] What is rescued in his model is a commitment to "the bare survival or the minimal liberty of (some substantive number of) its members" suffering from an abusive policy of a government; in such a case, intervention should be pursued "against the enslavement or massacre of political opponents, national minorities, and religious sects."[21] His judgment regarding the regime that commits human rights violations indicates his enthusiasm for the value of human rights. He considers governments and armies engaged in massacres to be criminal ones, and hence regards humanitarian intervention as law enforcement and police work against them. Given the dysfunction of the UN security system, he even goes so far as to say that morality provides no obstacle to unilateral intervention, so long as there is no immediate alternative available.[22]

Most parts of his book are not devoted to analyzing the real case in contemporary world affairs. However, it is possible to judge that this normative character conversely enhances the value of prescriptions articulated by liberalism, as defined in his book. Given the fact that this originally peripheral part of his book is frequently quoted in today's studies,[23] it would be no exaggeration to say that the Walzer model is one of the liberal normative prototypes of humanitarian intervention.[24] It expressly problematizes the degradation of the humanitarian situation as contrary to human morality and proposes the imperative for other people to address such a situation. It resolves the problem over the validity of the use of force in implementing this mission by formulating it as a law enforcement action.

## Legal Norms and Humanitarian Intervention

As described so far, both just war thinkers and liberal moralists have offered normative arguments regarding the problem of humanitarian intervention. Nevertheless, much of the debate in this area rests in the hands of international legal scholars. Legal principles such as sovereignty, nonintervention, prohibition of the threat or use of force, and human rights visualize and problematize humanitarian intervention. Given limited space, I will attempt here just to highlight representative legal arguments concerning humanitarian intervention in order to demonstrate its fundamental normative logic.[25]

The positions of legal scholars on humanitarian intervention can be classified into three types: first, those who consider it a legally established activity prior to 1945; second, those who regard it as a proscribed activity without Security Council authorization; and third, those who hold it to be a plausibly legal activity under the charter, even without Security Council authorization.

While the principle of nonintervention was widely known and respected, some international jurists recognized some exceptions to that principle in favor of humanitarian intervention prior to 1945. Although the late nineteenth and early twentieth centuries witnessed the emergence of the principle of nonintervention, there existed many prominent international jurists who admitted a right of humanitarian intervention.[26] Even a scholar like Vattel, having laid down the principle of nonintervention, admitted that intervention may be permitted on behalf of "cities rebelling against tyrannical rule," as well as to "preserve the balance of power."[27] Along the same line, Ellery C. Stowell defines humanitarian intervention as "the reliance upon force for the justifiable purpose of protecting the inhabitants of another state from treatment which is so arbitrary and persistently abusive as to exceed the limits of that authority within which the sovereign is presumed to act with reason and justice."[28] Such a legal theory was corroborated by prewar reality and state practices accumulated sufficiently to induce jurists to incorporate this normative factor into their legal thinking.[29]

Of course, it is not unreasonable that we might find Christian bias and hesitate to admit authentic altruism in these interventions. They were directed mostly toward the brutal behavior of the Ottoman Turks (not toward Christian states) and were generally motivated by other interests.[30] Moreover, the right to intervene was widely recognized at that time as not only for humanitarian assistance, but also as a means of reprisal or self-preservation. Needless to say, a general prohibition of war had not as yet been established. Thus, one might argue that humanitarian intervention, at least as a legal concept, had no special or distinctive meaning, given the existence of many other justifiable military goals. Nevertheless, I do not support this conclusion. It is important to recognize that even in this earlier period, when international relations were dominated by power politics, the roots of our current concept of humanitarian intervention had begun to emerge, at least among "Western civilized states." It would, of course, be incorrect to superimpose a traditional doctrine on the present international legal order without regard to the criteria that formed the basis of past decisions, and I do not intend to do so. The most important thing is to acknowledge that early on some legal scholars began to present the normative logic of humanitarian intervention and some states justified their interference in other states as a humanitarian mission.

In the postwar period, we confront the legal stance toward humanitarian intervention under the UN system. Unlike in the previous era, legal arguments about humanitarian intervention under the UN Charter have undergone a significant transformation, and proponents face new challenges. The most outstanding factors demarcating the watershed, in the post–World War II legal system, are the reaffirmation of state sovereignty and the strict prohibition of the offensive threat or use of force. It is especially significant that humanity has largely agreed to confine the scope of the use of force to the charter framework, creating a collective security system and setting forth mutual respect for sovereignty as the fundamental rule governing international relations. According to the charter, we can no longer justify humanitarian intervention only on the basis of human conscience and morality or on Christian ethics, as was the case in the era before the UN.

UN Charter, Article 2, paragraph 7 prohibits intervention "in matters which are essentially within domestic jurisdiction," and Article 2, paragraph 4 proscribes the threat or use of force against other member states. This may be interpreted to mean that no military actions are permitted other than self-defense and forcible measures under Chapter VII. The General Assembly has reaffirmed these strictures by subsequent resolutions, strengthening the norm against intervention.[31] This new code of conduct in international society appears to call on states to behave as follows: however cruel a ruler's policies are, such as mass killings, persecution, or blatant violations of human rights, even when people in other states want to take actions against them, any state action outside the framework of the UN—particularly military action against the country—must be abstained. Merely appealing to human morality no longer seems a sufficient justification in the contemporary world for intervention.

It is possible, however, to deduce a norm justifying humanitarian intervention from the charter. When the Security Council determines that a certain situation (in this case, a disastrous humanitarian condition) constitutes a "threat to the peace" and authorizes military measures to "maintain and restore peace," humanitarian intervention is legally or procedurally justified. Reflecting on the failure of this mechanism to work as expected during the Cold War period, Richard B. Lillich argues for alternative criteria to justify humanitarian intervention. Citing the two major purposes of the UN—the maintenance of peace and the protection of human rights—Lillich concludes that humanitarian intervention by states—even unilaterally, without Security Council authorization—is consistent with the purposes of the UN, would not violate Article 2, paragraph 4, and therefore can be legitimate.[32] Ian Brownlie vigorously criticizes this proposition on the grounds that it is "completely outside the general consensus of state practice and the opinion of experts of various nationalities."[33] To be sure, unilateral military intervention on behalf of human rights has rarely been considered legitimate. Without judging which view is correct, it is important to note that these scholars actually work on the same presumption of the plausibility of humanitarian intervention authorized under Chapter VII.[34] Neither camp undervalues the UN or seeks to overhaul the UN system as a norm provider, but rather each one advocates ways to achieve substantive improvements in humanitarian situations under a malfunctioning UN in the real world. It is widely admitted that the UN collective security system, if it functions well, would provide legitimacy to justify humanitarian intervention as a sanction against illegal actions.

The debate over what constitutes a threat to international peace and security continues. Yet, there does seem to be a consensus that some human rights issues, especially gross and flagrant violations, are no longer strictly domestic matters.[35] The conspicuous and outstanding evolution of legal documents relating to the humanitarian idea reinforce the validity of this position.[36] Therefore, it is reasonable to argue that a norm justifying humanitarian intervention has already been established, even from a legal point of view, although it has to be carried out with Security Council authorization.

In summary, theologians, liberals, and jurists have continuously discussed how to justify the use of force and have addressed similar issues about what we should do to respond to human rights violations in other countries. First, the just war theory provides embryonic normative foundations to articulate the reasons and criteria in undertaking humanitarian intervention. Second, liberalism, focusing on humanitarianism or the moral conscience of humanity, emphatically urges states to implement the norms. And third, international law, while embracing and interacting with the former two perspectives, indicates the most authoritative normative framework of humanitarian intervention. We can say that the ideal type of humanitarian intervention is that in which the Security Council recognizes some grave humanitarian situation (resulting from either an intentional policy of government or an internal conflict in which a government has collapsed) as constituting a threat to international peace and security and authorizes forcible measures under the UN

Charter, Chapter VII. Then, some member states may collectively carry out this mission, while attempting not to deviate from the principle of proportionality. This approximates the normative stage or prototype of humanitarian intervention that we can see in contemporary international society.

## Humanitarian Intervention and Politics

In the previous section, I attempted to pick up ideational arguments and clarify the logic of norms in the case of humanitarian intervention. However, the ideal type of humanitarian intervention raised there is neither a description of the reality of the empirical world, nor of my own value-laden demonstration. It is no more than a conceptual framework within which a certain aspect of state behavior is judged and evaluated. What concerns me most in this section is not an empirical analysis of the normative criteria of specific cases, but an inquiry into the extent to which state actors do or do not defy this normative proposition and the extent to which they invest their resources in goods that can be basically conceived as international public goods. In other words, the fundamental concern at this point is to detect the pattern of outcomes being generated through the interplay of the logic of norms and politics.

As a discussion of the "collective-action problem" indicates, one must be pessimistic about the possibility of attaining common goals or goods in an anarchical structure with no enforcement mechanism. It is possible to define humanitarian intervention more broadly so as to include an action of humanitarian assistance chiefly implemented by humanitarian international organizations and nongovernmental organizations (NGOs). However, it is undoubted that their missions cannot be pursued without the protection or security provided by state actors, who are the most effective and competent in keeping or enforcing peace. Given that the UN lacks a capable standing army independent of member states and that the permanent members in the Security Council possess veto powers that are vulnerable to consideration of national interests, we cannot ignore the political logic of state behavior in assessing the success or failure of humanitarian intervention. I explicate this logic of politics by presupposing state rationality.

### *Political Factors as Impediments to Humanitarian Intervention*

As previously mentioned, the ideal type of humanitarian intervention is one in which the Security Council recognizes a threat to international peace and security and adopts a resolution mandating forcible measures under Chapter VII; then some member states collectively carry out this mission. There is contemporary concern not only with the norm being abused in pursuit of extraneous national interests, but also with the reluctance of egoistic states to intervene in inhumane internal conflicts. Do these political factors take over the implementation processes and distort the realization of the norm? In order to answer this question, it is useful to consider the simplest form of state calculation implied in most rational actor model explanations.[37] As Graham Allison and Philip Zelikow assert, the general principle of the rational actor models yields two simplified but explicit propositions:

[A] An increase in the perceived costs of an alternative (a reduction in the value of consequences that will follow from an action, or a reduction in the probability of attaining fixed consequences) *reduces* the likelihood of that action being chosen.

[B] A decrease in the perceived costs of an alternative (an increase in the value of consequences that will follow from an action, or an increase in the probability of attaining fixed consequences) *increases* the likelihood of that action being chosen.[38]

In terms of the political analysis considered in this section, proposition A reflects the logic of political factors as impediments to humanitarian intervention. The calculation of perceived costs must be performed in almost every decision (not limited to the case of intervention) before deploying military forces. However, judging from the altruistic features inherent in humanitarian intervention, it is easily inferred that these expected costs tend to be even more highly counted in a humanitarian mission than in a military operation with a view to maximizing other values, such as national security or survival. The strong consciousness of prospective military costs (e.g., military budget, deployed equipment or technologies, and the lives of soldiers, and so on), generally impedes the promotion of humanitarian intervention in two ways. The first is by reducing the willingness of states, who may otherwise be in a dominant position due to resources, to intervene. These potential intervenors, especially if they have veto powers in the Security Council, are inclined not to authorize military action or to block it under the council unless the expected military costs are within their permissible range. This type of calculation must have effected the willingness of Western countries to authorize a humanitarian operation in Rwanda in 1994. Not only did the Hutu majority escalate a campaign of killing many members of the local Tutsi population, but they also attacked Belgian peacekeepers deployed there to enforce the UN-authorized peace deal, leading to the expected intractability of this conflict.[39] The second way is when consideration of expected further military costs causes the state that has already intervened to refuse to become involved more intensely. In some cases, such a state may abandon efforts to settle the conflict and stop its operations. In the Kosovo case, after the beginning of the operation, the United States persistently refused to deploy ground troops, contrary to the British proposal for a more effective operation. The Clinton administration was devoted to keeping its military costs as low as possible.[40]

Second, derived from proposition A, the value or benefit expected from humanitarian intervention must be large enough to induce intervention. Otherwise, similar to the expected working of variable costs, the variable benefit in this fundamental utility function would favor nonintervention. Put differently, the value that will be acquired by maximizing the security of other nationals cannot be equal to or more than that of maximizing the intervenor's own national security. More realistically, unless the target country where conflict wreaks havoc on many people is conceived as part of the area offering a lucrative opportunity to the intervening states, humanitarian intervention is less likely to occur, however disastrous the humanitarian situation is. This kind of political consideration, however inimical or contrary to the norm of altruistic humanitarian intervention, may well tally with the thinking of realists.[41] Indeed, the analogy of Somalia, a geographically costly location of negligible strategic and material value, is instructive.[42]

In terms of extraneous values or interest, the exercising of veto powers in the Security Council, which is often simply the result of state interest calculations, can do great damage to the legitimacy that would otherwise be conferred on a humanitarian mission. This extraneous value often has nothing to do with the mission or the targeted country itself, but has a great effect on the decision making of some veto-wielding powers. A country seeking to block the passage of a resolution authorizing intervention may emphasize the self-serving character of the action. In fact, this kind of calculation may have accentuated the opposition expressed by China and Russia to the North Atlantic Treaty Organization military intervention in Kosovo. They had no positive intention of participating in military attacks and thus no anticipated costs. They, nevertheless, resisted passing the resolution authorizing the use of force, lest any precedents be made for an interference in their own domestic ethnic matters. This calculation was fundamentally extraneous to the Kosovo intervention.[43] Quite apart from considering what is most urgently needed for preventing the atrocities in Kosovo, China and Russia attached greater importance to an expected loss of security that might be suffered from authorizing humanitarian intervention in another country. Their emphasis on the principle that human rights do not overcome state sovereignty was never derived from the value of protecting the people tormented under the oppression in Kosovo, but from the value of protecting their own discretion to settle their internal problems.[44]

### Political Factors at Work in Inducing Humanitarian Intervention

As proposition B shows, if the perceived costs of humanitarian intervention decreases or the value of consequences following from the action increases, then the probability of that option being chosen will increase, even if we do not relax the assumption of egoistic rationality.

So far, I have pointed out the general tendency for the variables of both costs and value to work to markedly reduce the probability of humanitarian intervention. Thus, it may seem contradictory to remark that we can find out the pattern of calculation leading to the increased probability of the outcome. However, logically speaking, it is impossible to exclude the scenario that can be deduced from the model, irrespective of its empirical validity. Furthermore, I believe that the conditions on which humanitarian intervention may occur are well worth analysis, given the fact that actual humanitarian intervention has occurred and that it is composed of a sequence of various decisions and events. Thus, here I will expressly examine the logic of politics that would induce humanitarian intervention.

Following the rational actor model propositions and the previous discussion, it is necessary to specify what factors should change the variables of costs and value so as to give a positive incentive to a potential intervenor. Nevertheless, as long as we assume a rational egoistic state actor, it is unimaginable that a state will pursue the policy of intervention entirely for the value of authentic humanitarianism. First of all, if a state were to intervene in another state where there exists a gross infringement of human rights, we cannot help under this model but infer that the intervenor must have aspired to gaining some value excepting a humanitarian one. Namely, we have to conclude that the undertaken humanitarian intervention must have resulted from an expectation of positive political values relating to the strategic or economic interests of the intervenor.

The following three empirical cases during the Cold War are relevant to my argument: the Indian intervention in East Pakistan (now Bangladesh) in 1971, the Tanzanian intervention in Uganda in 1979, and the Vietnamese intervention in Cambodia in 1979. They share similar characteristics: brutal violations of human rights by the government in the target country, causing grave humanitarian disasters; action by the intervening state without any authorizations by the Security Council (in this respect, far from my ideal type); and each intervenor's pursuit of egoistic political values. As most analysts argue, none of these cases should be regarded as pure humanitarian intervention.[45] In each case, the intervenor decided to take a military action to achieve a highly selfish value while, in greater or lesser degrees, trying to utilize humanitarianism as a means of justification.[46] Although it is true that the betterment of the humanitarian situation was indeed a consequence of each of the three interventions, we have to reason that the logic of politics behind humanitarianism, rather than humanitarianism itself, rendered positive service to moral imperatives as unintended effects.[47]

If we want to cause a rational egoist to respond promptly to the humanitarian needs in another state, it is obvious that we would not appeal first to the political values that I have mentioned earlier. Rather, it might be wiser to make state actors perceive the refugee problem or other costs expected from not addressing the crisis. As Hoffmann remarks, "there is no way of isolating oneself from the effects of gross human rights violations abroad: they breed refugees, exiles, and dissidents who come knocking at our own doors."[48] A worsening humanitarian situation in another country would not only bring heartwrenching images to our television screens, but also burden the neighboring states with huge costs for dealing with the inflow of numerous refugees. In the premodern era, "population was usually viewed as wealth, both in economic terms and as the foundation of military power." Until that changed, expelled refugees from another country had often been welcome. However, in the contemporary world, "the impact of a refugee flow . . . can be measured in direct and indirect economic costs, in negative social and cultural consequences, in threats to security both internally and externally."[49] All this suggests that leaving a disastrous humanitarian situation in another country unattended has the potential of multiplying the total costs not only to the neighbors, but also to other states in the region and elsewhere. Forcible intervention at an early stage of a crisis may be less costly in the long run, and thus an increasing awareness of the refugee problem may enable a rational state to expect that a high value will be gained from intervention.

The U.S. intervention in Haiti, in coordination with the UN in 1994, may have resulted from a perception of refugee costs. While its main purpose is said to be the restoration of a democratically elected leader who had been overthrown by the military, it was true that, at that time, "approximately 20,000 refugees left Haiti," and "it was rumored that 300,000 more lay in wait. Moreover, by the time the intervention occurred, the Haitian refugees held at the U.S. military base in Guantanamo, Cuba, had already cost the U.S. government $200 million."[50] While admitting that there are a variety of causes in the specific case, refugee costs as a variable offers one of the explanations for decisions by states to engage in humanitarian intervention.

Last, I will address the political possibility of inducing rational states to measure up to the expectations of international society. The previously mentioned political calculations, even if they cause or promote humanitarian intervention, are not so desirable in terms of the implementation of the ideal type articulated earlier. Thus, the important task is to incorporate a normative factor into the workings of the political logic. In order to support this argument, I believe that it is productive and insightful to utilize a strategic politician model. In this model, the political leaders are simply assumed to be rational actors who, while searching for a foreign policy, attempt to maintain themselves in office.[51] Through applying this assumption to our theme, it can be inferred that egoistic politicians would have incentives to pursue humanitarian intervention insofar as their constituencies or public opinion support the intervention strongly enough to lead to rising value and diminishing perceived costs. Maybe this seems to some critics to be quite trivial or add nothing new, but this way of governmental calculating is probably the most effective or only way to urge a rational state to redress human rights abuses around the world.

There is no doubt that individuals, groups, and the media are intermediaries in this decision process. Theoretically, every individual (except the political leader) can be a candidate for promoting this kind of action. Even if people do not devote their lives to consolidating humanitarian norms in the International Committee of the Red Cross and the Geneva Conventions like Henri Dunant,[52] it is possible for them, as "norm entrepreneurs," to contribute to the realization of norms through working as members of NGOs, demonstrating on the streets, contacting legislators, or merely not opposing intervention in an opinion poll. The working of moral motives such as altruism, empathy, and ideational commitment can be observed in some persons.[53] If adequate support from citizens for humanitarian intervention is gained or sufficiently expected by the leader, public power to influence the political calculation can work through the leader's desire to continue in office.

Today, the media probably have the greatest impact on the decision-making process. Although, in a globalized world, "individuals have undergone . . . a skill revolution" and expanded their "capacities to focus emotion as well as to analyze the causal sequences that sustain the course of events,"[54] it is difficult to convey the ideas or actions of individuals to leaders without media coverage. If the media function as transmitters that communicate popular values to leaders, their multiplier effect is often too large to be ignored. The effect of the media on decision making for humanitarian intervention—the so-called CNN effect—has been too significant to be dismissed.[55] Media coverage of humanitarian disasters throughout the world frequently arouses public moral consciousness and puts pressure on leaders to do something about such situations. As a result, this can lead to the decision to intervene, because governmental leaders almost always have to care about what the public wants and feels, if only (according to my framework) to continue in office. For example, Martin Shaw concludes that there was a causal relation between media reports and the Western decision to intervene to support the Kurds in Iraq,[56] and Jonathan Mermin identifies the causal influence of televised images of starving children in Somalia on changing the U.S. administration's reluctant position in favor of a humanitarian mission.[57]

This is not to say that the media can invariably influence the calculations of strategic politicians so directly or that they will always succeed in promoting humanitarian intervention.[58] What I want to emphasize is rather that there can be a process in which a norm, shared by some citizens, generates an additive political value through the media. This leads strategic politicians calculating in terms of their personal political benefit to support or not support humanitarian intervention. While strong public support for humanitarian intervention increases the expected benefit for the leader, it might also serve to reduce the perceived military costs that would accompany the intervention. As noted earlier, the expected costs help to determine whether states intervene or not, and also whether they will continue or reinforce the mission. For example, if many people, who had internalized international norms were expected to tolerate more military costs, President Bill Clinton might not have withdrawn the U.S. mission in Somalia immediately after the deaths of some soldiers. The norms could have provided the military personnel with "the prestige that would presumably accrue to their being identified as responsible for unusually challenging humanitarian tasks,"[59] and he could have appealed to such norms.

In summary, through examining the kinds of political factors that will affect the making and carrying out of decisions for humanitarian intervention, I have shown the limits and possibilities of such interventions. During the Cold War, intervention was often thought to generate important political benefits, such as strategic or material value to the intervenors. Even after the Cold War, rational calculation influenced by variables such as operational costs and national values will continue to have negative effects on the pursuit of "pure" humanitarian intervention. On the other hand, despite all these constraints, we may find that it is possible to find some opportunities for incorporating material or normative factors into governmental political calculations, so as to promote humanitarian intervention. These include those national interests that are accompanied by actual improvements in the humanitarian situation, such as reduction of costs relating to refugees, and gaining the strong support of the domestic public and the media. We can find the most positive interplay between norms and politics in the last factor, and its mechanism can work to induce egoistic states to act most desirably, according to the behavioral model derived from the ideal type of humanitarian intervention.

## Conclusion

Under what conditions and with what objectives military force should be exercised are crucial matters in international relations. Thus, questions associated with humanitarian intervention have attracted the attention of thinkers and analysts for two millennia. The arguments of theologians, liberals, and international lawyers have been accumulated, and we have acquired the norm of humanitarian intervention, which especially legitimizes interventions associated with legal authorization within the UN system. Along these lines, I have briefly traced the development of these norms and set forth the ideal type of humanitarian intervention in the context of the contemporary international society.

On this basis, I clarified that in the process of realizing the norm of humanitarian intervention, various political factors or calculus can impede or promote humanitarian action taken by rational egoistic states. Given the very fact that the primary intervening actors are still egoistic states, if we are resolved to settle humanitarian disasters with effective military force, that is, by means of humanitarian intervention, we, as global citizens, must influence the structure of state calculations. Otherwise, strategic rational politicians will, without any hesitation, refuse to act according to the logic of norms. In the end, the most important thing is to perceive that the key to promotion of humanitarian intervention rests not directly with national leaders enmeshed in egoistic political logics, but with the citizens holding transcendental values, with the power of votes or voices to influence the way of rational political calculation.

## Notes

I wish to thank David Wessels for his invaluable help and efforts in completing this chapter.

1. Michael Akehurst, "Humanitarian Intervention," in Hedley Bull, ed., *Intervention in World Politics* (Oxford: Clarendon, 1984), pp. 95–118; Jack Donnelly, "Human Rights, Humanitarian Intervention and American Foreign Policy: Law, Morality, and Politics," *Journal of International Affairs* 36 (1983): 311–328.

2. For elaboration of the concept of two logics, see James G. March and Johan P. Olsen, *Rediscovering Institutions: The Organizational Basis of Politics* (New York: The Free Press, 1989), pp. 24–26; James G. March and Johan P. Olsen, "The Institutional Dynamics of International Political Orders," *International Organization* 52, no. 4 (1998): 943–969, 948–952.

3. See Jack Donnelly, "Human Rights, Humanitarian Crisis, and Humanitarian Intervention," *International Journal* 48, no. 4 (1993): 607–640.

4. See Jeffery T. Checkel, "The Constructivist Turn in International Relations Theory," *World Politics* 50, no. 2 (1998): 324–348; Martha Finnemore and Kathryn Sikkink, "International Norm Dynamics and Political Change," *International Organization* 52, no. 4 (1998): 887–917.

5. Martha Finnemore, "Constructing Norms of Humanitarian Intervention," in Peter J. Katzenstein, ed., *The Culture of National Security: Norms and Identity in World Politics* (New York: Columbia University Press, 1996), pp. 153–185.

6. David Fisher, "The Ethics of Intervention," in Robert J. Art and Robert Jervis, eds., *International Politics: Enduring Concepts and Contemporary Issues*, 4th ed. (New York: HarperCollins, 1996), pp. 537–544.

7. This theology begins with the biblical command to "love your neighbor," an injunction to extend the grace of charity to all human beings as created in God's image. See Thomas L. Pangle and Peter J. Ahrensdorf, *Justice among Nations: On the Moral Basis of Power and Peace* (Lawrence: University Press of Kansas, 1999), p. 73.

8. Kenneth N. Waltz, *Theory of International Politics* (Reading, Mass.: Addison-Wesley, 1979), p. 105.

9. Pangle and Ahrensdorf, *Justice among Nations*, p. 77.

10. J. Bryan Hehir, "The Ethics of Intervention: Two Normative Traditions," in Peter G. Brown and Douglas MacLean, eds., *Human Rights and U.S. Foreign Policy: Principles and Applications* (Lexington, Mass.: Lexington, 1979), pp. 121–139, 124.

11. Hersch Lauterpacht, *International Law and Human Rights* (London: Stevens and Son, 1950), p. 84.

12. Hehir, "Ethics of Intervention," pp. 125–127; R. J. Vincent, "Grotius, Human Rights, and Intervention," in Hedley Bull, Benedict Kingsbury, and Adam Roberts, eds., *Hugo Grotius and International Relations* (Oxford: Clarendon, 1990), pp. 241–256.

13. R. J. Vincent, *Nonintervention and International Order* (Princeton, N.J.: Princeton University Press, 1974), pp. 20–63.

14. Kenneth N. Waltz, "Structural Realism after the Cold War," *International Security* 25, no. 1 (2000): 5–41, 11.

15. Stanley Hoffmann, "The Crisis of Liberal Internationalism," *Foreign Policy* 98 (1995): 159–177, 160.

16. Stanley Hoffmann, "The Politics and Ethics of Military Intervention," *Survival* 37, no. 4 (1995–1996): 29–51, 34.

17. Charles R. Beitz, *Political Theory and International Relations* (Princeton, N.J.: Princeton University Press, 1979), pp. 67–105.

18. Michael Walzer, *Just and Unjust Wars: A Moral Argument with Historical Illustrations*, 3rd ed. (New York: Basic, 2000), pp. 93–94.

19. The other two cases are those in which secession (or national liberation) movements take place and counterintervention is at issue. See Walzer, *Just and Unjust Wars*, pp. 89–101.

20. Walzer, *Just and Unjust Wars*, p. 107.

21. Walzer, *Just and Unjust Wars*, p. 101.

22. Walzer, *Just and Unjust Wars*, pp. 106–107.

23. Walzer says in the revised edition of his book that his chapter 6, which deals with intervention, was not intended as one of the main concerns. See Walzer, *Just and Unjust Wars*, p. xi.

24. See Michael J. Smith, "Humanitarian Intervention: An Overview of the Ethical Issues," *Ethics and International Affairs* 12 (1998): 63–79, 72–75.

25. For a thorough examination of legal matters regarding humanitarian intervention, see Peter R. Baehr, chapter 2, in this volume; Tania Voon, chapter 3, in this volume; Robert Cryer, chapter 4, in this volume.

26. Manouchehr Ganji, *International Protection of Human Rights* (Paris: Minard, 1962), pp. 22–43; Richard B. Lillich, "Humanitarian Intervention: A Reply to Ian Brownlie and a Plea for Constructive Alternatives," in John Norton Moore, ed., *Law and Civil War in the Modern World* (Baltimore, Md.: Johns Hopkins University Press, 1974), pp. 229–251, 231–232.

27. Hehir, "Ethics of Intervention," p. 133.

28. Ellery C. Stowell, *Intervention in International Law* (Washington, D.C.: Byrne, 1921), p. 53.

29. Stowell, *Intervention in International Law*, pp. 51–277.

30. Ian Brownlie, "Humanitarian Intervention," in John Norton Moore, ed., *Law and Civil War in the Modern World* (Baltimore, Md.: Johns Hopkins University Press, 1974), pp. 217–228, 220–221; Simon Chesterman, *Just War or Just Peace?: Humanitarian Intervention and International Law* (New York: Oxford University Press, 2001), pp. 24–25.

31. They are the "Declaration on the Inadmissibility of Intervention in the Domestic Affairs of States and the Protection of Their Independence and Sovereignty," General Assembly Resolution 2131 (20), 1965, and the "Declaration on Principles of International Law Concerning Friendly Relations and Co-operation among States in Accordance with the Charter of the United Nations," General Assembly Resolution 2625 (25), 1970.

32. Lillich, "Humanitarian Intervention," pp. 229–251.

33. Brownlie, "Humanitarian Intervention," p. 227.

34. For instance, Brownlie admits the legality of intervention under Chapter VII. See Brownlie, "Humanitarian Intervention," p. 226.

35. Anne Julie Semb, "The New Practice of UN-Authorized Interventions: A Slippery Slope of Forcible Interference," *Journal of Peace Research* 37, no. 4 (2000): 469–488; Thomas Buergenthal, "Domestic Jurisdiction, Intervention, and Human Rights: The International Law Perspective," in Peter G. Brown and Douglas MacLean,

eds., *Human Rights and U.S. Foreign Policy: Principles and Applications* (Lexington, Mass.: Lexington, 1979), pp. 111–120.

36. Thomas G. Weiss and Cindy Collins, *Humanitarian Challenges and Intervention: World Politics and the Dilemmas of Help* (Boulder, Colo.: Westview, 1996), pp. 13–38.

37. I do not intend to formulate a "formalized rational choice model" that includes game theory or mathematical modeling.

38. Graham Allison and Philip Zelikow, *Essence of Decision: Explaining the Cuban Missile Crisis*, 2nd ed. (New York: Longman, 1999), p. 25.

39. Sean D. Murphy, *Humanitarian Intervention: The United Nations in an Evolving World Order* (Philadelphia: University of Pennsylvania Press, 1996), pp. 243–260.

40. Ivo H. Daalder and Michael E. O'Hanlon, *Winning Ugly: NATO's War to Save Kosovo* (Washington, D.C.: Brookings Institution, 2000), pp. 96–100, 130–140.

41. See Robert S. Chase, Emily B. Hill, and Paul Kennedy, "Pivotal States and U.S. Strategy," *Foreign Affairs* 75, no. 1 (1996): 33–51; Michael Mandelbaum, "The Reluctance to Intervene," in Robert J. Art and Robert Jervis, eds., *International Politics: Enduring Concepts and Contemporary Issues,* 4th ed. (New York: HarperCollins, 1996), pp. 527–536; Wyn Boen, "The U.S. National Interest and the Future of Military Intervention," in Andrew M. Dorman and Thomas G. Otte, eds., *Military Intervention: From Gunboat Diplomacy to Humanitarian Intervention* (Aldershot, UK: Dartmouth, 1995), pp. 83–107.

42. Richard N. Haass, *Intervention: The Use of American Military Force in the Post–Cold War World*, rev. ed. (Washington, D.C.: Brookings Institution, 1999), pp. 171–173.

43. Concerning China's position on intervention and some suggestions, see Michael C. Davis, chapter 13, in this volume.

44. This principle was "reaffirmed" at a meeting between two leaders held during the Russian military campaign against Chechnya. See *International Herald Tribune*, 10 December 1999.

45. See Akehurst, "Humanitarian Intervention"; Finnemore, "Constructing Norms of Humanitarian Intervention."

46. Thomas M. Franck and Nigel S. Rodley, "After Bangladesh: The Law of Humanitarian Intervention by Force," *American Journal of International Law* 67, no. 2 (1973): 275–305, 275–277; Stephen A. Garrett, *Doing Good and Doing Well: An Examination of Humanitarian Intervention* (Westport, Conn.: Praeger, 1999), pp. 122–125. Peter R. Baehr gave me an important comment on this point.

47. Garrett, *Doing Good and Doing Well*, pp. 128–129.

48. Stanley Hoffmann, *Duties beyond Borders: On the Limits and Possibilities of Ethical International Politics* (Syracuse, N.Y.: Syracuse University Press, 1981), p. 111.

49. Alan Dowty and Gil Loescher, "Changing Norms in International Responses to Domestic Disorder," in Raimo Väyrynen, ed., *Globalization and Global Governance* (Lanham, Md.: Rowman and Littlefield, 1999), pp. 199–221, 208–209.

50. Karin von Hippel, *Democracy by Force: US Military Intervention in the Post–Cold War World* (New York: Cambridge University Press, 2000), pp. 101–103.

51. Randolph M. Siverson, ed., *Strategic Politicians, Institutions, and Foreign Policy* (Ann Arbor: University of Michigan Press, 1998).

52. Martha Finnemore, *National Interests in International Society* (Ithaca, N.Y.: Cornell University Press, 1996), pp. 69–88.

53. Finnemore and Sikkink, "International Norm Dynamics and Political Change," pp. 996–999.

54. James N. Rosenau, "Sovereignty in a Turbulent World," in Gene M. Lyons and Michael Mastanduno, eds., *Beyond Westphalia?: State Sovereignty and International Intervention* (Baltimore, Md.: Johns Hopkins University Press, 1995), pp. 191–227, 204.

55. Piers Robinson, "The CNN Effect: Can the News Media Drive Foreign Policy?" *Review of International Studies* 25, no. 2 (1999): 301–309; Peter Viggo Jakobsen, "National Interest, Humanitarianism or CNN: What Triggers UN Peace Enforcement after the Cold War?" *Journal of Peace Research* 33, no. 2 (1996): 205–215; Jonathan Mermin, *Debating War and Peace: Media Coverage of U.S. Intervention in the Post-Vietnam Era* (Princeton, N.J.: Princeton University Press, 1999); Martin Shaw, *Civil Society and Media in Global Crises: Representing Distant Violence* (London: Pinter, 1996); see also Daniela Ingruber, chapter 10, in this volume.

56. Shaw, *Civil Society and Media in Global Crises*, p. 88.

57. Mermin, *Debating War and Peace*, pp. 120–137.

58. Both logically and empirically, we can easily expect that the effects of media activity can be negative through mere ignorance or through noncoverage of grave humanitarian disasters.

59. Garrett, *Doing Good and Doing Well*, p. 159.

# Part III

## The Philosophy of Intervention

# 8

# Redefining Human Beings—Where Politics Meets Metaphysics

## Franca D'Agostini

### Defining the Subjects of Rights

This chapter points to some philosophical premises of the themes treated in this book. The basic idea that will be developed is that in contexts in which a global (international) view is needed, some "connected" politics, some conscious connection of politics to its own reasons—that is, ontological and logical premises—is also needed.

In a very brief account, the philosophical assumption that is at the basis of humanitarian interventionism is the primacy of *human rights* over *national sovereignty:* the defense of human life is considered more compelling than sovereignty. This has created important consequences on an institutional and legal plane, as the principle entails some fundamental changes in the moral hierarchy that is supposed to give origin to international law. For instance, and typically: keeping peace becomes a less important goal than defending the individual rights of any single member of humanity. So, we have the contrast between two principles that are also the foundations of different moral hierarchies: the primacy of the territorial, political, and cultural identity of national states (as established since the seventeenth century, with the Peace of Westphalia) and the primacy of life, dignity, and freedom of individuals belonging to humanity.

The choice in favor of the second principle, as Jürgen Habermas observes,[1] may be referred to a "universalistic" or "cosmopolitan" conception of law and international organisms, a conception that aims at substituting the old intergovernmental international law with a global humanitarian regime. The same choice nevertheless soon revealed some embarrassing implications, the most important of which for my theme is that even if the second principle is evidently to be preferred on the basis of a common humanitarian sense, it is not completely ascertained that human rights, intended as individual rights (rights of living individualities), should be the only and ultimate values. The "individualistic" doctrine of rights, typically claimed by Western tradition, is actually opposed to the communitarian ethos of some Asian, African, and Native American cultures, and nobody tells us that the first should be better than the second.

Here we are evidently at the philosophical core of the problem: what is needed, as it seems, is some philosophical inquiry into the nature and reasons of this kind of cultural alternative, a reflection that could possibly orientate the choice in favor of one or another possibility or promote the dialogue between the two points of view. But we have to note that such an inquiry does not properly (or exclusively) belong to a philosophy of law or of politics, being rather a part of a more fundamental reflection about the definition of entities involved in political and legal reasoning and on the ways of reasoning that can take into account with equality the rights and needs of these entities.

Let us consider the two principles mentioned earlier: primacy of national sovereignty and primacy of individual entities. The defense of the latter is generally linked, as I said, to the hypothesis of a cosmopolitan universalistic point of view (which in Habermas's intention corresponds to the idea of a *Weltbürgerrecht*).[2] The opposite point of view has been defined as "particularism." Hence, the universalistic defense of human rights has been conceived as opposed to the particularism of nationalities or ethnic groups.

However, it is quite easy to acknowledge that the two principles may also be described as both defending on a universalistic plane two sorts of particularity: the particularity of individual living entities, that is, men and women, and the particularity of collective national entities, that is, states. Thus, it is not the case of pure pluralism or pure universalism, but rather of two different degrees of generality. In the first perspective, we see supranational entities formally committed to defend subnational entities (individuals): the latter being the source of legitimization for the former. In the second perspective, we see national organisms in interrelation, with a somewhat less grounded legitimization of the supranational power.

Evidently, we are dealing with two different structures, two different ways of articulating globality and particularity, but we are also dealing with two different pictures and descriptions of how things are and should be. Everything seems to depend on how you "cut" or "frame" the reality you are examining. The choice of one structure depends on the subjects you intend to benefit from the law, and it also depends on how your description of reality and your definition of the subjects of rights act in your judging political strategies. It is not only a matter of different descriptions of reality, but also of different uses of these descriptions in an argumentative context. Ontology and logic (intended as shared rules of reasoning) are at the same time involved.

Let us consider another example. Around forty years ago, most aspects of male domination over women were not culturally evident and acknowledged in Western culture. Now, many people know this; there are still many things to do, but most people know the existence of new political subjects who are marginalized and exploited women. This is only a particular case: in fact, new political subjects continually emerge, and no reflection over human rights can avoid taking this into account. But to acknowledge the existence of new political subjects is not enough: you also need some new way of thinking and arguing. This is the reason why "differential" feminism has stressed that you cannot defend women's rights in a male way of thinking. In the same way, Karl Marx described (or "constructed"?) the new proletarian class, but he had to use the new Hegelian logic to define and defend their rights.

So it seems that when one treats rights of political subjects (especially new political subjects), he or she is somehow committed to be aware of the ontology (the kind of entities) he or she is referring to, and the logic (the way of reasoning) of which he or she is making use. And this could be a first step, if you want, for entering into a dialogue with people who make use of other ontological and logical points of view. But only a *prima philosophia*, that is, what had once been called "metaphysics," should be delegated to give people some awareness about the foundations (i.e., namely the ontological and logical premises) of their reasoning and arguing, so we have to admit that in these contexts we need a *metaphysical* inquiry.

And yet, there are many doubts about the legitimacy and possibility of such an inquiry. Many people think—for example, as Habermas holds[3]—that a "fundamental" political theory (like the one concerned with international strategies) must be developed without any connection to metaphysics, and that there must be a radically postmetaphysical philosophy of politics and law. Is this the last word about the connection between metaphysics—or more generally philosophy—and politics?

The analysis that follows points to the possibility and legitimacy of a junction of politics and fundamental philosophy on new bases. The remark that suggests this inquiry is that as it seems nowadays, in each inquiry or discussion about main political topics, some typical philosophical questions come to light again and again, and we often find ourselves committed to ask if we have (or should have) a shared ontology that describes the new political subjects and strategies of our era; if we have (or should have) a shared logic for evaluating and treating the political reasoning referred to by these new entities and strategies; and if we have (or should have) then a philosophical foundation for new political projects, situations, and goals. Probably the answers should be generically negative in a double sense: we do not have a *prima philosophia*, and we should not have it, if we want to avoid dogmatism. But this cannot be enough: it is quite easy to acknowledge that many political inquiries nowadays are hindered by the difficulty of adapting old structures of reasoning to new subjects of rights, or old (implicit) metaphysical assumptions to new metaphysical problems, and this suggests an examination of the issue in more detail.

## Antifoundationalism in Contemporary Thought

As it seems, in problems such as the limits of humanitarian interventions, the ambiguous role of globalization, and the diverging definitions of human rights (let alone other typical political and philosophical problems, such as abortion, cloning, and so on), some properly fundamental issues are involved: issues concerning conceptions of being and use of reason. And as I hinted, we probably need some philosophical inquiry institutionally interested in the foundations of reason, in possible and effective descriptions of being, and in premises and principles of common, scientific, and philosophical reasoning.

Now, a large part of recent Western tradition tells us that such foundational inquiries are generally useless if not dangerous. They are useless because a serious attempt to describe the foundations and premises of reason are doomed to fail, and they are dangerous because if they do not fail, they risk dogmatism. This means that no international humanitarian or political strategy can be founded on the existence of a shared idea of "human nature" and on the use of a global, overcultural reason. But note that it also means that neither can any antiglobalist political and cultural action be founded on such universal and objective structures. Evidently, one may say that there is something wrong with the foundations of reason, but there is also something wrong with skepticism about the foundations of reason. I suggest it is worth examining the problem in detail.

The difficulties of foundational inquiries are a main topic of modern and contemporary philosophy, be they connected to the failure of the metaphysical enterprise in David Hume's thought, to Immanuel Kant's claim about the primacy of practice, to the supposed failure of Georg Hegel's dialectical method, via the dismissal of the Marxist project, to Friedrich Nietzsche's theory of nihilism and its developments in French structuralism, or finally to Martin Heidegger's rejection of metaphysics.

This is a well-known landscape, for continental European thinkers, while the analytic, Anglo-American tradition of philosophy (or at least a relevant part of it) has basically been, all along the twentieth century, a sort of stronghold for pure philosophical theory.

However, as Michael Dummett stresses,[4] also the classical analytical conception of philosophical theory has been strongly influenced by some antisystematic and antifoundational tendencies, which were typical of Ludwig Wittgenstein and of some other great analytical thinkers. So, while the continental tradition has been deeply influenced by the failure of theoretical reason (in Kant and/or Nietzsche), the analytic tradition, while not assuming this failure, has always been inclined to promote sectorial and particular inquiries. Contemporary analytical researches in ontology and the foundations of knowledge are very subtle and deep, but irreducibly particular, linked to some specific theoretical style, and fundamentally unable to enter into a dialogue with the whole of culture.

One may admit that both in analytic and continental philosophy there is a fairly similar situation as to the kind of philosophic enquiry concerned with the foundations, conditions, and premises of common, philosophical, and scientific reasoning. In continental philosophy, there is a wide tradition of global reflections over the destiny and nature of Western logos, but its results have been generally critical, if not destructive. In analytic philosophy, we have a tradition of deep and fairly accurate analysis over some specific point or problem concerning the basis of knowledge and reason, with positive but forcibly particular results. Hence, we have a positive particular theory side by side a general negative theory.

This is basically the state of our philosophical background. How can we use this in our thinking about global responsibility and human rights, and about the nature of human beings who are supposed to benefit from these rights?

## Diminishing Philosophy

A perfect and in a way extreme representative of this situation is Richard Rorty.[5] He cumulates the negative idea of philosophical theory that is typical of a large part of continental philosophy with the idea of the useless nature of general assertions (be they negative or positive) that is a typically analytical inheritance. This explains the particular nature of Rorty's philosophical style. This also explains the fundamentally self-refuting structure of his argumentation, as he often argues, in a strongly universalistic and essentialist way, for the impossibility of any universalistic and essentialist argumentation.

Hegel claimed that skepticism is irrelevant, or a lucky thing for philosophy, and actually we find that in Rorty's "hyperbolic" claims there are destructive but at the same time edifying suggestions for a new thought of globality, and maybe they also include some suggestions about revising our ideas of human nature (or better: human beings).

In his reflection over philosophy, literature, and intercultural confrontation, Rorty advances the reasonable and commonly shared thesis that most mistakes in history are specifically to be referred to the misleading idea that there could be a human nature with objective features, and that human rights should be related to it or molded on it. Extermination and slavery have always been legitimated by the reification of something vague and abstract, called human nature.

Rorty has many friends who share this idea. Isaiah Berlin, Karl Popper, Hilary Putnam, Bernard Williams, as well as Alasdair MacIntyre and Michael Walzer have variously claimed the same thesis.[6] But Rorty's particularity consists in thinking that this implies the necessity of diminishing (or getting rid of) philosophy. As it seems, the whole problem of Western tradition is, according to Rorty, somehow an excess of philosophy. Philosophy itself in a way is to him the excessive tendency to theorize, to fix definitions of essences, to search for an account of the global nature of our world.

Rorty criticizes essentialism, which he believes to be the misleading tendency to treat the objects of human sciences (history, sociology, anthropology, literary criticism, and so on) in the guise of "things," that is, objects one can examine and study "from outside." He also charges philosophy in general with aiming to articulate these reifying descriptions into some global, universal, and unique description; according to him, essentialism in philosophy is the false picture of a nonexistent "objective totality."

This particularly holds in multicultural contexts. How can we rightly redefine human rights starting with an image of human nature as fixed and defined and wanting this picture to be valid for all peoples, regardless of their geographical, cultural, and historical background? Rorty says that for these reasons Heidegger's criticism of Western thought is completely wrong and in a way dangerous. We would fare much better with Charles Dickens. Briefly put: self-identification of human beings, and self-identification of cultures, should be performed by fiction, rather than by philosophy. All definition of human rights, Rorty explicitly says, should not be based on "theses" on the nature of beings, on human nature, and on values alleged to be universally and atemporally true, but (and this is a relevant aspect of his claim) "on litigious confrontations" over concrete alternatives.

These "litigious confrontations" are of some use because all our life and thought, according to Rorty, are based on preferences, instincts, and desires, and it is not worth searching for an idea or a thesis that is not located and belonging to a whole of interests, passions, situations, and so on: there is no idea without the contextuality of its being expressed. This is the reason why fiction is better than philosophy for democracy: a novel openly shows the purely narrative relevance of moral ideas; it shows that peace and justice have to be strongly pursued, but without any description of their nature and any foundation of their primacy.

As we see here, Rorty develops some anthropological premises (shared by pragmatists as well as by existentialists and historicists) in a destructive (more than deconstructive) direction. We should not think that there is no ontological implication in his assertion. The ontological basis of his theses is basically a theory of *Zugehörigkeit* (so to say: a theory of "belonging") that has a lot of antecedents: human beings are "living thinkers"—claimed Søren Kierkegaard— hence, whatever we think is relative and moves along with life, and we cannot express our beliefs in an objective way, as they were separated from life; we are "centers of strength," pure *"Wille zur Macht"* willing its own willing— stated Nietzsche—hence, every claim to know an objective truth is evidently false; and we are "fragments of autobiographies"—asserted Wilhelm Dilthey— and our being is made by history and carried on by the flux of time.

### Self-Contradiction

We thus perceive a strong ontological commitment involved in Rorty's hypotheses: a lot of philosophical premises are needed for his project of getting rid of philosophy.

Rorty concludes by presenting this syllogism: When tolerance and the ability of getting along well together become the values of a society, there is no need to hope for a world greatness; if we need this greatness, we need Plato and Heidegger, we need philosophy. But who really wants something like "world greatness"?—probably only someone like Adolf Hitler or similar exaggerated ideologists (more than philosophers) do, and as it seems according to Rorty only people like Hitler or Napoléon Bonaparte (or possibly Ilich Lenin in 1905) are "philosophers" *strictu sensu.*

Evidently, if you admit the alternative—*world greatness + philosophy* or else *tolerance + the ability of getting along well together,* also admitting at the same time the obscurity of the first possibility—you are committed to conclude, along with Rorty, that the second possibility is to be preferred, insofar as it defends the rights of something normally good and advisable.

But by looking closer at Rorty's argumentation, we see an interesting implication. A strong traditionalist may easily use Rorty's argument, by translating it as follows:

- First premise: if we want to get along well together, we should not practice any kind of philosophy
- Second premise: if we want to transform the world, and if we wish to cultivate the hope for a better future (if we want either both or one of them), we need philosophy
- Conclusion: if we want to get along well together, we should neither want a better world nor cultivate the hope for a better future

The reasoning is formally correct, but there are three ways in which it can be discussed.

First, it asserts an abstract opposition between "getting along well together" and "changing the world" (or searching for a world greatness), but it is not so convincing, as evidently we may need to change the world exactly in order to get along well together (and probably, but less evidently, I admit, given the very aim of "getting along well," one should also aspire to world greatness).

Second, it is not clear why in order to get along well with each other we should not practice any kind of philosophy: a certain exercise of universalist and essentialist discourse might actually be a useful ingredient of a good conviviality. If, as Rorty himself repeatedly suggests, we consider philosophy to be a literary genre, one cannot see how such a genre, like any other, might be a threat for humanity. Obviously, the question deals with the place and role of philosophy in a culture. But if this is the problem, in which sense and for what reasons should essentialism and search for "greatness"—which evidently are to be considered literary features—be condemned? It is hard to see how, in themselves, essentialism and search for greatness must be such a threat for everyday agreement. Usually, ideas are not dangerous in themselves, but for the use one makes of them.

Third, Rorty is evidently practicing here a more associative than argumentative style: but also any associative style has some references to substantial theses, to some description of how things are or are supposed to be. Any associative style bears on that particular connection between descriptive (or reconstructive) and prescriptive (normative) sentences that is typical of any theoretical discourse. Actually, also the premise "if we choose tolerance we should not need to hope for world greatness" is based on some descriptive account of how things (human beings) essentially are or are supposed to be: namely, that descriptive account that we can reconstruct from Kierkegaard, Nietzsche, and Dilthey.

## Skepticism and Philosophy

The most important thing to note here is that Rorty's stance is self-refuting in the sense previously mentioned: Rorty does what he asserts is impossible to do. But precisely this self-refutation, I believe, gives us some relevant suggestions in order to free our foundational even if not foundationalist philosophy from the oscillation between "negative totality" and "positive particular thought."

Rorty's criticism of the descriptive attitude of essentialism (he also develops the same criticism in his famous *Philosophy and the Mirror of Nature*,[7] and practically in all his work) is misleading. In fact, there could hardly be any theory or relevant thesis without an even implicit and unaware *description* of how things are (be this description intended as weakly reconstructive or dogmatically "representative"). And we see perfectly well that Rorty's criticism is also self-contradictory, as even Rorty's theses include some descriptive premises: the implicit anthropological assumptions that I sketched earlier, but also other, more subtle devices.

"If we prefer getting along well with each other we should not think of world greatness" is a globally descriptive assertion. More significantly, it also includes an idea of human nature, ambiguously revealed by the use of the first plural person "we." How can Rorty use such a term? Who are the "us" that he associates? Who does legitimate him to use this term and to make this association? To what extent does the same use of "we" not entail some implicit idea of a "universal audience" functionally equivalent to a universal human nature?

The fact is, now we can conclude, that there is no real destructive skepticism in philosophy. Skepticism is a strength of reason, not a threat to it. This is Hegel's basic idea in his famous *Verhältnis des Skeptizismus zur Philosophie*.[8] Hegel distinguished two kinds of skepticism: one is antiphilosophical and hence self-destroying and irrelevant, the other is the best friend of philosophers as it reminds them of the foundations of knowledge and being. But in both cases, Hegel seems to consider skepticism to be highly useful since even its deficiencies are particularly enlightening.

Aristotle's claim about philosophy, which is at the basis of Hegel's dialectics, is actually a classical argument against skepticism, and it matches Rorty's weak point particularly well. The well-known Aristotelian argument was as follows: in order to reject philosophy, we have to philosophize, hence one cannot get rid of philosophy.[9] It is easy to extend the idea: in order to reject descriptive theory, we need a descriptive theory that substantiates the need of rejecting descriptive theory; in order to do away with totality, we need a vision or a conception of totality; and in order to get rid of essentialism, we need an essential vision of essentialism. We see that it is not so easy to do away with philosophy, theory, and essentialism.

## Minimal Reason and the Defense of Philosophy

To summarize, I have shown that Rorty's view is self-refuting, basically because he criticizes essentialism in an essentialist way; in moving from a philosophical description of human beings and an implicit use and conception of "us" as human beings, he implicitly shares his ontological ideas about human beings. We also saw that this objection is fairly commonplace in the dialogue between foundationalism and antifoundationalism, as Hegel already stressed in his youthful writing about skepticism and philosophy.

So, the first argument in favor of my thesis (the need and possibility of some new "foundational" philosophy for the new demands of politics) is that we cannot get rid of our foundational prejudices, as we always have some sort of global vision of totality and human nature, in the very moment in which we start theorizing about our lack of ideas about totality and the multiplicity of our ideas concerning human beings. The fact that this point was shared by Aristotle as well as Hegel to me suggests the following important consequence: humanity has never possessed universal moral or shared values and principles, but most likely it has always had the same "minimal reason," at least insofar as each theoretical position is committed to measure itself against the impossibility or difficulty of rejecting some fundamental structures of reasoning. Hence, even if we do not share all our substantive and positive ideas, surely we share the limits of our reasoning and arguing.

Does this mean we are consigned to foundationalism?

Karl Otto Apel, in his refoundation of ethical discourse, agrees on ideas similar to these, but he substantially promotes a traditional structure of philosophical foundation.[10] In contrast, I would stress that a definitive acceptance of the skeptical results leads to a minimal reason more than to a properly foundational reason intended in the traditional way. This minimal reason is probably our effective philosophical *koiné* (i.e., our common philosophical language). And I suppose this is the right starting point of an evaluation of the new particular and/or universal entities with which our global thought is currently dealing.

Obviously, everything depends on which kind of foundational philosophy one embraces. The unique way in which Rorty's thesis is not to be considered as self-refuting is looking at it as the positive asking for a new style of philosophizing, or as the motion in favor of a particular type of foundational philosophy: based on narrative reconstructions more than on logical descriptions. The matter is not so clear, as Rorty seems frequently to play both the role of self-refuting antiphilosopher and of self-asserting new narrative philosopher.

However, there are two reasons why I think we need some type of foundational philosophy (which to some extent could still be called "metaphysics").

## Two Reasons for Philosophy

First, Rorty's idea is, in order to come to terms with our problems of globality, we need Dickens more than Heidegger, Milan Kundera more than Plato. But what can Dickens tell us, say, about the empire of multinational enterprises? He can surely teach us pity for poor people and a sense of human dignity, but as Rorty himself acknowledges, there is no real divergence on this point: the strategies for humiliating people are fairly equivalent all over the world, and fairly equivalent are the words used to condemn them. On the contrary, suppose that, without consideration of totality and uniquely occupied by the effort to get along well together, we should find ourselves one day without a world in which to get along, well or badly? Here we find the classical suggestion of Hans Jonas's Prinzip Verantwortung.[11] Jonas claims that ethics is ultimately founded on the responsibility for future generations: we cannot act in a way that can threaten the same existence of the world, that is, the existence of the same possibility of acting in the future. And the evaluation of this is linked to a global vision of the world, of its destiny and nature. We need to think of totality and universality, as these are the conditions of our very life. If we risk to destroy the world, we risk losing the same conditions of thinking, in either a philosophical or narrative style.

Without some thought of totality, or better, without some critical control of our views about totality, we are bound to submit, without knowing it, to our philosophical prejudices. We need a thought of totality in order to criticize totality, and we need a fundamental-preliminary theory in order to confront the different cultures and conceptions of being that a correct vision of totality presents us with. (This was Theodor W. Adorno's basic idea in his criticism of totality developed simultaneously with a defense of theory—the latter conceived precisely as a vision of global relations and responsibilities[12]).

Second, Western tradition is alleged to be founded on philosophy. A certain—probably mistakable and misleading—dominance of the philosophical way of seeing the world still constitutes more or less consciously the basis of Western culture. In a way, the whole world of technology and science (as Heidegger believed),[13] displays the triumph of a sort of Hegelian

Platonism, insofar as this world is based on the reality of things that are not properly real in a plain sense.

So, we seem to have an excess of philosophy, as Rorty holds. But note that in this deeply philosophical culture and life there is no clear cultural place for fundamental philosophy, for philosophy concerned with the ontological basis of thought and reason. Heidegger labeled this situation by the expression "oblivion of being." We may note that this oblivion creates an odd result: we have great resources for theory, but joined to a lack of conscious, and culturally acknowledged, philosophical foundation—if you want, an excess of theorizing without any kind of philosophical *koiné*.

And the specific important aspect of this situation is that the lack of philosophical orientation that affects recent Western culture led to a certain move toward pragmatism and fragmentation of political discourse. In Italy, this surely created the fertile background for the victory of a particular type of conservatism: a conservatism that is typically "without thought," characterized by a lack of ideal and critical orientation, joined with a proliferation of fallacious discourses. The dream of "transforming the world by means of philosophy" surely created historical damages, but it is fundamentally dangerous to infer that therefore we do not have to articulate politics with some sort of connected and general theory, or philosophical reflection over the premises of thought and reason.

**Dialogue in Foundational Contexts**

Surely, in our recent tradition of foundational philosophy (i.e., in recent philosophical enterprises more or less critically concerned with the analysis of the ontological and logical foundations of reason), there have been a lot of "nonbrutally essentialist" philosophical practices. Rorty has often misunderstood, for instance, the theoretical commitment of Hegel and hermeneutics (that he basically considers in the light of a weak pragmatism), and the ethical reasons of Heidegger (whom he fundamentally charges with theoreticism).

A good hermeneutical approach in my view should be committed to change Marx's formula, "transforming the world by means of philosophy, instead of interpreting it,"[14] by substituting "instead of" with "while." Hence, the question that hermeneutics could help to solve should still be part of Antonio Gramsci's questions: "How can philosophy transform the world while interpreting it?" "Can it really still perform such a double process, and if yes, how?"[15] In the hermeneutical account, foundational philosophy should be the art of dialogue, and any inquiry into the possibility of this kind of philosophy should be an inquiry into the methods and ways of maintaining such a dialogue in the face of the plurality of our descriptions and redefinitions of being. Hence, we see that the two main goals of recent political discourses indicated at the beginning of this chapter are one and the same in the hermeneutical view.

Should there be or can there be shared rules of dialogue in a foundational context? I wish to conclude by presenting some suggestions about what could be a "postskeptical" consideration of the different conceptions of political subjects and actions, a consideration that basically aims to make these conceptions interrelate or converge.

During the 1990s, the main currents of political philosophy were concerned by the problem of pluralism, conceived in these terms: how can we achieve some shared principles and procedures that make us able to comprehend a common core of political legitimacy? Basically, two main solutions were found. You can arrive at it by "subtraction," leaving aside your own conception of good, or by "dialogical convergence," favoring a confrontation of disparate stances. This alternative is particularly relevant for us, as it has been mainly conceived in order to connect single conceptions of values to political choices globally or universally oriented, that is, global decisions, committed to articulate single values. Bruce Ackerman and Charles Larmore propose the subtraction thesis—you succeed in rational political decision dismissing your own moral choices.[16] John Rawls and Ronald Dworkin propose the convergence thesis—you always have to promote the convergence.[17]

But note that subtraction and convergence could be seen as the basic principles of two kinds of weak foundationalism. And in this perspective, they both have some relevant defects. A self-subtraction attitude can hardly avoid the risk of leaving more room to dogmatism, to political integralism, to all those who are strongly oriented toward self-assertiveness more than to self-subtraction. On the other side, the dialogical convergence is a good but formal principle. How can it be performed, between which kind of entities, represented by what and who? If convergence is intended as a simple will to communicate, it is the obvious starting point of any search for a shared basis of political discourse; if instead it is intended as a regulative principle, one may always object that other principles are to be pursued, and hence we fall again in a situation of irreducible pluralism.

Probably a combination of subtraction and convergence is the right attitude for a foundational yet nonfoundationalist philosophy. As subtraction could allow us to avoid dogmatism in evaluating different ways of describing and "cutting" reality, and convergence could yield the conditions of confronting different constructions or descriptions of reality. Note that in a way Rorty's attitude is typically subtractive: In his theses, Western culture gives up its own proper and typical premise, that is, philosophy. We see that one cannot choose this solution without self-contradictions and/or dangerous consequences.

## Conclusion

The hypothesis put forward by this chapter, as hinted in the first section, is that the specific nature of political problems raised by globalization and international intervention might recall a new reflection about the ontological and more generally philosophical foundations of political reasoning. It is fairly evident that in order to get a good (shared and reasonable) definition of human rights—a definition that can support or possibly criticize international policies—some preliminary awareness about the nature and limits of possible definitions of human beings is needed. In a first approximation, it is difficult to project a global policy without having an idea of the human rights that should orient this policy, and supposedly, it is difficult to get this idea without any kind of preliminary definition of human beings (and/or without challenging and revising some already established definitions of this kind). So, it seems that some "fundamental" (general and preliminary) philosophy should be activated in these contexts.

But many questions arise, and this chapter has addressed some of them. Should philosophy still give an orientation to political thought? If yes, could there or should there be such kind of foundational philosophy? If yes, how would a foundational philosophy develop in order to avoid cultural dogmatism?

After a brief examination of the most destructive approach to these problems—the one performed by Rorty in the past twenty years—we arrive at four basic and provisional conclusions:

1. that a foundational philosophy is, more or less knowingly, already active in Western political thought (even Rorty's attempt to get rid of philosophy is firmly based on strong philosophical bases, namely on the anthropological assumptions of the so-called postmetaphysical tradition)
2. that awareness about the hidden philosophical assumptions of (supposedly) nonphilosophical theory is needed in order to avoid the devastating effects of a lack of critical orientation (one should be aware of one's own philosophical prejudices in order to avoid the deviate effects of these same prejudices)
3. that particularly, in intercultural confrontations, Gramsci's typical question "How can philosophy transform the world while interpreting it?" could find an answer in a Platonic-hermeneutical idea of philosophy as "the art of dialogue"
4. that much depends on how the dialogue is intended and practiced, as the main strategies of dialogical theory suggested in the last decade have been somehow partial and need to be integrated

Many things still remain to be said about this evidently demanding topic, but probably these could be the first steps on the way of a reconsideration of the role of foundational philosophy (which once was called metaphysics) in politics. And—in particular for the Italian situation—it is important to remember what Susan Haack stresses while discussing "vulgar Rortysm": that Benito Mussolini was enthusiastic for "pragmatism," intended as a perspective that subordinates intellectual life to politics.[18] So, we can see that there could be a certain affinity between political totalitarism and the philosophical project of diminishing philosophy.

## Notes

1. See Jürgen Habermas, *Die Postnationale Konstellation* (Frankfurt am Main: Suhrkamp, 1998, which presents the reasons and premises of Habermas's interventionism); see also the discussion in Harald Wohlrapp, "Krieg für Menschenrechte?" *Deutsche Zeitschrift für Philosophie* 48, no. 1 (2000): 107–132.
    2. Habermas, *Die Postnationale Konstellation*.
    3. A recent development of Habermas's postmetaphysical point of view is to be found in Jürgen Habermas, *Die Zukunft der menschlichen Natur: Auf dem Weg zu einer liberalen Eugenik?* (Frankfurt am Main: Suhrkamp, 2001).
    4. See Michael Dummett, "Can Analytical Philosophy Be Systematic and Ought It to Be?" in Michael Dummett, *Truth and Other Enigmas* (Oxford: Clarendon, 1978).
    5. I mainly take into account Rorty's essay about literature, philosophy, and intercultural confrontation. See Richard Rorty, "Heidegger, Kundera and Dickens," in Richard Rorty, *Essays on Heidegger and Others: Philosophical Papers* (Cambridge: Cambridge University Press, 1991), pp. 66–84; see also Richard Rorty and Anindita N. Balslev, *Cultural Otherness: Correspondence with Richard Rorty*, 2nd ed. (Shimla, India: Indian Institute of Advanced Study, in collaboration with Munshiram Manohar Lal, 2000).
    6. See Hilary Putnam, "The French Revolution and the Holocaust: Can Ethics Be Ahistorical?" in Eliott Deutsch, ed., *Culture and Modernity: The Authority of the Past, East-West Philosophical Perspectives* (*Proceedings of the Sixth East-West Philosopher's Conference*) (Honolulu: University of Hawaii Press, 1991), pp. 191–214.
    7. Richard Rorty, *Philosophy and the Mirror of Nature* (Princeton, N.J.: Princeton University Press, 1979).
    8. Georg Hegel, "Verhältnis des Skeptizismus zur Philosophie, Darstellung seiner verschiedenen Modifikationen und Vergleichung des neuesten mit dem alten," *Kritisches Journal der Philosophie* 1, no. 2 (1802).
    9. This kind of argumentation, mentioned in the pseudo-Aristotelian *Protrepticon*, is openly adopted by Aristotle in *Metaphysics*, Γ, 3, 1005 a-b. See Jonathan Barnes, ed., *The Complete Works of Aristotle: The Revised Oxford Translation*. (Princeton, N.J.: Princeton University Press, 1984).
    10. Karl Otto Apel, *Auseinandersetzungen* (Frankfurt am Main: Suhrkamp, 1998).
    11. Hans Jonas, *Das Prinzip Verantwortung* (Frankfurt am Main: Insel, 1979).
    12. Theodor W. Adorno, *Negative Dialektik* (Frankfurt am Main: Suhrkamp, 1966).
    13. See Martin Heidegger, *Vorträge und Aufsätze* (Tübingen: Mohr, 1954).
    14. Marx's famous eleventh thesis on Paul Feuerbach (1845) can be read in Karl Marx and Friedrich Engels, *Werke*, vol. 2, ed. by Institut für Marxismus-Leninismus (Berlin: Dietz, 1957).
    15. The typical connection that Antonio Gramsci individuated between philosophy and politics was openly inspired by an elaboration of Marx's theses on Feuerbach. See Antonio Gramsci, *Quaderni del carcere*, ed. Valentino Gerratana (Torino: Einaudi, 1975). An English selection from *Quaderni del carcere* is Antonio Gramsci, *Selections from the Prison Notebooks*, trans. and ed. Quintin Hoare and Geoffrey Nowell-Smith (New York: International, 1971).

16. Bruce Ackerman, *Social Justice in the Liberal State* (Cambridge, Mass.: Harvard University Press, 1980); Charles Larmore, *Patterns of Moral Complexity* (Cambridge: Cambridge University Press, 1987).

17. John Rawls, *Political Liberalism* (New York: Columbia University Press, 1993); Ronald Dworkin, *Taking Rights Seriously* (London: Duckworth, 1977); Ronald Dworkin, *Law's Empire* (London: Fontana, 1986).

18. Susan Haack's reconsideration of pragmatism can be found in Susan Haack, *Manifesto of a Passionate Moderate* (Chicago: University of Chicago Press, 1998).

# 9

# Preceding "Global Responsibility"
## Autonomy, Knowledge, and Power

### Nathalie Karagiannis

> I tremble in my uncertainty;
> I fear the daylight;
> The breezes I hear around me
> Make my heart beat fast.
> I would hide away,
> I would reveal the error;
> But I lack the courage either to hide
> Or to speak out.[1]

Some days after the departure of the French from Rwanda in the summer 1994, I was walking in an orphanage. Béatrice was walking with me: she was one of the women who took care of the orphans; she had lost two of her own children in the genocide. Suddenly, a cry of pain rose from the direction toward which we were heading. As we turned a corner, we saw a man—a soldier—lying in his own blood. His head was wounded on one side and he was still. Three other soldiers were standing around him. They waited for us to pass.

I have seen people more wounded, more sick, and more definitely dead than this soldier. But his memory is disturbing in a particular way. Unlike all the other instances where I could either do nothing or did something, in this case, I did not do anything but felt that I could have. Did I have a duty to act? Was I responsible for the future of the situation? Was I responsible in a way for its past? Was I anyway inscribed in a system of power relations that precluded any responsibility? Was I responsible *even though* I was inscribed in these power relations?

If questions of responsibility are inevitably posed at the individual level, they are acutely present at the collective level as well. Thus, when the French soldiers allowed perpetrators of crimes to exit Rwanda along with other refugees, were they responsible for "following the orders"? If the failure to distinguish between ordinary refugees and their political leaders was unintentional, as some still claim, is it not more convenient to eschew the question of responsibility altogether and instead talk about the power politics at stake? And can there be another responsibility, not bound by intention? An answer to this type of question is that the responsibility of the French is negotiated against the particular horizon of the "others" judgment on their actions. This answer points to a responsibility that is as dependent on others as on the self and that arises out of the event. This is the answer that this chapter favors, and it is an answer that challenges the current usage of "global responsibility."

The way to conceive of the coexistence or the mutual exclusion of power politics and responsibility is an epistemological and political choice. We must conceive of power politics and global responsibility both as situated in a chronological continuum (and thus one coming *after* the other) and as existing at the *same time.*

On the one hand, the passage from power politics to global responsibility can be thought of in terms of justification. In these terms, international intervention—having step by step grown out of its assurance that there is no need to justify intervention and later that intervention is justified on the grounds of sovereignty[2]—is nowadays increasingly justified through reference to (global) responsibility. Increasing reluctance to assert a world ruled by power politics and the proclaimed renaissance of morality have yielded this result. But things are more complicated: Thus, morality succeeding to realist politics must be viewed as an unacceptable reductionism, in the light of works that have shown the enormous potential for silencing alternatives that realism has had—be it in the political or the academic sphere. Realist politics was an era's and a geography's morality: certain questions of responsibility did not fail to be raised under the reign of realism.

On the other hand, the simultaneous presence of the two is apparent—power politics is a condition of possibility of (global) responsibility in the sense of the former constituting the horizon against which the latter is being invoked. This is due to the equivocy of responsibility. Responsibility—and global responsibility—can have different sorts of meaning; additionally, from the present political-theoretical viewpoint, responsibility is equivalent to accountability. In the context of power politics, responsibility can be either a liberal responsibility (liberal power politics corresponding to liberal responsibility because in a society of autonomous states each is responsible for itself in the name of a universal law), a realist power politics (each state is responsible for itself as it is characterized by an autonomous will), or an authoritarian power politics (in an authoritarian and paternalistic version of power politics, the strongest state will dominate the weakest and endorse responsibility for it). Power politics can therefore be conceptualized as the wider framework in which responsibility is invoked. Finally, another version of the coexistence approach would claim that responsibility is instrumentalized by power politics; that it is *just* a screen of smoke that hides the true intentions of states acting on (neo)realist premises. However, such an approach belongs itself to a power-politics framework.

To grasp how the concept of global responsibility is currently used, we need to identify its origin and its opposition. This chapter focuses on what precedes global responsibility, in an effort to elucidate which of the *problématiques* surrounding responsibility are still posed and which are not.

## Autonomy, Knowledge, and Responsibility

The ordinary imagery of responsibility fails to convey the historical transformations that the concept has undergone. Responsibility has been conceptualized in wholly different terms by thinkers like Aristotle, St. Augustine, or Max Weber. The current understanding of the concept is a relatively recent one, born in a secularized context and thus intimately bound to a characteristically secular idea of autonomy. Before "modernity," however, notions that approximate responsibility are always bound to a social context. In the ancient Greek context, one of the most famous examples is Antigone's revolt against Kreon's interdiction to bury her brother/father, Polynices. One authority, that of the moral and religious duty, that of honor and *doxa*, is stronger than the other, that of the state. The divine and the social responsibilities are mingled in Antigone's discourse, in a way that renders her responsible before the gods, before the memory of her brother, and before a certain understanding of custom, and hence not responsible before the tyrant.[3]

Likewise, three centuries before Rudyard Kipling urged the United States to seize the Philippines in his famous "White Man's burden," the burden of the first wave of colonizations had been viewed as a duty dictated by God and as a responsibility in front of the divine guidance. This triangle is typical of a religious (not only Christian) understanding of the giver, the receiver, and the divinity in whose name the giving is done. It characterizes both the domestic and the external affairs of the Europeans—and it was transformed into the welfare state and development cooperation policies that have more in common than has ordinarily been supposed.

But since the Enlightenment, it is autonomy that takes the place of the condition sine qua non of responsibility. In the simplest version of this relation between responsibility and autonomy, one can be held responsible only if one is autonomous—the translation from an individual to a larger state level presents no particular problem insofar as a (neo)realist or liberal (Kantian) perspective is taken. As a consequence, being deprived of one's autonomy renders one incapable of being responsible. This is, for instance, the sense in which we must understand the metaphor of childhood, very often encountered in the colonizers' discourse and that has left a trace in the idea of development.[4] Children—the colonized—are dependent on adults—the colonizers: lacking autonomy, they are irresponsible. This argument is thought to be valid until the colonized areas attain the legal international status of a state, the status of adulthood. Once this has been reached, they become sovereign, and hence, by this logic, responsible. However, if the former colonies are promoted to the state level, they remain backward, underdeveloped, or, in the most recent version, developing states. In fact, their autonomy can be questioned—and it has been not only by "Third-Worldist" theories of the *dependencia* type, but even, currently, by official development discourse. An asymmetry between "developed" and "developing" is thus always present in a way that renders the connection between autonomy and responsibility shaky. One's own definition through the other takes a twisted turn, since it is not denied and even recently proclaimed on the one hand, while, on the other hand, autonomy is also assumed.

Jacques Derrida's work on responsibility is precious but remains hesitant on the issue of autonomy. Looking at Derrida's understanding of responsibility reveals both the ambiguous uses of autonomy and how closely heteronomy (from *heteros* and *nomos* in ancient Greek: the other's law, the law outside oneself) is tied to responsibility, instead of or before autonomy, which in turn places responsibility in the context of a community.[5] In *Principles of European Responsibility,* Derrida discusses the historicity of responsibility— another way of talking about its dependence on a specific time (and space) context.[6] He points at the difficulty that is commonly encountered of acknowledging the historicity of responsibility, its Platonic and Christian versions and components. One can see how admitting a fundamental historicity of responsibility can be perceived by a certain type of thought as an annihilation of responsibility. The very possibility of speaking in favor of autonomy and responsibility seems to vanish, as it is thus thought, when a person is understood to be *free in a certain context* and responsible within this context. These are contradictions in terms, according to this logic. Is that still freedom, it is asked, and is that still responsibility?

But the idea of autonomy is part of a larger framework in which responsibility is a fact that follows the establishment of a causal link between a person and a state of affairs, as in "A caused B." Thus, the modern secular understanding of responsibility is based on a double assumption: the first part of this assumption is that causation equals (moral) blameworthiness and blameworthiness equals responsibility.[7] This entails that if it can be established that there is a causal link between a state of affairs and its precipitant, as William E. Connolly puts it, then the precipitant will be blamed and therefore held responsible.[8] However, establishing such links of causality is an endeavor that pertains more to the realm of nature and the social sciences than to the realm of the social life of human beings. Unless the dangerous fiction of all things social taking place as in a chemical bowl is adopted, we must reject the possibility of observing causal links between A and B.

The second part of the assumption on which the common sense responsibility is based concerns the factual character of the concept. The previous equations are grounded on a belief in the nonjudgmental character of responsibility. In this sense, to say that someone is responsible describes a fact not a judgment. However, despite being a secular responsibility, this common sense responsibility pertains to specific moral standards. This moral standard can in fact be viewed, according to Marion Smiley,[9] as an ideal liability that is ideal per se. In the absence of God or Nature defining these moral standards, we must look for a different place where they are constituted: in an enriched version of the social realm.

It is now clear that the understanding of autonomy we have encountered up to now is based on a view of the social life and responsibility that depicts them as woven by causal ties and understandable through facts. Indeed, the extreme version of autonomy can be found in liberal individualism where the freedom of choice is understood as centrally constituting the individual and her actions. In this approach, the individual (and here, also the state at least in Immanuel Kant's liberalism) is autonomous and rational and therefore responsible for (the consequences of the) actions that he or she *causes*.[10] Such responsibility is as clear-cut as a fact can be. There is an undeniably strong positive undertone in this version of autonomy's link to responsibility, one that speaks of emancipation and rendering accounts in one's own name and also, conversely, of the impossibility to escape responsibility in the name of the supernatural or natural blamer. In this sense, although the connection between the two concepts can and should be seriously discussed, the broader emancipatory horizon in which, historically at least, it made sense cannot be disregarded.[11] However, grasping the historically meaningful change of these concepts must not prevent us from questioning their use and misuse in the current international context.

**Responsibility and Knowledge**

In the recent past, the North Atlantic Treaty Organization's excuse for being sloppy in its bombings of Kosovo and thus successfully though mistakenly targeting the former Chinese embassy or a bus was that its maps were old and its technique inadequate, in a word *that it did not know or was not able to know*. This points to the endorsement of the idea that it is knowledge (and by extension, intention) that determines responsibility and that ignorance excuses one from responsibility. Indeed, uncertainty or the unknown can offer an effective grasp on how the direct relationship between autonomy and responsibility is questionable; it is particularly relevant in the case of international politics, not least because it has been the background assumption of all theoretical endeavors in the field. More generally, it is the different answers to, precisely, the issue of uncertainty that have yielded different results in terms of social-scientific and societal arrangements.[12] In relation to responsibility, we may follow Derrida when he says that if one is in possession of the full knowledge of what will happen, responsibility is not at stake. Indeed, to assume responsibility means to agree to render an account for consequences that are not fully mastered; by contrast, if one's decision reflected a full knowledge, it would only amount to the technical, as it were, application of this knowledge.

Saying that a responsible decision must be taken on the basis of knowledge seems to define the condition of possibility of responsibility (one can't make a responsible decision without science or conscience, without knowing what one is doing, for what reasons, in view of what and under what conditions), at the same time as it defines the condition of impossibility of this same responsibility (if decision-making is relegated to a knowledge that it is content to follow or to develop, then it is no more a responsible decision, it is the technical deployment of a cognitive apparatus, the simple mechanistic deployment of a theorem).[13]

As is obvious in Derrida's quoted text, this aporetic situation of responsibility with regard to knowledge enlightens our discussion of the issue of autonomy. The part of knowledge that is necessary to a responsible decision ("knowing what one is doing") points to autonomy—this is the classical understanding of responsibility, also in the juridical domain. According to this view, it is the *free* (autonomous) choice of the individual, based on knowledge, that implicates responsibility. The childhood metaphor of colonial discourse is based on exactly this intimate relation between (autonomy) knowledge and responsibility. To put it differently, only the adult depicted as autonomous *because* of his or her knowledge can be called developed. Conversely, the child—the colonized or the underdeveloped—does not *know what he or she does* and depends, for reversing this, on the parent.[14]

On the other hand, "not fully knowing what one is doing"—simultaneously at play in responsibility—can by extension be conceived as pointing to the nonautonomous part of responsibility. And indeed, if we must sometimes avoid linking responsibility to full knowledge, if we must understand that the moment of the decision (or the nondecision) is a moment where there is never full knowledge, we must actually start conceiving of a responsibility without the necessity of full knowledge.[15] "Not fully knowing what one is doing" ceases to view the person, and for our present purposes the state, as a fully rational individuality that masters perfectly all the relevant information and can act accordingly. It takes into account the big part of knowledge that depends on others, the other types of rationality that are expressed through actions and the fact that it is necessary sometimes to not be excused from responsibility because of the lack of full knowledge: responsibility is often at stake when (full) knowledge is not.

Thus, when I am walking next to a tortured man, I can take the decision to revolt against this or not. The full knowledge of the situation and, in particular, of the possible consequences escapes me. *And* (not but) at the same time, I know that this man is being tortured. To give another example: In one of

Primo Levi's "Moments of Reprieve," another Italian—but Christian, and thus, privileged in the camp—steals soup for him every day. This is an absolutely forbidden act that could provoke his murder. Were he caught doing this, not only would he most probably be judged responsible, but he would also have to be thought as responsible *ex ante,* that is, as a priori assuming responsibility. Such an endorsed responsibility is, however, wholly different from a full knowledge of what would happen to him. There remains a fundamental uncertainty, which is a necessary condition for any decision. This person knows that the Jews are hungry, he knows that offering food to them is forbidden, *and* he does not *fully* or exactly know what would happen to him if he were caught. But the illustrations of this necessary uncertainty need not be so admirable and can be found in any type of development policy, starting, for instance, with the international financial institutions' notorious structural adjustment programs. The ironic fact that institutions that function on the criterion of expertise, coming to realize the failure of their policies, claim that they could not know or foresee the consequences must be irrelevant to the judgment of whether they are responsible.[16]

### Responsibility and the Other

Autonomy and responsibility are always bound by alterity, and Derrida acknowledges and works with this. In *Politics of Friendship*, he distinguishes between three types of response (responsibilities—components of responsibility) that are not "juxtaposable; they are enveloped and implied in one another": the response for self, the response to the other, and the response to the institutionalized other.[17]

First, "one answers for self, for what one is, says or does, and this holds beyond the simple present."[18] This is the secular type of responsibility as defined by autonomy. It can be exemplified by Weber's ethic of responsibility, an ethic that is crucially turned toward its own origin.

As Daniel Warner shows with regard to the "domestic analogy" in international relations theory, Weber's charismatic leader or worthy politician is conceived as responsible toward himself; even if he is actually answering to an external calling, we will always be left out of this calling.[19] Based on such a view of Weber's responsibility, the domestic analogy leads to a realist international politics in a very straightforward way: the image of the actor conveyed here is that of the atomistic state seeking relative power—there is no objective law on which action can be based or justified. But Weber's thought on this point is fundamentally ambiguous—and R. B. J. Walker, whom Warner quotes, has accurately formulated it: in Weber, "the meaning of responsibility is hanging between a Kantian imperative to autonomous action in conformity with a universal law and an imperative to decide on the basis of one's own autonomous will (or in terms of international relations, on the non-rational will of one's autonomous action)."[20] A basis of responsibility as absolutely autonomous will is at variance with a responsibility based on autonomy *in conformity with a universal law.* To put it crudely, applying this in international relations yields radically different approaches: in the first case, realism, as in Warner's interpretation; in the second case, liberalism. It is this very ambiguity that has allowed a smooth passage from the era of colonialism (own will) to the era of human rights (own will according to a standard), or also, in another area, the inclusion of states in a "civilized" international society, as Gerrit W. Gong shows.[21]

But this ambiguity and the chronological transformation that it accounts for is not obvious in Derrida's phrase. On the contrary, he talks of a response of *one* that transcends the present—a oneness (and also a uniqueness) of the person is assumed. As with the typical, as it were, secular understanding of responsibility, the ultimate necessity of this oneness that transcends time is easy to grasp. The multiplicity of the self and its chronological (if not historical) transformation cannot be excuses, in particular at the international level where the juridical fiction of the "moral persons" serves precisely the purpose of allowing legitimate action as well as of rendering "one" responsible.

This first position of Derrida shifts with the second type of response: the *response to the other.* This type of response has two characteristics that render it fundamental: first, one is not responsible in front of (or *before,* in Derrida's terms that point to an anteriority) oneself but responsible in front of/before the question of the other. Unless the other asks (explicitly or implicitly) for one's account, story, or response, there cannot be responsibility. The second characteristic is that the very name that identifies one as responsible for oneself "is in itself *for the other,*" in some cases chosen by the other and in all cases implying the other. For both of these reasons, response (and responsibility) is conditioned by the other, by alterity.[22]

This situation *precedes* the response for oneself or, in other words, the depiction of responsibility as stemming from autonomy. Responsibility is an interdependent condition, but an interdependence that has a limit. Indeed, contrary to Emmanuel Levinas, Derrida's other is an absolute other, an irreducible other.[23] For Derrida, confounding self and the other would be neutralizing their alterity.[24]

Such an understanding of responsibility depicts people as ethically situated, as facing the others, and—to tie this with the initial, more conventional, vocabulary—is adjacent to a responsibility that depends on a socially negotiated judgment rather than on a fact. Additionally, the weight of the argument is on responsibility as it involves oneself and the other rather than on the "causal" link between one's actions and its consequences.

The social and political implications of such a responsibility become clearer in the light of the third type of response that Derrida proposes, which involves "answering *before.*" This type of response is the response to the "institutionalized agency of alterity," one that, in some instances, "is authorized to represent the other legitimately, in the institutional form of a moral, juridical, political community."[25] The response *to* becomes response *before,* the former preceding and being the reason for the latter. The novelty here is the introduction of the idea of community, be it through one of its institutional expressions such as law.[26]

Thus, for Derrida, there is no doubt surrounding the possibility to change scales: concerning responsibility, the same phenomenon is taking place at the individual and the collective (and a fortiori international) levels. How do we make sense of this unproblematized leap in view of all the literature that for twenty years has criticized the "domestic analogy"?[27] Derrida must be assumed to have thought about the international community level, at least via the issue of international justice, Nuremberg, the war in former Yugoslavia, and so on. Other writings of his witness this.[28]

One answer lies in the idea of a theoretical displacement: what is crucial to Derrida is how the demand of the other conditions one's ability, need, and obligation to respond—not who this other might be.[29] Furthermore, it is almost by principle that he leaves this untheorized. For, with his third type of response, he elevates the relation to alterity to a universality. Ironically, that this response before a community is *universal in its principle* does not prevent it from being at the same time profoundly historical. With this, we have reached the limit where Derrida's deconstruction stops: (the universality of) the relation to the other.

**European Responsibility**

That responsibility is defined within the community (also by the "institutionalized agency of alterity") and a fortiori, the international community, has important implications with regard to global responsibility. Who is responsible in global responsibility? For whom, for what? To whom is he or she responding and before which institutionalized version of the other? In global responsibility, all are responsible for everything, responding to all and before all. The evolution of the European development discourse vis-à-vis the African, Caribbean, and Pacific (ACP) countries helps make some more sense of global responsibility because the globality of the European Union (EU; earlier the European Community [EC]) and of the EU-ACP relationship is a good example of the ambiguities that are present in any discourse on the global; and because it underlines two observations concerning global responsibility: that it is rooted in a reflection on responsibility that has always been present in development, albeit in different forms, and that it nevertheless represents a break with the previous understandings of responsibility, in that it is a responsibility wholly turned to the future.

With regard to our initial concern with the relation between power politics and global responsibility, a chronological overview shows that there is a very clearly perceptible movement in the evocation of responsibility from a hierarchical to an egalitarian understanding. The earlier, hierarchical responsibility is rooted in a paternalistic vision of the relations between the two collectivities, while the egalitarian responsibility—much more ambiguous and susceptible to varying interpretations—can be seen as solidarious or pluralist.

The issues of autonomy and community or the importance of the other in responsibility, as well as that, concomitant, of uncertainty, also appear in different versions. Thus, in the first chronological phase, a process of autonomization of the EC (vis-à-vis mostly its member states), on the one hand, and the strong acknowledgment of the other's demands, on the other, constitute the background of a hierarchical responsibility. It is a responsibility that has a strong root in the past but also looks toward the future in a very open effort to reduce uncertainty through a (but not one only) linear vision of history.[30]

In the 1970s, the EC was responsible for the development of the ACP; it even had a *political will* to promote this, an element of the political identity of the EC that will interestingly later fade away, precisely as the political character of the EC is strengthened. This evolution can be encountered in the more general development discourse of the "international community" in the later years—when things tend to increasingly appear as inevitable and out of reach of any actor's will, as with globalization. In the 1970s, however, the responsibility of the EC is openly a matter of *wanting* to assume it—and it is, to a large extent, a responsibility for the future. Thus, the EC emerges as an autonomous actor through the performance of this responsibility.

This responsibility of the EC for itself, as Derrida would have it, has however an easily discernible origin in the responsibility toward (response to) the developing countries: the negotiating position of the ACP group is very strong, and its demands are acknowledged, praised, and answered. But acknowledging the other's demand does not eliminate inequality. In some sense, it can be surmised that the other's demand is somehow always inscribed in an inequality, the attribution of responsibility being thus the prerogative of the powerful. It is on such grounds that the powerful, and in this case the EC, can have a duty, as it were, to be responsible. Once again, this hints at autonomy as a prerequisite of responsibility, since autonomy (or freedom or, in some instances, independence) is generally understood to be a condition determining power.

As time passes and we advance toward the emergence of global responsibility, a movement that is inverse to the previous one takes place: autonomy becomes evident, and this is the case not only for the EC/EU, but also for the ACP. At the same time, however, the demand of the other—the ACP—is gradually vanishing with regard to responsibility. Indeed, during the 1980s the exercise of autonomization of the EC is being completed and the attribution of responsibility starts shifting to a less hierarchical understanding. Responsibility is now surrounded by notions pointing more to equality, like interdependency. If one depends on the other, then both are equally prone to ask for a response, a certain responsibility: this is best illustrated by the broader shift in the answer to the question of what can be done for the developing countries: from giving to sharing. Responsibility, too, starts to appear as something that can be shared.

To share a responsibility immediately points at a situation where both (or more) actors involved are equally autonomous, according to the common-sense understanding. It is an attribution of autonomy onto the "developing countries." However, in a sense anything else than the self-attribution of autonomy (and thus responsibility) amounts to robbing away autonomy: what is given with one hand is taken with the other—autonomy should only be conceived as emanating from the autonomous. There are numerous examples in the international life of how this is not so, starting with the strive for *recognition* of peoples, nations, or territories by the international community. But if autonomy so crucially depends on others, should we not talk about heteronomy?

In the 1990s, the trend toward egalitarian responsibility is strengthened, as this shared responsibility is increasingly mentioned. In a context of dismissal of Marxist claims and suspicion vis-à-vis strictly liberal approaches, it becomes difficult to decide what this responsibility *of all,* this *shared* responsibility, and ultimately this *global* responsibility mean. There are, however, some indices that help form an overall picture.

The first and more straightforward is that the African renaissance does not take place as was expected: the economic situation of the countries of the continent on the whole deteriorates. At the same time, there is internally, in the ACP countries, a multiplication of new movements and an intensification of those already existent, that criticize not only the hierarchical attribution of responsibility in the EU-ACP relations, but also the lack of accountability of their governments. This coincides with a wider return of "ethics" in development studies and policies, and with an increasing sense of a theoretical and practical impasse in the area. As a consequence, the place of ecological and environmental issues in the wider development agenda becomes bigger, as do gender and children's issues. For the EU, equality stops being an assumption and becomes an aim to be achieved.

In this context, the egalitarian responsibility that is the 1990s' trademark is a responsibility borrowing elements from conceptual *frameworks* that pertain to the market and to civic organization.[31] In the first case—the market—responsibility belongs *to each.* Here, one perceives the influence of liberal proceduralism that offers no legal correctives to power inequalities. In the second, wholly different case of the civic world, all are responsible for all. The world is viewed as one and there is a certain understanding, shared by all, of how this world should be. The links binding the developed and the developing countries are extremely strong—and the responsibility ensuing falls on all in order for the weaker to be supported (see note 26). In development, responsibility takes on different faces.

## Power and the Attribution of Responsibility

Apart from the conceptual level, which remains mesmerizing in that it shows how vague, ambiguous, or equivocal responsibility is, there are very practical political matters that beg the question of the concept's usage. For example, as Zygmunt Bauman and others point out, the issue of responsibility was shockingly absent or devoid of any possibility of application in the bombings of Kosovo. The Persian Gulf War provoked the same type of questioning, as is witnessed by Michael Walzer's new preface to his book *Just and Unjust Wars* or in Jean Baudrillard's *The Gulf War Did Not Take Place.*[32]

The mere evidence of a priori justification of different situations by means of responsibility should be a sign of a certain distancing of the Europeans from crude power politics. In another, more methodological way, we could disregard any problematization in terms of intentionality (something always underlying an analysis is terms of power politics), simply because very often trying to find out what the intentions are does not reveal much either about relations of power or about their consequences. In any case, whether or not intervention takes place, whether or not it is a moral one ("new moral interventionism"), it can be questioned without reference to some hidden layer of reality.

Nevertheless, if it can be done by means other than from a power-politics framework, a reflection on power is unavoidable in the context of a discussion on responsibility in development because of the simple question of who attributes responsibility. Indeed, underlining that responsibility is (also) determined heteronomously, as it were, is not a full answer to this question for one fundamental reason: that as with any decision, the decision to attribute responsibility is ultimately a decision that is taken by someone, and thus we must at least ask by whom this decision is taken. In other words, is there someone responsible for attributing responsibility? (The importance of looking at responsibility as a judgment, rather than as a fact, becomes evident.) This issue is none other than that of democracy and its procedures, and it amounts to asking what sort of democracy, if any, is at play in times when international intervention is as intense as it is in the cases of war, humanitarian assistance, or development.

These are perennial questions of political philosophy—in the sense of a necessity to keep democracy as a horizon while at the same time striving for its constant amelioration—that can never fully be answered. In the meantime, with changing historical contexts, the efforts to give answers to these questions change and so, to a certain extent, do the questions. Thus, in the historical period that is ours, we must, for instance, deal with a particular configuration of the international scene, greatly different than the one before 1989 and that, to give another example, is characterized by a new type of war.[33] Who, in this wholly new context, attributes responsibility is absolutely crucial to an understanding of this configuration. We can thus ask an interminable series of questions, such as who decides that there is no responsibility involved for such and such unfortunate mistake in the war, but also who decides who is responsible? Who decides that there is a responsibility of a certain part of the planet to give aid to another part of the planet? Who decides that the other part of the planet is responsible for itself? Perhaps more relevantly, who decides that responsibility should be global? Three aspects of this type of questioning are considered, as they cut across all these areas.

The first issue is that of the emerging "global social movement." The adjective "global" has been added to the previous "civil society" that referred to the intrastate situation. If this intrastate/interstate analogy were to be strictly maintained, then we would have to ask which is the global government to which global civil society corresponds.[34] Before attempting to answer this, we must observe that, in terms of responsibility, one of the evolutions regarding nongovernmental organizations (NGOs) is the crystallization of a rupture within global civil society, between, to put it quickly, radicals and reformists.[35]

In relation to responsibility, and a fortiori global responsibility, two questions follow: the first one is that of a co-opted civil society. Thus, the remedy to the problem of nonaccountability of the international financial institutions—a pervasive feature of the politics of structural adjustment programs (SAPs)—seems fallacious. With the new discourse of participation, responsibility is reported onto those (the co-opted civil society) who participate in the poverty reduction strategy process, the successor of the SAPs. Such a distortion of responsibility is unacceptable not only because the actual input of "civil society" organizations is minimal—and sometimes amounts to approving given documents—but mainly because it is always, without exception, the financial institutions that have the initiative of the programs (even of their format): responsibility should thus not even be shared, but fully endorsed by these institutions.

There is a second question that concerns NGOs' responsibility. Despite the certain social and community needs to which these organizations set out to give voice, and despite their undoubted participation in rendering a society (an international society?) more pluralistic, their lack of any sort of democratic mandate cannot be ignored. One does not need to resort to an old sort of (party) politics to see how, at a certain moment—precisely the moment when these organizations are deemed to "share" responsibility for certain policies—the question of their "representativity" or a more direct mandate for decision making ("in the name of") is posed. Thus, although it is inevitable and right that such organizations have found their own autonomy, as it were, instead of being "robbed" of it, they are faced with a fundamental problem of responsibility.

Another important aspect of responsibility in an international context concerns the very existence of the international community. In the globalization era, the reality of this international community must be problematized, as Bauman suggests in a thought-provoking paper on war.[36] This line of argument can be questioned by pointing out that the name of the international community is used on an everyday basis in every Third World country—and that it is attached to affairs that, though they might seem to represent only a small part of the northern, Western, or developed world's budget and interests, are woven in the daily practices and discourses of anyone and anything concerned with politics in a country not belonging to the "developed" world. For politicians, academics, or NGO members that live on a part of the planet that is not "developing," it might be almost impossible to imagine how present the international community is in other settings.

Hence, whether there is indeed anything like a "real" international community becomes, to a certain extent, an irrelevant question. The workings of "the myth" of an international community are far too real, in terms of which policies should be followed, how democracy is to be attained, what human rights must be protected, and how development should become the business (in every sense) of the people who are exposed to all the above. Here, the question of responsibility must once again be viewed strategically: there must be an international community since there must be a responsibility that can be attributed to it by the people subjected to decisions taken in its name.

Apart from a practical and crucial concern with who (in the name of international community) should endorse responsibility in local settings, however, a widely shared view holds that the absence of a horizon of global law transforms the interventions of the international community into a mere veil under which the crudest power politics must be at play. In the light of this possibility, the debate of sovereignty-solidarity, also at the origin of the welfare state, is crucial.

As David Chandler shows, international law—with its cornerstone, sovereignty—is being increasingly pushed aside in the name of international justice—with its cornerstone, the "duty" for intervention.[37] In the first case, international society (the society of nation-states) is the conceptual framework; in the second, it is the ambiguous global civil society. But if sovereignty seems a rather old excuse for the absence/refusal of intervention, one might want to consider that at least when it was a valid excuses there were no casualties without a corresponding responsibility (responsible person). Thus, there is a struggle against sovereignty that is founded on the ethical principle of a duty for intervention—the self-attribution of who must bear this type of duty is done by those who have the prerogative and the capacity to intervene. This new "return of morality" could be nothing more than unavowed (power) politics, a view espoused on other occasions by thinkers as different as Cornelius Castoriadis or Walzer.[38] But, although the suspicion remains strong, our attention could once again be shifted to the exact way in which responsibility is being used. In a situation like the bombings of Kosovo or Iraq, is there a serious basis for an argument of global responsibility? Or does the designation of the enemy, an exclusion, erase such a globality?

## Responsibility in Time

The third question on responsibility in the international context considers the affinity between war, humanitarian assistance, and development. From a certain point of view, war (time parenthesis), humanitarian assistance (urgency), and development (stages) are interventions on time and memory; as such, they face resistance. The most telling case is that of development, not least because its "time" lies at the heart of the concept and because it has been much theorized by any social and political theorist who was pre-occupied with social change outside the north. For our purposes, the way responsibility has participated in this intervention on time is interesting. There are two separate aspects of this issue.

The first is that responsibility has been increasingly divided between responsibility *ex ante* and responsibility *ex post*. If it is analytically possible to distinguish between these two times (I accept to be held responsible in the future *or* I am judged responsible for the past), it is practically impossible to do so, on the basis of the common autonomy-understanding of responsibility. Indeed, responsibility *ex ante,* as, for example, in Weber's ethic of responsibility, takes into account a responsibility *ex post.* In other words, a politician adopting an ethic of responsibility is now a politician who accepts the possibility of being held responsible for his or her later actions. This double understanding has prevailed in development discourse.

However, with the introduction of global responsibility these two times of responsibility become separable as a rule. Indeed, global responsibility can only be a responsibility *ex ante*—one can hardly see how all things and people global would be held responsible as in the case of a government that is democratically accountable. It is a responsibility for the future rather than the past. This raises a question on the practical application of accountability "in the name of." The cases of "wars in the era of globalization," as well as the ongoing development practices, reveal the lacunae of this global reasoning.

I will conclude with the second aspect of this question, which concerns the tendency of global responsibility to produce a radical rupture from the previous era—it is closely linked to its facing only the future. In this sense, this is a responsibility that works against memory too, and in particular in the European development discourse, against the (post)colonial memory. To use our initial vocabulary of power in relation to responsibility, the question of power (and power politics) does not cease to be posed once the—dubious—end of realism is decreed. On the opposite, it is perhaps more intensely present in locations such as that of memory and, more precisely, when there is a certain imposition of forgetting. But such an imposition inevitably provokes resistance, and it is in this resistance that we must look for the emergence of a more precise meaning of global responsibility or for its substitution by more precise responsibilities.

# Notes

I am grateful to Armin Rabitsch, Bettina Scholdan, and Peter Wagner for their suggestions.

1. Pietro Metastasio, libretto for Christoph Gluck's *La Clemenza di Tit*, in Cecilia Bartoli, *Gluck Italian Arias*, track 1, DECCA, 2001. Translation is from the record booklet.

2. See David Chandler, "International Justice," *New Left Review* 6 (November–December 2000): 55–66.

3. This is one reading of Antigone's revolt. Romantically, she has been seen as the emblem of the individual against the oppression of the state.

4. See John Stuart Mill for the period of the second colonialist wave:

This doctrine [of liberty] is meant to apply only to human beings in the maturity of their faculties. We are not speaking of children, or of young persons below the age. . . . Those who are still in a state to require being taken care of by others, must be protected against their own actions as well as against external injury. For the same reason, we may leave out of consideration those backward states of society in which the race itself may be considered at its nonage. . . . Despotism is a legitimate mode of governance in dealing with barbarians, provided the end be their improvement, and the means justified by actually effecting that end.

See John Stuart Mill, *On Liberty* (London: Dent, 1964), p. 73. For the contemporary equivalent in U.S. foreign policy, see Roxanne Lynn Doty, *Imperial Encounters: The Politics of Representation in North-South Relations* (Minneapolis: University of Minnesota Press, 1996), pp. 128–137.

5. In this chapter, "heteronomy" does not carry the customary negative connotations of imposition of a hegemonic (external) law.

6. Derrida writes on responsibility:

On the one hand, the history of responsibility is tied to a history of religion. But there is always a risk in acknowledging a history of responsibility. On the basis of an analysis of the very concepts of responsibility, freedom or decision, it is often thought that to be responsible, free or capable of deciding cannot be something that is acquired, something conditioned or conditional. Even if there is undeniably a history of freedom or responsibility, such a historicity, it is thought, must remain extrinsic.

See Jacques Derrida, "Secrets of European Responsibility," in Jacques Derrida, *The Gift of Death*, trans. David Wills (Chicago: University of Chicago Press, 1992), pp. 1–34, 5.

7. The discussion on blameworthiness is inspired by Marion Smiley, *Moral Responsibility and the Boundaries of Community, Power and Accountability from a Pragmatic Point of View* (Chicago: University of Chicago Press, 1992), pp. 4–14, 72–92.

8. William E. Connolly, *The Terms of Political Discourse* (Oxford: Robertson, 1983), chapter 3.

9. Smiley, *Moral Responsibility and the Boundaries of Community*.

10. On the relation of the individual-state(s) in Kant, see Fernando R. Tesón, "Kantian International Liberalism," in David R. Mapel and Terry Nardin, eds., *International Society, Diverse Ethical Perspectives* (Princeton, N.J.: Princeton University Press, 1998), pp. 103–113; see also Doty, *Imperial Encounters*, p. 120.

11. That is, for instance, Cornelius Castoriadis's view—a recurrent theme of his work, "But we cannot reiterate that the question will remain intractable so long as autonomy is understood in the Kantian sense, that is, as a fictively autarchic subject's conformity to a 'Law of Reason,' in complete misrecognition of the social-historical conditions for, and the social-historical dimension of, the project of autonomy." See Cornelius Castoriadis, "Individual, Society, Rationality, History," in Cornelius Castoriadis, *Philosophy, Politics, Autonomy* (Oxford: Oxford University Press, 1991), pp. 47–80, 75.

12. See Peter Wagner, *Theorizing Modernity* (London: Sage, 2001), chapters 2–3.

13. See Derrida, "Secrets of European Responsibility," p. 24; see also Jacques Derrida, "Force of Law: The 'Mystical Foundation of Authority,'" in Drucilla Cornell, Michel Rosenfeld, and David Gray Carlson, eds., *Deconstruction and the Possibility of Justice* (New York: Routledge, 1992), pp. 3–67.

14. Even Bauman illustrates his discussion of responsibility and development with an example where a child asks his mother what to do. See Zygmunt Bauman, "On Universal Morality and the Morality of Universalism," *The European Journal for Development Research* 10, no. 2 (December 1998): 7–18. Let me add that by contrast to the relation between responsibility and autonomy, that the relation between autonomy and knowledge is as old as the Old Testament and not characteristic of a secular context. In addition, how are we to take into account that "*ignorantia legis no excusant*" is a principle that takes the form of adage or even law in many contexts? The necessity of this principle in the face of the possibility of dubious excuses is clear. It implies that whether one ignores or not something that one is supposed to know is irrelevant: the law is applicable, and responsibility at stake. It is slightly different from what I say, following Derrida, that ignorance/uncertainty is always part of the decision and that it is also on the basis of this ignorance/uncertainty that the decision is taken. And that, therefore, responsibility ensues.

15. See Derrida, "Force of Law"; David Campbell, "The Deterritorialization of Responsibility, Levinas, Derrida, and Ethics after the End of Philosophy," *Alternatives* 19 (1994): 455–484.

16. Primo Levi, *Moments of Reprieve* (London: Abacus, 1987), pp. 149–160. A normative horizon of emancipatory knowledge can be maintained, as was done with autonomy. See Boaventura de Sousa Santos, "On Oppositional Postmodernism," in Ronaldo Munck and Denis O'Hearn, eds., *Critical Development Theory: Contributions to a New Paradigm* (London: Zed, 1999), pp. 29–43, 36.

17. Jacques Derrida, *Politics of Friendship*, trans. George Collins (London: Verso, 1997), p. 250.

18. Derrida, *Politics of Friendship*, p. 250.

19. Daniel Warner, "An Ethic of Responsibility in International Relations and the Limits of Responsibility/Community," *Alternatives* 18 (1993): 431–452.

20. R. B. J. Walker, *Inside/Outside: International Relations As Political Theory* (Cambridge: Cambridge University Press, 1993), p. 58.

21. Gerrit W. Gong, *The Standard of "Civilization" in International Society* (Oxford: Oxford University Press, 1984).

22. Heteronomy is at play in this alterity, not because it is in any way the absolute law "of the other" (with all the tyrannical potential that it carries) that is at play. On the contrary, it is perhaps even a prerequisite that this possibility of demand-response be instituted in a social-imaginary way. But exactly because of this (imaginary) moment of institution of society, the "other" is defined strictly as the other for whom the law exists, whom the law protects. It is in this sense that in the situation where

responsibility is at stake, the law will be the other's. This is confirmed by Derrida's example of the institutional alterity, which is—as will be seen—precisely, law. From a strategic point of view, heteronomy can be conceived as the condition of response, because if responsibility (as accountability) is instituted to counter unlimited power, then it must be the law of the weaker (the one who demands) that is operating. In this respect, see Derrida's own words, "I would be tempted, up to a certain point, to compare the concept of justice—which I'm here trying to distinguish from law—to Levinas's . . . *because of the heteronomic relation to others*, to the faces of otherness that govern me, whose infinity I cannot thematize and *whose hostage I remain.*" See Derrida, "Force of Law," p. 22, emphasis added.

23. Denise Egea-Kuehne, "The Challenge of Freedom in Eastern Europe: Derrida's Ethics of Affirmation and Educational Responsibility," in Ursula E. Beitter, ed., *The New Europe at the Crossroads* (New York: Peter Lang, 1999), pp. 25–38, 28.

24. Campbell, "Deterritorialization of Responsibility," p. 468. But as Campbell underlines in his discussion on the "deterritorialization of responsibility," both authors see in alterity the basis for ethics and responsibility.

25. Derrida, "Force of Law," p. 252.

26. This remark's fruitfulness should not be ignored just because of the long-standing discussion between communitarians and their opponents. Abandoning the crucial concept of community, in the sense of Hannah Arendt's common world, because it has been used in infelicitous ways seems an unfortunate choice: this has implications in the advocacy of a solidaric development world.

27. The "domestic analogy" sees the relation between the individual and the state as the model for the relation between the state and the states.

28. For instance, see Jacques Derrida, *The Other Heading*, trans. Pascale-Anne Brault and Michael B. Nass (Bloomington: Indiana University Press, 1992); see also Derrida, "Force of Law" (in particular its postscript).

29. A crucial difference exists with Levinas who, as Campbell notes, has casually and in repeated instances restricted the notion of the other to the neighbor—and, in one case, shockingly excluding Israeli responsibility for Palestinians. Apart from every other implication, this is radically at odds with the Levinasian proclaimed confusion of the other and "I." See Campbell, "Deterritorialization of Responsibility," p. 466. On this point, I might also add that Derrida's insistence of keeping one and the other separated, as mentioned earlier, can be thought as part of the more general antitotalitarian effort of deconstruction. This is also a way of reading social and political theoretical approaches that privilege (theoretically) dispute over solidarity and plurality of justifications over consensus. See Luc Boltanki and Laurent Thévenot, *De la justification: Les économies de la grandeur* (Paris: Gallimard, 1991).

30. References to the colonial past, or the absence thereof, serve as a significant sign for the direction of change in the discourse: this is close to the reflection on time and responsibility at the end of this chapter. The gradual disappearance of these references is concomitant to the EU's autonomization. See Nathalie Karagiannis, "Giving Development: Responsibility and Efficiency in the European Development Discourse towards the ACP States (1970s-1990s)" (Ph.D. diss., European University Institute, Florence, 2002), p. 148.

31. For an original mapping of different social worlds and the justifications functioning within each, see Boltanki and Thévenot, *De la justification.*

32. Michael Walzer, *Just and Unjust Wars: A Moral Argument with Historical Illustrations*, 3rd ed. (New York: Basic, 2000); Jean Baudrillard, *The Gulf War Did Not Take Place*, trans. Paul Patton (Bloomington: Indiana University Press, 1995).

33. This is epitomized both by the September 11, 2001, terrorist attacks on New York and Washington and by the response to them.

34. But currents as influential as Foucauldian poststructuralism or Gramscian Marxism have insisted on the possibility of thinking of society not as "fixated on notions of the state." See Laura Chrisman and Patrick Williams, "Colonial Discourse and Post-colonial Theory: An Introduction," in Patrick Williams and Laura Chrisman, eds., *Colonial Discourse and Post-colonial Theory: A Reader* (New York: Harvester Wheatsheaf, 1995), pp. 1–20.

35. One could argue that such "reformists versus radicals" debates are rather usual in resistance movements or even politics more generally. But this debate has a particular significance, not least because of its massive scale. Manifestations like those evident in the mass demonstrations that took place in Seattle, Gothenburg, or Genoa make more noise than one can hear about civil society in other settings. The debate within this global civil society is thus emblematic both of a certain unavoidable horizon of politics and resistance and of a novelty relevant to the mobility and rapidity of the networks, the great capacity for mobilization, the domains they cover, and their origins (the mythologization of the "grassroots"), as well as the areas they cut across (e.g., the national territories).

36. Zygmunt Bauman, "Wars in the Globalization Era," *European Journal of Social Theory* 4, no 1 (February 2001): 11–28.

37. Chandler, "International Justice."

38. Cornelius Castoriadis, "Le cache-misère de l'éthique," in *La montée de l'insignifiance* (Paris: Seuil, 1996), pp. 206–220; Walzer, *Just and Unjust Wars*.

# 10

## Reflections on the War on Terrorism

*Daniela Ingruber*

Interpretation is that which, shattering appearances and the play of manifest discourse, will set meaning free by remaking connections with latent discourse.[1]

### The End of Innocence

The implementation of the European Convention on Human Rights and Fundamental Freedoms has been one of the most important steps taken toward normal life after World War II. After the horror of the Holocaust and an unimaginably cruel war where civil society suffered tremendously, human rights seemed like a symbol of hope for new generations. During the last few decades, the Western idea of human rights started its image tour around the world. Human rights turned more and more into a global commitment. Optimists thought that this triumphal march would not end anywhere else but at the global acceptance of those Western human rights. The dream was the following: a new form of innocence in political and social action would come into being, and a new form of human being would emerge, though this time in a completely new shape with new attitudes.

Then one of those incidents happened that are powerful enough to change the world and even mark the end of an era. The terrorist attacks on September 11, 2001, created not only a tremendous humanitarian catastrophe, with various political and economic consequences on a global level, but also marked the end of innocence. This meant a change in every tiny detail of life. It meant fear in previously ordinary situations, such as traveling by airplane, using elevators, and visiting skyscrapers. Later terrorist attacks, like the one against a hotel in Kenya on November 28, 2002, perpetuated the fear without repeating the shock. September 11 changed the psychological situation of at least two entire societies—North America and Europe—and the consequences that followed the event will be felt for quite a while. Even watching the news reached a new dimension: who could get the pictures of terrorism out of his or her head? But who ever saw pictures of the war against terrorism proving its achievements?

Since that day, life has changed in many places. Within hours after the collapse of the World Trade Center (WTC) and parts of the Pentagon, the word "war" formed the headline of every television station and newspaper. First, the attacks were called the "war against America," then the title switched to the "war on terrorism," soon afterward, it became clear that the word "war" meant more than a polemic headline on the news. Nothing less than human rights themselves became an object of that state of war.[2] The terrorists responsible for the attacks supposedly wanted to destroy monuments that embodied Western culture and values. The twin towers of the WTC were a fabulous representation of capitalism and its power throughout the world; another symbol—one encapsulating military power—was the Pentagon. By killing 3,000 people, the terrorists knew that the West—respectively in this case the United State of America—would react and would have to react. They probably also knew that the reaction against terrorism would weaken another symbol of the West: human rights. Their theory came true when the collapse of the WTC and parts of the Pentagon led to political measures that not only strengthened the war against terrorism, but also weakened civil rights by passing new laws on surveillance instruments and opportunities.[3]

The lesson to learn leads to a reflection on human rights that accepts that their interpretation is anything but objective. Behavior considered a human rights abuse by one group may be acceptable to others. Many studies about human rights and their future within the so-called war on terrorism have been written, all of them offering important thoughts but no solution for the question which part of human rights could be sacrificed for security measures or to determine the point in time when a humanitarian intervention turns into a simple war (even though it might be a war on terrorism).

I acknowledge the changes, but one has to admit that events only have the power to "change the world" if people let them change it. This normally happens by talking about them repeatedly and looking at the same pictures over and over again, trying to understand but without any kind of deep reflection. In times of catastrophes, there is no time to reflect, no chance to think about the incidents with the necessary distance. Any attempt at reflection stays at best fragmentary. How should it be possible to reflect on something unbelievable, something that goes beyond human understanding and whose consequences have only started to unfold, but will be felt for many years?

Events may be powerful on a general scale, but eventually it is civil society, together with the system of mass media, that lends power to events in a way that influences opinion more than necessary. Hannah Arendt illuminates these workings with her definition of power: power is offered to a person, another group, or an event by a particular set of people.[4] Once this group denies power to someone, that person can still be strong but will be powerless in respect to that group. Keeping this in mind, it seems especially important to consider the globalization and monopolization of the mass media. In the Western world, there are more or less seven big press agencies deciding on the agenda of world news. It is they who determine the influence of a message. A Reuters headline, for example, will be a headline in many newspapers throughout the Western world, featuring the same images, the same headline, and the same interpretation to a global audience, regardless of state boundaries.[5]

Many Western people have certain "concrete" images in their mind, images that tell the story of the so-called important news of a specific time. For some, it may be the Vietnam War, for others the Prague Spring, and for others the Solidarity movement in Poland or the fall of the Berlin Wall. Some pictures became so famous that they influenced a part of people's lives and now belong to their personal history, even if they just know them from the news. One example is the little girl Kim Phuc in the Vietnam War who runs down a street, trying to flee, wearing no clothes but plenty of tears. Millions of people have her facial expression imprinted on their minds. For two or three generations, September 11, 2001, will be a similar shared mental image. That day, terrorism entered living rooms through TV sets. The images of the airplanes crashing into the WTC killing thousands by now form a collective memory of that day.

What, however, about the Pentagon and the plane that crashed in Pennsylvania? Why do we tend to forget that several hundred human beings died in the Pentagon building or in another hijacked plane the same day? The answer is cruel but simple: there were fewer pictures about it on TV, and even worse, there do not exist any pictures in real time. Hearing about an event at the Pentagon after having seen the pictures of two airplanes destroying both the geographical center of capitalism and uncountable human lives at the same time is too little to form a collective memory. At the WTC, there were many witnesses at the very moment when it occurred. Although we merely received reports about the other incidents, without concrete pictures of the Pentagon or the crash of the fourth hijacked plane, the latter one entered people's consciousness when TV stations broadcasted the last phone calls of the passengers. But, in regard to the WTC, the TV consumer did not only receive visual images. Some TV stations were cynical enough to broadcast the last phone calls of policemen or firefighters buried below the leftovers of the buildings. The audience heard their desperate words, their last breaths, and, of course, the silence of their deaths.

But the capacity to accept victims is limited. After learning of a certain number of victims, the individual fate cannot be understood any more; even mourning the individual gets impossible without knowing the victim personally. Death then turns into a mere figure, allowing voyeurism to easily take the disguise of the charity and compassion many felt after September 11. In most cases, the distinction between these three emotions vanishes. This is exactly the moment where politics can come in to tell the audience that someone has to strike back against terrorism; at that moment of shock the acceptance of counterviolence is the highest. The media and politics around the Western world cooperated perfectly, drawing pictures of the "good guys" on the one side and the "bad guys" on the other side; black-and-white paintings re-emerged rapidly. No human rights convention protected Western/U.S. citizens from falling for those stereotypes. As the Human Rights Watch wrote in a report, "Instead, the country has witnessed a persistent, deliberate, and unwarranted erosion of basic rights against abusive governmental power that are guaranteed by the U.S. Constitution and international human rights law. Most of those directly affected have been non-U.S. citizens."[6]

Another extraordinary element of the images of that day is related to the basics of life in the modern world: for the first time we, as Westerners, could convince ourselves on TV that our much praised technologies could not pro-tect us against unexpected manipulation through human intervention. We also can state that we somehow "had" to watch this on TV, as the incidents were so incredible that most of us were watching them over and over again, searching for an answer. Actually, one only saw the proof on TV that there is no protection that could emerge from the hyperarmament of secret services and the further development of the most modern war machines. The risk of human failure and human manipulation is unpredictable. The fragility of human existence in the age of technology still depends more on the educa-tion of those working with technology than on the machines themselves.

In general, fragility is nothing bad as long as we can accept it. Western civilization has ignored it for ages. The idea of infallibility brought about fallibility. It has led to false calculations and false, unjustified confidence in what cannot be controlled completely; technology and the belief therein. It seems ironic that the very media that had been presenting the miracles of technical progress now were the ones to show the uncontrollable telecast about the powerlessness of technological control.

Could it be that since September 11 the media now has a new role? I recognize a surprising unity within Western governments, not in the sense of a state interfering with the media, but more the way the issue of control through technology has been dealt with. People's belief in the project of modernity sank a little after September 11. In order to keep their faith alive, some sort of damage control had to be found. Criticism was seen as the wrong tool, even if the criticism itself was not directly related to the inci-dents of terrorism. A good example was a study conducted by several U.S. newspapers about a new count of votes in Florida for the last presidential election. The result was not spectacular, but the newspapers still decided to postpone the publication in order not to trigger a debate about the legitimacy of the U.S. president. As Timothy Besley, Robin Burgess, and Andrea Prat state, "In a democracy, citizens require information that they can use to se-lect politicians who serve their needs and to punish those who do not, other-wise formal democracy has no bite."[7]

For many Europeans, this patriotism of critical newspapers was difficult to understand. Of course, Europe was in a different position. In the end, however, the reactions of anticriticism were similar. Politicians, as well as journalists, functioned like perfect masters of the enlightenment, trying to hinder the population from doubting the project of modernity. The idea of a "we" and an "other," another element of black-and-white paintings, obviously was a perfect tool. Samuel P. Huntington's "The Clash of Civilizations,"[8] strongly criticized in the last years, was suddenly back on the news, this time without much contradiction.

## Fighting Terrorism—The Reinvention of War

As soon as the first shock of September 11 was over, it became obvious that something had to be done. In the beginning, there was only a feeling, not so much an intellectual knowledge. Neither the economic destruction nor the thousands of assassinated human beings could stay unpunished. Each person killed through violence was called one too many. This is common sense. The consequence was that the victims had to be expiated. They were civil victims in a new form of crime: the postmodern war. The only possible answer was another postmodern form of war: a war that was not declared, a war without battlefields, a war without concrete goals, a war without human faces, a war against an unknown enemy that received the virtual face of Osama bin Laden. The terrorists themselves could not get punished. They were dead, having used their bodies like weapons. The conspirators behind this attack had to be found and were assumed to live in Afghanistan. The politicians of numerous countries thought along similar lines: war was necessary to defend human rights! One of George W. Bush's sentences during his speech on October 7, 2001, cleverly related to the common good, "Terrorists are enemies of humanity who deliberately murder innocent people."[9] With these words, the U.S. president defended the then commencing war on terrorism and left no space for war opponents. President Bush went on, "At the same time, the oppressed people in Afghanistan will know the generosity of America and our allies. As we strike military targets, we'll also drop food, medicine and supplies to the starving and suffering men and women and children of Afghanistan."[10] Nobody seemed to have understood the humiliating tendency of these words, that misinterpretation of the human right for food. The United Nations (UN) did not intervene. Its resolutions backed the war on terrorism in a rare way.

I note that many scholars kept extremely quiet. They watched the news, and some wrote articles about how they watched the news, but the clearing work was not done mentally, but physically by firefighters. Was there no time left for the scholarly research of definitions? Politicians need to act, and, in this case, to react. A new kind of intervention was chosen: the war on terrorism. Scholars were not needed to criticize and reflect, but to work on studies about the consequences of a war on terrorism—studies that kept them busy but could be ignored in action by a simple reference to their existence.

In the past, it seemed so easy to define the meaning of an "international intervention," arguments in its favor, and eventually to discover the definition of violence itself. By using "intervention" to impose Western ideas on other political systems, and at the same time renaming it "humanitarian intervention," meanings were blurred: the term "violence," paired with "good intentions," and the legitimization to use violence with best intentions became ambiguous—but this ambiguity also left room for contestation. Could one say today that we thought we knew and tried to do our best, when "we" decided that the humanitarian aspect weighs more than the need to refrain from violence? But who would decide, and who would be critical of interventions as violence? Was there anything like a unified "we" crying for war against Slobodan Milosevic?

Then, after September 11, the definition of what constitutes violence was suddenly reinforced. "We" are against terrorism, "we" want to fight terrorism—these are statements that allow for no opposition. The fact that some members of civil society—a different "we"—would use other measures against terrorism than, for example, politicians or military personnel was not part of this process of redefining violence.

War became part of political argumentation. But the so-called war on terrorism soon turned into an ordinary war against the Taliban in Afghanistan, trying to free the people who had been suffering different forms of occupation and civil war for the last twenty years. Suddenly, the media became interested in women's rights in a region where nongovernmental organizations (NGOs) had been fighting in vain for years to put the dismal situation of women on the international agenda. There was a sudden abundance of reports on the extreme violation of women's rights under the Taliban regime. A war in the name of human rights emerged, but weren't human rights being again violated in their own name? Hundreds of thousands of refugees tried to escape the bombings;[11] the freedom fighters of the Northern Alliance killed hundreds of civilians on their way to Kabul. Warlords took over in the shadow of liberation and airplanes dropped bombs as well as food, simultaneously killing and nourishing the Afghan people. The thoughtlessness of this double-blind act verged on the edge of cynicism. People all over the world sat in front of their TV sets, trying to witness, imagining being part of the so-called just war or revenge. Bush articulated their hopes perfectly, "Peace and freedom will prevail."[12] Who, however, defines freedom and peace at a moment when war starts? Who would have imagined a situation where truth was folded and torn in such a way to fit into war-speak, all of this in the name of human rights?

At the same time, never before was it easier to manipulate reports from a war zone and to manipulate the people reporting. What exactly did we see? Dying children and burqa-covered women trying to flee over 5,000–meter-high mountains into refugee camps without water. We saw fighters of the Northern Alliance as well as people who had been captured and tortured, yet we only saw very few destroyed houses. And finally corpses, the so-called collateral damages, emerged everywhere. Marc W. Herold, in his effort to count the civilian victims,[13] was suspected of antipatriotism in a war considered to be just.

The war took place on territory beyond the battlefields. Battlefields did not even exist in this postmodern war. The enemy was something rather than someone or a concrete country. In a state of war, it is essential to give a face to the enemy—at best an ugly face—to create hatred. This time, bin Laden was seen as the perfect enemy, even before there could be proof of his guilt. Unlike other mass murderers such as Adolf Hitler, Milosevic, or Saddam Hussein, bin Laden simply turned into the essence of evil itself. President Bush defined it this way, "[O]ur responsibility to history is already clear, to answer these attacks and rid the world of evil."[14] Usually, deliverance from evil is associated with religion, and Bush's choice of words on this and countless other occasions shows how much the war on terrorism is regarded as a just war that must be fought in the name of the good.

The European discussions of the events of September 11 were similarly biased, leaving no room for shades of gray or uncertainty. There were those—the very few—who wrote and shouted against the feeling of revenge, and those who stuck to the assumption that a war had to be fought in the name of humanity, even in the name of humanism. They referred to the human rights declaration, to all moral belief and the natural sentiment of justice. It seemed they did not remember that humanity could not be defended with weapons. Humanism has to survive for its own sake, or the best intentions will kill it.

Finally, the war on terrorism was fought not only in central Asia. In the European Union, strict laws that previously could not win legislative majorities were accepted as a measure and tool against terrorism.[15] Europeans accepted the restrictions of their liberties, an intervention into their lives, while bin Laden remained free.

Little consideration was given to the significance of the military and legal protection of human rights, weakening human rights in the name of the defense of democracy and human rights.[16] Democracies rarely go to war against each other. The most vehement wars are fought against enemies that are not considered democracies. Ideology and values enter the equation, influencing people in a way similar to religion. A military intervention only needs to be called "humanitarian" in order to be accepted.

## Losing Human Rights

Terrorism shocks Western societies intensely not only because of its violence, but also with the fact that it threatens their very institutions of freedom. It attempts to destroy them directly and purposefully. It is shocking that these institutions have a lot to offer civil society, but provide no methods and tools for the fight against terrorism, as long as we do not want to abolish the institutions themselves together with terrorism. The difficulty of living in a democracy and fighting wars recalls eternal questions about the honesty of our Western position toward democracy and human rights.

The great strength of humanitarian intervention is its appeal to American liberal and European social democratic leaders who find themselves without effective economic policies to promote the social justice they claim to serve, but still need a virtuous cause to distinguish themselves from "the right," presumed to be indifferent to human suffering.[17]

Human rights and democracy are precious values, but they are taboo, with some of their aspects beyond discussion. As consent emerged, they suffered a most significant loss: the freedom to rethink. In the 1990s, when it became acceptable or even heroic to fight wars in the name of human rights, to kill to break the same thing that is called a human right, in the name of human rights, an avenue to the war on terrorism was opened.

Any war touches on human rights. The danger of destroying them forever accompanies every single bomb being dropped with the purpose to destroy and/or kill. This is especially true at a time when human rights tend to be summoned as a reason for war. War in the name of human rights is still a war, but not necessarily a just war. Never in human history was there a war we could call just, not even the war against Hitler. It may be called necessary because preventive measures had not been taken early enough. There should be a debate on what constitutes a necessary war, but it needs to be led without out reference to ideology.

The terrorists tried to provoke war. Now they have the proof that the Western system is also a cruel one, not caring too much about the fate of civilians. In August 2002, the Human Rights Watch published a study on U.S. human rights abuses against detainees after September 11.[18] Many of those detainees were sent to prison simply because they looked like Arabs. Not much was heard about those persons again, whereas Guantánamo became a symbol for the cruelty of postmodern international interventions.

All over the world, former pacifists said for the first time after a very long time that sometimes it is unavoidable to use violence in the fight against violence. September 11 closed the ranks: people in the Western world, but also in other parts of the world, knew they had to fight against terrorism, and they let their governments do it. What kind of war was this? What kind of violence targets terrorists but affects civilians?

Scholars are searching for definitions of violence and war, because even if we, as civilians, do not understand (or do not want to understand) the reasons behind violence or war, we need definitions, first of all in order to express ourselves, but also to defend our ideas about violence and its legitimate use.

Talking about human rights logically means to eventually talk about violence. Breaking any kind of human right is always violent, mostly expressed in the violent act of depriving someone of his or her personal liberty. Human rights should protect people, though this is not always what they do. Wolfgang Sützl writes, "Human rights, first designed to regulate the behavior of governments in relation to their citizens, now play an increasing role in enabling governments to regulate each other."[19] As a consequence, human beings—including state rulers—assume the right to regulate other human beings, based on the idea of a superior democracy, but ultimately depending on a balance of power. Eventually, these inflictions on the original purpose of human rights are considered small wounds that have to be accepted in a war fought for the very idea of human rights. Is a fight for human rights based on violence still a fight in the name of human rights? Or is it a simple war?

Human rights are still something filigree, easy to hurt, easy to abuse. Human rights get hurt regularly. Very often they also get abused by politics and economics, but not only in the way of direct and daily abuses, which we hear about. Many times one does not even read or hear of these abuses in the media, as many of them seem to be too ordinary, not sufficiently spectacular for the world of news.

Human rights get abused as an institution in and of itself, if they are used as an excuse for revenge. Still, they seem extraordinarily important to us, given that even ancient rules of international law, such as sovereignty, are questioned in their name. Going to war with the idea of fighting for freedom, democracy, and human rights will ultimately lead to the demolition of those cherished ideas. The terrorists knew this. And they took a war into account. For them, a human life was worth nothing at all. It is the world's various cultures, though, that understand the value of life. If politics dares to use those values as a tool and, in the worst case, as a military tool, they threaten human beings and destroy the work of hundreds of years to end the circle of violence.

The defense of Western values can only be found in other ways. Those values have to be reflected before politics can find an appropriate method to defend "our" freedom. Otherwise the West will end up with leftovers of something we used to call freedom and human rights.

But what do we do with this knowledge? Where do we go from here? (And in the "here" there definitely exists a "we" as a shared interest in our common need for freedom.)

One hundred years ago, when the German philosopher Friedrich Nietzsche wrote down his now most popular and mostly misquoted sentence about the death of God, a new religion was already born, but still quite invisible. In the twentieth century, this new religion became more and more powerful, nourishing hopes for a better human life. But suddenly, at the beginning of the twenty-first century, this religion, too, is in deep crisis. This new religion was human rights. Remembering Nietzsche, we often forget the exact quote and interpret it as a tale about the death of God. Nietzsche, however, talks about murder: "Gott ist todt! Gott bleibt todt! Wir haben ihn getödtet!"[20]

On the other hand, today, human rights stand for the "one and single" truth of some still undefined civil society. Ages ago, they were one of the first and most impressive common goods of modernity. One might even consider human rights the natural children of modernity. One of their tasks seems to be to take care of morality once God had lost his power. Like God, human rights are not visible, but contrary to God, they at least become obvious in their absence. This makes it easier to believe in them and increases the urge to act in their name. Like any other religion, human rights have a pool of interests behind them, insinuating what is wrong and what is right. To apply this understanding to the war on terrorism is an easy game for the ones in power.

A new definition that human rights intellectuals try to re-create time and again will not change anything for the better. New tools are needed that go beyond the fixation of meanings. Wim Wenders's movie *The End of Violence*[21] starts with the words "Define violence!" followed by a long break. Wenders does not suggest a definition and it is obvious why. Instead, he shows people trying to fight violence, only to end up frightening, torturing, and murdering. This way he uncovers the cynicism of violence in the name of nonviolence.

**Truth Is the First Victim of War**

Reports about human rights abuses vary in everything but background. The reports resemble one another to the degree of nondistinction. In the cases of Iraq, Turkey, the Congo, or Macedonia, for example, reports about torture and death and pictures of crying refugees, supposedly helpless old people, and dirty and anxious children are all too common. We know the pictures. We recognize the eyes of the starving or frightened children. It was pictures like those that made many people speak out for a military intervention in Kosovo. The staggeringly high number of refugees and potential victims were also used to make Europeans and North Americans believe in the necessity of a North Atlantic Treaty Organization (NATO) intervention. Later, however, it turned out that many of the pictures and stories we saw on TV had been manipulated.

War captures our minds. Those involved cannot be neutral even if they try. The sight of the battlefields, the damages, and the victims leads to a clear opinion about the good and bad sides of war. This impression is not directly related to truth, as truth is one of the first victims in wartime. Journalists agree on the fact that they know about the fragility of truth. Helplessness is the response. All of this, of course, is done in the name of human rights.

If everything can be manipulated, it is us as human beings, more than "anything else," that can be manipulated and misinformed. An ironic detail is that in many cases, we manipulate ourselves by looking at pictures or listening to stories about human rights abuses. It is very easy and tempting to believe in the so-called facts that one seems to see with his or her own eyes.

In reality, however, most of the time, "seeing them with our own eyes" means to look at photographs. As Jean Baudrillard so aptly states, "Photography conveys the state of the world in our absence."[22] It can especially be manipulated to misinform about the so-called reality of a war. The misinforming party is always called the other one, the enemy.

Photography produces a kind of thunderstruck effect, a form of suspense and phenomenal immobility that interrupts the precipitation of events. The freeze-frame is a freezing of the world.[23]

How is this connected to the war on terrorism? For security reasons, civilians are prevented from hearing or seeing anything of the war that would help them understand and judge the actions going on. Citizens of nations at war have to accept the involvement of the Western world in war without hearing or seeing details. Looking at war from this perspective reminds me of wars in antiquity. In those times, the population knew there was a war. And that was it. The news did not bring them information every day. In the end, they would see the surviving soldiers returning home in triumph or in shame, bearing signs of victory or loss. The progress of the war was a secret. Today, civilians are in a similar position, even though we have the technological tools to be witnessing war scenes at any time and in real time. But we are not allowed to. The war fought in the name of the people is fought with the acceptance to lock them out, and yet, all that happens in vain. As Paul Virilio states, "The balance of terror is thus a mere illusion in the industrial stage of war, in which reigns a perpetual imbalance, a constantly raised bid, able to invent new means of destruction without end."[24]

As terrorism disturbs the Western dream of feeling secure, the word "security," as in the Cold War, received a new, important, or nearly miraculous meaning. The necessity to establish security again after September 11 forces all parts of Western society and their allies to sacrifice a piece of their freedom. Censorship was a natural but astonishing and extreme consequence, as it started deliberately. The translation of the bin Laden videos—distinctly different in their German and English versions—is a good example of this permanent manipulation of truth.

Though human, we are well behaved and act cowardly. We do not cry out against the cutting of our basic rights in this world of war. We accept this as a tool against terrorism, not understanding that this is what the terrorists tried to provoke. In the end, only the taboos remain. But taboos are a sign for the end of discussion. How much worse if we accept them deliberately.[25]

## From Victims to Cases of Damage

In every war, language is one of the essential victims. Words turn martial and militant. They tend to exaggerate. They hurt people just as much as weapons. They might get more dangerous because they sometimes use the disguise of an ordinary word but still have the intention to hurt. A physical wound heals. A hostile word walks through our consciousness and comes out unexpectedly.

We all know that. Sometimes, however, we seem to forget that words cannot do anything on their own. It is human beings that use them, in certain cases, like weapons. In the age of (dis)information, we believe in depending on the news, which can be considered ironic in itself. We still trust their words. What else can we do?

Without any coincidence, propagandist lies are regarded as some of the most effective tools of war. With the help of propaganda—simultaneously using the tools of pictures and words—each little incident acquires a surprising meaning. Language is never neutral. Words living in war change their meanings. In the end, we call it war-speak.

Some examples of this war-speak are very well known, like the special one that we all remember from the recent wars in which NATO was involved. In former times, civilians who lost their lives during a war were called victims. In war reports, they were called victims and were mourned. Most recently, in the aftermath of the Persian Gulf War and Kosovo intervention, a quasi-neutral word has emerged for it. The civilians have turned into "collateral damage," a phrase that tells us everything about international collaboration in the name of human rights.

Damage is a leak in a boat, a broken window, a bombed house, a factory that has been burned down. Anything can get damaged. But human beings get wounded and suffer. Certainly, the civilians of today do not get attacked by the defenders of human rights (in this case, NATO). They are left out of the fighting and war strategizing, as only such a behavior can justify warlike commitment in the name of human rights. Civilians are not supposed to die in war. But they might get transformed by collateral damage, which means an unplanned side effect. This is what NATO taught us. And the media as well as the intellectuals assisted perfectly. The really shocking fact is not so much that NATO's public relations department must have invented that striking word, but that the media accepted it nearly without any contradiction in the name of defending human rights.

The intellectuals had a special role in Kosovo. They had been calling for an international intervention for several weeks. They cried out for NATO as if it were the ancient Greek goddess of revenge. As a consequence, they accepted the "collateral damage." They deliberately adopted the word with the intent of hiding the ugly face of war. The generation of 1968 that had been the shining example of peace for so many years whenever it tried to be revolutionary or resistant against its governments also used the phrase, as if it were absolutely natural to do so. Thus, the ideology of collateral damage was developed, constituting a peripheral damage in itself.

In the war on terrorism, intellectuals were supposed to be patriotic and support their governments. None of them seemed to long for silence. Thousands of words were printed. Suddenly, there existed experts on Afghanistan and Iraq. Objectivity was no category in this topic. The new story goes like this: during the search for bin Laden and Saddam Hussein, civilians stood in the way. They could get damaged, without intention, of course. So once again, we call them collateral damage. Others argue that they are equally innocent victims, as those human beings who were murdered on September 11. The suffering of children and civilians, but also the pictures of desperation, provoke contradiction and hatred. And each war (on terrorism) increases the lack of understanding the necessity of those wars.

Of course, the issue of collateral damage can be used as a tool of war as well. Schools and mosques or other civilian buildings tend to be situated close to military targets. The intervening enemy has to make the decision of whether to risk killing innocent civilians or to abandon the target. In this case, geographical proximity denies the possibility to damage only military targets. This is where the camera comes in again, demonstrating its important role. It shows the picture of tortured or murdered civilians. But it also shows the deeds of the Taliban, who were prepared to sacrifice their own people—while one could mention that this sacrifice of the population is considered normal during a state of war (without necessarily condoning it), few newspaper reports did so.

## The Role of the Media

In times of war, there is always intense pressure for reporters to serve as propagandists, rather than journalists. Although the role of the journalist is to present the world in all of its complexity, giving the public as much information as possible in order to facilitate a democratic debate, the propagandist simplifies the world in order to mobilize the public behind a common goal.[26]

The mass media is irreplaceable in its influence on public opinion, and, to a certain extent, it is the media that decides the status of human rights and international intervention, though they themselves are only instruments. On special occasions, governments prefer selected reporting. The war on terrorism made this issue obvious.[27] Exactly in times of crisis, when it is most important to read or hear about facts, media freedom was restricted. Governments and conflicting parties tried to influence and put pressure on the media, restricting its right of free movement. This was one of the democratic abuses during the Persian Gulf War and the Kosovo intervention. It was in this respect that Baudrillard was right to state during the Persian Gulf War what remains true today, "The war is also pure and speculative, to the extent that we do not see the real event that it could be or that it could signify."[28]

In the meantime, governments have learned how to cope with critical media. The latter has to be treated in a more friendly manner. That is what governments do, holding them high, demonstrating a shared responsibility. In the end, it is the newspapers, magazines, and TV programs that allow us to believe in our political system, that use war as a political tool. The media hold the very important role of reporting and analyzing situations. But they also need to reach a large audience, as the World Bank's report *The Right to Tell* mentions.[29]

Consumers of such media reports just learn what they should know, very often in the name of those in power. Their position could not have been different this time. Finally, it is the population who supports and pays the soldiers. They are the ones who provide the government with the power to start or end a war.

Without a network of media supporting the government, the war on terrorism would not be able to take place. This is how politics works. The most cunning representation wins space in the news and gets valuable minutes at prime time. This is very often as a picture instead of as words because pictures tend to be more impressive and suggestive. Baudrillard writes, "The world in itself resembles nothing. As concept and discourse it relates to many other things—as pure object, it is unidentifiable."[30] States and governments (in fact, politicians and spin doctors) know about the power of the media just like civic organizations or civil society. And all of them use this power if they can.

It is especially the new media, the information and communication technologies, that standardize the news. People lose control of distinguishing between truth and lies. Any manipulation is possible with the help of the news media; and many manipulations are already impossible to prove technologically.

What happened to our eyes, our capacity to see? Indeed, we are not only capable, but also prepared to overlook that sometimes behind the picture of terrified faces of people in need lies manipulation, the placing of the photograph and the report in our minds to push through the interests of a particular group. Manipulations or disinformation are the most important tool, no matter whether the "good" or "bad" ones win the prime-time slot. It always happens in the name of something important, something valuable. But this time, there is a difference. There are fewer voices to speak out against the propagandā of war. Reflection is given less weight than usual in wartime.

History makes it easier to reflect on the things that lie in the past. The war on terrorism, on the contrary, is still part of our daily media consumption and daily life. Reflection through mass media is very limited. They are expected to inform us about the latest news. There is always something particularly new or urgent and reflection has to be postponed repeatedly. The velocity of messages turns into an acceleration without a break. The relatively unanimous and uncritical opinion about the reasons behind terrorism results in an even less critical position toward the war on terrorism.

**The Fall of the Peace Movement: The Fall of Civil Society, Too?**

Certainly, human rights and humanism, and even peace, cannot get defended through the means of violence. Walter Benjamin argues that violence can neither be legitimate nor legal.[31] The actual danger for the ones in power, who decide about war or peace, is not so much a counterpower that was thought to be found in civil society. Civil society does not exist in the way of a counteraction anymore. No one is left civilian, since the majority was in favor of war as a form of revenge, thought to be a just decision. Civil society ended up as an actor in the war game, precisely because patriotism asks for unconditional support of the state.

Other persons with different ideas about war and patriotism, speaking up against violence and remembering the moments of the ancient peace movement—a different "we"—were not heard. They also form part of civil society. The peace movement thus still exists, but has spread into thousands of NGOs without any common goal. Each group is talking for itself. Regional and small alliances stay that way. The borders between the internal interests in such movements seem to be higher than the borders between civil society and the ones in power.

There is no one left to talk about substance. The freedom of criticism has been abolished. The voices of peace cannot be heard anymore because the voice of war and international intervention is louder. This is exactly why the terrorists have won already. With the decision to go to war and not to fight with civil tools, the issue of further civil victims was accepted. The peace movement was too shocked to understand the threat. The helplessness of a formerly strong movement made it easier for the ones in favor of war. The peace movement—now called civil society—remained immobile, watching, and paralyzed.

### The Necessity of Reflection with Unusual Tools

The war might be fought already, yet there are still ways to avoid further violence in the name of human rights, falsely called "humanitarian intervention." First of all, those who oppose violence should acknowledge their own helplessness and then speak out. The silence of the "good people" leads to the victory of the "bad ones," only adding to the misery and eventually contributing to a self-fulfilling prophecy. It would be wiser to take one's time for reflection. But it is time that we least have.

A new definition is not enough for human rights. Rather, the process of discussion is an important element. Without it, communication is cut. If the West is actually still interested in changing something in this world and does not only want to appear as a sum of dreaming persons taking care of abused human rights, it needs a culture of talking and exchanging ideas, even if some ideas at the first moment seem provocative. Sützl writes, "One of the traditions of modernity is to view difference as a defect to be corrected."[32]

Immanuel Wallerstein says that science can only predict the past by predicting a posteriori.[33] Huntington sticks to the contrary by telling the future.[34] His most famous article has been quoted over and over again since September 11. The Northern Hemisphere searches for interpretations as to why the

terrorists did what they thought they had to do. The "clash of civilizations" presents a model of various types of cultures. But contrary to
postmodern thinking it argues for strict boundaries. Most fatally, it does
not present any hope for the future. Other interpretations for the reason
behind the terrorist attacks at least offer a model of escape. Actually, however, the idea that neocolonialism and poverty, injustice, and the marginalization of huge numbers of people provoked the violence cannot help us
either. The war on terrorism demonstrated that there is no interest in changing
political views in favor of stopping violence. The chance to rethink global
power politics was not taken. The latest meetings of the World Trade Organization show this in a very sad way.

It seems tempting to assert the error in Huntington's paradigm of a clash
of civilizations, but this will not change the war on terrorism into a less
military one. His ideas are assumed to reflect reality. Even Huntington does
not manage to prove the contrary when he attempts to disassociate himself
from his own ideas.[35] He simply is not heard.

What we call the war on terrorism is, at a minimum, two wars: there is the
one in Afghanistan and another one in Iraq, countries that supposedly give
shelter or support to terrorists. In fact, this war on terrorism is against people,
most of all extremely poor and marginalized people. It does not take much to
imagine that the violence of this war will provoke new hatred against the so-
called civilized nations. In addition, this war diverts much needed funds from
the fight against poverty.

Such war will not help anyone to feel better after the grief of September
11. Neither can the ancient biblical idea of revenge—"an eye for an eye, a
tooth for a tooth"—be seen as fulfilled, because the wrong ones, the civilians, suffer from such war. The liberation of the Afghan people from the
Taliban (or the Iraqis from Hussein's regime) seems to be a necessary and a
humanitarian issue, but the tools are too immense. Whether it leads to something better on a political level will be shown within the next years. By then,
we will understand that the peace process was the crucial factor, not the
bombs on Kabul. In the end, it will be the UN that will present the last bit of
hope for the Afghanis to guarantee maybe not peace, but at least a calmer
atmosphere for the long process of recovery for an entire nation.

The long-term consequences are frightening. The war on terrorism has
turned into a war against the Taliban, which will eventually be seen as a war
against Islam. Together with Huntington's famous paradigm, the bombs stand
for the ignorance and arrogance of the Western world, and it remains doubtful whether they can bring about lasting peace. In the long term, a destabilization in the region, most visibly in Pakistan, but also notable in Kazakhstan
and in Uzbekistan, has become inevitable. The Western countries rushed into
the war in Afghanistan without understanding the responsibility for their allies. Civil society, despite a number of studies and evaluations on the impact

of a war in Afghanistan, still cried for war as the only possible solution it could imagine. And as on September 11, civilians had to die for it.

But the real war on terrorism has to be fought on a different level. Bombs will not save anyone from terrorism. Economics play a much bigger role in that war. The war against Islamic regimes is nothing else than a game to distract people's attention away from the real war on terrorism. In their own countries, the people's civil rights were taken away by measures of surveillance.

The civilians suffering and dying were the collateral damage in that game. The failure of the secret service will lead in two different directions. On the one hand, there is a strong movement, mostly from within the secret service, to invest more money in technologies, to be better prepared next time; and everybody seems to believe in a next time. On the other hand, there exists a small movement that tries to take the crucial chance and change foreign policy. Instead of investing in technology, which limits people's freedom, this movement may seek other paths to fight crime and terrorism.

## Epilogue

No one is immune against barbarity. As human beings, we decide for ourselves who we are by acting and by letting our governments act for us. This is part of democracy, too.

Today, we are not in a position to fully reflect on issues related to the war on terrorism. It might be the work of historians to judge our actions. If the fight against what we judge to be "evil," however, leads to a point where we—as civil society this time—have to give away or ignore those principles that once gave us the power to start fighting against that very "evil," then it is a clear sign that we have to stop. Otherwise, we will end up realizing that we have betrayed ourselves.

We have the opportunity to let the incidents of September 11 and all the following horrible acts of terrorism crush us and, as a consequence, let the terrorists know that they won by destabilizing our interpretations of a peaceful life. In that view, war is the only answer, combined with a number of internal security laws that deprive us of our freedom in favor of bureaucracy and security. Eventually, it depends much more on us than on the terrorists whether terrorism wins or loses. I would rather have it lose.

The best way to let September 11 stay in the collective knowledge is a warning that this shall never happen again. In this case, weapons will not do us any favors. But people living in the North will have to give away Western/ Northern ignorance and try to find the common qualities between cultures, instead of seeing the differences like Huntington does. This does not mean an attempt to eliminate the differences, but to hold up diversity. There is only one possibility to have the terrorists lose, to act in a way they did not expect us to react. They relied on counterviolence and have been right until now. They did not count on respect.

Postmodern thinking has provided the present time with one wonderful tool, the deconstruction of our minds stuck in ways of thinking without exit. The reinterpreting of our acting and thinking and respect for "the other" could be such a deconstruction. Reflecting on the war on terrorism, I adhere to the words of Bertolt Brecht:

> that the rain
> falls from above to the bottom
> is totally unbearable for me.[36]

## Notes

1. Jean Baudrillard, "On Seduction," in Jean Baudrillard, *Selected Writings*, ed. Mark Poster (Cambridge: Polity, 1988), pp. 149–165.

2. In respect to this, Kenneth Roth, the executive director of Human Rights Watch, states, "Personal liberty should not be a casualty of the campaign against terrorism." See Human Rights Watch, "Human Rights Watch Criticizes Anti-terrorism Legislation," October 22, 2001, available at www.hrw.org/press/2001/10/terrorism1022.htm (accessed March 24, 2003).

3. For more information, see Human Rights Watch, "Human Rights Watch Criticizes Anti-terrorism Legislation."

4. Hannah Arendt, *Macht und Gewalt* (Munich: Piper, 1995), pp. 54–55.

5. In discussing reflection, it would be a mistake of perspective to write about the entire world and people's opinions. There is no definite "we," there are only groups that come together for certain events and spread again afterward. The feeling of a community appears and disappears; the differences are part of the program.

6. Human Rights Watch, "Presumption of Guilt: Human Rights Abuses of Post-September 11 Detainees," *Human Rights Watch* 14, no. 4 (August 2002): 3.

7. Timothy Besley, Robin Burgess, and Andrea Prat, "Mass Media and Political Accountability," in *The Right to Tell: The Role of Mass Media in Economic Development* (Washington, D.C.: World Bank, 2002), pp. 45–60.

8. Samuel P. Huntington, "The Clash of Civilizations," *Foreign Affairs* 72, no. 3 (Summer 1993): 22–28; see also Samuel P. Huntington, *The Clash of Civilizations and the Remaking of World Order* (New York: Touchstone, 1996).

9. George W. Bush, "U.S. Message on Terrorism," October 7, 2001, quoted from U.S. Embassy, Vienna, Austria, Unedited paper, October 2001.

10. Bush, "U.S. Message on Terrorism."

11. For more information on the use of the imagery of refugees, see Terence Wright, *Collateral Coverage: Media Images of Afghan Refugees during the 2001 Emergency*, New Issues in Refugee Research, Working paper, no. 62 (Geneva: UN High Commissioner for Refugees, 2002).

12. Bush, "U.S. Message on Terrorism."

13. Marc W. Herold edited a list on the Internet counting the civilian victims of the war on terrorism in Afghanistan (during the first months of war—from October 2001 till March 2002). See Marc W. Herold, "A Dossier on Civilian Victims of United

States Aerial Bombing of Afghanistan: A Comprehensive Accounting," revised March, 2002, available at www.cursor.org/stories/civilian_deaths.htm (accessed March 24, 2003).

14. George W. Bush, "President's Remarks at National Day of Prayer and Remembrance," September 14, 2001, available at www.whitehouse.gov/news/releases/2001/09/20010914–2.html (accessed March 24, 2003).

15. For more information, see Human Rights Watch, "Human Rights Implications of European Union Internal Security Proposals and Measures in the Aftermath of the 11 September Attacks in the United States," October 15, 2001, available at www.hrw.org/press/2001/11/eusecurity-memo.htm (accessed March 24, 2003).

16. "Human Rights Watch is concerned that public demonstrations and protest could be subject to the provisions of the proposal, thus quelling legitimate peaceful dissent." See Human Rights Watch, "Human Rights Implications."

17. Diana Johnstone, "NATO and the NEW World Order: Ideals and Self-Interest," in Philip Hammond and Edward S. Herman, eds., *Degraded Capability: The Media and the Kosovo Crisis* (London: Pluto, 2000), pp. 7–18.

18. See Human Rights Watch, "Presumption of Guilt."

19. Wolfgang Sützl, "The Contamination of Universalism: Nihilism and Human Rights after Kosovo," *Human Rights Review* 2, no. 1 (October–December 2000): 71–83.

20. Friedrich Nietzsche wrote, "God is dead! God stays dead! We have killed him!" ("Die fröhliche Wissenschaft"). Aphorismus 125, in Friedrich Nietzsche, *Sämtliche Werke Kritische Studienausgabe*, vol. 3, ed. Giorgio Colli and Mazzino Montinari (Munich: DTV, 1988), pp. 343–651, 480–482, my translation.

21. Wim Wenders, *The End of Violence* (Buena Vista International, MGM-UA Home Entertainment Inc., and Metro-Goldwyn-Mayer, 1997).

22. Jean Baudrillard, *Photographies 1985–1998*, ed. Peter Weibel (Graz: Hatje Cantz, 1999), p. 136.

23. Baudrillard, *Photographies 1985–1998*, p. 134.

24. Paul Virilio, *The Virilio Reader* (Oxford: Blackwell, 1998), p. 54.

25. For more information on the imagery surrounding refugees, see Wright, *Collateral Coverage.*

26. Seth Ackerman and Jim Naureckas, "Following Washington's Script: United States' Media and Kosovo," in Philip Hammond and Edward S. Herman, eds., *Degraded Capability: The Media and the Kosovo Crisis* (London: Pluto, 2000), pp. 97–110.

27. Compare with Norman Solomon, "War Needs Good Public Relations," October 25, 2001, available at www.fair.org/media-beat/011025.html (accessed March 24, 2003).

28. Jean Baudrillard, *The Gulf War Did Not Take Place*, trans. Paul Patton (Bloomington: Indiana University Press, 1995), p. 29.

29. Besley, Burgess, and Prat, "Mass Media and Political Accountability," p. 50.

30. Baudrillard, *Photographies 1985–1998*, p. 141.

31. Walter Benjamin, "Zur Kritik der Gewalt," in Walter Benjamin, *Zur Kritik der Gewalt und andere Aufsätze* (Frankfurt: Suhrkamp, 1965), pp. 29–65.

32. Sützl, "Contamination of Universalism," p. 81.

33. Immanuel Wallerstein, "Uncertainty and Creativity" (talk at Forum 2000: Concerns and Hopes on the Threshold of the New Millennium, Prague, September 3–6, 1997), available at http://fbc.binghamton.edu/iwuncer.htm (accessed March 24, 2003).

34. Huntington, "Clash of Civilizations."

35. Alexandra Föderl-Schmid, "Es darf kein Kampf der Kulturen entstehen, US-Politologe Huntington: Krieg gegen Terror dauert Jahre" ("There Must Not Be a Fight between Civilizations, U.S. Political Scientist Huntington: War against Terror Will Take Years"), *Der Standard Online*, 16 October 2001, available at http://derstandard.at/ archiv (accessed March 24, 2003).

36. Bertolt Brecht, "Der untergang des egoisten johann fatzer," quoted in Heiner Müller, *Textmontage (Unpublished Fragments of Brecht's Work on the Fatzer-material)* (unpublished manuscript, on file with author), p. 101: "daß der regen von oben nach unten fällt das ist mir ganz unerträglich."

# Part IV

## Regional Dialogues

# 11

# The New NATO

## An Instrument for the Promotion of Democracy and Human Rights?

### *Rebecca R. Moore*

As evidenced by the preamble to the 1949 Washington Treaty, the members of the North Atlantic Treaty Organization (NATO) have long committed themselves to the defense of a common set of principles, namely, "democracy, individual liberty, and the rule of law." Since the end of the Cold War, however, these principles have assumed a higher profile in NATO's mission, largely because the "new NATO" has deemed them central to security in a globalizing world. Indeed, NATO is now committed, not simply to safeguarding its values from an outside threat, but to extending them outside its territory, to the fledgling democracies of central and eastern Europe. The notion that NATO could help secure democracy to its east was, in fact, one of the Clinton administration's principal arguments on behalf of enlargement.

NATO's increasingly political mission has also had important implications for its military dimension. NATO's interventions in Bosnia and Kosovo were both justified to some degree on human rights grounds, and, in the case of Kosovo, NATO went so far as to effectively declare that the human rights of the Kosovar Albanians took precedence over the Federal Republic of Yugoslavia's claim to sovereignty. The allies' willingness to abridge the sovereignty of a state that had threatened no NATO member, without the authorization of the UN Security Council, marked a significant departure from past practice. Yet, it was both fully consistent with the definition of security embraced by the "new NATO" and reflective of the growing salience of human rights concerns in international politics. NATO's venture into the democracy promotion business does, however, raise two important questions. First, why has the promotion of democracy and human rights come to enjoy such a prominent place in NATO's post–Cold War mission? And, second, does NATO actually constitute a viable vehicle for the promotion of these values?

## An Individual Rights–Based Concept of Security

The current prominence of human rights in NATO's political and military missions derives from a variety of factors, among them the nature of the threats confronting Europe since the end of the Cold War. NATO's new Strategic Concepts issued in 1991 and 1999 both conclude that security threats are now "less likely to result from calculated aggression against the territory of the Allies" and more likely to stem from instabilities precipitated by ethnic and religious rivalries, territorial disputes, failed reform efforts, human rights abuse, and the dissolution of states. Indeed, the vast majority of armed conflicts since the end of the Cold War have been intrastate rather than interstate conflicts.

Over the past decade, NATO has made a concerted effort to adapt its own mission and capabilities to the challenges associated with this new environment. In 1999, for example, the alliance formally added peacekeeping and conflict prevention activities to its stated military mission. Such changes reflect NATO's larger determination that the consolidation of democracy and respect for human rights within states is essential to the future of peace and stability in Europe. Based on the assumption that shared liberal values were critical to the stabilization of western Europe, NATO has committed itself to constructing, in the whole of Europe, a new security order that is ultimately grounded on those values. As Lord Robertson, the NATO secretary-general, has explained it, NATO's "task now is to build the Euro-Atlantic security environment of the future—where all states share peace and democracy, and uphold basic human rights."[1] Although NATO remains committed to the collective defense of its territory, its evolving conception of security is now less state-centric, less deferential to the Westphalian principle of nonintervention, and dependent to a considerable extent on the triumph of democratic values. Ultimately, it is a concept of security that rests as much on the rights of the individual as it does on the right of sovereignty traditionally enjoyed by states.

Conceiving security in this way has had far-reaching implications for the alliance's military dimension, as was well demonstrated in the case of Kosovo. As NATO representatives pointed out at the time, the massive human rights violations taking place against the Kosovar Albanians represented "a fundamental challenge to the values for which NATO has stood since its foundation."[2] Failure to confront the crisis would have threatened to jeopardize the very security order that NATO sought to construct. Had NATO not acted in Kosovo, argues former secretary-general Javier Solana, "the entire logic of turning Europe into a common, political, economic and security space would have been invalidated."[3] Lord Robertson later explained the intervention in similar terms, "This issue goes to the very heart of our morality. If we had allowed this ethnic cleansing to go unanswered, we would have fatally undermined the basis of the Euro-Atlantic community we are trying to build, as we enter the 21st century."[4]

Indeed, the intervention in Kosovo reflected a larger shift in thinking about the relationship between security and human rights. As Jessica T. Mathews observes, the growing prominence of intrastate conflicts and instabilities has "fed a growing sense that an individual's security may not in fact reliably derive from their nation's security."[5] Growing concern with this apparent disconnect between the fate of human beings and the security of the state has given rise to an alternative perspective for thinking about security labeled "human security," which focuses primarily on the safety and basic needs of individuals, rather than the survival of the state.[6] The essentially liberal security order NATO envisions encompasses this notion of human security. As Richard Cohen notes, human security—or what he terms "individual security"—"stands at the center of any real international security system built around liberal democratic ideals."[7]

Growing interest in the notion of human security reflects what many believe to be the emergence of global norms of democracy and human rights—a trend with potentially far-reaching implications for the sovereignty of the state. As Cohen observes, "the Westphalian concept of the absolute right of states to act as they see fit within their own territories is no longer accepted by liberal democratic states nor, increasingly, by nations within international organizations such as the United Nations."[8] Rather, the current trend is to understand state sovereignty as contingent on a government's ability to implement norms of democracy and human rights. United Nations (UN) secretary-general Kofi Annan, in fact, told the UN Human Rights Commission during NATO's 1999 bombing of Kosovo, "Emerging slowly, but I believe surely, is an international norm against the violent repression of minorities that will and must take precedence over concerns of sovereignty."[9] Although Annan subsequently expressed concern over NATO's decision to act in Kosovo without Security Council authorization, he affirmed the need for intervention in the situation and endorsed the notion that state sovereignty must not serve as a shield for the abuse of human rights. As he put it in September 1999:

> State sovereignty, in its most basic sense, is being redefined—not least by the forces of globalisation and international co-operation. States are now widely understood to be instruments at the service of their people, and not vice-versa. At the same time, individual sovereignty—by which I mean the fundamental freedom of each individual, enshrined in the charter of the UN and subsequent international treaties—has been enhanced by a renewed and spreading consciousness of individual rights. When we read the charter today, we are more than ever conscious that its aim is to protect individual human beings, not to protect those who abuse them.[10]

Although most international law experts nevertheless concluded that NATO's intervention in Kosovo was at odds with the UN Charter, the growing acceptance of human rights discourse in international politics did serve to provide a normative basis for NATO's action. Indeed, Lord Robertson later sought to justify the intervention by pointing to "an ever growing body of international law, including . . . the Universal Declaration of Human Rights that requires the international community to respond when massive violations of human rights are being committed."[11]

NATO has also clearly contributed to the tendency to understand sovereignty as dependent on democracy and respect for human rights. Although NATO officials maintain that Kosovo was a unique case and not a precedent-setting event, scholars argue that NATO, through its intervention in Kosovo, set a precedent in favor of military intervention in humanitarian crises.[12] Moreover, the intervention reflected NATO's determination that security can no longer be understood purely in terms of preserving political borders. The rights of the individual merit at least as much attention as those of the state.

## NATO's Political Dimension

Indeed, NATO's vision is that of a Europe in which all states respect human rights and resolve their disputes through dialogue rather than through force. Although NATO ultimately opted to use force in Kosovo, the allies clearly prefer an essentially peaceful approach to constructing this new security order. As NATO leaders recognized early on, achieving this goal would not only necessitate an interest in the internal affairs of central and eastern Europe, it would also require that NATO develop the capacity to foster its values through essentially political means. NATO's recognition of this fact dates to mid-1989 when the administration of George H. W. Bush concluded that, by enhancing its own political dimension, NATO might act as a sort of catalyst for democratic reform in central and eastern Europe.[13]

Affirming that "security and stability do not lie solely in the military dimension," the NATO allies issued a declaration during the July 1990 summit in London stating their intention "to enhance the political component of the Alliance as provided for by Article 2" of the original NATO Treaty.[14] The Declaration on a Transformed Atlantic Alliance (more commonly known as the London Declaration) asserted that changes in the Soviet Union and eastern Europe would allow NATO to "help build the structure of a more united continent, supporting security and stability with the strength of our shared faith in democracy, the rights of the individual and the peaceful resolution of disputes."[15] The fact that NATO's first order of business was to ensure that its values prevailed throughout the former Soviet bloc bore witness to the allies' own conviction that shared democratic values were the key to their success in stabilizing western Europe. Enlarging the zone of peace in Europe required first extending eastward the values on which that peace was to be built. NATO's new mission, as articulated by former president Bush during a speech at Mainz, Germany, in late May 1989, was to be the creation of a Europe "whole and free."

Enhancing NATO's political dimension also encompassed the creation of new institutions, whose ultimate purpose was the extension of NATO values beyond NATO territory. In 1991, NATO invited all former Warsaw Pact members to join the newly created North Atlantic Cooperation Council (NACC), an institution designed to promote cooperation on political and security matters and encourage the development of democracy in central and eastern Europe. The NACC, which was succeeded in May 1997 by the Euro-Atlantic Partnership Council, reflected NATO's desire to pursue dialogue with its former adversaries, but it also revealed the allies' conviction that genuine security could be achieved only on the basis of democratic values and within a community that included the whole of Europe. As U.S. secretary of state James Baker put it in an address before the NACC in 1991, "For forty years, we stood apart from one another as two opposing blocs. Now, history has given us the opportunity to erase those blocs, to join together in a common circle built on shared universal and democratic values."[16] Reaching out to former adversaries represented an essentially political means by which NATO sought to influence the direction of domestic reform in central and eastern Europe.

The Partnership for Peace (PFP) constituted a second institution through which NATO sought to shape domestic affairs to its east. Proposed by the Clinton administration in October 1993, the PFP, which was open to all NACC and Organization for Security and Cooperation in Europe (OSCE) members, was designed to promote defense-related cooperation and "enhance stability and security throughout Europe."[17] The goal of a democratic and undivided Europe meant that the PFP would also embrace a democracy promotion mission. The institution's Framework Document, in fact, declares the "protection and promotion of fundamental freedoms and human rights" to be "shared values fundamental to the Partnership" and requires member states to reaffirm their obligations under the UN Charter, the Universal Declaration of Human Rights, the Helsinki Final Act, and all subsequent CSCE documents.[18]

Ultimately, however, it was not the PFP but the decision to admit new members that drew the most attention to NATO's democracy promotion mission. Opening NATO's door to new members, the Clinton administration argued, would allow the alliance to "do for Europe's East what it did for Europe's West."[19] Administration officials asserted that admitting new members would project stability to the east by allowing fledgling democracies to consolidate internal reforms, which in turn would serve to enlarge the zone of peace in Europe. Yet, they also made it clear that prospective members would be required to demonstrate their commitment to democratic reform prior to being admitted. President Bill Clinton, in fact, stated publicly during the period preceding the first phase of enlargement that "countries with repressive political systems, countries with designs on their neighbors, countries with militaries unchecked by civilian control or with closed economic systems need not apply."[20] Enlargement, therefore, became a means by which

NATO could reward those central and east Europeans who had made strides in the direction of the political and economic reforms essential to achieving a liberal European security order.

## Can NATO Promote Democracy?

Yet the question remains: Does NATO truly have the capacity to promote its values outside its territory? Proponents of the realist school of international relations theory have expressed considerable skepticism that NATO enjoys any real influence over the process of democratization in central and eastern Europe. Generally speaking, the criticisms of NATO's democracy promotion venture can be divided into three primary strands. The first focuses on NATO enlargement and argues that the process is simply not essential to the democratization of central and eastern Europe. Democratization has been driven by factors other than NATO, so it would occur even in the absence of enlargement. Second, critics argue that NATO has played little or no role in the regional cooperation and reconciliation that have occurred in the region. Plenty of other incentives existed to encourage the states of central and eastern Europe to patch up their differences with one another. Finally, NATO's skeptics argue that NATO's Cold War record in democracy promotion is poor. Hence, there is little reason to be optimistic about the alliance's capacity to promote democracy and respect for human rights in the future.[21]

Many of these criticisms, however, are somewhat misleading with regard to the claims made by NATO members. Even the Clinton administration, whose rhetoric regarding NATO's democracy promotion potential may have been somewhat overblown at times, never suggested that NATO enlargement was *necessary* for democratization or even that it constituted a primary incentive for democratization. More importantly, critics fail to acknowledge that free elections and a firm commitment by political elites to democratization—while certainly important first steps in the democratization process—do not constitute the consolidation of *liberal* democracy, as NATO's new mission requires.[22] Scholars who focus on democratization commonly cite as essential elements of liberal democracy: respect for individual rights, including minority rights; the rule of law; civil society; civilian control of the military; and the embedding of democratic values throughout society.[23] In states with a long legacy of communist rule and little prior experience with democracy, achieving all of these elements is, at best, a lengthy and difficult process.[24]

As for NATO's role in facilitating the process of democratization, the record suggests that NATO has had an impact on both the direction of domestic reform in prospective member states and the interrelationships between these states. Although NATO has never established strict political criteria for membership, it did release an internal study on enlargement in September 1995, which was distributed to prospective members. The study stressed that new members would be expected to conform to the basic principles of the

Washington Treaty—democracy, individual liberty, and the rule of law—and demonstrate a firm commitment to the principles and objectives of the PFP Framework Document, which also commits its members to democratic principles and the peaceful resolution of disputes.[25] Prospective members were also put on notice that they would be expected to subscribe to OSCE norms and principles, which included resolving ethnic and external territorial disputes by peaceful means, "promoting stability and well-being by economic liberty, social justice and environmental responsibility," and establishing civilian control over their militaries. Following the study's release, NATO officials emphasized repeatedly that the willingness and ability of states to meet NATO's political as well as military standards would be a critical factor in decisions about who would be invited to join the alliance.

Those criteria appear to have been taken seriously by both current and prospective NATO members. Although it's likely that many of the domestic reforms that have transpired in the region would have occurred even in the absence of NATO enlargement, central and east European leaders have stated publicly that the prospect of NATO membership has influenced their domestic and foreign policies. For example, during a series of three public hearings conducted in April 1997 by the U.S. Commission on Security and Cooperation in Europe to assess the progress of prospective NATO members in meeting their obligations under the Helsinki Final Act and OSCE agreements, invited representatives from ten states stressed that the prospect of NATO membership had served as an important incentive for both domestic reforms and improved relations with neighbors.[26]

These public acknowledgments suggest that NATO and its expectations have, at least, been a factor in internal political decisions. Moreover, the fact that even those states that were not included in the first phase of enlargement declared their continuing commitment to making the required reforms further demonstrates that NATO membership is still highly desired in the region. It also reflects the extent to which prospective members recognized that NATO's expectations, as outlined in the *Study on NATO Enlargement*, would continue to be a critical factor in decisions about new members. For example, even though Romania did not receive an invitation to join the alliance at the 1997 Madrid Summit, its leaders subsequently expressed a renewed determination to make the reforms necessary for NATO membership. During a visit by President Clinton just following the Madrid Summit, Romanian prime minister Victor Ciorbea remarked, "We would have been very happy if we had been invited in the first wave. But at the same time we are looking at things realistically. Romania has real and great chances to integrate by 1999 if we continue with reforms."[27]

The impact of NATO and European Union (EU) enlargement has perhaps been even more evident in the case of Slovakia. When NATO enlargement was first announced in 1994, Slovakia was widely considered a leading candidate. However, it was ultimately excluded from the first phase of enlargement because of widespread concerns about the authoritarian nature of Prime Minister Vladimir Meciar's government. The lesson was undoubtedly not lost on either the Slovaks or other prospective members. Beginning in late 1998, the post-Meciar government of Prime Minister Mikulas Dzurinda stressed repeatedly that it was committed to making the reforms necessary to join both NATO and the EU. Dzurinda even stated publicly that "NATO and the promise of membership play a key role in directing the behavior of new democracies."[28] Prior to parliamentary elections in September 2002, representatives from NATO member states visited Slovakia and repeatedly stressed that if Meciar's party (the Movement for a Democratic Slovakia) were returned to power, Slovakia would again be denied an invitation to join NATO.

## Regional Cooperation

The lure of NATO membership also appears to have encouraged the resolution of long-standing ethnic and border disputes throughout central and eastern Europe. As noted earlier, the *Study on NATO Enlargement* alerts prospective members that resolving such issues will be a significant factor in making membership decisions. Included among the many agreements reached since the mid-1990s are two treaties Hungary signed in 1995 and 1996 with Romania and Slovakia, establishing mechanisms for dealing with the large Hungarian minorities in both states.[29] Romania, as did Poland, also signed an agreement with Ukraine over border disputes and past recriminations.[30] For its part, the Czech Republic took a significant step toward improving relations with Germany in January 1997 when the two governments signed a much debated declaration acknowledging previous wrongs committed against each other, namely, Nazi crimes against Czechs and Czechoslovakia's expulsion of 2.5 million Sudeten Germans after World War II.[31]

Prospective NATO members also launched a variety of regional cooperation mechanisms. These arrangements include an interparliamentary assembly established by Lithuania and Poland to strengthen cultural relations and protect minority rights, and a forum known as the "Five Presidents," which has brought together the leaders of Poland, Ukraine, Lithuania, Latvia, and Estonia to discuss regional security, economic cooperation, and cultural exchange issues.[32] Referring to these various agreements, Daniel Fried, the U.S. ambassador to Poland, observed in 1998, "When Poland and Hungary became more confident of their NATO membership, they increased their outreach to their neighbors—Hungary to Romania, and Poland to Lithuania."[33]

Perhaps the best-known association for regional cooperation is the Visegrad group, which emerged in 1991 when Poland, Hungary, and Czechoslovakia met to coordinate their efforts to join NATO and the EU. Although cooperation among the group members lapsed after 1993 due partly to Czechoslovakia's "Velvet Divorce," the Visegrad group revived itself in 1999 when its members, including Slovakia, met in Bratislava and proclaimed a new beginning. During the course of the meeting, NATO's three newest members also pledged to help Slovakia join the alliance.[34] Given that the Visegrad group initially materialized in 1991 long before NATO announced its intention to enlarge, it's clear that NATO was not the sole factor mobilizing regional cooperation. Yet, in certain instances, cooperation does appear to have been encouraged by the enlargement process. In an analysis of the Czech Republic's security policies, Stephen J. Blank observes that the Czechs' desire for NATO membership was the one issue that had prompted regional defense cooperation between Prague, Warsaw, and Budapest. In his view, the cooperation occurred largely because NATO had advised new members that they would not be accepted until they could work together on both economic and defense issues. According to Blank, the Czech Republic's willingness to engage in such cooperation at the behest of NATO, given its earlier lack of interest in other forms of cooperation, reflected its "priority goal of gaining NATO membership."[35]

The Clinton administration also made frequent reference to these various regional agreements to support its case that the enlargement process was indeed generating stability and reform in central and eastern Europe. "To align themselves with NATO these states are resolving problems that could have led to future Bosnias," Madeleine Albright observed in 1998. "This is the productive paradox at NATO's heart: by extending solemn security guarantees, we actually reduce the chance that our troops will again be called to fight in Europe."[36] Solana also suggested that NATO had prompted various regional agreements completed between 1996 and 1998 by telling prospective members, "You have no chance of being in this club [unless] you make a real effort to solve minority problems."[37]

In his study of Romanian-Hungarian relations since the end of the Cold War, Ronald H. Linden also ties the generally peaceful nature of the relationship directly to the process of NATO enlargement. Linden argues that when NATO released its 1995 study on enlargement, it became clear for Hungary and Romania as well as other prospective NATO members that "simply reflecting Western norms would no longer be enough; action to put these into practice had to take place." It was at that point, he says, that both Hungary and Romania "realized that resorting to the 'old' ways of interethnic and interstate conflict would severely retard their chances of gaining entry into Western institutions." Indeed, Linden notes that Hungarian prime minister Gyula Horn acknowledged that his government had "recognized from the outset that the community of European states will under no circumstances admit into its ranks countries that squabble relentlessly among themselves."[38]

The willingness of Bulgaria, Romania, and other surrounding states to cooperate with NATO during the conflict in Kosovo, despite a lack of support by their respective publics, might also be construed as evidence of NATO's continuing appeal. Indeed, Bulgaria's prime minister said, at the time, that support for the alliance was "a question of Euro-Atlantic solidarity, and choosing European values."[39] Similarly, the Bulgarian ambassador to the

United States said of Bulgaria's supportive stance, "What we're trying to achieve now is not just a safe Bulgaria, a safe home. . . . Now we want a safe neighborhood."[40] In the wake of September 11, 2001, NATO's appeal was no less evident. Prospective member states demonstrated their continuing interest in joining the alliance by behaving as "de facto" allies. Bulgaria and Romania, for example, contributed military assets to the war in Afghanistan, and both also offered the United States military bases for a possible attack on Iraq.

## A "New NATO"

As noted earlier, at least some skeptics of NATO's capacity for democracy promotion draw their conclusions as much from the Cold War period as from the experience of the past decade. They commonly point out that Turkey, Spain, Portugal, and Greece all experienced periods of undemocratic rule and manifested poor human rights records subsequent to becoming NATO members, and, yet, not one was ever threatened with the loss of its membership. The critics therefore conclude that because NATO demonstrated minimal influence over the domestic politics of its members during the Cold War, there is little reason to believe that it can serve as a vehicle for democracy promotion today.[41]

This comparison is not a useful one, largely because of the growing importance of NATO's political dimension since 1989. NATO now operates in a fundamentally different environment than it did during the Cold War, and decisions regarding new members follow from a different set of criteria— one in which democratic values have achieved a significantly higher profile. New members, NATO declared at its 1999 summit in Washington, must be in a position to "enhance overall security and stability in Europe." Today, that means upholding the values underpinning the liberal security order NATO envisions for the whole of Europe.[42] Greece, Turkey, and Spain, on the other hand, were admitted for reasons that were primarily strategic in nature. Given NATO's new mission and the radically altered strategic environment in which it currently operates, it seems unlikely that states that lack a demonstrated commitment to democracy would be deemed the security *producers* NATO demands today. In fact, former NATO secretary-general Willy Claes explained in 1996, "We do not need security consumers," but rather states that can "bear the full responsibility of membership, including the risks and financial costs of membership." An anonymous NATO official quoted by the *New York Times* put it more bluntly, "We don't need any more Frances, Spains, Greeces, or Turkeys."[43]

## The EU versus NATO?

Those who doubt NATO's democracy promotion potential have also tended to argue that the EU is far better equipped than NATO to assist in the consolidation of political and economic reforms in central and eastern Europe. However, to the larger task of consolidating a liberal order in Europe, NATO contributes two crucial commodities that the EU cannot provide: military power in defense of shared values and a strong link to the United States, whose military strength continues to be regarded as vital to the defense of the values for which NATO stands. NATO therefore possesses a leverage for influencing reforms that the EU does not enjoy. As Petr Lunak observes, the paradox associated with the desire of central and east Europeans to join west European institutions is that it has been "marked by a mistrust of purely European institutions."[44] This mistrust is likely grounded not only in the region's World War II experience, but also in the EU's failure to prevent or stem the violence emanating from the former Yugoslavia in the early 1990s.

Numerous statements by central and east European leaders emphasize the importance of security to the consolidation of democracy in the region. Polish foreign minister Bronislaw Geremek, for example, has said that Poland chose to join NATO because it "is an alliance which has put its immense military might in service of fundamental values and principles that we share. NATO can make Europe safe for democracy. No other organization can replace the Alliance in this role."[45] Vaclav Havel echoed these thoughts in slightly different terms, "While the European Union focuses on political and economic integration, NATO constitutes an irreplaceable instrument for the collective defense of these values."[46] The region's leaders have also insisted that a U.S. presence is essential to security on the European continent. In the words of Polish president Aleksander Kwasniewski, "The two world wars proved to the peoples of Europe and America that without a U.S. presence in Europe, European security is unlikely to be achieved."[47] A Polish official quoted by the *New York Times* just prior to Poland's accession to NATO made the same point even more explicitly, "We want to be good Europeans. But more than anyone except perhaps the British, we understand how important it is to keep the Americans involved in Europe."[48]

Furthermore, as Zbigniew Brzezinski suggests, it is the security that NATO provides that has made reconciliation in Europe possible, both today and during the Cold War.[49] Referencing the numerous examples of regional cooperation witnessed in central and eastern Europe since the mid-1990s, Brzezinski writes:

[T]he ongoing reconciliation between Germany and Poland would not have been possible without the American presence in Germany and the related sense of security that Poland's prospective membership has fostered in Poland. The same is true of the Czech Republic and Germany, Hungary and Romania, Romania and Ukraine; and the desire to get into NATO is also having a similar influence on Slovenia's attitude toward Italy and Lithuania toward Poland.[50]

Moreover, as Linden notes, while the EU and NATO both made democratic institutions and processes a necessary condition for admission, only "NATO insisted that the East European states also pursue peaceful policies among each other, that they commit themselves to settling rather than replaying old conflicts and to setting up a system for settling present and future disputes."[51]

Ultimately, it would be impossible to sort out methodologically the precise impact of various external forces on the process of democratization and reconciliation in central and eastern Europe. Institutions such as the EU and NATO, as well as the broader process of globalization generated by global markets and information technology, have all influenced the direction of political, economic, and military reform taking place throughout the region. Indeed, the phenomenon of globalization, which many scholars view as narrowing appreciably the economic and political choices available to states, is likely having a greater impact on the states of central and eastern Europe than any one outside institution. However, both NATO and the EU can be understood as part of this phenomenon. Both contribute to increasing political and economic integration. And, by championing their own democratic values and practices, both serve to foster the emergence of so-called global norms of democracy and human rights.

## A "Return to Europe"

Certainly, NATO's role in articulating democratic values as the linchpin of the peaceful and prosperous Euro-Atlantic community after World War II should not be underestimated. Indeed, one of the most interesting aspects of the enlargement process thus far is the way in which central and east Europeans have characterized their desire to join NATO and the EU. According to the region's leaders, their primary motivation for joining NATO has more to do with its identity as a "Western" institution than it does with security. The majority of these states, in fact, perceive their respective security environments to be relatively benign.[52] NATO, however, is an institution to which they believe they rightfully belong by virtue of their cultural and historical ties to the West. As John Gerard Ruggie puts it, "for NATO's most likely-would be members, expansion has become less an issue of security than of identity politics, an affirmation that they belong to the West."[53]

Indeed, central and east Europeans tend to view their post–World War II history as marked by an artificial separation from the West and subjugation by an alien power and culture.[54] Hence, they have characterized joining NATO and the EU as part of their "return to Europe." Explaining Poland's desire to join NATO, Polish foreign minister Bronislaw Geremek put it this way, "We have . . . spared no effort to return to the roots of our culture and statehood, to join the Euro-Atlantic family of democratic nations. We will not rest until Poland is safely anchored in Western, economic, political, and military structures. This is the essence of our aspirations to join NATO."[55] Hungarian foreign minister Janos Martonyi echoed these thoughts following Hungary's accession to NATO in March 1999. "Hungary has come home," he declared. "We are back in the family."[56] Generally speaking, this sort of rhetoric captures the notion that NATO is not simply a military alliance, but a political community whose members share a common culture, values, and interests.

The notion of a "return to Europe," however, casts NATO's role in the region in a slightly different light than do portrayals of the alliance as a vehicle for projecting democratic values eastward. The sentiments expressed by central and east European leaders suggest that NATO is not so much projecting its values eastward as it is "moving westward," embracing opportunities denied to it during the Cold War. As Hungarian president Arpad Goncz put it, "The rhetoric of NATO enlargement suggests that NATO is moving eastward at the instigation of the present 16 allies. Instead, what is happening is that the countries of Central and Eastern Europe are moving westward. Separated from West-European and Euro-Atlantic institutions for 40 years, these countries now have the freedom and opportunity to join institutions such as NATO, the European Union and the Western European Union."[57]

NATO secretary-general Lord Robertson later used similar language in discussing alliance efforts to persuade the Russians that they have no need to fear the expansion of NATO. Robertson acknowledged that NATO "may not convince Russia fully," but he also expressed optimism that "if a realistic attitude in Russia prevails, Moscow will see that NATO is not 'moving East,' but that Central and Eastern Europe—and Russia itself—are gradually moving West."[58]

If one accepts this perspective, NATO's ability to assist in the democratization and stabilization of central and eastern Europe derives as much from its pull as a guardian of democratic values as it does from the force of its military might. NATO, the initial enlargement experience suggests, does not so much project its values as it pulls others to its core, in the process encouraging the necessarily indigenous reforms required of NATO members. Indeed, former NATO commander Wesley K. Clark said of the alliance in his farewell address, "Together we have demonstrated that there is nothing stronger than the power of ideas . . . ideas of freedom, law and justice and that democratic peoples united in a vision of a common imperative form an irresistible and magnetic force which is transforming the nature of Europe."[59]

## Interests, Identity, and Values

The notion that NATO's values are themselves the source of the alliance's influence in central and eastern Europe also raises theoretical questions about the relationship between values, identity, and interests. Traditional realist thinking tends to define interests and values as mutually exclusive entities. Yet, the concept of a "return to Europe" suggests that identity—informed by history, culture, values, and ideas—has influenced the way in which the governments of central and eastern Europe have defined their interests and, consequently, how they have behaved internally and externally. Indeed, simply being identified as part of the West appears to have become an important interest among the states of the region.

NATO's leaders have themselves unabashedly identified the alliance with Western civilization and the democratic values commonly associated with the "West." Czech president Havel, for example, called on NATO in a 1997 *New York Times* op-ed piece to "urgently remind itself that it is first and foremost an instrument of democracy intended to defend mutually held and created political and spiritual values. It must see itself not as a pact of nations against a more or less obvious enemy, but as a guarantor of Euro-American civilization."[60] During his visit to Poland in June 2001, President George W. Bush also stressed that NATO is unique because its members share common values and a common civilization—a civilization that he was careful to say was not confined to western Europe. "Yalta did not ratify a natural divide: it divided a living civilization," he proclaimed, "The partition of Europe was not a fact of geography; it was an act of violence."[61]

Emphasizing the link between NATO, Western civilization, and democratic values has served as one means of alerting prospective members to the fact that being identified as a member of the "West" requires first actively embracing and implementing its values. In effect, NATO leaders have used the concept of identity as a means of influencing how the states of central and eastern Europe conceive their interests and therefore interact with others. NATO's new mission is contingent on constructivist assumptions that states' interests are not wholly material as realist theory maintains, but can be shaped or, as Alexander Wendt argues, even constituted by ideas.[62] The very notion that security can be constructed or understood in terms of democratic values presumes that states' interactions with each other are governed to some degree by their perceptions of each other, and that these perceptions are influenced by values or ideas. By promoting its own values as norms that should govern the entire Euro-Atlantic region, NATO has sought to further a sense of collective identity underpinned by shared liberal democratic values.

**Democracy Assistance**

Importantly, NATO has not confined itself to popularizing democratic values. Its members have also provided practical assistance to partner states seeking to implement these norms. In 1992, for example, the North Atlantic Assembly, which serves as NATO's collective parliamentary arm, established the Rose-Roth initiative, which is "a series of special parliamentary seminars and staff training programmes designed to assist the development of parliamentary democracy" in central and eastern Europe. A particular theme of Rose-Roth activities has been civil-military relations, especially democratic control of the armed forces.[63] The George C. Marshall European Center for Security Studies, which is based in Garmisch-Partenkirchen, Germany, and is supported jointly by the United States and Germany, also hosts courses annually for civilian and military leaders from central and eastern Europe that are aimed at assisting the democratization process in the region, including the establishment of civilian control of the military.[64] These various activities led *Washington Post* reporter Dana Priest to suggest in 1998 that the center had "become the intellectual center for the inconspicuous revolution taking place inside the militaries of Eastern Europe."[65]

NATO also established a Membership Action Plan (MAP) in April 1999 to assist NATO aspirants in meeting the alliance's expectations. The plan, which reaffirms the political guidelines set forth in the 1995 *Study on NATO Enlargement,* requires participants to submit an Annual National Program detailing its preparations for NATO membership. NATO then provides each individual member with feedback on its progress. Additionally, NATO offers MAP members the opportunity to participate in meetings and workshops with NATO political and military personnel on a variety of membership-related issues.[66]

**The Future of Enlargement**

Recognizing that enlargement remains perhaps the most important means by which NATO can influence the domestic affairs of those states still outside the alliance, NATO has emphasized that its door remains open and that the seven invitations issued during the Prague Summit in November 2002 would not be the last. The notion of unlimited enlargement, however, is a highly troublesome one for a variety of reasons, including fears of diluting the alliance's military capabilities and rendering decision making more difficult. Also problematic is the question of NATO's relationship to Russia and, specifically, whether NATO should be open to eventual Russian membership as Vladimir Putin suggested in mid-2001.[67]

Within the alliance, enthusiasm for this idea has been scarce. Indeed, Havel, who favors opening the alliance to all European states who demonstrate a commitment to democracy, has intimated in not so subtle terms that Russia does not belong in NATO because NATO is an alliance of Western civilization of which Russia is not a part. During a gathering of representatives from ten NATO aspirants in Bratislava several weeks before the 2001 NATO summit in Brussels, Havel declared that NATO can and should expand to include the territory "from Alaska in the West to Tallinn in the east," but he also cautioned that "a somewhat desperate effort to integrate everybody at all costs could finally lead to nothing but confusion and ruin."[68] Former U.S. secretary of state Henry Kissinger had earlier taken a similar position, writing in 1997 that Russia is not a wholly European power and thus has interests that are not necessarily consistent with NATO objectives. Opening NATO to Russia, Kissinger concluded, would "dilute the Alliance to the point of irrelevance."[69]

In the wake of September 11, however, Putin's cooperation in the "war on terrorism" and his apparent efforts to move Russia closer to the West have served to generate greater cooperation between Russia and NATO. In May 2002, the allies agreed to establish a new NATO-Russia Council, which allows Russia a seat at the table during NATO discussions of certain, specified issues, including terrorism and the proliferation of weapons of mass destruction. Still, as Timothy Garton Ash suggests, Putin's efforts to draw Russia closer to NATO present the West with the difficult question "of how far we should compromise our own standards in order to encourage Russia's admirable impulse toward greater cooperation with the rest of Europe."[70]

The issue of Russian membership also begs the question of whether NATO has the capacity to influence democratic reform in areas not historically regarded as part of the "West." The notion of a "return to Europe" suggests that central and east Europeans are rejoining a community grounded on a common culture, history, and values—a community that both preceded and outlived the Cold War. Does NATO have the capacity to enlarge this community or are there cultural and historical limits to NATO's ability to promote norms of democracy and respect for human rights outside its territory?

Yet another unresolved issue with potentially important implications for NATO's political dimension concerns the lack of a remedy for states who, once inside the alliance, fail to abide by NATO's values. Indeed, the original Washington Treaty contains no provision for removing or sanctioning members who fail to maintain the political and military standards that prospective members are now expected to meet. This could in the future prove troublesome for an alliance whose political dimension has become increasingly important.

At the same time, however, NATO's efforts to construct and maintain a Europe "whole and free" may again require that NATO be willing, if necessary, to use force in defense of its values. In an age of terrorism and weapons of mass destruction, NATO will need to think seriously about just what the defense of its values requires. At Prague, the allies agreed that "effective military forces . . . are vital to the freedom and security of [their] populations" and made preparations to transform and reinvigorate NATO's military dimension in order to address new threats.[71] Indeed, it seems likely that in the foreseeable future, defending NATO's values will not be a purely political task.

# Notes

1. Lord Robertson (speech at NATO Parliamentary Assembly, Amsterdam, November 15, 1999), available at www.nato.int/docu/speech/1999/s991115a.htm (accessed July 2001).

2. "Statement on Kosovo, Issued by the Heads of State and Government Participating in the Meeting of the North Atlantic Council in Washington, D.C.," April 23–24, 1999, available at www.nato.int/docu/pr1999/p99—062e.htm (accessed July 2001).

3. Javier Solana, "Fresh Cause for Hope at the Opening of a New Century," in William Joseph Buckley, ed., *Kosovo: Contending Voices on Balkan Interventions* (Grand Rapids, Mich.: Eerdmans, 2000), p. 218.

4. Lord Robertson, "Law, Morality and the Use of Force" (speech at the Institut de Relations Internationales et Strategiques, Paris, May 16, 2000), available at www.nato.int/docu/speech/2000/5000516a.htm (accessed July 2001).

5. Jessica T. Mathews, "Power Shift," *Foreign Affairs* 76, no. 1 (1997): 51.

6. See Barry Buzan et al., *The European Security Order Recast: Scenarios for the Post–Cold War Era* (London: Pinter, 1990), p. 9.

7. Richard Cohen, "From Individual Security to International Stability," in Richard Cohen and Michael Mihalka, *Cooperative Security: New Horizons for International Order*, The Marshall Center Papers, no. 3 (Garmisch-Partenkirchen: George C. Marshall Center, 2001), pp. 7–8.

8. Cohen, "From Individual Security to International Stability," p. 8.

9. Quoted in Ove Bring, "Should NATO Take the Lead in Formulating a Doctrine on Humanitarian Intervention," *NATO Review* 47, no. 3 (1999): 24–27.

10. Kofi Annan, "Two Concepts of Sovereignty," *The Economist*, 18 September 1999, p. 49.

11. Robertson, "Law, Morality and the Use of Force."

12. See Michael J. Glennon, "The New Interventionism: The Search for a Just International Law," *Foreign Affairs* 78, no. 3 (1999): 2–7; see also Michael Mandelbaum, "A Perfect Failure: NATO's War against Yugoslavia," *Foreign Affairs* 78, no. 5 (1999): 3–5.

13. It is no doubt also true that as the Soviet threat receded, NATO's own future depended on its ability to make a credible case that it was not simply a military alliance, but a political institution as well.

14. Article 2 of the original Washington Treaty declares that NATO members will "contribute toward the further development of peaceful and friendly international relations by strengthening their free institutions, by bringing about a better understanding of the principles upon which these institutions are founded, and by promoting conditions of stability and well-being. They seek to eliminate conflict in their international economic policies and will encourage collaboration between any or all of them." See "The North Atlantic Treaty," available at www.nato.int/docu/basictxt/treaty.htm (accessed March 25, 2003).

15. "Declaration on a Transformed North Atlantic Alliance Issued by the Heads of State and Government Participating in the Meeting of the North Atlantic Council ('The London Declaration')," July 6, 1990, available at www.nato.int/docu/basictxt/b900706a.htm (accessed March 25, 2003).

16. Quoted in David S. Yost, *NATO Transformed: The Alliances' New Roles in International Security* (Washington, D.C.: U.S. Institute of Peace Press, 1998), p. 101.

17. See "Partnership for Peace," in *The NATO Handbook, 50th Anniversary Edition* (Brussels: North Atlantic Treaty Organization, 1998–1999), pp. 86–87.

18. See "Partnership for Peace (PfP)," *NATO Basic Fact Sheet*, no. 9 (March 1996), available at www.nato.int/docu/facts/1996/PfP.htm (accessed September 2000).

19. U.S. Department of State, NATO Enlargement Ratification Office, NATO Enlargement Fact Sheet; see also Madeleine Albright, "Enlarging NATO," *The Economist*, 15 February 1997, p. 22.

20. U.S. Commission on Security and Cooperation in Europe, "Report on Human Rights and the Process of NATO Enlargement," June 1997, p. 7.

21. For example, see Dan Reiter, "Why NATO Enlargement Does Not Spread Democracy," *International Security* 25, no. 4 (2001): 41; see also Michael Mandelbaum, "Preserving the New Peace: The Case against NATO Expansion," *Foreign Affairs* 74, no. 3 (1995): 10.

22. Importantly, the liberal security order NATO envisions is built on a shared commitment to liberal values, not simply the establishment of electoral or majoritarian democracy.

23. For example, see Larry Diamond, *Developing Democracy: Toward Consolidation* (Baltimore, Md.: Johns Hopkins University Press, 1999).

24. One particular difficulty has to do with the consolidation of civilian control over the military. For a useful discussion of the difficulties confronted by the states of central Europe in making this transition, see Jeffrey Simon, *NATO Enlargement and Central Europe: A Study in Civil-Military Relations* (Washington, D.C.: National Defense University Press, 1999), p. 313.

25. *Study on NATO Enlargement*, 1995, available at www.nato.int/docu/basictxt/enl-9501.htm (accessed September 2000). At approximately this same time, U.S. secretary of defense William Perry issued what became known as the "Perry Principles." Enlargement, Perry argued, must be guided by the same principles on which the stabilization of western Europe depended: collective defense, democracy, consensus, and cooperative security. See William J. Perry, "The Enduring Dynamic Relationship That Is NATO," *Defense Viewpoint* 10, no. 9 (1995), available at www.defenselink.mil/speeches/1995/s19950205—perry.html (accessed March 25, 2003).

26. Representatives from Bulgaria, the Czech Republic, Estonia, Hungary, Latvia, Lithuania, Poland, Romania, Slovakia, and Slovenia participated in the 1997 hearing. See U.S. Commission on Security and Cooperation in Europe, "Report on Human Rights and the Process of NATO Enlargement," June 1997.

27. "Clinton Is Welcomed by a Jubilant Poland," *International Herald Tribune*, 10 July 1997, p. 5.

28. "Slovak Prime Minister Says NATO Enlargement Boon to Stability," *Central Europe Online*, 16 June 2000, available at www.centraleurope.com (accessed March 25, 2003).

29. Hungary and Romania also supported each other's inclusion in the first phase of enlargement and have established a joint peacekeeping battalion.

30. For discussion of the significance of these various examples of regional rapprochement, see Elizabeth Pond, *The Rebirth of Europe* (Washington, D.C.: Brookings Institution, 1999), pp. 14, 74–77.

31. Craig R. Whitney, "Germans and Czechs Try to Heal Hatreds of the Nazi Era," *New York Times*, 22 January 1997.

32. Pond, *Rebirth of Europe*, pp. 76–77; see also Senate Committee on Foreign Relations, *The Debate on NATO Enlargement: Hearings before the Senate Committee on Foreign Relations*, 105th Cong., 1st sess., October–November 1997, p. 300.

33. Jane Perlez, "With Promises, Promises, NATO Moves the East," *New York Times*, 26 April 1998, p. A16.

34. See "NATO Front Runners Pledge Support for Slovak Membership" *RFE/RL Newsline*, 6 January 1999, available at www.rferl.org/newsline/1999/01/060199.asp (accessed July 2001); "Visegrad Countries Call for Rapid Entry of Slovakia into NATO," *Central Europe Online*, 20 January 2001, available at www.centraleurope.com (accessed March 25, 2003).

35. Stephen J. Blank, "Prague, NATO and European Security," U.S. Army War College, Strategic Studies Institute, 1996, pp. 4–5, available at www.carlisle.army.mil/ssi/pubs/1996/prague/prague.pdf (accessed March 25, 2003).

36. Madeleine Albright, "NATO Enlargement: Advancing America's Strategic Interests," statement before the Senate Foreign Relations Committee, February 2, 1998, in U.S. Department of State, *Dispatch* 9, no. 2 (March 1998): 14.

37. Quoted in Pond, *Rebirth of Europe*, p. 74.

38. Ronald H. Linden, "Putting on Their Sunday Best: Romania, Hungary, and the Puzzle of Peace," *International Studies Quarterly* 44, no. 1 (March 2000): 136.

39. John Tagliabue, "Bulgarians Bet Future on a Link to NATO," *New York Times*, 12 May 1999, p. 12.

40. Francis X. Clines, "NATO's Next Applicants Preen, Jostle and Hope," *New York Times*, 25 April 1999.

41. For example, citing the Cold War case studies of Turkey, Spain, Portugal, and Greece, Dan Reiter writes, "Overall, the cases provide almost no evidence that NATO membership significantly promoted democracy: The transgovernmental effects on civil-military relations were uneven, the stick of NATO ejection was never applied to members that reverted to autocracy, and in the instance of NATO entry there is no evidence of the NATO carrot spurring democratization." See Reiter, "Why NATO Enlargement Does Not Promote Democracy," pp. 56–57.

42. The Washington Declaration, April 23–24, 1999, available in *The Reader's Guide to the NATO Summit in Washington, April 23–25, 1999* (NATO Office of Information and Press), pp. 11–12.

43. Steven Erlanger, "Pressure on NATO to Expand," *New York Times*, 9 February 1996.

44. Petr Lunak, "Security for Eastern Europe: The European Option," *World Policy Journal* 11, no. 3 (1994): 128.

45. Bronislaw Geremek, address on occasion of the accession protocols to the North Atlantic Treaty, December 16, 1997, available at www.polishworld.com/polemb/nato/speech/address1.htm (accessed July 2001).

46. Vaclav Havel, "A Chance to Stop Exporting Wars and Violence," *Transitions* (December 1997): 17.

47. Aleksander Kwasniewski, "Isolationism Is an Anachronism," *Transitions* (December 1997): 23.

48. Steven Erlanger, "3 Fragments of Soviet Realm Joining NATO's Ranks," *New York Times*, 12 March 1999.

49. In the case of the Cold War, Brzezinski offers the examples of France's reconciliation with Germany as well as France and Britain's ultimate acceptance of German reunification.

50. Zbigniew Brzezinski, "NATO: The Dilemmas of Expansion," *The National Interest*, no. 53 (Fall 1998): 13.

51. Linden, "Putting on Their Sunday Best," p. 126.

52. Poland and the Baltic States are the likely exceptions to this rule given their history and geographic location. The statements of numerous Czech and Hungarian leaders, however, have reflected their relative sense of security. For example, Czech foreign defense minister Jaromir Novotny stated in 1997, "For the first time in this century, the geographical position of the Czech Republic is to our advantage. People feel safe." See Jane Perlez, "Czech Backing for NATO under 50%; Lack of Enthusiasm Worries U.S.," *New York Times*, 23 December 1997. Similarly, Hungarian president Arpad Goncz insisted that "Hungary's determination to become a member of the alliance is motivated by shared values and the desire to belong to a favorable security environment, not by fear." See Arpad Goncz, "The Least Expensive Way to Guarantee Security," *Transitions* (December 1997): 19.

53. John Gerard Ruggie, *Winning the Peace: America and World Order in the New Era* (New York: Columbia University Press, 1996), p. 85.

54. See Milan Kundera, "The Tragedy of Central Europe," in Gale Stokes, ed., *From Stalinism to Pluralism: A Documentary History of Eastern Europe since 1945*, 2nd ed. (New York: Oxford University Press, 1995), p. 223.

55. Bronislaw Geremek, address on the occasion of the accession protocols to the North Atlantic Treaty, December 16, 1997.

56. "Poland, Hungary, Czech Republic Formally Joins NATO," *New York Times*, 12 March 1999; see also Jeremy Bransten, "1999 in Review: New Challenges As NATO Moves East," Radio Free Europe/Radio Liberty report, available at www.rferl.org/nca/features/1999/12/f.ru.991220150049.html (accessed March 25, 2003).

57. Goncz, "Least Expensive Way to Guarantee Security," p. 9.

58. Lord Robertson, "NATO Challenges: Illusions and Realities" (speech at Chicago Council of Foreign Relations, June 19, 2001), available at www.nato.int/docu/speech/2001/s010619b.htm (accessed July 2001).

59. "NATO's Clark Hands over Alliance Military Command," *Central Europe Online*, 4 May 2000, available at www.centraleurope.com (accessed March 25, 2003).

60. Vaclav Havel, "NATO's Quality of Life," *New York Times*, 13 May 1997.

61. "Text: Bush in Poland," *Washington Post*, 15 June 2000.

62. Alexander Wendt, *Social Theory of International Politics* (Cambridge: Cambridge University Press, 1999), pp. 114, 135.

63. Simon Lunn, "NATO's Parliamentary Arm Helps Further the Aims of the Alliance," *NATO Review* 46, no. 4 (Winter 1998): 8–9.

64. U.S. Department of State, "Annual Report to Congress on PFP," July 29, 1997; see also Robert Kennedy, "Educating Leaders for the 21st Century—A Snapshot of the Marshall Center for Security Studies," *NATO Review* 46, no. 4 (Winter 1998): 28–29. For more information on the Marshall Center's activities, see the Marshall Center's website at www.marshallcenter.org (accessed March 25, 2003).

65. Dana Priest, "U.S.-Run Center Helps Shape Future Leaders," *Washington Post*, 14 December 1998, p. A29.

66. Feedback is to take place during annual 19+1 meetings of the North Atlantic Council. See "Factsheet on NATO's Membership Action Plan," April 20, 2000; see also "Membership Action Plan," Press Release NAC-S(66), April 24, 1999, available at www.nato.int/docu/pr/1999/p99—066e.htm (accessed July 2001).

67. Peter Baker, "Putin: NATO Should Disband or Allow Russia to Join," *Washington Post*, 18 July 2001.

68. "Czech President Says Space for Future NATO between Alaska, Tallinn," *CTK News Agency (Prague)*, 11 May 2001 (available through Lexis-Nexis). Havel has also suggested on several occasions that Russia distrusts NATO because it suffers from a sort of identity crisis. "Russia," he says, "must finally realize that NATO's mission poses no threat to it and that if NATO moves closer to Russia's borders, it brings closer stability, security, democracy, and an advanced political culture, which is obviously in Russia's essential interest." See *RFE/RL Newsline*, 16 May 2001 (available at www.rferl.org/newsline/2001/05/160501.asp (accessed, July 2001).

69. Henry Kissinger, "NATO: Make It Strong, Make It Larger," *Washington Post*, 14 January 1997, p. A15.

70. Timothy Garton Ash, "A New War Reshapes Old Alliances," *New York Times*, 12 October 2001.

71. "Prague Summit Declaration, Issued by the Heads of State and Government Participating in the Meeting of the North Atlantic Council in Prague," Press Communiqué PR/CP, November 21, 2002, p. 127.

# 12

# NATO's War Over Kosovo

## The Debates, Dynamics, and Consequences

### *Giovanna Bono*

Since the terrorist attacks on the United States on September 11, 2001, Western military intervention has officially two intertwined purposes: that of defeating international terrorism and simultaneously promoting democratization and human rights. In light of these developments, it is important to reappraise the war that the North Atlantic Treaty Organization (NATO) conducted over Kosovo. The war represented a watershed event in international relations: it was the first time in its history that the Western alliance attacked a sovereign state (the Federal Republic of Yugoslavia [FRY]/Serbia) by justifying the action on the basis of "humanitarian intervention."[1]

The aim of this chapter is not to provide an analysis of the causes of the Kosovo conflict. Such causes are to be found in the divergent aspirations of the Kosovo Albanian ethnic population and Serbian nationalists and the failure of the Western powers to address the problems in the region through comprehensive conflict prevention measures.[2] Instead, this chapter has two objectives: first, to reassess the pro- and anti-NATO narratives on the Kosovo war by analyzing the objectives of a "policy community" that shaped Western strategy toward the Balkans during 1998 to March 1999, and second, to outline the key lessons learned by the Western allies from the conflict and their likely impact on the current "war on terrorism."

To achieve the first objective, I briefly summarize the arguments of the pro- and anti-NATO narratives on the Kosovo war. After describing the hypothesis of the policy community and research findings, I provide an analysis of the key factors that influenced the dynamics of NATO's intervention.

### NATO's War on Kosovo: The Pro- and Antinarratives

A variety of competing pro- and antinarratives have coalesced over the NATO war in Kosovo. Supporters of NATO's intervention, at the simplest level, maintain that it was a humanitarian war undertaken to stop an "evil dictator" (Slobodan Milosevic, the Serbian leader) from committing acts of "genocide" and to prevent a potential "spillover" affect. As stated by British prime minister Tony Blair, "This is a just war, based not on any territorial ambitions but on values. We cannot let the evil of ethnic cleansing stand. We must not rest until it is reversed. We have learned twice before in this century that appeasement does not work. If we let an evil dictator range unchallenged, we will have to spill infinitely more blood and treasure to stop it."[3]

In academic circles, the official explanation was substantiated by the work of a number of commentators. Marc Weller, Adam Roberts, Ivo H. Daalder, and Michael E. O'Hanlon affirm that the Western alliance had a moral right to use military power.[4] In their view, even if NATO's threat of force of March 1999 did not have the full approval of the United Nations (UN) Security Council, there were other principles on which NATO was acting. These principles are those of "forcible humanitarian action" that had been approved by the events in October 1998, which had resulted in more than 200,000 refugees. According to these principles, if there exists a situation characterized by a fundamental dissociation between a population and a purported government, which becomes manifest by an actual or imminent humanitarian catastrophe of significant proportions, military action is justified. From this perspective, NATO's intervention was an answer to a humanitarian emergency and had a preventive aim.[5]

According to Daalder and O'Hanlon, the war was not about land and property but rather about human rights.[6] In their account of events prior to the NATO bombing, the Serbian policy was one of "ethnic extermination."[7] This view of the conflict was reinforced by the fact that in April 1999 the press reported an undisclosed source that argued that Milosevic had devised a plan called "Operation Horseshoe" for expelling and exterminating the Kosovo Albanian population.[8]

Two more explanations are commonly used in favor of NATO's action. One is that the international community had exhausted the possibilities for a diplomatic settlement to the crisis and that NATO's credibility was at stake. According to some analysts, although the international community proposed a variety of political solutions, the Serb leadership failed to seize the opportunity. The other explanation is that NATO was acting on the threat that the conflict would spill over to neighboring countries and lead to instability in southeastern Europe, threatening west European security.

Some assert that there was an element of diplomatic and military miscalculation on both sides. A belief common in NATO that a few days of bombing would suffice to resolve the issue proved inaccurate.[9] At the same time, Milosevic was allegedly persuaded that NATO would not undertake a sustained bombing campaign and that Russia would militarily come to his support. In other words, all the players in the drama had not properly thought through the consequences of their actions.[10]

Critics of the NATO intervention assert that the war was not so much about safeguarding the human lives of oppressed people, but rather had different dynamics. Some argue that geostrategic aims were at play. NATO and the United States wanted to expand their presence to southeastern Europe in order to gain access to an important transport system and thus consolidate their presence in the Caspian Sea and the Persian Gulf.[11] Others maintain that the war was fought because NATO needed to demonstrate its own relevance. At the same time, the United States wanted to show that it remained the world leader and wished to establish a right to use NATO in external military engagements, even without UN approval.[12]

Some analysts are of the opinion that NATO's decision to become militarily involved in the conflict between 1998 and March 1999 was influenced by its past experience in the Balkans. In Frédéric Bozo's view, for example, NATO's engagement was partly driven by a desire to give shape to the new Strategic Concept that was to be discussed in April 1999 at the Washington Summit.[13]

The critics of NATO's war over Kosovo also challenge the idea that what was happening in Kosovo prior to the launch of NATO's air strikes against Serbia could be defined as an act of orchestrated genocide. The critics state that those supporting NATO intervention have simplified the complex causes of the conflict so as to present the Kosovo Liberation Army (KLA) as an innocent victim and the Serbs as the villains. In the critics' view, this is an unbalanced account of the history of the conflict. They acknowledge that the Serbian police and the Serbian army were fully responsible for killing civilians and for most of the massacres committed in the region. But in their perspective, these deplorable actions were undertaken as a reprisal against the activities of the KLA, an organization also involved in the kidnapping and killing of Serbian policemen and alleged "civilian collaborators." In other words, there was guerrilla warfare, a conflict between two sides in which both engaged in violation of human rights.[14]

The critics use official figures for the Kosovo conflict, published by NATO and the Organization for Security and Cooperation in Europe (OSCE), that show that between the early months of 1998 and March 1999 there had been 2,000 dead and approximately 200,000 displaced people. Based on these figures, they argue that this human tragedy cannot be compared to the 6,000 Jews who were gassed every day in Auschwitz. They argue there has to be a clear definition of what is meant by genocide. From this perspective, what is described by officials and prointerventionists as ethnic cleansing prior to NATO's bombing could be better understood as the fleeing of civilians from the region for fear of war.[15]

Those opposed to NATO's military intervention also maintain that the Western allies never gave diplomacy a chance. During the Rambouillet negotiations, U.S. officials confronted the Serbs with a nonnegotiable version of the agreement and set up an ultimatum: they were told to either accept the conditions or be bombed. This final version of the new agreement contained a crucial new element expressed in Annex B, paragraph 8, which stated that "NATO troops would have full jurisdiction over FRY." NATO was to have "free and unrestricted passage and unimpeded access throughout the Yugoslav Federation (FRY), including associated airspace and territorial waters."[16] This was interpreted in Belgrade as signifying a total military occupation and political control of the FRY/Serbia by NATO. According to the critics, any independent state agreeing to this would be committing political suicide.[17]

## An Evaluation of the Debate: The Role of Policy Communities

Given the sufferings that the war caused, it is understandable that academics and officials have been engaged in heated controversy. In the analysis that follows, I hypothesize the existence of a policy community. This hypothesis takes the assumption from Robert O. Keohane and Joseph S. Nye that there is a phenomenon of transgovernmental policy coordination and transgovernmental coalition building in Western policy making. This assumption is combined with analysis of the role of ideological factors, as is addressed in the present literature on epistemic and policy communities.[18] Thus, I argue that a transgovernmental coalition can emerge not only because there is an intense pattern of interaction, but also because of the existence of common value systems and shared ideological perspectives toward a number of policy issues. The existence of "policy communities" in NATO is partly an expression of the breakdown of the consensus among the Western Allies that had characterized the Cold War period and the search for a new form of international governance. A policy community is thus defined as

> an alliance between sections of national government (composed of officials and politicians) and sections of an international bureaucracy. Members of a policy community have in common shared belief systems and perspectives on a number of foreign policy and security issues. They influence the policy-making process by intervening in setting agendas and proposing measures during periods characterized by high-level disagreement among political leaders at the international level.[19]

The hypothesis assumes that the existence of a policy community contributes to shaping the formulation of policies and their outcomes. It will be beyond the scope of this chapter to recount the findings based on a detailed analysis of events. Hence, I provide a summary of the key findings[20] and then discuss them in relation to the debate between the pro- and anti-NATO narratives.

### The Role of the Policy Community: Key Findings

The original research subdivided the analysis into three periods: January 1998 to early June 1998, mid-June to October 1998, and November 1998 to March 1999. The results are discussed in this sequence.

## Phase One: January to Early June 1998

The official beginning of the war was the result of the success of the KLA in undertaking guerrilla activities against the Serbs and the response of the Serbian armed forces. Initially, the strategy of the KLA was to create a corridor between Albania and central Kosovo that linked the Drenica valley to the Albania border.[21] Despite the attempts of the Serb forces to win back territory lost to the insurgent guerrilla movement, the KLA held on to its territorial conquest. During February and May, Serb police forces killed more than eighty civilians in cold blood. At the same time, the KLA undertook guerrilla warfare, which consisted in kidnapping and killing a small but significant number of Serb civilians. Between March and May 1998, the Serb military launched a counteroffensive in the Drenica valley region to regain territory lost to the KLA and attempted to seal off the borders with Albania.[22] The Serbian strategy initiated an internal refugee crisis.

Evidence for the existence of a policy community among Western allies can be found in the differential responses of Western organizations (the UN, OSCE, European Union [EU], and NATO) to the crises during this period. In the so-called Contact Group, the UN and the EU, the emphasis was on the use of diplomatic, political, and economic means to end the conflict. This can be found in the decisions taken by the Contact Group on January 8, March 9, and June 12, 1998, and by the UN in Security Council Resolution 1160. The Contact Group stressed the importance of political dialogue and called for the withdrawal of the special police units; an end of actions, directed by the security forces against the civilian population; access to Kosovo for the International Criminal Court Tribunal and other humanitarian organizations, as well as by representatives of the Contact Group and other embassies; and a demonstration of public commitment to begin a process of dialogue with the leadership of the Kosovo Albanian community. To enforce its demands, the Contact Group threatened to put a freeze on the funds held abroad by the FRY/Serbian government, to ban commercial air flights to and from the FRY, and to freeze international assets and investments. Resolution 1160 advanced a similar line of demands as those suggested by the Contact Group and threatened to introduce an arms embargo against the FRY.[23]

In contrast to the debate and decisions taken by the UN and the Contact Group, NATO was more ready to consider military means to resolve the crisis. In fact, despite the lack of a UN mandate, by the end of May, NATO became a key actor in the crisis. The NATO military started planning for a wider range of military options in Kosovo. At first, the North Atlantic Council (NAC) stated that it had a "legitimate interest in developments in Kosovo, inter alia because of their impact on the stability of the whole region which is of concern to the alliance."[24] Then, on May 29, 1998, NATO foreign ministers told the military authority to prepare to dispatch alliance forces to Albania and the former Yugoslav Republic of Macedonia and perhaps to Kosovo itself. NATO military authorities drew up preliminary plans to respond to Albania's request for a NATO force on its 140-kilometer-long border with Kosovo. General Wesley K. Clark, Supreme Allied Commander Europe (SACEUR), envisaged that about 20,000 to 23,000 troops would have been needed for the task. In addition, the ministers stated that NATO was to "consider the political, legal and, as necessary, military implications of possible further deterrent measures," implying a direct NATO intervention in the event that the conflict deteriorated into "massive violence."[25]

The Western alliance was successful in putting the military options on the table during this period thanks to the lobbying activities of British officials and the support that it found among the members of the NATO international military staff. In a speech in Rome, Prime Minister Blair declared his determination to ensure that Kosovo would not degenerate into another Bosnia. British minister of defense George Robertson admitted that there was a growing awareness that NATO might have to use military force in Kosovo.[26] At the same time, General Clark went to Washington to present his idea of a dual strategy for Kosovo. This involved establishing a comprehensive proposal for a settlement and an approval that NATO would use military leverage to compel negotiations, involving the use of NATO military air power. In Clark's view, the worst-case scenario, requiring an air bombing campaign, had to be envisaged and planned for.[27]

Other EU member states, while not opposed to NATO's involvement in the conflict in principle, sought to contain some of the demands for military options by arguing that the use of NATO military power should require authorization by the UN Security Council. This demand formed a central piece of the EU Council declaration signed on June 15–16, 1998.[28]

*Phase Two: Mid-June to October 1998*

By June, the KLA succeeded in controlling up to 20 percent of Kosovo, and this territory included strategic locations such as the coal mine at Belacevac. The KLA was advancing toward central Kosovo and was nearly reaching Priština. The Serbian security forces concentrated their effort on restricting the human flow across the Albanian border and by so doing caused the number of internally displaced people to rise significantly. In a counteroffensive, they managed to retake a mining area northwest of Priština, reopened lines of communication to western Kosovo, and regained control in Belacevac. Yet, the Serbs were either unwilling or unable to retake all the territory held by the KLA in the southwest of the province. The country therefore remained divided. The KLA controlled much of the south, but the north and Priština were under Serbian control.[29]

During this period, the British and NATO positions found support among hawks in the State Department, who began to shape U.S. policy toward the crisis. This occurred mainly because, from the beginning of January 1998 until the second half of 1999, President Bill Clinton was caught up in the Monica Lewinsky sex scandal. Having less time to dedicate to foreign policy issues, Clinton came to rely more on the advice of Madeleine Albright, the U.S. secretary of state, rather than on the advice of other members of the National Security Council (NSC).

The emergence of the new U.S. approach can be noticed in two aspects of the policy pursued: a more open support for the KLA and a stronger reliance on NATO's threat of force. This approach ignited a transatlantic controversy over the handling of the crisis.

*Support for the KLA?*

On June 25, 1998, Richard Holbrooke, newly appointed by the United States to mediate between the international community and Serbia, met the KLA leaders publicly.[30] Most EU member states did not want to negotiate with the KLA. A few days after the encounter, the EU Council of Ministers stressed that Kosovo president Ibrahim Rugova remained the key interlocutor for the negotiations and reaffirmed that the KLA should not be given any hope of independence.[31]

*Use of Force?*

By early August, the U.S. State Department spokesman James Rubin announced that NATO was fine-tuning its contingency plans for a possible military engagement in Kosovo, thus implying a readiness on the part of the United States to take military action.[32] He also made clear that in NATO's opinion existing UN resolutions on the former Yugoslavia provided sufficient authority for any military intervention that could be undertaken. French, German, and Russian officials thought differently.

*The Tactics of the Policy Community*

The key influence of the policy community was its success in persuading NATO defense ministers to introduce an activation warning on September 24, 1998. The order was for a "limited air option and a phased air campaign," thus opening the door for increased preparation for military operations.[33]

The initiative was the result of learning to modify tactics in order to obtain agreement from Western political leaders. As previously mentioned, throughout the spring and summer of 1998, SACEUR and NATO international staff had prepared for the eventuality of a land invasion and large-scale military air strikes modeled on the Desert Storm operation during the Persian Gulf War. During that period, NATO international staff learned how to win the support of dovish European NATO allies, who were inclined to believe that the mere threat of air strikes or a few days of strikes would get Milosevic to the negotiating table. The tactics consisted in focusing on getting agreement for the early stages of the operations and refraining from extensively discussing the long-term options that had to be contemplated if the strategy of a few days of air strikes did not get Milosevic to comply.[34]

Obtaining approval for an activation warning was a central preoccupation of the policy community. In fact, it should be remembered that despite the decision taken at the defense minister level, the NAC did not immediately approve the step. It took another month for the go-ahead to be given at such a level. This occurred only after intense activity by Albright, British officials, and NATO secretary-general Javier Solana. In early October 1998, Albright sent a personal letter to every NATO foreign minister in which she argued, "This is not a time to back down. Yes, it is dangerous and we genuinely want a political solution. But we have made our commitment clear and we must follow through." The letter was followed by personal phone calls from Albright and Robin Cook, the British foreign minister.

The final decision made on October 13 was to issue activation orders for limited air strikes and a phased air campaign in Yugoslavia to begin in approximately ninety-six hours; the orders required Secretary-General Solana's intervention.[35]

Another example of the influence of the policy community can be found in the introduction into the agreement of specific demands placed on Milosevic after he had agreed to comply with the ultimatum set by NATO and Security Council Resolution 1199. In his book, Clark explicitly states that he, together with U.S. ambassador Alexander Vershbow and Secretary-General Solana, was unhappy with the agreement that Holbrooke had at first negotiated with Milosevic because it did not include a role for the Western alliance. Hence, he sought to persuade Holbrooke of his point of view and obtained backing from Albright. This resulted in Milosevic assenting to NATO's reconnaissance flights over Kosovo and to the deployment of 2,000 unarmed monitors under the auspices of the OSCE to be supported by an "extraction force" stationed in Macedonia.[36]

The agreement between Milosevic and Holbrooke was a victory for those policy makers who, like Albright and Robertson, had long argued that Milosevic would only negotiate if threatened with bombs. This was one of the reasons why NATO took the historic step to keep the activation orders in operation months after that the agreement was signed.

*Phase Three: November 1998 to March 1999*

From late 1998 to March 1999, the influence of the policy community can be found in the response to a number of events: the breaching of the cease-fire by the KLA, the response to the Racak massacre, and the manner in which the Rambouillet Conference was held.

*The Breaching of the Cease-Fire*

By mid-October 1998, 4,000 members of the Yugoslav Special Forces had left Kosovo and a cease-fire was established. During November, the KLA broke the cease-fire by taking control of the territory left by the Serbian police. The KLA used the cease-fire to regroup, rearm, and prepare for a new offensive in the spring. Sporadic fighting also occurred. On December 14, Serb police forces killed thirty-six KLA men. In retaliation, the KLA killed six Serb civilians.

Despite this return of war in Kosovo, U.S. voices in support of the aims of the KLA became stronger. On January 6, 1999, Clark blamed the Serbs for escalating military tensions in the province. He also maintained that in the long run the Serbian military would have to face the KLA because the Kosovo Albanians could not risk the catastrophe of falling under the political repression of Belgrade. As one commentator pointed out, this implied a legitimization of KLA's existence and of its methods.[37]

Albright shared Clark's vision that Milosevic was responsible for the continued conflict in the region. On January 15, 1999, at an NSC meeting that included National Security Adviser Sandy Berger, Defense Secretary William Cohen, Chief of the Joint Chiefs of Staff Henry Shelton, Director of the Central Intelligence Agency George Tenet, and top aides, Albright stated that the October agreement had no future. In contrast to the position taken by the Pentagon's representatives and by Cohen and Berger, Albright argued that the administration was faced with three options: "stepping back, muddling through, or taking decisive steps." In her view, the third option would deliver better results and stressed that the threat of NATO action had to be maintained.[38]

*The Racak Massacre and Western Allies' Response*

On the same day that the NSC meeting took place, a massacre at Racak in Kosovo hit the news headlines. Forty-five Kosovo Albanians, including three women, a boy, and several elderly men, were found dead.

NATO ambassadors, at an urgent session on January 18, decided to send Clark and Klaus Naumann to Belgrade for diplomatic talks. Meanwhile, Albright worked in collaboration with Vershbow, the U.S. ambassador to NATO, and her staff on a proposal that would allow for NATO military action. Her strategy consisted of an ultimatum to the parties to force them to accept an interim settlement by a certain date. If the parties accepted the deal, they would commit themselves to its enforcement with the help of troops on the ground. But if Belgrade refused to accept the plan, NATO would launch air strikes. Because of inertia on the part of other sections of the U.S. policy-making structures that were opposed to Albright's view, Clinton decided to adopt the secretary of state's position on the issue.[39]

Albright then embarked on a series of meetings in European capitals to persuade reluctant allies. Most European officials argued that the threat of the use of force should not be used to punish Milosevic for the Racak massacre, but rather to extract from both parties a long-term political solution. In their view, the Serbs were not the only one responsible for the worsening situation. The KLA had also failed to respect the cease-fire and made substantial military advances. Hence, the EU foreign ministers agreed that it was better to seek international negotiations with both Milosevic and the Albanian leadership. This invitation was to be backed by a NATO warning against Belgrade, but not an ultimatum, and the threat to cut off financial and arms support for the KLA. In some European capitals, renewed doubts were raised as to the international legal authority for NATO's air strikes.[40] As a compromise, and particularly under pressure from the French government,[41] it was decided to make a last-ditch negotiation effort. However, Albright won the argument that there had to be a clear threat of air strikes in case Milosevic refused to endorse a settlement.[42] The negotiations were to become known as the Rambouillet Conference.

*The Rambouillet Conference*

During the Rambouillet Conference, which was to last from February 6 to February 20, the influence of NATO international staff along with British and U.S. officials surfaced openly. The conference was to negotiate an interim agreement of three years that established substantial autonomy for Kosovo.

Despite the introduction of a number of rules and procedures, the Rambouillet talks were not conducted on the basis of an equal dialogue among the participants. From the beginning, U.S. and British officials lent support to the KLA. Despite the fact that the Kosovo population had elected Rugova as their leader, it was decided that the KLA would be represented at the negotiations and would have substantial voting power. Hence, only one-third of the delegation came from the elected government of President Rugova. It was therefore not so much of a surprise when Hashim Thaci, a twenty-five-year-old member of the KLA, rather than President Rugova, was elected to head the delegation. The collusion between the position of U.S. officials and that of the Kosovo Albanian delegation is also demonstrated by the fact that the KLA hired Morton Abramowitz, a former U.S. State Department official, the president of the International Crisis Group, and a close friend of Albright, as an adviser during the Rambouillet negotiations.[43]

From the start, there was no real dialogue between the two delegations. Rather, the representative of the Western leaders engaged in a one-way conversation with Milosevic. When Milosevic refused to sign the agreement, the content of which is not publicly available, the negotiators panicked. They presented to both parties a short document of less than a page.

The two delegations were to indicate acceptance of the agreement, subject only to technical changes, to be made later by experts. Since this meant giving the negotiators carte blanche, neither of the delegations accepted it.

Lacking an agreement, the negotiations were prolonged until February 23. It is at this point that Albright officially entered the negotiations. It was clear that, even if Milosevic did not accept the agreement, there would not be sufficient grounds for bombing Serbia unless the KLA did agree to it. In order to persuade the Kosovo Albanian delegation to do so, Albright pursued the following strategy: first, she invited Clark to visit the delegation to reassure it of the nature of the demilitarization of the KLA, and second, she addressed the Kosovo Albanian demand for a referendum on independence. She proposed to include in the agreement that the "expressed will of the people" would be an element to be included in the final agreement. She insisted that the efforts made by parties involved would be an element that would be considered in determining a final settlement in Kosovo. These points were presented in an unsigned letter to the Kosovo Albanian delegation. Most of the members of the Kosovo Albanian delegation were swayed by Albright's concessions. However, Thaci refused to endorse it. As a compromise, the KLA was given two weeks to obtain support in Kosovo for the agreement.[44]

Then, a day before the deadline, the negotiators put forward the annexes on the military and civilian implementation that were to be nonnegotiable. Appendix B, entitled "Status of Multi-national Military Implementation Force," included the controversial points in paragraph 8 that gave NATO personnel, together with their vehicles, vessels, aircraft, and equipment, free and unrestricted passage and unimpeded access throughout the FRY, including associated airspace and territorial waters.[45]

These paragraphs were interpreted in Belgrade as a capitulation to NATO in that the Western alliance would have taken control of the territory of the FRY. The talks ended in failure: the Kosovo Albanian delegation signed up to the agreement, and the Serbs rejected it. NATO had the go-ahead for military action.

### Examining the Findings against the Pro- and Anti-NATO Narratives

The findings indicate that there is some evidence for the existence of a policy community that included NATO international staff, along with British and U.S. officials. The key influence of the policy community was to ensure that at crucial moments the military options were put at the forefront of diplomatic efforts; this simultaneously sidelined any open discussions about the long-term implications of military actions if NATO's threat of air strikes failed. The findings however do not fully explain why other European allies decided to go along with the strategy of the policy community.

To explain these changes, we need to take into account some of the assumptions contained in the current conflicting narratives on NATO's war over Kosovo. By comparing the findings on the policy community with the current literature, I will outline some of the key factors that can help explain the complex dynamics of NATO's decision to intervene militarily in the conflict.

## Did NATO Intervene Because of Humanitarian Reasons or Because of Hegemonic Factors?

The findings reveal that there was a genuine concern within the international community about developments in Kosovo, particularly abuse of human rights. However, by demonstrating that the members of the identified policy community were inclined to use NATO as a tool in support of the efforts of the KLA, the findings challenge the idea that NATO's actions were purely humanitarian, that is, politically neutral.

### The Influence of Other Factors

The anti-NATO narratives maintain that the Western alliance intervened because the United States wanted to prove its hegemonic role in the Balkans and NATO aimed to expand its area of influence. These arguments are not fully supported by the findings. In Washington, there was no consensus among policy makers about how to react to the crisis. The United States took a leading role because domestic events allowed the State Department, led by Albright, to shape the policy-making process by default. In other words, the influence exercised by leading members of the State Department was not part of an overall strategy conceived in the Pentagon and in the White House. Rather, U.S. policy makers were divided. The leading position that the State Department and the British officials took was facilitated by specific domestic factors.⁻

### The Influence of the Human Rights Discourse on British and U.S. Officials

Blair, who had become the British prime minister in 1997, represented a new generation of British politicians, less influenced by the ideology of realism and power politics and more by the discourse of human rights. Blair, along with many other members of his party, believed that past British interventions in the Yugoslav wars (1991–1995) had been based on a wrong understanding of the causes of the conflict and therefore was a stain on the British reputation. His conceptualization of international relations was shaped by the belief that human rights should be given more attention in the formulation of foreign and security policy. In fact, this new understanding even came to be included in the new British Ministry of Defense Strategic Defense

Review, which was announced in 1998. The review committed Britain to enhancing the flexible capacity of its armed forces to undertake peace support and humanitarian operations. From the perspective of the government and the Ministry of Defense, the United Kingdom had a responsibility to act as a force for good in the world.

Similarly, Albright was influenced by the politics of human rights because of her personal background, in that her family had suffered in the Nazi concentration camps. Moreover, the Clinton administration brought into the State Department a new layer of officials, who, affected by the civil rights movement of the 1960s, believed that human rights deserved a high priority on the U.S. foreign policy agenda.

Hence, when the conflict erupted, some British officials and influential sections of the U.S. policy-making community were inclined toward viewing the situation in the Balkans as a simple question of denial of human rights by Serbia over the Kosovo population. In addition, in contrast to the view of other Western allies, leading figures in the Labour government and in the Clinton administration had long considered Milosevic the key culprit in the Balkan tragedy. The presentation of Milosevic as an "evil" dictator was not merely propaganda to justify going to war. Rather, it was based on deeply felt convictions.

Although there is no doubt that Milosevic was a nationalist, the causes of the conflict in the Balkans cannot be reduced to the existence of his regime. Rather, as many studies have demonstrated, there were complex dynamics in operation, even during the wars in Croatia and Bosnia.[46] In the case of Kosovo, it is difficult to argue that Thaci, the KLA leader, was a more legitimate leader than Milosevic or that KLA military tactics lived up to Western standards of international law.

**The Lessons Learned from the Balkans**

Rather than hegemonic factors, it appears that Western policies came to be dominated by the position taken by British and U.S. officials because there was already an existing consensus about the need for the use of a threat of force when dealing with regional conflicts.

This belief had been the product of the lessons learned in the Bosnia wars (1992–1995). While at the beginning of the war in Bosnia, some Western allies wanted to hold on to traditional notions of neutrality, by 1995 they agreed that the use of force was legitimate. The military success of NATO's Operation Deliberate Hope in obtaining a diplomatic agreement meant that the belief in the use of force became entrenched in the security policies of all Western allies.[47]

Hence, the debate within the Western alliance was restricted to the exact dosage of military and diplomatic tools and the level of legitimacy to be obtained from the UN. This consensus allowed the members of the identified policy community to raise the stakes easily. At the same time, another factor came into play: the relationship that was established between NATO's internal renewal process and its presence in the Balkans.

## Internal Renewal and Balkan Presence

During NATO's intervention in the Bosnian wars, the renewal of the NATO integrated military structure had become closely linked to the ability of its member states to deploy troops for peacekeeping/peace-enforcement operations. U.S. officials and leading NATO international staff had in fact, throughout the early part of the 1990s, argued that the structure, force posture of west European armed forces, and the related equipment, military doctrine, and operational planning had to change to meet "external threats." The ad hoc nature of Western policy making in the Bosnian wars, the strategies of the warring parties in the region, and the conscious efforts by NATO's international military staff and officials to link the planning of a large peacekeeping/ peace-enforcement operation to the testing of the Combined Joint Task Force and the Partnership for Peace concepts all contributed to the idea that what was at stake in Bosnia was the survival of NATO.[48]

Although by 1997 the Implementation Force had demonstrated NATO's ability to sustain peacekeeping/peace-enforcement tasks, in the minds of influential military experts and U.S. officials within NATO, it had not succeeded in generating sufficient changes in the force posture and force planning of the organization. In fact, when the conflict in Kosovo erupted, NATO officials were undertaking studies of the new alliance's structure and posture. Hence, when General Clark and his subordinate thought about Kosovo, they were also preoccupied with the process of renewal and the general status of NATO's presence in the region. By late 1998, the discussion about the extent to which European NATO allies should contribute to modified-force-generation planning by restructuring their own military forces became an element of the discussions on how to respond to the Kosovo crisis.

In the autumn of 1998, the United Kingdom, with the consent of U.S. officials, proposed to allow the Western European Union to be integrated into the EU in order to give the latter a military muscle. At the heart of the change in the British position was a desire to ensure that European allies upgrade their military commitment to the NATO alliance. Britain would concede to an EU autonomous role only if politicians in Paris and Bonn committed themselves to restructuring their military forces to achieve military targets for the new Strategic Concept that was being drawn up by staff at the Supreme Headquarters Allied Powers Europe (SHAPE).[49]

The deployment of forces in Kosovo was perceived at SHAPE headquarters as a test of the ability of European partners to commit themselves to the new targets drawn up and later to be known as the Defence Capability Initiative and the Headline Goals. Furthermore, U.S. officials made it clear that they wanted Europeans to deploy the bulk of the troops in Kosovo in the event of a land invasion.[50]

## Pressures on the Doves and the Nature of Policy Making within NATO

The doves within the Western alliance complied with the demands made by the policy community because of a number of pressures.

First, the fear of regional destabilization and the televised sufferings of the civilian displaced population played an important role in forcing the doves to take a tough stance.

Second, the German and Italian electorate voted for two new governments in 1998 that were composed of politicians (Joschka Fischer and Massimo D'Alema, respectively) whose parties (the German Greens and the former Italian communists, respectively) had traditionally been opposed to the Western alliance. Because of this, there were some domestic and external pressures on the new German and Italian coalition governments to show their allegiance to NATO.

Third, a linkage was established between, on the one hand, the preparation for the potential deployment of troops in Kosovo and, on the other, the promise made to key NATO European allies, especially France, of an independent EU defense force. This dampened concerns among dovish European allies about the military strategy that was being drafted at NATO headquarters to deal with the crisis. Even if some French, German, and Italian policy makers had some doubts about the nature and means to resolve the Kosovo conflict, they were not inclined to distance themselves from the line pursued in London and Washington for fear of missing a historical chance to realize a more independent European defense.

Fourth, the policy-making process within the Western alliance has specific characteristics that limited the influence of the doves. There is no veto power at the NAC level, and countries are reluctant to withdraw from the Western alliance on one single issue because of the security benefits that each member state obtains from participating in NATO. Many decisions with a military content are framed at a lower level of the policy-making process, thanks to the operational ability of NATO international military staff. But these decisions are highly political in nature. Officials in the lower-level policy-making structures have a significant influence on the policy-making process in that they shape the questions that are discussed at a higher level. Because of these factors, individual countries or a coalition of a few acting on a specific policy have limited room to maneuver.

## Conclusion

In relation to the pro- and anti-NATO narratives on intervention, the findings do not refute the proposition that Western leaders were sincerely moved by human rights concerns. However, they challenge the idea that NATO acted as a neutral actor and that its motives were purely humanitarian.

The difference between these findings and the prevalent critical literature on NATO's war over Kosovo is that it refutes the idea that hegemonic factors can help explain the conflict. In contrast, it argues that critics of NATO's war in Kosovo have insufficiently paid attention to the following dynamics: the influence of domestic factors (the human rights discourse among British and U.S. officials), the "lessons" from past interventions (the unquestioned belief in the use of military force to resolve regional crises), the linkage that came to be established between the renewal of the integrated military structure and NATO's presence in the Balkans, and the constraints and pressures on the doves.

The findings provide support for the notion that diplomacy was not given a chance at Rambouillet, in that the key role played by the British and U.S. officials (who were more openly sympathetic to the aims of the KLA) in the negotiations strengthened the belief among the Serbian leadership that there could be no room for compromise. The findings allow for a reinterpretation of the geostrategic argument: it was no so much territorial control of the southern Balkans that some NATO officials and politicians wanted; rather, one of the many factors that came to influence the Western alliance's strategy toward the Kosovo war was the ability of the Western alliance to continue with its process of transformation of its integrated military structure based on force projection.

Given these results, what are the lessons that can be drawn for future dynamics of Western military intervention in light of the current war on terrorism?

The key lessons that many European members of the Western alliance drew from intervention in the Kosovo war was that to have a say in international crises one needs to possess military power independently of the United States. In fact, despite the apparent "victory" of NATO in the Kosovo war, the intervention intensified demands for a new "burden sharing" among the Western allies. Immediately after the war, some European member states (re)interpreted Blair's proposal for an independent European army as allowing the creation of political and military institutions within the EU, partly to counterbalance the weight that the United States has in NATO.

At the same time, on both sides of the Atlantic, the experience of the war has given support to those who want to plan for external military operations through ad hoc coalitions of the willing. This will allow a group of countries to intervene externally using the economic and military facilities available within the UN, NATO, and the EU without being fully accountable to the political authority of these institutions. The recent Western military interventions in Afghanistan and Iraq and their aftermath are an example of this trend.

The experience in Kosovo thus accelerated the dynamics of the breakdown of the international order as it existed in the Cold War period, in that it has contributed to a transformation of the Western alliance into a "service provider."

# Notes

1. For an overview of the theoretical, historical, and legal debate about "humanitarian intervention," see Danish Institute of International Affairs, *Humanitarian Intervention: Legal and Political Aspects* (Copenhagen: Danish Institute of International Affairs, 1999); James Mayall, "The Concept of Humanitarian Intervention Revisited," in Albrecht Schnabel and Ramesh Thakur, eds., *Kosovo and the Challenge of Humanitarian Intervention* (New York: UN University Press, 2000), pp. 319–333.

2. Miranda Vickers, *Between Serbs and Albania: A History of Kosovo* (London: Hurst, 1998); Stefan Troebst, *Conflict in Kosovo: Failure of Prevention? An Analytical Documentation, 1992–1998* (Flensburg: European Centre for Minority Issue, 1998).

3. Tony Blair, "Doctrine of the International Community" (speech to the Economic Club of Chicago, Hilton Hotel, Chicago, April 22, 1999).

4. Marc Weller, "The Rambouillet Conference on Kosovo," *International Affairs* 75, no. 2 (1999): 211–251; Adam Roberts, "NATO's 'Humanitarian War' over Kosovo," *Survival* 41, no. 3 (Autumn 1999): 102–123; Ivo H. Daalder and Michael E. O'Hanlon, *Winning Ugly: NATO's War to Save Kosovo* (Washington, D.C.: Brookings Institution, 2000).

5. Marc Weller, *The Crisis in Kosovo, 1989–1999: From the Dissolution of Yugoslavia to Rambouillet and the Outbreak of Hostilities* (Cambridge: Centre of International Studies, University of Cambridge, 1999), pp. 395–396.

6. Daalder and O'Hanlon, *Winning Ugly*, pp. 1–6.

7. Daalder and O'Hanlon, *Winning Ugly*, pp. 22–87.

8. For a background to the issue, see Tim Judah, *Kosovo: War and Revenge* (New Haven, Conn.: Yale University Press, 2000), pp. 240–242.

9. Michael Mandelbaum, "A Perfect Failure: NATO's War against Yugoslavia," *Foreign Affairs* 78, no. 5 (September–October 1999).

10. "Was the Kosovo Campaign a Success or a Failure? A Brutal Quagmire," *International Herald Tribune*, 31 March 2000.

11. Tania Noctiummes and Jean-Pierre Page, "Yougoslavie: une guerre impérialiste pour instaurer un nouvel ordre mondial," in Samir Amin et al., eds., *Maitres du monde? ou les dessous de la guerre des Balkans* (Pantin: Le Temps des Cerises, 1999), pp. 7–9.

12. Noam Chomsky, *Le nouvel humanisme militaire* (Lausanne: Editions Page, 2000), pp. 197–199. Other commentators have added that the United States also intervened to demonstrate that the security of the continent needed its presence and to discredit any vague desire for an autonomous European defense. See Pierre D'Argent, "Au nom des droits de l'homme," in Bernard Adam, *La guerre du Kosovo: Eclairages et commentaires* (Brussels: Complexe/GRIP, 1999), pp. 79–81; Eric Rouleau, "Lessons of War: French Diplomacy Adrift in Kosovo," *Le Monde Diplomatique* (December 1999).

13. Frédéric Bozo, "Continuity or Change? The View from Europe," in S. Victor Papacosma, Sean Kay, and Mark R. Rubin, eds., *NATO after Fifty Years* (Wilmington, Del.: Scholarly Resources, 2001), pp. 53–72.

14. James G. Jatras, "NATO's Myths and Bogus Justifications for Intervention," in Ted G. Carpenter, ed., *NATO's Empty Victory: A Postmortem on the Balkan War* (Washington, D.C.: CATO Institute, 2000), pp. 21–30; Bernard Adam, "Aprés la guerre du Kosovo, quelles leçons pour la sécurite européenne?" in Adam, *La guerre du Kosovo*, pp. 147–162.

15. Chomsky, *Le nouvel humanisme militaire*, pp. 40–41,131, 135, 230, 245.

16. Original reprinted in Weller, *Crisis in Kosovo*, pp. 468–469.

17. Chomsky, *Le nouvel humanisme militaire*, p. 161. A critical perspective of the Rambouillet negotiations can also be found in Emanuele Arielli and Giovanni Scotto, *La guerra del Kosovo, anatomia di un' escalazione* (Rome: Editori Riuniti, 1999); Roberto Menotti et al., eds., *L'intervento della NATO in Kosovo: riflessioni su una escalation coercitiva* (Rome: CeSPI, 2000), pp. 39–40, available at www.cespi.it/ Laboratorio/Lab__3=2000.pdf (accessed March 25, 2003).

18. Robert. O. Keohane and Joseph S. Nye, "Transgovernmental Relations and International Organizations," *World Politics* 28, no. 1 (1974): 38–62; Peter Haas, "Introduction: Epistemic Communities and International Policy Co-ordination," *International Organization* 46, no. 1 (1992): 1–35.

19. Giovanna Bono, *NATO's Peace-Enforcement Tasks and "Policy-Communities," 1990–1999* (Aldershot, UK: Ashgate, 2003), see especially the introduction.

20. Bono, *NATO's Peace-Enforcement Tasks*, chapter 5.

21. Judah, *Kosovo*, p 145.

22. Georges Berghezan, "Les coulisses du rapide developpment de l'UCK," in Bernard Adam, *La guerre du Kosovo*, p. 60; Judah, *Kosovo*, pp. 140, 157–167.

23. Weller, *Crisis in Kosovo*, pp. 188, 235–237.

24. Weller, *Crisis in Kosovo*, p. 272.

25. "NATO Prepares for Crisis in Kosovo," *Financial Times*, 29 May 1998.

26. "NATO Urged to Intervene As 11,000 Refugees Flee Kosovo," *Financial Times*, 5 June 1998; "Kosovo Crisis," *The Guardian*, 6 June 1998, p. 12.

27. Wesley K. Clark, *Waging Modern War: Bosnia, Kosovo and the Future of Combat* (Oxford: Public Affairs, 2001).

28. Weller, *Crisis in Kosovo*, pp. 230–231.

29. Judah, *Kosovo*, p. 169; Tim Youngs and Tom Dodd, *Kosovo* (London: House of Commons Library, 1998).

30. "L'émissaire americain rencontre des combattants albanais du Kosovo," *Le Monde*, 26 June 1998, p. 3.

31. "Les Occidentaux veulent amener les combattants du Kosovo à négocier," *Le Monde*, 1 July 1998.

32. "US Says NATO Is Ready for Military Intervention in Kosovo," *The Independent*, 4 August 1998, p. 1.

33. Reprinted in Weller, *Crisis in Kosovo*, p. 277; Clark, *Waging Modern War*, pp. 134–137.

34. Clark, *Waging Modern War*, pp. 123, 177–187.

35. Daalder and O'Hanlon, *Winning Ugly*, p. 44.

36. Clark, *Waging Modern War*, pp. 141–143.

37. "Blaming Serbs, NATO General Says Kosovo Nears New War," *International Herald Tribune*, 6 January 1999.

38. Daalder and O'Hanlon, *Winning Ugly*, p. 70.

39. Daalder and O'Hanlon, *Winning Ugly*, pp. 71–72.

40. "More NATO Air Strikes on Serbs? A Daunting Test for Alliance," *International Herald Tribune*, 20 January 1999; "Divergences occidentals sur la crise du Kosovo," *Le Monde*, 27 January 1999, p. 3.

41. Massimo D'Alema, *Kosovo: gli Italiani e la guerra* (Milano: Arnoldo Mondatori Editore, 1999), p. 14.

42. Barton Gellman, "The Path to Crisis: How the United States and Its Allies Went to War," *Washington Post*, 18 April 1999, p. A31. The NATO ultimatum is reprinted in Weller, *Crisis in Kosovo*, p. 416.

43. Judah, *Kosovo*, p. 205.

44. Reprinted in Weller, *Crisis in Kosovo*, p. 452.

45. Weller, *Crisis in Kosovo*, pp. 468, 469.

46. Susan L. Woodward, *Balkan Tragedy: Chaos and Dissolution after the Cold War* (Washington, D.C.: Brookings Institution, 1995).

47. Bono, *NATO's Peace-Enforcement Task*, chapters 3, 4.

48. Bono, *NATO's Peace-Enforcement Task*, chapter 7.

49. Julian Lindley-French, "NATO, Britain, and the Emergence of a European Defence Capability," in S. Victor Papacosma, Kay, and Rubin, eds., *NATO after Fifty Years*, pp. 43–53.

50. Clark, *Waging Modern War*, p. 164.

# 13

## The Reluctant Intervenor
### The UN Security Council, China's Worldview, and Humanitarian Intervention

*Michael C. Davis*

In the 1999 United Nations (UN) General Assembly meeting, UN secretary-general Kofi Annan signaled a new era of activism in humanitarian intervention, highlighting the increasing need for UN intervention and proclaiming, "state sovereignty is being redefined by the forces of globalization and international cooperation."[1] Tang Jiaxuan, China's foreign minister, quickly responded that "the issue of human rights is . . . an internal affair of a country, and should be addressed mainly by the government of that country through its own efforts."[2] He emphasized the preeminence of sovereignty and nonintervention as the guiding principles of the international system and the primary role of individual state actors in implementing human rights commitments. These opposite views distill one of the central human rights issues today. What is the appropriate response of the UN and regional international organizations to vast humanitarian crises emerging from within member states? What is the appropriate response of other member states? Should the UN or other international bodies yield to the claims of sovereignty, even when confronted with a serious human tragedy? In this chapter, I consider China's views and policies in respect to these questions and the likely role of China in shaping the humanitarian intervention regime.

Given China's permanent membership in the UN Security Council and its status as a major power, it would seem unwise to ignore China in addressing the humanitarian intervention debate. This consideration requires us to address central elements of China's worldview and to consider their relationship to the emerging global view on appropriate responses to humanitarian crises. In a world of uneven responses to these tragic events, the political views of China and other non-Western states will ultimately be critical to the development of satisfactory global norms.

Any analysis of China's contribution to this debate must recognize that China's views on sovereignty and related global issues are intertwined with

China's domestic politics and political structure.[3] China's current status as an authoritarian unitary state with several restless peripheral communities clearly shapes its present resistance to humanitarian intervention. Its ongoing political conflicts with Taiwan, Tibet, and Islamic ethnic groups in central Asia loom especially large among the factors shaping its policies. China's responses to these types of issues are further complicated by its domestic political system. A government with little democratic resources may be prone to more often mobilize nationalist sentiments as a source of support for its views in this area, encouraging further resistance to incursions on sovereignty. Under the current political regime in China, there is little room for dramatic change in these policies. If there was future domestic political reform in China—including democratization and possible confederal arrangements with its peripheral communities—this formula could be altered and China's resistance relaxed. But the short-term prospects either for democratization or altering its territorial paradigm are not great.

China has tended to take a hard line on sovereignty and nonintervention. In the philosophical terms discussed in chapter 1, China has taken a firm position in favor of the Millian conception of sovereignty and nonintervention and has had less use for the Kantian notion of perpetual peace built on the foundation of a federation of republican states, which underlies democratic peace theory. The UN Charter appears to harbor conflicting commitments to both this Kantian federation and the Millian commitment to sovereignty. China has placed considerable weight on the sovereignty-protecting view of the UN Charter. Under existing political conditions, this narrows the scope of acceptable solutions to humanitarian crises in respect of the UN regime. One must doubt the Chinese support for the new Canadian-UN report recasting intervention as a "responsibility to protect."[4] China will either see a suspicious threat to sovereignty in this conception or will seek to shape it to lay heavy emphasis on the nonintervention norm, while depreciating options in the report that seek to get around UN immobility.

China's lukewarm response to the "war on terrorism" and U.S. initiatives in the UN Security Council respecting Iraq have well illustrated China's contradictory concerns in respect to sovereignty issues. On the one hand, it shares the concerns of the so-called war on terrorism, attributing some of its own separatist problems to the same sources.[5] On the other hand, it fears that giving the United States and its allies a blank check to intervene in the internal affairs of a state such as Iraq may redound to its own disadvantage. These fears were certainly not assuaged by the rather shaky arguments offered by the U.S. administration for the recent intervention in Iraq. That these arguments, on the available evidence, appeared to come down largely to regime change could not have been reassuring to the regime in Beijing.

This chapter will contrast China's views with the emerging world practice discussed elsewhere in this book. This analysis considers both the likely contribution of the current Chinese regime to the intervention debate and the likely effect of domestic political reforms and settlements on China's role in this debate. The discussion throughout relates Chinese perspectives to a variety of perspectives in the emerging global debate introduced in chapter 1 and developed throughout the book. Evident here is a certain Chinese (and non-Western) distrust of contemporary largely Western motivations for intervention. At the same time, Western powers often distrust China's intentions.[6] The source of this latter distrust relates especially to China's existing regime type and strong defense of sovereignty and nonintervention. Given the directions the intervention debate has taken, this analysis also considers the likely effect of democratization and the potential for federal or confederal arrangements to contribute to China's intervention policy.[7] As China's rapid development proceeds, it will be important for scholars and political strategists to anticipate different political scenarios. For a democratizing China, would confederal arrangements with the periphery contribute to patterns of peace?[8]

In terms of global norm development, this chapter anticipates the development of a humanitarian intervention principle that will increasingly relate nonintervention to the presence of democracy and respect for international human rights. It is not the present argument that these conditions are now established. It is likely, however, that regional norm development will increasingly shape strategies of crisis prevention and expectations regarding intervention. Regional institutions may ultimately place greater emphasis on human rights and democracy. Regional commitments to democracy and human rights may, in turn, contribute to the avoidance of the types of conflict most likely to produce humanitarian crises and to the peaceful resolution of conflicts when they occur. Regional developments are in many respects already moving in this direction, though Asia's relative lack of regional security and human rights institutions may leave it out of the picture. Given China's importance in the global debate and its existing regime type, China may turn out to be an obstacle to evolving global norms in this area. Its resistance to change may reduce its role in the development of a humanitarian intervention norm. As a consequence, this type of region-focused reform process is likely to minimize China's role in devolving norms of humanitarian intervention. On the other hand, if China takes up substantial political reform, its role in developing intervention norms will be enhanced and the likelihood of norm development on a global scale increased. Whether through a long arduous path of regional and ad hoc development or through a formal global UN-sponsored treaty regime, the long-term development of a firm link between democracy/human rights and nonintervention seems likely.

## China and Humanitarian Intervention

It is noteworthy that in the plethora of academic articles and books addressing humanitarian intervention the position of China on these issues is hardly mentioned.[9] Either China is perceived to be irrelevant to the emerging post–Cold

War norms in this area or it is viewed as simply an insurmountable obstacle, so far out of step with the rest of the world that it should be ignored. As noted earlier, China has taken a skeptical position on a variety of fundamental questions associated with the humanitarian intervention question. It has, in many respects, positioned itself on the opposing side of past global trends in regard to sovereignty, human rights, democracy, and intervention. China has articulated a fundamental sovereignty principle that puts it at odds with an expanding intervention regime. It has made its five principles of peaceful coexistence, nearly all of which speak of nonintervention, the centerpiece of its foreign policy.[10] These principles lend a moral grounding to its nonintervention principle. An assessment of China's role in respect of the humanitarian intervention question ought to consider the current regime's likely flexibility on these issues and ways in which domestic political reforms are likely to shape China's future policies.

China's current views on sovereignty and nonintervention implicate nearly all of the issue areas in the humanitarian intervention debate, including the transformation of the state system, the nature of sovereignty, the role of the UN, the role of regional international institutions, globalization, and the foreign policies of global powers.[11] At the same time, Chinese policies in these areas implicate China's reform process at home and its patterns of identity formation and global participation. The intervention question serves to sharpen the focus of our attention to these long-standing world order questions and offers an opportunity to view these questions through a more concrete and narrow lens. The Chinese response to these events and developments serves to highlight a competing side of this debate that will certainly influence the intervention regime to come.

## China's Current Position

China's formal position in respect to international responses to humanitarian crises can be broken down into two issue areas: crises arising out of internal conflicts and crises arising out of cross-border incursions. In respect of humanitarian crises arising out of internal conflicts, China opposes any form of military intervention, unless the sovereign power and the UN Security Council both approve such action. China clearly has its own territorial problems in Taiwan and Tibet, which it characterizes as internal, in mind. Its resistance to such intervention proposals is usually passive, exercised by some form of abstention on a Security Council resolution on intervention. This policy is effectively characterized by passive participation or reluctant intervention. Although China has often articulated strong views against potential intervention actions, it has rarely used its Security Council veto power, fearing the undermining of its UN standing. Such veto actions are usually reserved for more directly Taiwan-related matters. China's opposition to intervention takes a particularistic quality where relations with Taiwan are involved. As of 2000, it had exercised its Security Council veto power four times, and three of these related to matters where Taiwan relations were directly implicated.[12] It may simply refuse to support a country that has relations with Taiwan.

China's position is more flexible regarding military intervention in respect of cross-border incursions, where only UN Security Council approval would be viewed as essential. In respect of such international conflicts, it has also been more amenable to nonmilitary forms of intervention, such as sanctions and boycotts. And when a military response has seemed necessary, China has usually gone along with such a response, only insisting on Security Council approval. The recent U.S. response to terrorist attacks on the World Trade Center, the so-called war on terrorism, tested this general approach seriously. Although China went along with the U.S. claim to be exercising self-defense, as permitted in the UN Charter, it strongly favored Security Council approval. At the same time, China's own concerns about separatist resistance in Xinjiang, which China attributes to the same radical Islamic groups in Afghanistan, and other geostrategic considerations favored participation in the coalition against terrorism mobilized by the United States. In spite of this specific self-interest, a deeper and long-standing concern with the sovereignty principle tended to dampen China's support for U.S. intervention in Afghanistan. Concerning U.S. military intervention in Iraq, China's resistance increased even more. Even after that intervention, China continued to encourage a more substantial UN role, being truly a reluctant intervenor.

Where UN approval for intervention has been obtained and the UN is involved, China has even shown a willingness to participate in military operations. It has taken up limited roles in the UN peacekeeping process.[13] It has served on the relevant UN Special Committee on Peacekeeping Operations and has contributed about 1 percent of the separate peacekeeping budget. China is credited with filling 532 peacekeeping slots in 9 missions from 1989 to 2000.[14] Overall, from 1990 to the present, it has contributed about 650 military observers, liaison officers, or staff officers and 800 engineering troops (in Cambodia in 1992).[15] At the end of 2002, it had fifty-three Chinese military observers in the field in six regions of the world.[16] In its *National Defense White Paper, 2002*, China emphasized its commitment to greater security cooperation, especially in the East Asian region.[17]

### The Domestic Chinese Context

Beyond these broad principles, China's position on international intervention is shaped in important ways by very practical domestic concerns.[18] China's resistance to democracy at home and its human rights practices have been visible components of its resistance to international intervention. Domestically, its view is often expressed as opposition to "interference in its internal affairs." Beyond a general concern with outside meddling, a powerful myth is attached to the notion of national unity in the Chinese leadership's conception of its political history. Disunity is viewed as an invitation to chaos. Detractors challenge the authenticity of this unitary claim, its contribution to peaceful order, and the appropriate territorial scope of China's historical claims—the latter especially regarding Taiwan, Tibet, and parts of central Asia.

China's claims to Taiwan, its occupation of Tibet, and its communal conflicts with Muslim separatists in central Asia have played especially significant roles in respect to China's territorial anxieties.[19] Intervention is viewed as a direct threat to its claims to these peripheral communities. Taiwan has inspired China to impose its conception of sovereignty in its international relations at every opportunity. Tibet has presented China with a serious contradiction, as it is credited with resisting imperialism abroad and pursuing it at home. This contradiction has encouraged a rather absolutist official view of state sovereignty, sometimes tempered by practical considerations, as it seeks resolution of its territorial crises. At the same time, such a view of state sovereignty has contributed to a tense relationship with popular communal leaders of its peripheral communities. As the difficulties that China has confronted in response to the war on terrorism attest, China's most intense internal confrontation of a military nature in recent years has arisen in respect to the peripheral Muslim communities in central Asia.

These tense conditions often leave little room to maneuver, and the current Beijing government can be expected to persist in its resistance to an expanded intervention regime. Nevertheless, it should be appreciated that the Beijing view is not monolithic. A variety of human rights and trade agreements or practices may depreciate its otherwise hard view of sovereignty. The Hong Kong model is the most striking case in this regard. The Sino-British Joint Declaration over Hong Kong appears to invite outside interests and participation. At the same time, the Hong Kong agreement commits China to maintain democracy and human rights in the territory.[20] China has shown less flexibility over Tibet. Though there has been dialogue with the Dalai Lama about autonomy for Tibet, few concrete concessions have been made on Beijing's part.[21] Global agreements have also demonstrated some movement. China has signed but not ratified the International Covenant on Civil and Political Rights (a treaty that already applies in Hong Kong), though again the degree of ultimate compliance is suspect. Accession to the World Trade Organization (WTO) has likewise relaxed the sovereignty barrier in China's international economic relations. China's flexibility on the sovereignty issue, conceived in terms of outside interference, appears to be most visible in respect of economic development and least pronounced in respect of territory and security. The economic reform process in China is continuing to raise the prospects for further political reform. Do flexibility in developing an intervention regime, domestic democratization, and solutions to China's peripheral anxieties come as a package?

## Assessing the Chinese View

China's hard line on sovereignty comes at a cost. As suggested earlier, it is largely excluded from discussions concerning reform of the intervention regime. One hardly ever sees China even mentioned in such reform discussions or the academic literature. An authoritarian hard-line regime such as China is not much trusted in a Kantian world. That the current U.S. administration, for its own reasons of hostility to multilateralism and the UN, has come to share Beijing's resistance to such a Kantian world may only stiffen Beijing's resolve. China's hard legal positivist or statist view of international law and sovereignty poses a serious challenge to an emerging more interventionist global order. The 1999 events in Kosovo and East Timor and the more recent war on terror and intervention in Iraq have especially tested China's worldview and put China in opposition to evolving trends. One can see China's peripheral communities in its considerations when it opposed the UN Security Council's taking action in Kosovo and when it later supported a resolution to condemn the North Atlantic Treaty Organization (NATO) regional action.[22] This was also evident when it opposed UN-sponsored intervention in East Timor. This intervention, in China's view, involved an internal conflict, and, accordingly, China withheld its consent to military action until the sovereign power in Jakarta had agreed. China's reluctant participation in the war on terrorism and resistance to U.S. intervention in Iraq further testifies to its continuing status as a reluctant intervenor.

China's view of human rights more generally has been deployed to give theoretical underpinning to its formal hard-line position on sovereignty. This Chinese conception "transposes the notion of individual freedom into the conceptual framework of nationalism."[23] The Chinese government, in its white paper on human rights, emphasized the role of sovereignty in assuring basic human rights.[24] With historic colonial imposition in mind, sovereignty is viewed as the foundation for human rights and for resisting Western encroachment. Turning the Western conception of rights on its head, in this conception, the interests of the state override individual rights in the collective national interest.[25] Taken as a whole, this tends to conceptually assign indivisibility to territorial sovereignty. As noted earlier, in practice, some degree of exception has been made in respect of Hong Kong and Taiwan and in respect of some multilateral trade and human rights treaties.[26] As China becomes more engaged in global processes of trade and human rights, one can expect further easing of its hard-line position on sovereignty. The accession to WTO represents major movement in this regard. Without substantial political reform, however, the current regime will likely remain fundamentally at odds with the notion of global integration and the resultant depreciation of sovereignty. This contrast highlights the difficulty with humanitarian intervention in Beijing's current conception.

Under these circumstances, China's foreign partners and the international

community have a substantial interest in China's internal political development. A full analysis of China's contribution to the intervention regime therefore requires reflection on the consequences of political reform in China. It
is important to consider the impact and likely character of domestic political
reform, considering both democratization and the possible use of federalism. A democratically reforming or liberalizing China would likely embrace
international human rights and would have more difficulty pursuing harsh
policies toward peripheral communities. Under reform, China may be expected to adopt the more widely held conception of human rights as limiting
or constraining the state. Democratization would likely reduce China's resistance to importing democratic principles and human rights considerations
into an intervention regime.

Federalism may offer even broader options under democratic reform. Federalism on the mainland of China has been discussed throughout the twentieth century as an option in China's democratization process. I have argued
elsewhere that domestic conditions in China tend to suggest that the direction of democratic reform would likely include federalism.[27] Discussions
emanating from Taiwan have especially considered this aspect.[28] While the
current authoritarian Beijing government has resisted this model, it has engaged in decentralizing economic reforms that have produced what some
have characterized as economic federalism.[29] It has also offered proposals
for unification with Taiwan that appear to leave open the option of confederation. Is there lurking in this posturing the possibility of movement on the
intervention question? As noted in chapter 1, confederal arrangements could
actually include the potential for mutual intervention among confederal members to uphold democracy. This may shore up confidence in the confederal
agreement. In some respects, through NATO, Europe has a similar form of
military security for democracy under its unification process.[30] The Organization of African Unity (OAU), now Africn Union (AU), has used intervention to restore democratic governments in Liberia and Sierra Leone.[31] The
Organization of American States (OAS) has likewise been proactive on democracy and similar sentiment attaches to the Summit of the Americas, which
requires democracy as a condition of membership.[32] In this context, China's
reform process may open avenues to more directly address the development
of a global regime on intervention. China's current worldview clearly stands
in opposition to devolving such a regime. In a sense, this process is held
partial hostage to current statist Chinese views.

## Looking Ahead

Using the emerging global discourse in respect to sovereignty and intervention as a template, the previous discussion considers China's likely contribution to the evolving norm respecting humanitarian intervention along two
tracks: China's likely role under its current regime and the likely role of

China under political reform. China's current regime is fundamentally at odds, both in principle and in reality, with the sovereignty deprecating features of a substantial humanitarian intervention regime along the lines suggested by Annan. China can be expected to marshal its considerable influence in the UN Security Council and in the developing world more generally to obstruct any substantial alteration in the nonintervention principle. It will certainly resist expanded use of intervention in the Asian region.

For China, the nonintervention principle requires both sovereign consent and UN Security Council approval for any outside intervention in respect to an internal conflict and Security Council approval in respect to intervention in an international armed conflict. Any attempt at formal global change in this regard would therefore be rejected. China's current slight flexibility in sovereignty conceptualization revealed in its Hong Kong, Taiwan, and multilateral agreement policies allows some room to maneuver in respect of the sovereignty principle, but little in respect to an intervention regime. I would judge that this, at most, points to a sustained nonintervention principle with limited exceptions on an ad hoc basis. It is doubtful that China would agree to formal standards for such limited exceptions but, faced with continuing humanitarian crises, may permit such to arise from practice. It has already to a limited extent tolerated such practice. The war on terrorism has so far taken on such an ad hoc quality in Chinese policy. The Chinese worldview and its role as a permanent member of the Security Council leave little scope in this regard. There is some hope that China's increased participation in peacekeeping operations and its limited participation in the coalition against terror may ease its anxiety about the global process, but fundamental differences seem sure to remain.

The largest space for maneuver around the present regime on a systematic basis will be to focus on regional development of intervention principles. Under current circumstances, regional action will likely shape global norms. When the UN Security Council appears immobilized in the face of humanitarian crises, we can expect regions to increasingly go it alone to solve problems in their backyard. China can do little about such efforts and may eventually feel pressure to be more accommodating, especially if these efforts leave it out of the process. Though the UN Charter appears to require prior Security Council approval for regional interventions, the Security Council is hard pressed to resist regional intervention in the face of humanitarian crises on the scale of Kosovo or East Timor. Regional blocks in Europe and the Americas, and to a lesser degree in Africa, may proceed to carve out more substantial democratic and human rights standards for regional humanitarian intervention actions. In the face of increased resistance to ad hoc regional actions such as Kosovo, this more systematic effort to devolve acceptable standards appears essential. Even the Association of Southeast Asian Countries (ASEAN), itself tied to a troubled region, may someday move in this direction, as it begins to develop its regional security arrangements. It appears, as in Kosovo, China will be in no position to stop these developments. China's resistance in this regard may simply operate to count it out of the discussion. The absence of a substantial Asia-wide or East Asian regional multilateral community may further depreciate China's contribution. China's inability or unwillingness to participate in this process, or its doing so only in a limited and ad hoc fashion, will come at some strategic costs in this respect. A more accommodating posture, however, is not presently ensured.

The second track of analysis considers the possibility that domestic reform in China will open the door to a more substantial commitment to an intervention regime. This pressure may ultimately point in the direction of full Chinese engagement in the processes of shaping the global regime on sovereignty and intervention and the relationship between these and democracy. For the most part, a democratic China may be expected to have a more liberal view in respect to evolving norms in this area. More of a long shot is the possibility of intervention being employed as security for potential Chinese confederal arrangements with its peripheral communities. A democratic confederal agreement with such peripheral communities as Taiwan and Tibet may open opportunities to employ intervention provisions as confidence-building measures.

Whether or not an intervention regime is used as security for unification, a democratic confederal China could be expected to be more accommodating of a reformed intervention regime. Generally, coherent rules are better than uncertainty. Reform would allow China greater opportunity to participate in and shape the global order in this regard. This reform prospect raises the much debated question of whether a more democratic China will be less or more nationalistic, less or more difficult. Although I see transition problems, I believe that in the long run a democratic China will be less prone to nationalistic outbursts. The institutional arrangements of democratic governance tend to encourage avenues of interaction, discussion, and mutual accommodation, making China a more productive player in developing the global regime. Democracy may produce episodes of retrenchment, as has been evident in the conservative resistance to multilateralism in the current U.S. administration, but over the long term, democracy should favor greater global engagement and integration.

The previous discussion highlights the many options under consideration and the sources of Chinese anxiety. The character of China's regime type will certainly shape this debate in the short run. Under existing circumstances, regional multilateral solutions may be the best way to respond to an immobile UN. Democratic peace theories also underlie and have shaped the intervention debate in ways that generally put the major democracies at odds with China. China's position has historically challenged this democratic peace thesis, claiming that it is a much more peaceful country then the hegemonic Western powers who might use human rights as an excuse for unwarranted intervention. Given the long history of colonialism, the Chinese and non-Western mistrust of internationalist intentions is not surprising. This mistrust of outside intentions will certainly shape any intervention regime that develops around China's current political circumstances and future concerns that may shape the role of a politically reforming China in the intervention debate.

## Notes

1. Kofi Annan, "Secretary-General Presents His Annual Report to the General Assembly," September 1999. Annan argues that the core challenge is to "forge unity behind the principle that massive and systematic violations of human rights—wherever they may take place—should not be allowed to stand. . . . If states bent on criminal behavior know that frontiers are not the absolute defense; if they know that the Security Council will take action to halt crimes against humanity, then they will not embark on such a course of action in expectation of sovereign immunity." See Thomas M. Franck, "Are Human Rights Universal?" *Foreign Affairs* 80, no. 1 (2001): 191–204, 194.

2. In many respects, these 1999 statements at the General Assembly meeting reflected earlier statements by both officials' predecessors. The earlier UN report "Agenda for Peace" had met similar criticism in the early 1990s from former Chinese foreign minister Qian Qichen.

3. See Andrew Nathan and Robert S. Ross, *The Great Wall and the Empty Fortress: China's Search for Security* (New York: Norton, 1997); David Shambaugh, "China's Military Views the World," *International Security* 24, no. 3 (Winter 2000): 52–79 (noting the insular view of the Chinese military and the significance of Taiwan in its strategic calculus).

4. International Commission on Intervention and State Sovereignty, *The Responsibility to Protect* (Ottawa: International Development Research Centre, 2001). As this report was largely prepared for the UN secretary-general and was submitted to the UN, it will be referred to as the "UN Report on the Responsibility to Protect."

5. Information Office of the State Council, *China's National Defense in 2002* (Beijing: Information Office of the State Council, 2002) (hereafter *China's National Defense White Paper, 2002*).

6. Although Western powers are often suspected of using human rights as a tool of imperialist strategies, the regime in Beijing is suspected of abusing human rights and resisting cooperation with humanitarian objectives merely to sustain authoritarian power. This mistrust has been evident in a variety of strategic issues ranging from missile defense and weapons sales to intervention. See Erik Eckholm, "Experts Try to Make Missile Shield Plan Palatable to China," *New York Times*, 28 January 2001, pp. 1, 4; Jane Perlez, "The General Picks up Where He Left Off," *New York Times*, 28 January 2001, Week in Review, p. 5.

7. Scott A. Silverstone, "Federal Democratic Peace: Domestic Institutions, International Conflict, and American Foreign Policy, 1807–1860" (paper presented at the annual meeting of the International Studies Association, Chicago, Ill., February 20–24, 2001).

8. Michael C. Davis, "The Case for Chinese Federalism," *Journal of Democracy* 10, no. 2 (1999): 124–137.

9. See Louis Fielding, "Taking the Next Step in the Development of New Human Rights: The Emerging Right of Humanitarian Assistance to Restore Democracy," *Duke Journal of Comparative and International Law* 5 (1995): 329.

10. These five principles include (1) mutual respect for sovereignty and territorial integrity, (2) mutual nonaggression, (3) mutual noninterference in internal affairs, (4) equality and mutual benefit, and (5) peaceful coexistence. See Samuel S. Kim, "Sovereignty in the Chinese Image of World Order," in Ronald St. John Macdonald, ed., *Essays in Honor of Wang Tieya* (London: Nijhoff, 1994), pp. 425–445, 428. Kim argues that even China's pursuit of economic integration with the outside world is "neomercantilist." It aims to gain the benefits of economic development with minimum costs to state sovereignty. See Kim, "Sovereignty in the Chinese Image of World Order," p. 429.

11. For an analysis of how various strategic and policy issues interact in China's international relations, see Marc Lynch, "Why Engage? China and the Logic of Communicative Engagement," *European Journal of International Relations* 8, no. 2 (2002): 187–230.

12. There were two vetoes in 1972 and two in 1997–1999. The first one in 1972 involved the premature recognition of Bangladesh and the other was related to Israel. In 1997–1999, China opposed UN missions in Guatemala and Macedonia, both of which had flirted in their foreign policy with Taiwan. See Sally Morphet, "China As a Permanent Member of the Security Council, October 1971–December 1999," *Security Dialogue* 31, no. 2 (June 2000): 151–166.

13. Bates Gill and James Reilly, "Sovereignty, Intervention and Peacekeeping: The View from Beijing," *Survival* 42, no. 3 (Autumn 2000): 41–59.

14. Such a figure may involve a larger overall number of troops, with some being replacement troops. These operations include Kuwait, Western Sahara, Mozambique, Cambodia, Liberia, Sierra Leone, and East Timor. See Gill and Reilly, "Sovereignty, Intervention and Peacekeeping."

15. *China's National Defense White Paper, 2002.*

16. *China's National Defense White Paper, 2002.* It has provided civilian policemen and has been quite active in contributing to the UN Transitional Administration in East Timor. See "What's behind China's Support of East Timor?" *The La'o Hamutuk Bulletin* 3, no. 4 (May 2002).

17. The report noted China's participation in a variety of regional security organizations, including the Shanghai Cooperation Organization, the ASEAN Regional Forum, the Conference on Interaction and Confidence-Building Measures in Asia, the Council on Security Cooperation in the Asia-Pacific Region, and the Northeast Asia Cooperation Dialogue. See *China's National Defense White Paper, 2002*, pt. 6.

18. This aspect is of theoretical interest in current international relations academic debates over variations of neorealism, neoliberalism, and constructivism. See Andrew Moravcsik, "Taking Preferences Seriously: A Liberal Theory of International Politics," *International Organization* 51, no. 4 (Autumn 1997): 513–553; Jeffrey W. Legro and Andrew Moravcsik, "Is Anybody Still a Realist?" *International Security* 24, no. 2 (Fall 1999): 5–55; Kenneth N. Waltz, "Structural Realism after the Cold War," *International Security* 25, no. 1 (Summer 2000): 5–41; Thomas Risse, "'Let's Argue': Communicative Action in World Politics," *International Organization* 54, no. 1 (2000): 1–39.

19. Davis, "Case for Chinese Federalism."

20. Michael C. Davis, "Constitutionalism under Chinese Rule: Hong Kong after the Handover," *Denver Journal of International Law and Policy* 27, no. 2 (1999): 275–312.

21. Michael C. Davis, "The Future of Tibet: A Chinese Dilemma," *Human Rights Review* 2, no. 2 (2001): 7–17.

22. The military technology of NATO's war in Kosovo was also of great Chinese interest. See Shambaugh, "China's Military Views the World."

23. Fernando R. Tesón, "The Kantian Theory of International Law," *Columbia Law Review* 92 (1992): 53–102, 62. Note that Tesón highlights this potential in a non-Chinese context.

24. Information Office of the State Council, *Human Rights in China II* (Beijing: Information Office of the State Council, 1991).

25. See Louis Henkin, R. Randle Edwards, and Andrew Nathan, *Human Rights in Contemporary China* (New York: Columbia University Press, 1986).

26. Jean-Marie Henckaerts, ed., *The International Status of Taiwan in the New World Order: Legal and Political Considerations* (London: Kluwer Law International, 1996); Davis, "Constitutionalism under Chinese Rule." China has signed a number of human rights agreements, including, for example, the Convention on Eliminating Discrimination against Women, the International Covenant on Civil and Political Rights (signed but not ratified), and the International Covenant on Economic Social and Cultural Rights.

27. Davis, "Case for Chinese Federalism," p. 124.

28. "KMT Shelves Confederation Policy," *South China Morning Post*, 26 July 2001, p. 8.

29. Yasheng Huang, "Central-Local Relations in China during the Reform Era: The Economic and Institutional Dimensions," *World Development* 24, no. 4 (1996): 655–672; Gabriella Montinola, Yingye Qian, and Barry R. Weingast, "Federalism, Chinese Style: The Political Basis for Economic Success in China," *World Politics* 48, no. 1 (1995): 50–81.

30. See Rebecca R. Moore, chapter 11, in this volume.

31. John Kwabla Akpalu, "The OAU and Humanitarian Intervention in Africa" (master's thesis, Harvard Law School, 1999). Note, however, the consensus requirements in the OAU decision process, which effectively assigned all thirty-five members a veto power.

32. The final communiqué of the 2001 Quebec meeting is reported to provide that "[a]ny unconstitutional alteration or interruption of the democratic order in a state of the hemisphere constitutes an insurmountable obstacle to the participation of that state's government in the Summit of the Americas." Note also the OAS condemnation of nondemocratic moves by former Peruvian leader Alberto Fujimori.

# 14

## Human Rights and Intervention in Africa

*Rasheed Akinyemi*

This chapter will focus on nonmilitary international intervention, especially in respect of international institutions concerned with Africa's economic development. While military intervention in Africa's domestic and interstate conflicts is the most commonly cited form of intervention in Africa, it is by no means the most pervasive. Many other forms of developmental and humanitarian intervention may precede and follow military intervention. Humanitarian intervention supported by military force and warfare is the common ground given to justify post–Cold War international engagement in Africa. These interventions often include airlifting food supplies, medications, and first aid necessities (e.g., sleeping bags, blankets, and materials to build refugee camps). International humanitarian organizations like the UN High Commissioner for Refugees and the International Red Cross complete the humanitarian package of such interventions. The political arguments to justify such post–Cold War interventions include the restoration of hope, nation building, installation of democracy, and finally protection of human rights. The precondition for all such interventions is conflict and violence, as well as the inability of African states to resolve or manage their conflicts. It is sometimes not sufficiently appreciated that African conflicts and the inability of African leaders to resolve them are expressions of deeply rooted crises that precede the immediate conflict.

This chapter will address the nonmilitary forms of international intervention that often precede and presage a humanitarian crisis, focusing particularly on the politics of structural adjustment and the post–Cold War politics of conditionality that attach to economic aid. We will consider how these policies contribute to human rights violations in Africa. These human rights violations especially concern the deprivation of basic needs, which increase in regions that contain poverty and deprivation of the right to development. The right to development is a key element of fundamental human rights and directly implicates issues of international responsibility. The politics of adjustment and its enforcement in many African states has led to direct conflict between the state and civil society, producing unjust arrests, excessive use of force, suppression of nonviolent protests, and frequent bloodshed.

This chapter aims to demonstrate the nature of power politics in the relationship between Africa and the Western world and the consequent effects of outside interventions in Africa. Reasons given by Western nations and their international institutions for their intervention may appear to demonstrate their global responsibility, but a critical analysis into the politics of structural adjustment and political conditionality exposes the rhetoric and cynicism that often lies behind Western demands for democracy and human rights. Human rights rhetoric is often used to establish a new regime of control and is sometimes more a reflection of the power politics of the Western world than a signal of global responsibility. This power politics may amount to arrogance of power, as was openly demonstrated recently by the American government during the August to September 2001 Durban World Conference on Racism.

## Background to Africa's Crisis

In order to understand why it is always easy to intervene in Africa's domestic conflicts, it is necessary to look into the nature of the present crisis. The African crisis is a complex and multifaceted one. First, it is a crisis with historical origin. Second, it is a crisis confined within limiting structures as will be explained, and third, it is a crisis of the political economy of Africa. It is an accepted fact that both exogenous and endogenous forces influence the African crisis. Their relative weight is contestable.

The endogenous and exogenous roots of Africa's crisis is captured in Ali A. Mazrui's exploration of Africa's triple heritage and the impact of such heritage on Africa's identity.[1] The first heritage is the African personality that existed long before and survived alongside Islam, Western Christianity, and colonialism. This concept involves the complex problem of searching for the African identity in an indigenous cultural context. Leopold Sedar Senghor adopts the concept of Negritude for the same purpose of defining the African identity.[2] Using stronger political language, Kwame Nkrumah presents the context of the African personality, "For too long in our history, Africa has spoken through the voice of others. Now, what I have called an African Personality in international affairs will have a chance of making its proper impact and will let the world know it through the voices of Africa's own sons."[3] For those who have been concerned with the African identity, including those who have supported the concept of African socialism, a common conviction is that Africa's past identity contains some cultural and traditional values that must be revived for the purpose of Africa's development. This position conflicts with concepts of modern Africa formed alongside the imaginary visions of colonial empires.

The second heritage is religion and language and their impact on the cultural personality of the African continent. This especially refers to the Semitic impact on Africa's identity. "The most successful Semitic religion in the world is Christianity; the most successful Semitic language is Arabic; the most successful people globally are the Jews."[4] If we put the elements of this heritage in proper context, it will not be difficult to arrive at some series of conclusions regarding the impact of the Jewish culture, the Arabic culture, and the religious and political impact of Islam on African identity. "Another impact of Islam on Africa has been in the realm of political culture. This includes Islam's impact on political values, institutions and vocabulary. Again identity, especially political identity, is at stake."[5] This is another major source of crisis in many African countries.[6]

Africa's third heritage is Western influence, which includes slavery, Western imperialism, the mapping of Africa into modern nation-states, colonialism, and modern institutions (political, economic, and military). The power of the colonial master's languages, which also corresponds with the neocolonial states and their boundaries, is the most impressive element of Western heritage in Africa. Language is obviously a very important influence in Africa's current crises. The impact of language on Africa's development can be evaluated by considering education in Africa. The majority of Africans who go to school receive their education in foreign languages (Arabic, French, English, Portuguese, Afrikaans, and, in a few places, German). This same predicament also applies to many other colonized areas such as Latin America, where Spanish dominates other indigenous languages. The English read and write in English, the French in French, and the Italians in Italian. It is therefore not surprising that these colonized societies, with such heritage of foreign languages, remain behind in the fields of modern science and technology. What actually is the advantage of Western heritage on Africa? "Europe's greatest service to the people of Africa was not Western civilization, which is under siege, or, even Christianity, which is on the defense. Europe's supreme gift was the gift of African identity, bequeathed without grace and without design, but a reality all the same."[7]

### Structural Impediments

There is a common agreement among scholars that Africa's structural weaknesses contribute much to the present-day crisis, as well as to Africa's inability to handle its affairs by itself. This leads to structural dependency, as well as Africa's vulnerability to external interventions. Different approaches have been adopted to analyze these structural problems. While some scholars look far beyond the colonial episode, others concentrate on the colonial legacies and their aftermath in Africa. The realities of Africa's triple heritage are confined within structures that are impediments to Africa's development. According to Bade Onimode, "Fundamentally, the African crisis is one of underdevelopment, the central problematic of the African continent and the Third World generally. This makes the crisis basically structural and historical."[8]

Looking into the causes of conflicts in Africa, Keith Somerville confirms the structural basis of Africa's crisis and relates it to the consequences of the persistence of arbitrary colonial borders. He notes, "If Africa had not been colonized, the political map of the continent would be very different. It might still be troubled by conflict and subject to foreign influence, but the pattern would be different. The conflicts and forms of foreign interference we see now cannot be divorced from the colonial inheritance."[9] Referring to domestic policy failures in African countries, Onimode identifies five broad areas that are directly related to inherited structural problems. These endogenous factors have immensely contributed to Africa's crisis. He notes,

> Post-colonial Africa has failed to transform these inherited structures of production, consumption, distribution, technology, power, institutions and values. It was wrongly assumed that these structures could be used as a basis for nation-building and the development of African economies and societies. The maturing contradictions of this error have contributed to the agrarian crisis, socio-economic stagnation and decline as well as political strife throughout Africa.[10]

The failure to identify and tackle Africa's crisis within its inherited structures has led to the deepening of the crisis and escalation of its symptoms. Symptomatically, the problems express themselves in such forms as environmental degradation, relative population growth, famine, shortage of food supplies, poverty, social unrest, political decay, civil strife and conflicts, and economic and financial difficulties. The economic and financial difficulties have led to debt crises, state bankruptcy, and state collapse. Various attempts have been undertaken to bring these problems under control, such as through poverty alleviation programs, but progress has been minimal in most cases because the root causes of these issues are not being objectively addressed.

Transitional and adjustment programs have failed to bring long-term solutions because policies are not tailored toward the transformation of the structures and economic relations, especially the political economy of African societies. Transition policies and programs often cannot address structural problems accurately. They also confront radical changes in power politics within the African polities, as well as Africa's relations with the outside world, especially in the economic and trade areas. Power politics keep Africa underdeveloped and very dependent on external military, political, and economic intervention.

Power politics here refers to the struggle for control of state power and resources by African leaders. This leads to various forms of political exclusion of the majority of the people and amounts to deprivation of rights to political participation and the right to development. As Claude Ake aptly

describes it, in politics everything is second to the struggle for power between those who hold it and those who want it. All kinds of human rights
violations are a common by-product of this struggle.[11]

However, few were able to effectively react to this situation. The majority
of Africans were not in a position to form a credible force to challenge those
in power. Their best way of survival was through the patronage system that
eventually gave legitimacy to those who hold state power. Power politics
also refers to the relationship with external powers and major international
financial institutions (IFIs) and donors, who constantly seek political influence and engage in economic exploitation. Intervention from outside is
expressed through political intimidation, blackmailing, threats to withdraw
economic and military assistance, and the enforcement of political and economic conditions. Such conditions lead to new forms of violations of rights
or to the exacerbation of already existing forms of human rights violations
in Africa.

I have deliberated on some of the historical causes of Africa's crisis, as
well as the inherited structures, applying endogenous and exogenous explanations. It is now time to turn to the politics of structural adjustment, beginning with the debt crisis of the 1980s.

## The Debt Crisis and the Development Paradigm

> Since it started around 1979, the African and Third World debt crisis has
> unfolded into an act of international aggression and war. . . . It is another
> episode of silent surrender . . . [and] satisfies the motives, mechanisms and
> effects of conventional war. . . . [It] has decreased prices of raw materials
> and silenced demands for new international economic order, thrown Nige-
> ria and other debtor countries wide open to imperialism, and allowed physi-
> cal occupation by the IMF and World Bank staff of the Central Banks and
> Ministries of Finance and Trade of debtor countries. . . . [It] has led di-
> rectly and indirectly to thousands of deaths from riots, demonstrations,
> starvation and epidemics. It has also visited social-psychological vio-
> lence on millions of unemployed, undernourished, diseased and demor-
> alized people.[12]

The above quotation reflects not only the position of many African scholars,
but also of some Western scholars.[13] It is apparent that the debt crisis represents one form of power politics and another form of forcing African states,
in collaboration with Western financial institutions, to violate human rights
and deprive people of their rights to development. The International Monetary Fund (IMF) and World Bank adjustment policies are rationalized on
the grounds of the fiscal and debt crises. The debt crisis of African states in
the middle 1980s served as a justification for the international donor community and the IFIs to directly intervene in Africa's political and economic

affairs. This action has received a lot of criticism and is another example of how issues are addressed on the surface without addressing their deeper causes.

The following discussion argues against the popular view that Africa's debt crisis is merely financial or economic. It is important to consider the historical and political background to this crisis. There are several important factors to consider. First, the fiscal and debt problems of the 1980s are symptoms of structural problems inherent in capitalist economic systems, generally, and are an outcome of the triple colonial heritage discussed earlier. These difficulties have been carried over into the postcolonial period. Second, Africa's economic fiasco and the debt problems are due to the ideology of development that dominated the early periods of the 1960s going into the 1970s, when military regimes took over political power. Third, the debt crisis had the exogenous and endogenous dimensions noted earlier. From the African leaders' position, development was to compensate for all that was suffered during colonialism but also was perceived as the easiest way to redistribute resources. "Without exception, all the nationalist leaders believed that one important lesson to be learned from the humiliation of colonization was the need to overcome not only political weaknesses but also military, economic, and technological ones."[14]

When Ghana gained independence in 1958, one of Kwame Nkrumah's priorities was development. He figured that there were abundant raw materials ready for exploitation and a "free world" market ready to pay the just price. The returns of such trade relations, according to the expectations of African leaders, would be enough to carry out development programs. With much optimism, Nkrumah's government designed a bogus development program that would transform Ghana's economy and raise the people's social standards.[15] It did not take too long for Nkrumah to realize that Africa was not in a position to determine the prices of its raw materials and that Africa would need other resources if development was to be achieved. The prices of Africa's raw materials, including Ghana's most prominent production, cocoa, fell drastically on the world market, and Nkrumah had to look for foreign aid to carry out his development plan. By the time Nkrumah was overthrown by the military in February 1966, Ghana had incurred enormous foreign debt, the economy had not been industrialized, and the country had not been modernized. Poverty and underdevelopment remained the order of the day.

Such was the attitude of postcolonial African leaders toward development. They relied much on the inherited colonial economy of dependency, where cash-crop production for export formed the basis of the economy and of state income. It was an economic structure that was based on import substitution, where Africans were encouraged to produce and export what they did not need and to import and consume what they did not produce. As Ake assesses it, the ideology of development and the elaboration of development plans served to legitimize African regimes, but had virtually no influence on the economic situation in their countries.[16]

Another characteristic of the postcolonial economy that was influenced by the ideology of development was the role of the state. This was, in turn, influenced by the rural-urban dichotomy in development agendas and the contradictions in development ideology. First, the neocolonial state saw itself as the sole agent of development, the so-called developmental state. Second, the postcolonial state saw itself as a symbol of modernization, as well as an agent of modernization. Third, the state's main goal was to design development programs to meet the "ideals" of a modern nation-state, including rigorous urban development, industrialization, and a modern national army.

While designing flamboyant development programs in these urban sectors, rural development, especially agricultural development, received second-class attention. Farmers and peasants did not receive the appropriate financial and social attention that would enable them to sustain production, even for the export sector, which was the first source of state income.

While relying heavily on income from cash-crop production, Africans were spending more money and attention on other development sectors to the detriment of agriculture. African governments gave priority to prestigious development projects, often referred to euphemistically as the "white man's elephant projects." These were projects that could not be financed from the meager income from cash-crop sales and that did not serve the purposes of the majority of the people. These projects were financed by foreign borrowing, called "development aid." Just as colonial political and economic structures created unequal development,[17] so did neocolonial states and the postcolonial ideology of development. As mentioned earlier, the ideology of development had its exogenous dimension, which gave support to these internal factors, while promoting neocolonial ties. "For when the rising tide of nationalism showed that colonialism could not survive, they [the former colonial masters] had contrived the concept of partnership in development to maintain a presence and some leverage in the colonies and to gain allies in the battle against communism."[18]

The failure of African states to follow an independent development path was not due to the lack of alternatives,[19] nor was it due to a lack of resources. Rather, it was due to inherited structures from the triple heritage dilemmas, as well as the inherent contradictions in the social structures of African social relations. The struggle by a small group of the elite for control of state power, the promotion of an ideology that served to sustain the status quo, and the resultant economic deprivation of the people are fundamental to the crisis of the 1980s. Ake sees the ideology as one big problem due to the conflict between its manifest and latent functions.[20]

Furthermore, this struggle for power and survival was a good political reason for the Bretton Woods institutions (BWIs) and for the donor community to enforce orthodox economic policies on these leaders. It was well known that these leaders lacked a base of legitimacy and would do anything to remain in power, even if it required implementing unpopular social and economic policies that would lead to violations of human rights. Africa is still being haunted by this historical legacy, such that stages of development have been characterized by one crisis or another.

What was the real situation of the African debt crisis in the 1980s that called for the structural adjustment intervention policies of the IMF–World Bank? Between 1974 and 1982, the nominal dollar value of the debts of developing countries rose from $140 billion to $560 billion. By the end of 1984, the external debt of Africa alone reached $145 billion, representing a sevenfold increase in indebtedness from 1974. By December 1987, Africa's total debt stood at $228 billion, about half of that of Latin America and double that of Brazil. By 1990, Africa's debt had grown to $250 billion. Some 70 to 80 percent of this debt was owed to official creditors. From $8 billion in 1985, the interest and amortization charges on Africa's debt jumped to $19.5 billion by 1987. Total debt as a proportion of exported goods and services increased from 167 percent in 1982 to over 228 percent by 1987. The debt service ratio or total debt service payments, as a percentage of annual export earnings, which was 15 percent in 1980, soared to over 50 percent in 1987 for sub-Saharan Africa.[21]

The reactions to this situation from the international community were directed toward solving the crisis based on the real debt situation, rather than dealing with the historical and structural problems on which the African state and economy is founded. The IMF–World Bank responses to Africa's debt crisis, according to Onimode, were structural adjustment program (SAP) ideology, co-option of African governments, use of fifth columnists, the spreading of conditionality, and attempts to co-opt foreign nongovernmental organizations (NGOs).[22] For the purposes of this chapter, I shall concentrate on the SAP and conditionality politics.

**The Politics of Structural Adjustment**

The most unpopular adjustment programs experienced so far in Africa and some other developing countries are the economic liberalization packages of the BWIs. The 1980s were known not only as the lost decade, but also as the decade of adjustment. It was the decade of the "neoliberal consensus,"[23] (Ronald Reagan in the United States, Margaret Thatcher in Britain, and Helmut Kohl in Germany.) The social and economic policies of these governments led to attacks on the role of the state on welfare issues giving justification to World Bank/IMF SAP policies. Social democratic values and the welfare state, the neo-Keynesian consensus, came under pressure, while privatization and the rolling back of the state became the (un)popular economic slogans. If the Cold War was an ideological war between two political doctrines, then the politics of structural adjustment was an economic war between two economic doctrines. "The neo-Keynesian consensus was breaking up quite unexpectedly, challenged from the political Right by the rather simple and implausible doctrines of monetarism and supply-side economics, and from the political Left by no less simple and implausible varieties of neo-Marxism and other radical critiques."[24] The victims of these ideological wars, both political and economic, are the poor developing countries.

The IFIs under the BWIs were called on to follow suit in the promotion of the neoliberal ideology, as well as in its practical implementations through economic adjustment programs in developing countries. The phrase "structural adjustment" goes back to the birth of development economics in the 1940s.[25] World Bank president Robert McNamara articulated its objectives in his closing speech to the annual meeting of the Board of Governors of the World Bank in Belgrade in October 1979, highlighting "a sudden and dramatic reversal of the locus of responsibility for ensuring successful world development, from the shoulders of the economically strong to those of the economically weak."[26]

An important factor in the shift in responsibility, according to analysts, were the oil shocks of 1973 and 1980 and their impact on the economy of the Western world. The oil shocks led to a slackening of economic growth in the West, with real gross domestic product (GDP) per capita falling back from 4.7 percent from 1965 to 1973 to 2.8 percent from 1973 to 1980 and in the developing countries from 3.7 to 2.8 percent.[27] In economic terms, "The commodity power of the [so-called] Third World oil producers appeared to have succeeded in shifting the balance of advantage towards themselves and away from the industrialized countries, within a more generally turbulent economic environment. This perception helped to undermine the post-war consensus that the adjustment burden should rest with the industrial world."[28]

Instead of burden sharing, the West moved toward a burden-shifting policy, forgetting that the majority of the so-called Third World countries were not oil producers. The impact of the oil shocks and the reactions of the West had a devastating social and economic effect on the poorest of the developing countries. One could argue that the reaction of the West was selfish, unjust, and imperialist. The West would not accept a redistribution of wealth based on fair trade relations or even paying the right prices for raw commodities coming from the developing world. In fact, the West had always maintained a strong policy of "no New World Order," treating this as a cornerstone in the North-South dialogue. The desire for a New World Order by the countries of the South principally focused on trade relations between the two hemispheres, as well as on the demand for more acceptable "terms of trade." The rejection of such adjustment in trade relations, from the Western world, and the insistence on imposing structural adjustments on Africa and other developing countries shows a lack of global responsibility. This arises in one of those moments in the political outlook of the Western countries where they believed that there was a threat to their living standards or to their "civilization."

In reality, during the oil crisis the economic situation in Africa was generally poor and the situation in sub-Saharan Africa was more serious than in the developed economies. There was a fall in real GDP growth in sub-Saharan Africa from 6.7 percent from 1965 to 1973 to 3.2 percent from 1973 to 1980. Exports stagnated between 1973 and 1980, and the growth rate of real GDP per capita fell from 3.6 to 0.3 percent due to an increase in population growth. These combined factors gave rise to the perception that Africa's economic crisis of the 1980s was purely due to endogenous forces. External shocks that triggered Africa's economic crisis included deflation and restrictive monetary and expansionary fiscal policies in developed countries, especially in the United States. This triggered the debt crisis. World interest rates rose from an average of only 1.3 percent from 1973 to 1980 to just below 6 percent from 1983 to 1986. The seriousness of the debt crisis became real when in August 1982 Mexico declared the suspension of its debt payments. This reality revealed further that the other fourteen highly indebted countries would also be declaring debt payment suspensions.

By the time the first structural adjustment loans were being initiated by the BWIs, at the very point where the world economy was in trouble, lending to developing countries by Western private and commercial banks went on as usual. According to John Toye, there was perhaps a lack of awareness among the developing countries that a substantial part of this debt carried variable interest rate terms. The lending banks, especially British and American private banks, still believed that higher incomes from export activities of the borrowing countries would guarantee debt repayments and services. This turned out to be a dream. "The international financial institutions realized the deflation of the industrial economies invalidated their commodity price forecasts and their failure to supervise the investment practices of borrowing countries made their approval of massive commercial lending foolhardy, to say the least."[29] It was not only the dreaming of the banks that was on display, but also their power. Western commercial and private banks were very well aware of the weak positions of African countries, politically and economically; hence, it was easy for them to determine how and when to declare the fate of African states. "As external creditors, these banks exercise great power over debtor countries. Besides sharply raising interest rates, they have typically depressed the credit worthiness of African and other Third World countries, diminished their access to foreign credit, and raised financial charges against them. These practices, combined with the rapid deterioration of export earnings have severely aggravated the crisis in African countries."[30]

## Political Conditionality and Human Rights Abuses

Human rights abuse is a crisis of the African state. Poverty and underdevelopment are not necessarily a natural phenomenon, but they are phenomenal. Structural poverty exists where there is an unequal distribution of wealth and resources, leading to a huge gap between those who have and those who are deprived. It is largely caused by the absence of political and legal frameworks that guarantee rights to equitable distribution and redistribution, among which I also count the right to political decision making and the right to development. When policy reforms demand the state to withdraw from its obligations of providing the basic needs of its citizens, especially when those affected are the most vulnerable in the society, then this amounts to an abuse of human rights. When, in the processes of citizens demanding their rights, the state brutally intervenes, this also amounts to human rights violations. When economic rationalization policy leads to deprivation of work, without compensation or without legal rights to challenge that deprivation, it is an abuse of human rights. All these abuses have taken place in many African countries where IMF–World Bank SAPs had been implemented. In extreme cases, governments have responded to frequent popular protests against these policies with unstructured violence, leading to the death of hundreds of anti-SAP demonstrators across Africa. The worst cases occurred in Sudan, Sierra Leone, Morocco, Nigeria, Zambia, and Zimbabwe.

The most outspoken reactions to structural adjustment policies in Africa and in some other developing countries are popular unrest and strikes. These are championed by the middle class and other coalition groups (e.g., doctors, journalists, lawyers, university teachers, and other representatives of the middle-class professions), labor and trade unions, students and other groups ranging from market women to taxi and bus drivers, unemployed citizens, and some representatives of NGOs. The protests are directed against government decisions to accept IMF–World Bank adjustment loans, as well as against government policies to implement structural adjustment demands, eradicate subsidies, and reduce social and welfare spending. They are also targeted toward policies that result in increasing the prices of basic need commodities. The reactions of African governments to food riots are clear indications of the nature of Africa's political leadership. The political environment that was needed for the implementation of adjustment programs undermined any democratic values, as well as the respect for human rights:

> The harsh character of these conditionalities has also been widely decried. They are so tough that few regimes, whether military or elected, have ever had the courage to implement them fully. And where they are implemented at all, this typically requires the imposition of authoritarian regimes—often through the militarization of politics, the overthrow of elected civilian governments and the scandalous undermining of democracy. The conditionalities are also harsh in terms of their actual or expected effects on people and the economy: massive unemployment from retrenchment, inflation after devaluation or social services crisis after subsidy withdrawal.[31]

In Sierra Leone, under the regime of Joseph Momoh, the IMF demanded the government to implement stiff austerity measures. "Petrol prices rose from Le15 to Le30 a gallon and kerosene from Le12 to Le13 a gallon in July 1986. School fees were abolished in government schools, while a flat rate of Le200 a month tax free was granted to all government employees towards the cost of educating their children and for transport."[32]

I shall concentrate on the experiences of Nigeria to demonstrate that the politics of the SAPs and conditionalities, in collaboration with postcolonial African states, brought about serious abuses of the political and human rights of Africans. Various scholars have carefully accounted for Nigeria's experiences with the SAPs.[33] The most debated period was during the military regime of General Ibrahim Babangida (1985–1993). When the military government of Babangida came to power in August 1985, one of its targets was to resume dialog with the IMF over the conditions that the fund would attach to the Nigerian application for an Extended Fund Facility (EFF) loan. This loan would be used for the financing of the SAPs forced on the country by the IMF–World Bank. For whatever reasons the Babangida regime might have had, the government decided to call a national debate on the IMF and the role that it should play in the management of the national economic crisis. "The decision to declare the debate was part of wider confidence-building measures such as the abrogation of Decree no. 4 which was promulgated in 1984 to limit the freedom of the press and prevent criticism of public officials, the unbanning of associations . . . the declaration by the government of its intention to respect human rights."[34]

The result of the national debate was rejection of any involvement of the IMF in the national economy, as well as rejection of the EFF loan. Instead of respecting public opinion, Babangida's government went on to declare the launching of the SAPs on June 27, 1986. Just like Nigeria, many other African countries, including Zambia, Morocco, Benin, Algeria, and Zimbabwe, that introduced SAPs had witnessed serious forms of protests that resulted in the loss of life. The Babangida military regime was confronted by a coalition of forces representing a large spectrum of Nigerian society that protested against the drastic austerity measures introduced by the government. The government responded with repressive measures, including the violation of rights to basic needs and other necessities of living. It introduced decrees that curtailed civil liberties and workers' rights. Decrees 17 and 19 prevented workers from appealing against retrenchment and automatic receipt of retrenchment benefits. Prices of food items such as gari, yams, beans, maize, plantains, and rice rose an average of about 150 to 330 percent between 1981 and 1987. Other items such as sugar, milk, and fish rose by more than 350 percent, while real wages fell sharply.

The adjustment program seriously hit Nigerian professionals, who are the backbone of the middle class. When elephants fight, it is the grass that suffers. Africa's middle class plays important social and economic roles in the maintenance of the social fabric. Theoretically, it is supposed to play the role of the mediator between the ruled and the rulers, especially during periods of crisis. It is also important in keeping the traditional structure of extended families alive. Such extended families engage other members of families in respect of educating children, taking care of aged family members, connecting people together for job opportunities, and so on. Any destabilization of the middle-class position in Africa affects the majority. This is why the middle class was identified as one of the most potentially disruptive groups during the implementations of the SAPs and conditionalities. According to Bjorn Beckman:

> Wage earners make up the most coherent and potentially disruptive social groups in the opposition bloc. They are acutely affected by the restructuring of incentives enforced by SAP including cuts in public sector employment, the fall in domestic industrial production, removal of price and rent controls and subsidies, and the rise in cost of imports. . . . Wage earners are those affected most by public service cuts and increases in fees as they are those who depend most on access to public transport, education, health, electricity and water supply in the reproduction of every existence.[35]

In Nigeria, groups that confront the government's economic and wage policies are organized under the umbrella of the Nigeria Labor Congress (NLC). Such groups take up industrial actions and public demonstrations. Sometimes, calls for such actions lead to nationwide strikes. Such strikes are articulated under the rights to public expression and are therefore protected constitutional rights of citizens. Some scholars have addressed the politics of labor and adjustment in Nigeria.[36] In April 1987, the NLC started a struggle against the SAP imposed by the military government of General Babangida. This included the refusal to raise the minimum wage and the removal of petrol subsidy. The IMF–World Bank insisted that the domestic price of petrol should be raised to the level of world market prices. Reactions from the NLC were articulated in such words as, "Enough is enough. The government must choose between the Nigerian people and the World Bank dictation. Remove subsidy and remove life! Workers stand up and be counted on the side of Labor or die on your knees."[37] The reactions of the government to the labor anti-SAP protests included changes in the running of the NLC administration. The government's actions led to a serious distortion in state-labor relations:

> The politics of Structural Adjustments affects workers and makes them vulnerable by the dominance of the public sector in the wage economy. When wages in the public sector are cut, consumers are affected. Consumers of public services are also affected. Thus, the industrial actions to fight against SAP policies on May Day in 1987 and the brutal reaction of the state security apparatus is due to the intervention of the IMF and World Bank in Nigeria's economic affairs. The workers articulated their objections as follows: "We know the IMF is strong. We also recognize the might of our enemies, but should we import SAP to kill Nigeria?"[38]

The state's reactions to the NLC mass rallies across the country included the banning of any rally in any part of the country, the storming of trade union offices by state police, brutal dispersion of demonstrators, and arrests and illegal detention of labor leaders. Nigerian newspapers reported the greatest manhunt for labor leaders in the history of the country. Labor leaders were accused of plotting to overthrow the government, and the director of public prosecution threatened labor leaders with sedition charges.[39]

The state not only suppressed the existing rights of the NLC, but also that of the courts. When the NLC challenged the dissolution of the Congress in the Lagos High Court, the state claimed that the court had no right to interfere in emergency decrees. When the NLC brought its case in front of the Federal High Court, the case was thrown out.

Another frontline movement against the IMF–World Bank adjustment programs came from Nigerian students as the "Petrol Price Uprising" of April to May 1989. "Provoked by authoritarian school authorities and encouraged by popular support, students initiated a nation-wide campaign in April 1989, linking local grievances to national anti-SAP movement, mobilizing support from local communities and from democratic organizations."[40] Nigerian students belonged to one of the social groups that had been adversely affected by the SAP:

> Since the introduction of SAP, many Nigerians, some having children in the universities, have been retrenched from their places of work. . . . In 1988 alone, for example, about 200,000 workers were retrenched, 5,000 dismissals at the Nigerian Ports Authority and 17,500 could equally lose their jobs at the Nigerian Railway Corporation. . . . The cumulative effect of this on the students has been manifest in the reduced allowances available to them from their parents, forcing many students to cut down on food, books, and clothing expenditure. . . . The environment for teaching and learning in Nigerian universities has also deteriorated in the face of the ever-declining grants from the state since 1980. The situation reached a crisis point in 1987 when the recurrent grant to the universities was reduced to just 30% of the amount normally granted.[41]

It was under this situation that the students came out to challenge the government's package of austerity measures. The 1986 crisis started at the Ahmadu Bello University, Zaria, when students organized to commemorate the anniversary of the death of a student killed in a 1978 student riot. The university authorities did not approve of this commemoration, so they called on the state security police to encircle the university. The confrontation with the police escalated, and by May 23, 1986, the police had killed four university students. Other Nigerian universities and institutions of higher learning became involved in the crisis, and violence spread across to many parts of the country. The government reacted by banning the National Association of

Nigerian Students (NANS) and some student leaders were dismissed, including a few of their teachers. Tekena Tamuno, one of the dismissed Nigerian professors, claimed that the student riots were not just due to the problem in Zaria, but also against the government's romance with the IMF.

Seeing how the SAP affected the students, as stated earlier, it is not surprising that the students decided to take to the streets during the 1988 and 1989 riots. The increase in fuel prices in April 1988 instigated major anti-SAP riots in Nigerian institutions of higher learning, starting at the University of Jos. By the end of May 1988, about thirty-three schools throughout the country had been closed down. The confrontation with the government lasted for four weeks, after which some of the universities were temporarily closed down. However, the minister of education issued a policy statement, saying that any institution shut because of future unrest would remain closed indefinitely and should not expect any subvention from the government. The relationship between the government and the NANS also remained tense, while the State Security Service hunted down student leaders all over the country. All attempts by the NANS to organize and convene meetings were interfered with by government security agents.

The peak of confrontation that led to the biggest showdown in April and May 1989 with the government started with an alleged money transfer by the president, General Babangida, his wife, and some top government officials into some foreign accounts. This took place while many Nigerians were suffering under the adjustment and austerity economic policies of the government and the IMF–World Bank.

The new anti-SAP demonstration started again on May 23, 1989, in what was initially alleged as a commemoration of the students massacred at the Ahmadou Bello University, Zaria, in 1986. The rumor about the Babangida money transfer encouraged students to organize anti-SAP riots again. By May 24 and 25, students, joined by other members of the Nigerian society, such as the market women, took to the streets to demonstrate against all SAP initiatives. In Benin, the prison was set on fire, prisoners were set free, and several government buildings, including the Benin High Court, were burned down. Many lives were lost in the Benin uprising, leading to reactions from other university students all over the country. On May 29, the riot engulfed other universities, such as the University of Ibadan and the Nsukka University. May 31 was declared "Black Wednesday" because of the number of lives that were lost in Lagos during a clash between students and police. The position of the police throughout this period of anti-SAP rioting was described as follows, "During the anti-SAP riot, the Nigerian Police used the best in their armory—armored cars, water spraying trucks, helicopters, different canisters of tear gas, rifles, pistols etc. In some parts of the country where the hostility was protracted and fierce, the police were assisted by the army, which led to the death of many Nigerians—children, students, policemen and a number of pregnant women."[42]

The public supported the student riots because of the widespread effects of the SAP on all Nigerian social classes and individuals. The society was heavily burdened with the question of who should be held responsible for the whole crisis, the massacre, and the destruction of public and private goods. In fact, the Nigerian society was briefly able to articulate its economic problems and make political demands. In the Benin riots of May 24, students and their sympathizers were promoting such political demands as "Babangida must go" and "the SAP must be abolished." "The actions of the students had the backing of most Nigerians. The groups that identified with the students were market women, unemployed youth, labor union officials, and radicals in the Nigerian society. Although nobody was ready to accept responsibility for the hoax that ignited the crisis, most Nigerians were convinced that the social hardship associated with the SAP could only breed more political instability."[43]

The earlier elaboration of the human rights abuses associated with economic intervention as demonstrated by the Nigerian case demonstrates that responsibility for the hoax rests with both the Nigerian state that allowed itself to be oppressed by external forces, such as the IMF–World Bank, and the Western powers (especially Organization for Economic Cooperation and Development states). In accordance with their new economic thought of neoliberalism and power politics, they had supported human rights abuses in Africa and other developing countries.

Onimode emphasizes the effects of the SAPs and conditionalities on the fledging democratization in Africa. According to him, "The effects on democratic experiments center around the negotiations of these programs, their implementation procedure, dissent management and response mechanism. Thus, it is disturbing that the negotiations of the Fund-Bank programs are rarely ever subjected to broad national discussion or debate."[44] Furthermore, the political participation and mobilization necessary in a fledging democratic process are hindered by the top-down approach with the BWIs and African governments. "Avoiding political process with mass mobilization and popular political participation of broad social forces, the high-handed and elitist implementation of these programs make them extremely unpopular. Hence the need for authoritarian regimes and neo-fascists coups for their adoption and execution. Orthodox stabilization and adjustment programs encourage the pervasive undermining of democracy and the militarization of politics in Africa."[45]

The nature of the African state and the impact of the IMF–World Bank fundamental economic policies on the flag independence of postcolonial African states raises a question as to their political legitimacy and their constitutional legal rights. The fact that these two IFIs were able to blackmail, pressure, and undermine respect for Africans calls into question the dependency of African sovereignty. As Onimode puts it:

There are several alarming aspects of this phenomenon. One is the atomi-zation of the state which is the political analogue of the informalization of the economy. The African state, like its counterpart in the rest of the Third World, has been reduced to a mere "adjustment state"—to adjust the na-tional economy and population to the rapacious requirements of the credi-tor countries, for the repayment of immoral external debts, the dumping of manufactured food imports, repatriation of profits for multinational corpo-rations . . . and unhindered penetration and domination of foreign capital. . . . In such ways, the political impact of Fund-Bank stabilization and ad-justment programs has been a systematic weakening and essential marginalization of the state in Africa, through a direct affront on its tradi-tional sovereignty and the reversal of the gains of democratization since flag independence.[46]

What one must add here is that this political impact amounts to abuse of the political rights of the African people and a gross violation of human rights. It also offends the political rights of African states. Actually, there is a significant indication that political conditionality justifies calls for democra-tization, human rights, accountability, and good governance from African leaders. The West and the IFIs have demonstrated their double-standard in many ways in their dealings with Africa and other developing countries. They use the stick-and-carrot mechanism to intervene and destabilize fragile societies. They may cause political instability with their overzealous demands. No wonder that apartheid South Africa took so long before it was forced to change, and it is no wonder that the United States so arrogantly walked out of the 2001 Durban Conference on Racism in South Africa.

This concluding statement will remind us of the initial position of this chapter, that the New World Order and the new forms of global intervention in Africa have nothing to do with the global responsibility of the interven-tionist powers. Rather, such economic intervention in Africa is a clear dem-onstration of the power politics of the Western world and the international donor community. Economic intervention, ostensibly to stabilize Africa's economic situation, has produced a serious social, political, and economic crisis. These interventions have resulted in various forms of human rights abuse. This is the distinctive quality of post–Cold War African interna-tional relations.

## Notes

1. Ali A. Mazrui, *The Africans: A Triple Heritage* (Boston: Little, Brown, 1986).
2. See Paul Sigmund Jr., *The Ideologies of the Developing Nations* (New York: Praeger, 1963), pp. 248–250.
3. Kwame Nkrumah, *I Speak of Freedom: A Statement of African Ideology* (New York: Praeger, 1961), p. 125.
4. Mazrui, *Africans*, p. 81.

5. Mazrui, *Africans*, p. 95.

6. Social and political crises in countries like Sudan, Nigeria, Algeria, Chad, Egypt, and even in the Great Horn of Africa are such that they have their origins in this triple heritage. The present consequence is outside intervention.

7. Mazrui, *Africans*, p. 113.

8. Bade Onimode, *A Political Economy of the African Crisis* (London: Zed, 1988), p. 2.

9. Keith Somerville, *Foreign Military Intervention in Africa* (London: Pinter, 1990), pp. 183–184.

10. Onimode, *Political Economy of the African Crisis*, pp. 8–9.

11. Claude Ake, *Democracy and Development in Africa* (Washington, D.C.: Brookings Institution, 1996), p. 7.

12. Onimode, *Political Economy of the African Crisis*, p. 25.

13. Patricia Adams, *Odious Debts* (London: Earthscan, 1991).

14. Onimode, *Political Economy of the African Crisis*, p. 8.

15. Nkrumah, *I Speak of Freedom*, p. 242.

16. Ake, *Democracy and Development in Africa*, p. 9.

17. See Samir Amin, *Unequal Development: An Essay on the Social Formations of Peripheral Capitalism* (Sussex, UK: Harvester, 1976).

18. Ake, *Democracy and Development in Africa*, p. 8.

19. See Samir Amin, *Delinking: Towards a Polycentric World* (London: Zed, 1990); Reginald H. Green and Ann Seidman, *Unity or Poverty? The Economics of Pan-Africanism* (Baltimore, Md.: Penguin, 1968).

20. Ake, *Democracy and Development in Africa*, p. 9.

21. The IMF reported the terms of trade of sub-Saharan Africa as: -0.3 on the average for 1970–1979, -3.3 in 1980, -4.5 in 1981 and 1982, 1.6 in 1983, 6.4 in 1984, -1.6 in 1985, -15.2 in 1986, and 4.8 in 1987. See Onimode, *Political Economy of the African Crisis*, pp. 26–32. For a detailed analysis of the debt-export ratios, see Ake, *Democracy and Development in Africa*, pp. 103–106.

22. Onimode, *Political Economy of the African Crisis*, pp. 31–32.

23. Lionel Demery, "Structural Adjustment: Its Origins, Rationale and Achievements," in Giovanni A. Cornia and Gerald K. Helleiner, eds., *From Adjustment to Development in Africa* (London: Macmillan, 1994), pp. 25–48.

24. John Toye, "Structural Adjustment: Context, Assumptions, Origin and Diversity," in Ralph van der Hoeven and Fred van der Kraaij, eds., *Structural Adjustment and Beyond in Sub-Saharan Africa* (London: Currey, 1994), pp. 18–35.

25. Toye, "Structural Adjustment," p. 18.

26. Toye, "Structural Adjustment," p. 19.

27. Toye, "Structural Adjustment," p. 19.

28. Toye, "Structural Adjustment," p. 19.

29. Toye, "Structural Adjustment," p. 21.

30. Onimode, *Political Economy of the African Crisis*, p. 13.

31. Bade Onimode, *A Future for Africa: Beyond the Politics of Adjustment* (London: Earthscan, 1992), p. 53.

32. Amadu Sesay, "In the Land of the Voiceless: Economic Austerity and Popular Protest in Sierra Leone," in Thandika Mkandawire and Adebayo Olukoshi, eds., *Between Liberalisation and Oppression: The Politics of Structural Adjustment in Africa* (Dakar, Senegal: Codesria, 1995), pp. 186–216.

33. See Adebayo Olukoshi, *The Politics of Structural Adjustment in Nigeria* (London: Currey, 1992); Bjorn Beckman, "The Politics of Labour and Adjustment: The

Experience of the Nigerian Labour Congress," in Mkandawire and Olukoshi, eds., *Between Liberalisation and Oppression*, pp. 281–323.

34. Olukoshi, *Politics of Structural Adjustment in Nigeria*, p. 7.

35. Bjorn Beckman, "Empowerment or Repression? The World Bank and the Politics of African Adjustment" (paper presented to the symposium The Social and Political Context of Structural Adjustment in Sub-Saharan Africa, Bergen, Norway, October 17–19, 1990), quoted in Sesay, "In the Land of the Voiceless," pp. 186–216.

36. Beckman "Politics of Labour and Adjustment," pp. 281–323.

37. Beckman "Politics of Labour and Adjustment," p. 281.

38. Beckman "Politics of Labour and Adjustment," p. 288.

39. Beckman "Politics of Labour and Adjustment," p. 290.

40. Beckman "Politics of Labour and Adjustment," p. 303.

41. Isaac Olawale Albert, "University Students in the Politics of Structural Adjustment in Nigeria," in Thandika Mkandawire and Olukoshi, eds., *Between Liberalisation and Oppression*, pp. 374–392.

42. Albert, "University Students," p. 383.

43. Albert, "University Students," pp. 383–384.

44. Onimode, *Future for Africa*, p. 66.

45. Onimode, *Future for Africa*, p. 66.

46. Onimode, *Future for Africa*, pp. 67, 68.

# Part V

## Topics in Intervention

# 15

# Distributive Justice, Globalization, and International Intervention

## The New Roles of Multilateral Institutions

### Alice Sindzingre

International financial institutions (IFIs), especially the Bretton Woods institutions (BWIs)—the World Bank and the International Monetary Fund (IMF)—have increasingly placed social issues at the top of their agendas. After decades of "structural adjustment," global poverty has become one of the key issues, with poverty reduction being the main objective of such programs. Other dimensions of human development, such as health, education, and social protection, are equally considered to be priorities not only within countries, but also on a global scale. Global crises, such as the one that broke out in Asia in 1997–1998, have accelerated the analysis of social problems that are a consequence of global forces over which countries have sometimes little responsibility and control. Pressure has also been exerted on the World Trade Organization (WTO) to pay some attention to social issues. This has led to the widespread use of new concepts, such as international public goods, international architecture, or core labor standards. The latter have incited the financial institutions to focus more on such problems and to renew their dialogue with international organizations oriented to such problems, such as the International Labor Organization (ILO). Likewise, this has put at the forefront the themes of global economic justice and international intervention in addressing global distributive issues. Here, the BWIs and their economic reforms, or the WTO, are part of the solution as well as the problem. The relevance of their intervention has become both questioned and legitimized, particularly with the new notion of "global governance."

Simultaneously, academic thought in development economics, after a relative indifference toward topics like global inequality or redistributive policies, has attached greater importance to such issues. This is mostly thanks to the influence of Amartya Sen, especially after he was awarded the Nobel Prize. Many studies have developed a broader concept of poverty, focusing on inequality and redistribution, the absence of a trade-off between equity and efficiency, and notions of distributive justice and rights. These ideas are being adopted increasingly in international contexts and in assessments of the consequences of globalization.

This chapter analyzes the concept of global distributive justice and the related reflections of the international community. Then, it describes the impact of such notions in the relations between international institutions and developing countries. This includes especially the programs and conditionalities of financial institutions, the expansion of trade and the rules related to it, and the international handling of global economic crises. Finally, it questions the relevance of these concepts and instruments in terms of international and domestic political economy (e.g., aid, reforms, or trade). This analysis considers the feasibility of global governance as a solution to global distributive problems, which would come under the competence of multilateral institutions. At the end of the day, the success or failure of multilateral efforts may constitute the backdrop to the types of humanitarian crises and interventions addressed throughout this book.

## The Concepts: Poverty, Justice, and Inequality

### Poverty, Rights, and Distributive Justice

Distributive justice has to identify the nature of the deprivation: distributing what, to whom and by whom, and why. It is the object of a vast literature at the borders of welfare economics, social choice theory, and philosophy. It refers to the ways in which a society should allocate its scarce resources among individuals, given their competing needs and claims.[1] Likewise, the notion of poverty has been deeply renewed by the analyses of Amartya Sen,[2] who demonstrates its multidimensionality. Poverty encompasses not only monetary poverty, but also other dimensions of human life. It is a deprivation of "capabilities" and "functionings," along different dimensions, and is due to a lack of assets or opportunities, or of access to them. This includes, for example, the dimensions of human development, such as health, education, and social life, as well as the impossibility of participating with dignity in the activities of a society. Although they are not equivalent to poverty, social exclusion and discrimination are the result of a deprivation of rights and access to opportunities, which may be causes of poverty, as in the case of certain ethnic groups or castes. These features are intrinsic— "constitutive"—dimensions of poverty, but they may also be the causes of deprivation in other aspects. Deprivation is a cumulative process that creates poverty traps at the individual level, as well as at group or country levels. For example, a lack of income results in a lack of education and health, which in turn leads to handicaps in seizing job opportunities, thus triggering an intergenerational vicious cycle.

Poverty may also be apprehended in terms of a deprivation of basic rights and liberties, which may be considered as a core dimension of human well-being.[3] According to John Rawls, human rights express a minimum standard of well-ordered institutions rather than attributes of human beings.[4] Political and economic rights are not, contrary to the rights of the person (e.g., rights to life, liberty, and property), genuine human rights.[5] In contrast, for Sen, substantial freedoms imply essential capabilities. "Capability rights," that is, the fulfillment of people's rights to capabilities, should be the goal of a society. However, beyond differences of normative perspectives, human development is not viewed as separated from progress in human rights.

One question is the scope of human rights, which relates to what can be considered as the material minimum, or on the other side of the equation, the responsibilities of the wealthy. Human rights are linked to the corresponding duties of others in order to ensure the fulfillment of those rights. In Sen's view, legal rights are an essential basis for human rights, but certain laws may be unjust or certain rights are not being applied. Since human beings have certain rights by virtue of their humanity, governments should be helped to work toward achieving this goal, in particular in poor countries where resources are insufficient. In a context of scarce resources, the implementation of economic rights, such as rights to food, health, and education, remains a difficult question, especially because of their opportunity costs. Although rights may be considered relative to time and societies, some basic human rights should constitute minimum standards in all decent societies and across cultural variations. For such rights, universality and indivisibility can be asserted.[6]

The relationship between human rights and poverty is complex. At the aggregate level, some countries have achieved an impressive performance in growth and poverty reduction but poor results in terms of human rights. At the individual level, human rights constitute an intrinsic dimension of the multidimensionality of poverty. Extreme poverty can be considered as an affront to human dignity and a denial of human rights, an argument that has been adopted by the United Nations (UN). This extension to rights has given rise to diverse theories on the relevant justifications and policies that address poverty, on the duty of solidarity, and on the universality of rights—economic, social, and cultural rights. These rights are formally recognized by international institutions, in particular the UN and ILO Conventions. The IFIs, like the World Bank, using Sen's work, have added the dimension of "empowerment" to their analyses of poverty. However, the historical tension continues between the ethical stance—solidarity is a duty toward the poorer whatever the determinants of their situation—and the market-incentive stance. In the market stance, solidarity should be modulated according to the behavior of the poor, and rights are balanced against a notion of responsibility, following the implicit distinction between the deserving and undeserving poor.

*The Debates on Inequality*

The definition of poverty entails multiple conceptual problems, for example, the distinction between absolute versus relative poverty or the priority of one type of poverty over another, in terms of concepts as well as policies. What should be a priority for the policy makers? Should it be to focus on a certain threshold of income, as in the absolute poverty suffered in developing countries, or should the focus be on those deprived of most of the goods enjoyed by the other members of the society, in terms of income, health, or education?[7] The comparative importance of poverty versus inequality is the subject of many debates. This is intrinsically tied to political beliefs and divergences. Poverty and inequality are either mutual dimensions of each other or separate phenomena, and relative poverty may be assimilated to inequality. Depending on specific views of egalitarianism, the increase of global absolute poverty is more alarming than the fact that world inequality has increased or that the rich individuals are getting even richer. Consequently, distributive justice may put more emphasis on addressing world poverty, in particular absolute poverty, than on global inequality—between countries and/or individuals, or within countries. Inequality may itself be perceived both in terms of income inequality or of inequality of opportunities. As underlined by Sen, it leads to distinguishing between global and international equity: the domain of social justice either applies primarily within countries or it cuts across nations.[8]

The choice of the causal framework for poverty as well as inequality is essential because it differentiates between the concepts of distributive justice. Analyses may focus on relative versus absolute poverty, poverty of income, assets or opportunities, or inequality of income or opportunities. Goals may be aimed at lowering inequality or reducing poverty. Arguments and policies targeted on a better distributive justice clearly differ depending on the determinants and dimensions considered as the main causes. Such determinants and dimensions can be lack of income, assets, or opportunities, or less economic and more political and sociological determinants, such as notable inequalities, deprivation of rights, political exclusion, or discrimination. Another debated problem is the causal relationship between inequality and growth. Excessive inequality within a country has been demonstrated as impeding growth.[9]

## Justifications and Instruments of International Distributive Justice

*The Actors of International Distributive Justice*

Formal global institutions like the UN system, the BWIs, or informal ones like the G7, G8, G20, G24, or G77 are organized according to the principle of specialization, with specific fields and mandates. There is an underlying tension between the various multilateral bodies, in particular between the UN system and the BWIs. UN institutions are considered to be "democratic" ("one state, one vote"), but with little power to enforce their decisions and sanctions, and crippled by bilateral politics and interests. The BWIs claim to be more efficient, but are not democratic ("one dollar, one vote"), and the voting power of member states is proportional to their gross domestic product (GDP) and demographic weight. By mandate, they are not supposed to take decisions under the influence of political considerations. They base their legitimacy on technical expertise, though they are suspected of giving preference to particular models of economics, politics, and society under the guise of technical economic reform. In the case of bilateral arrangements, governments frequently promote their geopolitical and business interests and use aid as an instrument of their foreign policy.[10]

Multilateral institutions address a variety of concerns and have a variable range. The UN adopted the International Covenant on Economic, Social, and Cultural Rights in 1996, and it set up an autonomous Committee on Economic, Social, and Cultural Rights. The ILO, besides numerous other conventions, has established a set of "core" labor standards in its Declaration on Fundamental Principles and Rights at Work (1998). The creation of the WTO in 1996 has blurred the fields of competence between multilateral agencies on the issue of justice and rights, as some observers advocate linking the issues of equity and labor rights to the WTO agenda. Since the 1990s, the notion of the benefits of trade has gained an increasing visibility, to the detriment of the notion of development. Trade is supposed to be an effective instrument for stimulating growth in developing countries. The WTO is gaining increasing power because of its capacity to sanction and ensure compliance. Other observers defend the separation of moral considerations—rights and equity concerns—from the rules of WTO, since this is not its mandate but that of a UN agency like the ILO. The international community has initiated a global debate on the effectiveness of aid in the 1990s, facing the failure of adjustment programs and redistribution policies, especially in the poorest countries of sub-Saharan Africa.[11]

*Arguments and Justifications: Ethics, Efficiency, and Markets*

Distributive justice, like any action of redistribution, implies two sides: the collection side and the distribution side. The collection side may consist of revenues, that is, through taxation or voluntary grants, and may involve states or private actors. Redistribution may involve not only income and wealth, but also rights, assets (e.g., land), and opportunities through improved health and education.

*Ethical Arguments*

Distributive justice is usually based on ethical arguments. The polarization of the world and the existence of huge numbers of "have-nots" arouse moral and humanitarian demands. Among the vast literature on normative economics, John Rawls's theory of distributive justice has developed the argument of "justice as fairness": individuals should behave as they would if placed under a "veil of ignorance" in a hypothetical "original position" within a society. One principle is to give priority to the worst-off individual within a lexicographic order of allocation of primary goods. Sen disagrees with the concept of "primary goods" as the goods that should be distributed. The well-known question of Sen is "equality of what?" In his view, the dimensions to be equalized are not goods, but opportunities and capabilities, that is, freedoms. What kind of global distributive justice should be required to amend global inequalities?[12] For Rawls, at a global scale it should not be grounded on egalitarian principles (e.g., wealth transfers to poorer societies) but on mutual aid.[13] Other ethical stances justify the reduction of global inequality by principles of universality, responsibility, and altruism when being confronted with deprivation, humiliation, or exclusion.[14]

Ethical attitudes are confronted with the classical problems of norms and the philosophical stances of universalism, relativism, and the incommensurability of values. It is not always easy to make an unambiguous judgment on a situation that is unjust or to have a clear idea of the appropriate action to take. This is especially true with respect to other countries or different political and economic settings with, for instance, deep-rooted discriminatory norms against certain social groups. Moreover, assessments by rich countries of inegalitarian situations in poorer ones are easily contaminated by underlying power relationships, ignorance, or paternalism.[15] Furthermore, altruism is a variable and idiosyncratic feature of individuals, and it has no direct interpretation as a redistributive obligation. One example is the reluctance of citizens to redistribute vis-à-vis taxation. Sensitivity of social groups varies according to their history, explaining the well-known difference between the United States and Europe on issues of equality and justice.[16]

Mobility is an essential dimension here, beside that of equality. Preferences for redistribution seem to be connected with the relative positions occupied by individuals on the social scale and to their prospects of mobility. In the United States, individuals who have faith in equal opportunities have a lower preference for redistribution than individuals who feel that other factors interfere with this equality, like discrimination; the latter therefore adhere to redistributive policies.[17] Likewise, individuals may perceive themselves as sharing a social contract and membership and as pooling risks and rewards. In exchange for their efforts, they expect that they have a chance of climbing the economic ladder—the negative side being a greater flexibility of the labor markets. As reminded by Sen, inequality is multidimensional, and it is not easy to judge relative policies. Which is the more unequal system: high protection and high unemployment, or low protection and high mobility?[18]

## Economic Arguments

This is why distributive justice is also based on economic arguments, which use different channels. Redistribution and transfers may be grounded on the argument of risk pooling and can serve as an insurance mechanism, especially under the new hazards associated with globalization. Likewise, the environment provided by effective redistributive and equalizing mechanisms constitutes a guarantee against the risks of impoverishment. It confers a greater capacity to take risks and allows for a longer time span. Expectations of redistribution are an asset, an additional input in the productivity of individuals. They are compatible with the individualist-voluntarist perspective of the social contract—being a more inclusive social contract—or more efficient social norms because they are shared. The guarantees offered by a state committed to redistribution and providing risk-pooling mechanisms strengthen feelings of membership and protection, ease collective action and labor relations, reduce transaction costs, stabilize individual calculations, and offer longer time frames for individual decisions to invest, consume, produce, and save. They thus forge a positive relationship between these expectations of protection and productivity. At the aggregate level, economic stability may also be viewed as a public good. High public levies and taxation can lead to higher productivity and, therefore, higher growth.[19] Equality, egalitarian policies, and asset-redistribution can boost productivity.[20] In some developed countries, inequality would have increased more in the last decade if the state had distributed less.[21]

A second category of economic arguments justifying distributive justice is that distribution corresponds to the interests of the richer classes. To abandon the poor in their poverty increases negative externalities, such as the risks of communicable diseases, social unrest, and smaller market prospects for products made by the rich. These economic arguments have a long history and have been a recurrent way of legitimizing charity, philanthropy, and help to the "deserving poor."[22] The same arguments are also a justification for the global transfers advocated by the World Bank,[23] which has put forward poverty reduction as the main justification of its existence, along with calls for coalitions of governments, civil society, and the private sector. This argumentation may be linked to the academic reflection on the legitimacy of multilateral institutions, which now justify their status as being "international public goods." Such goods are said to ensure economic stability, binding the hands of governments that lack credibility, and to provide knowledge, vis-à-vis international markets and investors, to governments of emerging and developing countries.[24] Globalization has intensified international negative externalities, such as contagious diseases, the proliferation of conflicts, financial systemic crises, and global market failures. Nonfinancial multilateral institutions like the UN also use the argument of the interest of rich countries to increase their aid, against the indifference of public opinions toward international redistributive justice. Globalization not only involves financial flows, goods, information, or opportunities, but also risks,[25] such as vast migration movements or new types of insecurity like terrorism.

## Mechanisms and Instruments of Distributive Justice: Markets, Growth, and Public Redistribution

The trade-off between equity and efficiency is an old debate in public economics. At the domestic level, the instruments of redistribution are taxation, transfers, and public services. At the international and government levels, these may be taxation of external trade and preferential schemes, as well as transfers and program or project aid. The traditional debate on equity versus efficiency occurs at the international level, since all these redistributive instruments may create distortions and disincentives—trade barriers, aid, grants, and projects—that can cause serious negative disruptions on poor economies and local prices. Food aid is a good example. The opposition between efficiency and equity is increasingly criticized.[26]

Further instruments are market incentives and contractualization, markets requiring efficient contracts to function smoothly. Developed for national contexts, they may be questioned in an international context. The neoclassical notion of a global contract acknowledges that some markets may be missing (e.g., credit or insurance markets). Developing countries may be trapped in low equilibriums of the social contract, with low redistribution and strong inequalities.[27] At the international level, economic growth is considered the main instrument to alleviate poverty. However, heterodox economists justify public intervention specifically aimed at inequality. There is a tendency to advocate more trade than assistance, which is increasingly recognized as inducing dependence.

The emphasis may also be put on market failures and their correction. This legitimizes strong government intervention and the need for rules for corrective policies, that is, rules for sanctions and incentives. An example is the linkage by a multilateral institution of international trade rules with country policies aimed at improving social rights, for example, the European Union (EU) revised Generalized System of Tariff Preferences. To avoid being accused by developing countries of using labor standards as a protection mechanism, the EU proposes an incentive mechanism designed to encourage respect for labor standards, which links additional benefits to respect for core labor standards. Constraints may be associated to incentives. In order to benefit from the EU arrangement, countries must comply with the ILO core labor standards conventions.[28] For the EU, labor standards should not be included in multilateral trade agreements, nor should they be enforced through trade sanctions. Linking trade and social issues via multilateral rules, which seems to improve equity and rights, may be manipulated for protectionist purposes and private interests, and may also trigger a spiral of increased recourse to trade sanctions. Besides regulations, public intervention may take the form of redistributive policies. Redistribution addresses income or wealth, but also equality of rights, access, chances, capabilities, or functionings, according to Sen's concepts. This may, for example, include land reforms or positive discrimination.[29]

A general problem affecting mechanisms of international distributive justice is the extrapolation of analysis from instruments tailored for within-countries issues to between-countries issues. Another problem, which is more acute in developing countries, is that of efficient institutional channels, via governments or substate levels, given the often-weak institutional capacity or the illegitimate or nondemocratic aspect of some political regimes.

## *"Globalization": Its Effects on Inequality and State Capacities*

International distributive justice cannot be analyzed outside the issue of globalization, both as an idea and a set of facts. Globalization includes increased global flows of goods, services, financial transactions, individuals, and information. Beyond the explosion of analyses, the question remains open as to whether globalization is an old or a new phenomenon,[30] as well as regarding the diverse types of flows it refers to, and on its genuinely "global" character—as some regions seem to be left out. Globalization is relevant because it is viewed as having a negative impact on international wealth distribution and aggravating inequality between countries, within countries, and between social groups, creating losers despite its potential benefits for some. In theory, trade liberalization helps to reduce poverty, but it may have a negative incidence on income distribution, prices, wages of unskilled workers, and public revenues and spending. Thus, globalization has triggered rising criticism from the "global civil society" about its metonymic incarnation, that is, the multilateral institutions and global summits of the richer countries: G7/G8, IMF, World Bank, and WTO.[31] However, the fact that the last few decades have witnessed both globalization and an increase in global inequality does not imply that globalization is the cause of this increase. Antiglobalization protests are in fact not about globalization. As Sen notes, the central concern is the level of inequality and whether the distribution of gains is fair.

Globalization is also a major issue because it may weaken the capacities of nation-states to redistribute, resolve distributive conflicts, and address justice and equity issues. This challenges the basis of their legitimacy and the stabilization of democracy.[32] However, states seem to retain considerable power in some domains.[33] Nevertheless, states are under new pressure because the global liberalization of financial flows and the competition to attract international capital have the direct effects of diminishing state taxation capacity. The fact that globalization undermines the capacity of states in addressing injustice buttresses arguments for a global public sphere and international norms and intervention. It also legitimizes the role of multilateral institutions in matters of distributive justice, though this raises questions of domestic accountability. This is particularly challenged by the current marginalization of the poorest countries in terms of economic and geopolitical weight, as well as in terms of representation and influence in multilateral institutions.

## Multilateral Interventions, Poor Countries, and Distributive Justice

As in other domains of economics, whether the instruments are trade or aid, options are marked by theoretical choices on the determinants of distribution, their channels and mechanisms, and the desirable goals. This, in particular, includes the choice between the neoclassical framework versus heterodoxy and egalitarianism.[34] The latter positions are in the minority in the multilateral system. Debates are continuing on the appropriate devices for social protection, with the usual tensions over the role of government and the allocation of social responsibility between the individual and society. Should there be safety nets and market-based solutions such as insurance schemes, or more interventionist and redistributive public policies?

### Aid, Conditionality, and Economic Reform

Before aid and trade, growth is obviously a privileged mechanism for poverty reduction. However, discussions are ongoing over the necessity to accompany growth with active redistributive policies, since growth often modifies the shape of distribution in a given country. This is opposed to the old theory of "trickle-down" processes. These policies may be initiated by governments or promoted by external donors. Conditionalities attached to BWI loans may or may not have explicit redistributive components.

### Aid and Reform

Official development assistance has for a long time been the main instrument to help poor countries set in motion the virtuous cycle of development and, consequently, to redress international inequalities. It may originate from a moral obligation, whether humanitarian or distributive,[35] although sensitivity to international inequality is not homogenous among rich countries. The BWIs legitimize their prescriptions of economic reforms and conditionalities attached to new financing by their goals of higher growth, and thus poverty reduction—according to the orthodox theory of greater efficiency.

The BWIs are aware that economic reforms generate both winners and losers. With the recent insistence on poverty reduction as their main mission, they present their reform programs as a means of "making the poor the winners." Their recent emphasis on the negative effects of government corruption stresses the fact that reforms aim at making these corrupted elites the losers.

This is one aspect of the many contradictions between the conditionalities attached to BWI loans and the "ownership" of reforms by the recipients—the obvious condition of their effectiveness. BWIs expect that reforms should be "owned" by the poor and the majority of the population, since liberalization and the other reforms are supposed to break the rents of the elites and foster growth. The support of politicians is less required, albeit strategically necessary. This shows the political ambiguities of BWI intervention. By mandate, the World Bank and the IMF are apolitical, their prescriptions rely on technical grounds, and they lend to states and not to particular regimes. But simultaneously they justify their intervention by its benefits for the poor and need the support of the governmental elites. They often forget that developing countries are often highly unequal and that poverty is often the outcome of political exclusion and predatory regimes.

Some reforms, such as trade liberalization, may have negative distributional effects, especially in sub-Saharan Africa, where budgets strongly rely on the taxation of international trade.[36] Social expenditures in health and education were often the last priority of liberalization. The suppression of food subsidies, as well as the introduction of user fees, had negative distributional consequences.[37] The new programs (Poverty Reduction Strategy Papers) launched by the World Bank and the IMF, which are focused on social services, assess these failures—while exonerating the reforms—and aim at reversing this trend.

*The Political Economy Dimension*

A pivotal argument underlying the legitimacy of BWI programs is based on political economy. The case of governments in developing countries behaving in an antigrowth or antidevelopment political economy constitutes a clear argument for legitimizing a supranational interference in the domestic affairs of a country. This is true not only in the human rights domain, where it is now admitted, but also in the economic and institutional domains. Since many governments in developing countries are corrupt, rely on rents, and do not redistribute except to themselves and their clients or to oligarchies, BWI economic reforms have often the implicit justification that they break up these rents. This is why the reforms prescribed by the BWIs are sometimes welcomed by local opposition groups and leftist political movements, for they can destabilize such rents and interest groups remaining in power. Despite this, they are frequently rejected by civil society movements, especially in African countries—for instance, the dismantling of local marketing boards or monopolies, building of central bank independence, or establishing trade liberalization. In Southeast Asia, after the 1997–1998 crisis, BWI conditionalities on bank restructuring were explicitly targeted against local "cronies" and rent-seekers, among other sectors. Reforms are supposed to level playing fields, allow for better participation of individuals in economic activity, and improve justice in the sense of a more inclusive allocation of resources and opportunities.

However, African and Asian countries display differences in geopolitical importance and the capacity to attract private capital flows and, therefore, in respect to dependence on BWIs. This leads to different types of interventions on the part of richer countries, with obviously less room for maneuver for the poorest African countries, in negotiations on reforms, safety nets, and social policies. Owing to economists' conceptions of states and policy reform, and the dismissal of the dimensions of local history, social norms, or political economy, these equitable objectives are often immobilized at the discourse stage. The BWIs are ill equipped to redress unequal distribution if the majority of people suffer from social exclusion,[38] and reforms have often produced unintended effects. In fact, political considerations and the geopolitical weights of countries are always present behind the economic technicalities, and conditionalities are frequently not enforced by the BWIs.[39] Long-lasting support and lending to openly corrupt, authoritarian, and inegalitarian governments undermine the credibility of the official objectives of reforms, such as addressing the needs of the poorest, ensuring the broadest participation, and enforcing accountability on the part of the elites.

Conditionality and aid have the well-known negative dimension of international intrusion, for they create understandable resistance from recipient governments. The poorest countries, mostly in sub-Saharan Africa, are trapped in the vicious cycle of the lack of international credibility. Since the debt crisis in 1982, they have received very little private financial flows and have therefore become totally dependent on international public assistance and IFI financing. This lack of credibility is a justification of the penetration of the IFIs, conditionality, and the locking-in of government policies. This legitimizes the IFIs as acting in this case as global public goods. Assisted governments have no other choice but to accept, however reluctantly, whatever conditionalities are imposed, thus inducing multiple policy reversals that have spiraling negative effects on the credibility of local politicians and economic activities.[40]

### The Rise of Multilateral Institutions: The Benefits of Trade and Global Governance

In the last decade, the dominant paradigm within the "international community" became trade, its effects, and its virtues. This period witnessed an unprecedented explosion of trade flows: world trade grew at a rate of 6.5 percent in the 1990s, besides a rise in the world GDP per capita of 1.3 percent.[41] Many economic studies stress that trade openness and liberalization boost growth, poverty reduction, and efficiency, and are an essential aspect of development policies. On the other hand, the distributional consequences of trade liberalization can be regressive, depending on the institutional specificities of countries.[42] Trade liberalization needs to be accompanied by explicit redistribution whenever problems of equity arise and reform leads to adverse distributive effects.

The institutional translation of this phenomenon is the expansion of the global role of the WTO after its creation in 1995. The power of the WTO lies not within itself but in the governments of its 144 member countries. However, the consequences of the decisions taken by the Dispute Settlement Body (DSB) on economic activity within countries gives it power not only on trade issues, but also on many others that are related to social or developmental dimensions—a practice that is perceived as excessive and illegitimate by global civic groups.[43] The underlying conceptual paradigm is that a better integration of developing countries will bring about better welfare and that this is more efficient than aid, which has turned out to be ineffective. The WTO bases part of its global legitimacy on being the organization designated to help developing countries integrate more effectively into the world economy and to lay down global rules that can protect them from free-market forces, mercantilist interests, and crude power relationships. Its arguments are that developed countries can trade, bargain, or retaliate on a bilateral basis, while small and poor countries can be integrated and protected by multilateral rules applying to all.

*The Issue of Social Standards*

The improvement of global social justice has been activated by the idea of attaching conditionalities, not only to classical IFI financing in exchange for economic reform, as in structural adjustment, but also to the regulation of international trade flows. In the latter case, conditionalities focus not on the economic sectors but on social and labor relations and rights. According to this perspective, global inequality and justice issues may be addressed through rules on exported products. Those countries that do not respect social standards may be sanctioned through rules limiting their external trade, for example, "fair trade" and improvement of the comprehensiveness of WTO rules.[44] They seek the benefits of a genuine WTO "Development Round." Developing countries consider that the previous Uruguay Round did not work in their favor, revealed the asymmetries of the global trade game, and was not fully implemented by the rich countries. They are therefore reluctant to accept the inclusion of new issues and rules, which may be hidden protection for the richer countries. Paradoxically, the governments of developing countries may be seeking such equity while being inequitable vis-à-vis their own citizens.

However, just like the "authoritarian altruism" of governments deciding what is good for their citizens, richer countries seek to impose social standards for the sake of countries that refuse them, whatever their universal validity. Linking respect for social clauses with international trade rules, through an institution like the WTO, is strongly defended by some in the name of the global values of equity and social justice. So far, as reaffirmed in Singapore in 1996, the WTO accepts core labor standards, rejects their use for protectionist purposes, and recognizes the ILO as the competent body to deal with them. For partisans of a stronger linkage, social justice is the result of collective and voluntary choices, and it should be built into the architecture of trade and investment. However, this claim of universality is not fully credible. It is being advocated by civic groups in developing countries genuinely committed to ideals of justice and also by particular interests in developed countries (e.g., the U.S. government or the unions of developed countries). Interestingly enough, this link is sometimes hotly contested by the very people in the developing countries who are supposed to enjoy greater justice under it, and not only, as expected, by the elites or governments. Some developing countries see this as a new guise to protect rich countries, while some academic economists believe this link creates market distortions that are likely to be harmful to poor countries.[45]

Given its mandate, the ILO is the appropriate forum, but it currently lacks the enforcement capacities of other multilateral institutions, even though its constitution allows members to take measures against countries violating its recommendations. However, a consensus in some multilateral institutions seems to be emerging on the essential central role of the ILO. Most multilateral institutions, the BWIs, and UN agencies, such as the UN Conference on Trade and Development (UNCTAD) and the UN Development Program, agree on the necessity for a cautious analysis of trade, labor, and globalization. There is, however, resistance from some emerging countries and different agendas for decisions coming from the UN system.

*The Relevance of Global Institutions*

The new idea of "global public goods" is a response to the tension between the different forms of legitimacy embodied by the existing multilateral institutions, in particular the UN system and the IFIs, as well as to the widening criticisms of the "civil society." These criticisms see the IFIs as instruments dedicated to the interests of rich countries, especially the United States. This is shown in their biased treatment toward the financial crises in East Asia, Turkey, and Argentina. Multilateral institutions revamp their eroding global legitimacy by trying to present their missions as global public goods. Such goods are said to have the best capacities to support macrofinancial stability, provide credibility for weak states, prevent global crises, and leverage the financing of social public goods that private transnational firms will not produce, such as drugs or vaccines. In a context of questioning the capacities of nation-states and global externalities, one possible solution may be the transformation or extension of the missions of existing multilateral institutions. However, this option is weakened by their poor results, as well as by the criticisms both from conservative and progressive circles, which view them either as lacking credibility and efficiency, or being manipulated by rich countries. Multilateral institutions are pervaded by intrinsic democratic deficits. Democratic mechanisms are still defined in territorial-statist terms and national representative bodies generally exercise little oversight over their state's positions in multilateral fora. Moreover, these multilateral institutions are composed of states, with their intrinsic interests. In this sense, they are "international" rather than truly "global"—that is, able to address global problems, such as environmental issues.

Another solution may be the creation of new global institutions, but it threatens the principle of parsimony and entails the risk of overlapping and multiplication of multilateral entities focused on a specific problem. This may result in a potential loss of credibility and efficiency. Proposals have been submitted to create some new institutions, with a mandate on issues considered as global public goods, such as a world financial authority,[46] a world council of social and economic security, or an institution focused on the global management of taxation.[47] The issue of global governance is supported by some other multilateral institutions, such as the EU, which insists on global social governance.

### The Limits of Existing Instruments

#### *The Limits of Global Trade Rules*

There is an excessive emphasis on the positive effects of multilateral rules and the establishment of rights. This supposes that the rules are respected. The virtues of trade liberalization are equally exaggerated, especially for sub-Saharan Africa facing innumerable historical, political, and economic constraints. Since the 1980s, many least developed countries (LDCs) have lowered their barriers to trade, but they are still stagnating. "[O]penness does not deliver on its promise."[48] Trade openness is just one component of a development strategy, and it cannot be a substitute for it. Economic policy should focus on growth rather than on trade. The rare developing countries that achieved some success, for example, Mauritius and Botswana, did so by implementing a number of unorthodox policies.[49] Other trade arrangements have not provided the poorest countries with the promised growth and welfare. This is the case of bilateral or regional rules and agreements, such as the European Generalised System of Preferences or the Lomé Convention, which has been an overt failure in this regard. Likewise, the initiative of the EU, which removes restrictions on imports from the LDCs ("everything but arms"), may achieve fewer benefits than expected.

Global economic integration is often said to bring benefits and growth to developing countries. In the case of low-income countries, the benefits from WTO membership, in terms of improved market access for their traditional exports, seem to be limited.[50] Existing multilateral agreements, such as the General Agreement on Tariffs and Trade and the Uruguay Round, and then the WTO, did not succeed in reducing the income gap between developed and the poorest developing countries. During the last decade, sub-Saharan Africa fared worse, halving its share in global trade, which was 1 percent in the 1990s, while attracting a tiny amount of foreign direct investment (FDI). As pointed out by UNCTAD, too much is expected of the virtues of global institutions and global agreements for resolving the problems of sub-Saharan Africa. These are obvious examples of the failures of global governance due to lobbies, as well as private, national, and geopolitical interests. In contrast, global integration entails significant costs, especially the costs of complying with the new obligations accompanying WTO membership, as well as do-mestic institutional costs ensuing from openness (e.g., increased demands of social protection and intensified social conflicts).[51] More generally, WTO rules are affected by problems of credibility. Criticisms against the WTO and IFIs are recurrent within the global civil society, which perceives them as expressing mainly the interests of rich countries and their transnational cor-porations. They are especially thought to favor the United States and its policy of opening foreign markets to its own products. Indeed, rich countries fear the competitiveness of emerging countries and generalized openness. The labor unions of developed countries, working ideally in favor of a universal distributive justice, function in reality within their national boundaries and constituencies. Their fear is that the relocation of firms in developing coun-tries would apply pressure on lowering wages, and they therefore defend universal social standards by invoking the "race to the bottom" argument.

The rules established by the WTO now forbid the very economic strate-gies that allowed poor countries to develop three decades ago. These in-clude, for example, state interventions to create dynamic comparative advantages, as in the case of the "developmental strategies" of Korea and Taiwan, industrial policies, or control of the FDIs and their inclusion in a domestic development strategy.[52] These instruments are now limited by the multilateral rules of the WTO.[53] Moreover, the emergence and extension of mandates of global governance institutions, the IFIs, or the WTO, and the strengthening of the global financial architecture after the financial crises of the 1990s in East Asia or Russia may contribute to undermining the domestic governance of nation-states.[54] On the other hand, globalization may put a premium on the role of states. Trade openness seems to be associated with bigger-sized governments.[55] However, globalization and openness make more difficult the supply of state protection and its regulation.[56] Equally, for openness to be efficient, it requires the existence of effective local institutions that are able to manage social redistributive conflicts, as well as a minimal quality of public governance and noncorrupt bureaucracies. Nation-states seem to survive well, but a global governance regime should be innovative as to their new form, such as a global federalism.[57]

These limitations may be addressed according to different conceptions of rules, in particular the common-law and civil-law traditions. The ability to impose costly sanctions is also a strategic issue. Some analysts advocate global regulation, beyond contractual arrangements based on market instruments like incentives. They advocate a strengthening of the rules and a better capacity to enforce them. However, the legal means, which multilateral institutions increasingly use to enforce their rules—giving rise to a "judicialization" of relationships between states—are closer to the common-law model. This model of judicialization is shown by the explosion in the activities of the WTO's DSB.[58] The Dispute Settlement System (DSS) and the Dispute Settlement Understanding, which are the "central pillars" of WTO multilateralism, are supposed to help small countries. However, the DSS has been mostly used by the G4 countries (60 percent of all the complaints in the first three years of WTO operations), one explanation being that disputes are proportional to the diversity of a country's exports over products and partners.[59] The DSB works on a case-by-case basis, gradually creating an *ex post* legal corpus, in the tradition of the common law. However, it obviously reflects the preexisting economic and political asymmetries between countries, while global regulation may be regarded as a fairer system. Likewise, the constraints of "soft law," that is, the many codes of conduct on transnational corporations, are weak. Even if legal rules are the outcome of hegemony and interests, which has always been the case historically, a global and *ex ante* rule-based system may be a more equitable one. It could be a step toward a "global law," in contrast to "global governance." The latter is thought to be a synonym for a club of the wealthiest, which globalization and its social effects now make necessary.[60]

### The Limits of Aid and the Reform of Multilateral Institutions

Over the last few decades, aid has been particularly inefficient in addressing justice and equity issues, producing the well-known "aid fatigue" syndrome of public opinion. After decades of economic reform under the guidance of the IFIs, sub-Saharan Africa and Latin America exhibit high degrees of inequality. Asian countries, which show lower levels of inequality, achieved them through heterodox policies, sometimes in disagreement with the IFIs. They resorted to targeted state interventions and temporary market distortions.

Also, at the institutional level, global governance, as embodied by the IFIs, is basically financial governance. Rather than addressing the fundamental questions of international asymmetries and their structural determinants, it chooses to reproduce them.[61] Governance of the IFIs is based on weighted voting, according to the wealth of member states, rather than on equitable representation. While developed countries have 17 percent of the voting power in the UN, they account for 61 to 62 percent in the BWIs[62]—the United States has within the IMF much more power over decisions than its weight of 17 percent.[63] Bilateral members, at the levels of their own development policies, their activity within the multilateral system, and their domestic political agenda, should have played a role in complementing the multilateral institutions. However, the aid packages given by bilateral donors have been notoriously lacking in coordination and coherence among themselves. This has added to the inefficiency of development assistance in countries that were the poorest and had the weakest domestic institutions, as in sub-Saharan Africa.

In times of global crises, massive rescue packages and emergency financing were launched, but mainly because of a fear of systemic risk and the destabilization of the financial systems of developed countries, rather than to resolve the specific problems of developing countries. They were created for the emerging countries and not for the poorest, since the latter do not represent a threat to the world order. The initiatives relating to a new global architecture were mainly a response to financial crises, such as the Asian crisis. Preoccupations of distributive justice remained secondary. Moreover, economic reforms prescribed by the IFIs during the crises were strongly criticized, even by prominent scholars, as being inappropriate and sometimes even worsening them. These crises have revealed the fragility of welfare systems in emerging countries. Reflections on global governance should concentrate on more permanent mechanisms that are likely to cushion their impact in terms of poverty, the deterioration of living conditions, and the aggravation of inequalities.

## Conclusion

The concept of global distributive justice has gained a strategic importance with the emergence of "globalization," which may or may not erode states. It is the subject of increasing analyses on the mechanisms of multilateral institutions and global governance. However, there is a risk that these notions will just be the fads of an "international community," creating concepts to justify institutional existence. Moreover, global distributive justice is caught in a series of dilemmas. Global problems cannot be assimilated with multilateral ones, which continue to be treated within the framework of states. States are ill equipped to address global externalities as well as economic justice. The ethical, economic, and political duty of distributive justice may be assigned to multilateral institutions, even though they are not the outcomes of democratic processes, or to states whose governments may be illegitimate or corrupt. Another duty, in many developing countries, is to support and reconstruct states and public sectors, because many public goods (e.g., rights or stability) are so far only provided by states.

Reflections are trapped in debates on institutions—global institutions or global public goods. Existing "efficient" but nondemocratic institutions, such as the BWIs, are in sharp contrast with inefficient but more democratic ones like the ILO. There is also a dilemma between the use of existing institutions, often flawed by problems of credibility in matters of economic justice, or the creation of new institutions. This latter option contains the risk of an inefficient multiplication of entities, leading to competition and overlapping, and their juxtaposition with states that claim to have the only political legitimacy so far. Beyond the problems of appropriate multilateral institutions, global distributive concerns are addressed mainly by the instruments of aid and economic reforms. These instruments, particularly trade liberalization, have obvious limitations. The issues of global economic rights and justice require much more in-depth analyses. Solutions to these issues also depend on the political will of governments and a clarification of the objectives, rules, instruments, and institutions that are capable of enforcing commitments.

## Notes

1. See John E. Roemer, *Theories of Distributive Justice* (Cambridge, Mass.: Harvard University Press, 1996).

2. Amartya Sen, *Development As Freedom* (New York: Knopf, 1999).

3. See Isaiah Berlin, *Four Essays on Liberty* (Oxford: Oxford University Press, 1969); Robert Nozick, *Anarchy, State and Utopia* (New York: Basic, 1974).

4. John Rawls, *A Theory of Justice* (Cambridge, Mass.: Harvard University Press, 1971).

5. Charles Beitz, "International Liberalism and Distributive Justice," *World Politics* 51, no. 2 (January 1999): 269–296.

6. John Rawls, "The Law of People," in Stephen Shute and Susan Hurley, eds., *On Human Rights: The Oxford Amnesty Lectures, 1993* (New York: Basic, 1993).

7. Amartya Sen, "Poor, 'Relatively Speaking,'" *Oxford Economic Papers* 35, no. 2 (1983): 153–169.

8. Amartya Sen, "Global Justice: Beyond International Equity," in Inge Kaul, Isabelle Grunberg, and Marc A. Stern, eds., *Global Public Goods: International Cooperation in the Twenty-first Century* (New York: UN Development Program, 1999), pp. 116–125.

9. Roberto Perotti, "Growth, Income Distribution, and Democracy: What the Data Say," *Journal of Economic Growth* 1, no. 2 (June 1996): 149–187; Martin Ravallion, *Growth, Inequality and Poverty: Looking beyond Averages*, Policy Research Working Paper, no. 2558 (Washington, D.C.: World Bank, 2001).

10. Alberto Alesina and David Dollar, *Who Gives Foreign Aid to Whom and Why?* Working Paper, no. w6612 (Cambridge, Mass.: National Bureau of Economic Research, 1998).

11. Between 1980 and 1994, for the twelve countries that received fifteen or more World Bank and IMF adjustment loans, the median per capita growth rate was zero.

See William Easterly, *The Elusive Quest for Growth* (Cambridge: Massachusetts Institute of Technology Press, 2001).

12. David Miller, "Justice and Global Inequality," in Andrew Hurrell and Ngaire Woods, eds., *Inequality, Globalization, and World Politics* (Oxford: Oxford University Press, 1999), pp. 187–210.

13. Wilfried Hinsch, "Global Distributive Justice," in Thomas W. Pogge, ed., *Global Justice* (Oxford: Blackwell, 2001), pp. 55–75.

14. See Charles R. Beitz, "Does Global Inequality Matter?" in Thomas W. Pogge, ed., *Global Justice* (Oxford: Blackwell, 2001), pp. 106–122.

15. Cass R. Sunstein, *Free Markets and Social Justice* (New York: Oxford University Press, 1997), chapter 2.

16. Alberto Alesina, Rafael Di Tella, and Robert MacCulloch, *Inequality and Happiness: Are Europeans and Americans Different?* Working Paper, no. w8198 (Cambridge, Mass.: National Bureau of Economic Research, 2001).

17. Alberto Alesina and Eliana La Ferrara, *Preferences for Redistribution in the Land of Opportunities*, Working Paper, no. w8267 (Cambridge, Mass.: National Bureau of Economic Research, 2001).

18. Amartya Sen, "Economic Policy and Equity: An Overview," in Vito Tanzi, Ke-Young Chu, and Sanjeev Gupta, eds., *Economic Policy and Equity* (Washington, D.C.: International Monetary Fund, 1999), pp. 29–43.

19. Laurent Davezies, personal communication, June 20, 2001.

20. Samuel Bowles, Herbert Gintis, and Erik Olin Wright, eds., *Recasting Egalitarianism: New Rules for Communities, States and Markets* (London: Verso, 1998).

21. On England, see Anthony Atkinson, *Is Rising Inequality Inevitable? A Critique of the Transatlantic Consensus*, Annual Lectures 3 (Helsinki: WIDER, 1999).

22. Robert W. Fogel, *The Fourth Great Awakening and the Future of Egalitarianism* (Chicago, University of Chicago Press, 2000); Ethan B. Kapstein, "Distributive Justice As an International Public Good: A Historical Perspective," in Inge Kaul, Isabelle Grunberg, and Marc A. Stern, eds., *Global Public Goods: International Cooperation in the Twenty-first Century* (New York: UN Development Program, 1999).

23. Alice Sindzingre, "Institutions d'aide et enquêtes sur la pauvreté en Afrique," *Cahiers d'Economie et Sociologie Rurales* 42–43 (1997): 146–183.

24. Dani Rodrik, "Why Is There Multilateral Lending?" in Michael Bruno and Boris Pleskovic, eds., *Annual World Bank Conference on Development Economics* (Washington, D.C.: World Bank, 1995), pp. 167–193.

25. See United Nations, *Report of the High-Level Panel on Financing for Development* (New York: United Nations, 2001).

26. François Bourguignon, *Distribution, Redistribution and Development: Where Do We Stand?* Working Paper, no. 98–11 (Paris: DELTA, 1998).

27. Roland Benabou, "Unequal Societies: Income Distribution and the Social Contract," *American Economic Review* 90, no. 1 (March 2000): 96–129.

28. European Commission, *Promoting Core Labour Standards and Improving Social Governance in the Context of Globalisation* (Brussels: Communication COM [2001] 416 final, 18 July 2001).

29. Glenn Loury, "Social Exclusion and Ethnic Groups: The Challenge to Economics," in Boris Pleskovic and Joseph E. Stiglitz, eds., *Annual World Bank Conference on Development Economics, 1999* (Washington, D.C.: World Bank, 2000), pp. 225–252.

30. Kevin H. O'Rourke and Jeffrey G. Williamson, *When Did Globalization Begin?* Working Paper, no. w7632 (Cambridge, Mass.: National Bureau of Economic Research, 2000).

31. Andrew Linklater, "The Evolving Spheres of International Justice," *International Affairs* 75, no. 3 (July 1999): 473–482; Charles R. Beitz, "Social and Cosmopolitan Liberalism," *International Affairs* 75, no. 3 (July 1999): 515–530.

32. Bob Deacon, *Globalization and Social Policy: The Threat to Equitable Welfare* (Helsinki: Globalism and Social Policy Program, 2000); Geoffrey Garrett, *The Distributive Consequences of Globalization*, Leitner Working Paper, no. 2001–02 (New Haven, Conn.: Yale University, Center for International and Area Studies, 2001).

33. Linda Weiss, *The Myth of the Powerless State: Governing the Economy in a Global Era* (Cambridge: Polity, 1998); Peter Evans, "The Eclipse of the State? Reflections on Stateness in an Era of Globalization," *World Politics* 50, no. 1 (October 1997): 62–87.

34. Bowles and Gintis, *Recasting Egalitarianism*; George F. DeMartino, *Global Economy, Global Justice: Theoretical Objections and Policy Alternatives to Neoliberalism* (London: Routledge, 2000).

35. Brian R. Opeskin, "The Moral Foundations of Foreign Aid," *World Development* 24, no. 1 (1996): 21–44.

36. John Toye, "Fiscal Crisis and Fiscal Reform in Developing Countries," *Cambridge Journal of Economics* 24, no. 1 (January 2000): 21–44.

37. Frances Stewart and Albert Berry, "Globalization, Liberalization and Inequality: Expectations and Experience," in Andrew Hurrell and Ngaire Woods, eds., *Inequality, Globalization, and World Politics* (Oxford: Oxford University Press, 1999), pp. 150–186.

38. Amartya Sen, interview in *Challenge* 43, no.1 (January–February 2000): 22–31.

39. Alice Sindzingre, "Les bailleurs de fonds en quête de légitimité," *Esprit*, no. 264 (June 2000): 116–127.

40. Alice Sindzingre, "Crédibilité des Etats et économie politique des réformes en Afrique," *Economies et Sociétés*, no. 4 (1998): 117–147.

41. World Bank, *Global Economic Prospects and the Developing Countries, 2001* (Washington, D.C.: World Bank, 2001), tables 1.6, 1.7.

42. José Antonio Ocampo and Lance Taylor, *Trade Liberalization in Developing Countries: Modest Benefits but Problems with Productivity Growth, Macro Prices and Income Distribution*, Working Paper, no. 8 (New York: New School for Social Research, Center for Economic Policy Analysis, 1998).

43. On the DSB, see John H. Jackson, "Dispute Settlement and a New Round," in Jeffrey J. Schott, ed., *The WTO after Seattle* (Washington, D.C.: Institute for International Economics, 2000), pp. 269–282.

44. Joseph E. Stiglitz, "Two Principles for the Next Round or, How to Bring Developing Countries in from the Cold," *World Economy* 23, no. 4 (2000): 437–454.

45. Drusilla K. Brown, "Labor Standards: Where Do They Belong on the International Trade Agenda?" *Journal of Economic Perspectives* 15, no. 3 (Summer 2001): 89–112; Alice Sindzingre, *Economic and Social Rights, Globalisation, and Multilateral Institutions* (New Delhi: International Political Science Association and Jawaharlal Nehru University Conference on Globalisation, Development and Human Rights, 2002).

46. John Eatwell and Lance Taylor, eds., *International Capital Markets: Systems in Transition* (Oxford: Oxford University Press, 2002).

47. See Deepak Nayyar, ed., *Governing Globalization: Issues and Institutions* (Oxford: Oxford University Press and UNU/WIDER, 2002); Isabelle Daugareilh and Alice Sindzingre, *Strategies for the Development and Revival of Economic and Social Rights*, Discussion Paper (Geneva: UN Economic and Social Council, Committee on Economic, Social, and Cultural Rights, 2001).

48. Dani Rodrik, "Trading in Illusions," *Foreign Policy* (March–April 2001): 54–62; UN Conference on Trade and Development, *The Least Developed Countries: Report 2000* (Geneva: UN Conference on Trade and Development, 2000).

49. Dani Rodrik, *Trade Policy and Economic Performance in Sub-Saharan Africa*, Working Paper, no. w6562 (Cambridge, Mass.: National Bureau of Economic Research, 1998); Dani Rodrik, "Can Integration into the World Economy Substitute for a Development Strategy?" (paper presented at the annual World Bank Conference on Development Economics, Paris, June 26–28, 2000).

50. Rolf J. Langhammer and Matthias Lücke, *WTO Negotiation and Accession Issues for Vulnerable Economies*, Discussion Paper, no. 2001/36 (Helsinki: WIDER, 2001).

51. Dani Rodrik, *Where Did All the Growth Go? External Shocks, Social Conflict and Growth Collapses*, Discussion Paper, no. 1789 (London: Centre for Economic Policy Research, 1998).

52. See Ha-Joon Chang, *Kicking away the Ladder? Policies and Institutions for Economic Development in Historical Perspective* (London: Anthem, 2002).

53. Irma Adelman, "Fifty Years of Economic Development: What Have We Learned?" (paper presented at the annual World Bank Conference on Development Economics, Paris, June 26–28, 2000); Alice H. Amsden, *Industrialization under New WTO Law* (Bangkok: UN Conference on Trade and Development X, 2000).

54. Peter Evans, *Economic Governance Institutions in a Global Political Economy: Implications for Developing Countries* (Bangkok: UN Conference on Trade and Development X, 2000).

55. Dani Rodrik, *Why Do More Open Economies Have Bigger Governments?* Working Paper, no. w5537 (Cambridge, Mass.: National Bureau of Economic Research, 1996).

56. Robert Pollin, *Globalization, Inequality and Financial Instability: Confronting the Marx, Keynes and Polanyi Problems in the Advanced Capitalist Economies*, Working Paper, no. 8 (Amherst: University of Massachusetts, Political Economy Research Institute, 2000).

57. Dani Rodrik, "How Far Will International Economic Integration Go?" *Journal of Economic Perspectives* 14, no. 1 (Winter 2000): 177–186.

58. Geneviève Chedeville-Murray, personal communication, May 2001.

59. Henrik Horn, Petros C. Mavroidis, and Hakan Nordström, *Is the Use of the WTO Dispute Settlement System Biased?* Discussion Paper, no. 2340 (London: Centre for Economic Policy Research, 1999).

60. Mireille Delmas-Marty, *Droit et mondialisation* (Paris: Le Monde, Université de Tous les Savoirs, 2000).

61. José Antonio Ocampo, "Recasting the International Financial Agenda," in John Eatwell and Lance Taylor, eds., *International Capital Markets* (Oxford: Oxford University Press, 2002), pp. 41–73; Andrew Hurrell, "Global Inequality and International Institutions," in Thomas W. Pogge, ed., *Global Justice* (Oxford: Blackwell, 2001), pp. 32–54.

62. Ngaire Woods, "Governance in International Organizations: The Case for Reform in the Bretton Woods Institutions," *International Monetary and Financial Issues for the 1990s* (New York: United Nations, 1998), quoted in Gerald K. Helleiner, *Markets, Politics and Globalization: Can the Global Economy Be Civilized?* Tenth Raul Prebisch Lecture (Geneva: United Nations, 2000), p. 13.

63. Strom C. Thacker, "The High Politics of IMF Lending," *World Politics* 52, no. 1 (October 1999): 38–75.

# 16

## The Power of Responsible Peace
### Engendering Reconstruction in Kosova

*Chris Corrin*

In this chapter, I consider the reconstruction processes following international intervention in Kosova to exemplify significant shifts in dialogues on the importance of gender analyses in peace and security policy making.[1] Varying types of intervention into Kosovar society have taken place recently, including North Atlantic Treaty Organization (NATO) military intervention, United Nations (UN) peacekeeping intervention, and the intervention of activist women to construct a sustainable peace. Of these, I focus mainly on the latter two, considering how far the UN mission has included women and gender concerns in its processes and how women themselves have taken control in various ways to ensure some measure of gender equity.

Within this consideration is a focus on human rights from the perspective of women's rights. Building on developments within this field over the last two decades, human rights activists internationally have made great strides toward policy change to recognize specific crimes against women, such as the systematic use of rape in war. Following work undertaken in 2000 for the Gender Audit (GA), which reviews the reconstruction programs for southeastern Europe,[2] I consider the impact of these programs on Kosovar women and girls. This includes consideration of whether and how the international community is ensuring the participation of women and the inclusion of gender-based analyses in rehabilitation and re/construction efforts and policy making.

Recent thinking at international levels has been sharpened, since October 2000, with the UN Security Council Resolution 1325 on women, peace, and security.[3] The council underlined the vital role of women in conflict solution and mandated a review of the impact of armed conflict on women and girls, the role of women in peace building, and the gender dimensions of peace processes and conflict resolution. Arising from this resolution was the establishment of an interagency task force and the invitation to Kofi Annan, the UN secretary-general, to undertake a study on women, peace, and security, which was published in October 2002.[4] The UN Development Fund for Women (UNIFEM) also published its independent experts' report on women, war, and peace in 2002.[5] Having the power of the UN behind it might mean that future action promoting women as shapers of peace and key agents in re/construction processes could be more strongly supported.

Issues of power have long been central to political thinking. For theorists and activists concerned with analyses of power use and abuse, it has been shown that viewing the "political" by using the lens of gender analysis considerably broadens the field of politics. Feminist writers show that "malestream" accounts within political theory and political science are themselves political.[6] There is a noticeable shift from traditional perspectives on politics concerned with structures, functions, and activities to a focus on politics as working out relations of power throughout society. In circumstances of violent conflict and re/constructing sustainable peace, issues of power politics are highlighted. Standard accounts of war tend to focus on military might, battles, bombing, damage, and "success." For those viewing politics from a broader standpoint, inclusive of gender analysis and human rights standards, considerations involve aspects of the militarization of societies through ideas concerning masculinity and femininity, issues of family, ethnicity, and disability raised by damage (collateral and intended) and deaths in battle, plus issues of responsibility for creating sustainable, peaceful relations.

Considering interventions through women's activism for peaceful community building ranges from local political interventions to international feminist analyses in administering peace (through women's integration into UN governance structures) and gaining justice in women's human rights. Some of the courageous and tenacious work by women's community groups toward sustainable re/construction is assessed to explore how barriers against inclusion of women's voices and activities in peace and security matters are finally beginning to crumble. Assessments of Kosovar women's situations (rape in war and trafficking in women) highlight areas of ongoing work to achieve gender-based violence reduction and/or elimination. Many women survivors are unlikely to see justice but are involved in the creation of international legal frameworks to address grievances at all levels. Key means for gaining justice include the increased participation of women in politics and recognition that the absence of women in governance is an obstacle to democratization. As a result, steps were taken in the Kosovar elections from 2000 to 2002 to widen access and integrate women into governance structures. In considering fully peace building from postconflict work in Kosova to a conceptual rational for a gender framework in an operations context, the arguments come full circle in the recognition of gender analyses as a critical variable in peace building.

**Interventions**

A significant intervention into the way of life in Kosova happened in 1989 when the Yugoslav Serb administration removed all Kosovar Albanians from participation in government administration and civic institutions. A dual system came into effect whereby parallel social and political arrangements were developed by Kosovar Albanians. Cottage hospitals (run by the Mother Theresa Foundation) providing basic health services, community councils, and home-based education were established and sustained with funding from varying sources, including remittances from the diaspora of Kosovars overseas.[7] All this changed with military conflict and UN protection. In any transformation from conflict to sustainable, equitable peace, the full participation of civil groups is recognized as central. Human relations of all sorts, including gender relations, fluctuate in times of flight, exile, displacement, and return. Using gender analyses does more than identify and minimize discriminatory practices in providing a base from which to consider equal access. It begins to "change minds" in assessing the core of what motivates—in war and toward sustainable peace.[8]

Here, the very nature of "power politics" is challenged at national and international levels and considerations of "global responsibility" become embedded in the ideas and realities of international collaboration toward violence reduction and grounded in restructured power relations at all levels of our societies. Wars have differing trajectories, yet the violence can have parallel aspects (such as rape of women in war). The specific characteristics of war in Kosova included ten years of Serb-induced state terror and Kosovar Albanian nonviolent resistance. Many contributors to this book argue the "rights and wrongs" of NATO intervention. From a peace activist perspective, there are always other routes than violence, and many believe that the political negotiations had not been exhausted in the Kosova situation. Articles on the choice of nonviolent methods of intervention list many and varied alternatives to military warfare, and in terms of relative "success" these compare favorably.[9] In analyzing violent conflict, the old adage that "there are no winners" is now recognized as a truism.

In the Kosova context, failure to secure Slobodan Milosevic's agreement to peacekeeping forces following the Rambouillet Conference did not automatically signal a bombing campaign, except insofar as NATO had threatened military intervention and would lose credibility if no action were taken. Many legal and moral issues were at stake in terms of the intervention—with no specific UN Security Council authorization, the bombing was outside NATO's key rationale as a defensive alliance.[10] Arguments at the time were proposed in terms of "victory" over the violent Milosevic regime. Tony Blair argued that, "The most ambitious air campaign in military history is gradually destroying Milosevic's forces. We are doing it precisely, carefully—and with overwhelming success."[11] Commenting on this, John Sloboda argues that much of the Serbian military capacity survived and civilians bore the brunt of the bombing. "The claim that the bombing was 'careful and precise' is manifestly false. More than 75 per cent of the bombs dropped by the RAF were free-fall, including the 78,057 cluster bomblets released."[12] It remains a possibility that NATO forces killed more people than the Serb forces and that the NATO strikes provided cover for Serb forces to escalate the ethnic cleansing already begun. Long-term ecological damage, including leftover depleted uranium shells and land mines, is now part of everyday life in Kosova. While Kosovar women (and children) were among the most vulnerable groups in the conflict, given high civilian casualties and rape used as a war weapon, it is clear that they cannot be viewed only as victims. All-women mine-clearing teams were active in Kosova as early as November 1999.[13]

Of the "interventions" that I am concerned with, those of women activists for peaceful community building highlight intervention in how future civic, social, political, and economic relations can be developed. Such interventions take place at local, national, and international levels with *internationalism* a central aspect of the overarching frame. Physical intervention, such as the work of women's groups considered here (e.g., the Kosova Women's Network [KWN] and the Centre for Protection of Women and Children), coupled with intellectual stimulus from feminist thinkers involved in resistance to war, have struggled to gain space for local women's concerns and needs within an international/ist frame. There is evidence of success at this level, between the actions of women's community groups on the ground and the international recognition of the importance of such work, particularly from bodies such as UNIFEM and feminist international human rights groups. All interventions need to take this into account. Here, actions speak loudly—from women tackling difficult roles in nongovernmental organization (NGO) politics, to becoming part of UN administrative and legislative structures—as the activism based on strategic gender analyses is apparent.

**Administering Peace**

With ten years of Serb state oppression over Kosovar Albanians escalating in the 1990s, questions about ignoring the early warning signals coming from Kosova still remain. Julie Mertus notes that, "Human rights groups had long reported on the crisis in Kosovo and had long forewarned of impending disaster. Indeed Serbian politicians had announced to the press on several occasions their plan to rid Kosovo of ethnic Albanians."[14]

Elisabeth Rehn and Ellen Johnson Sirleaf write that "[w]hile the importance of gender is well recognized, concrete measures to improve the flow of early warning information from and about women have not been put in place."[15] Local women used various methods to protest the atrocities. In March 1998, women in Priština combined one of the oldest protests, a silent vigil while carrying only bread, with the most modern by spreading news of their plea through e-mail. Around the world, women activists were aware of the women's protest for their sisters in Drenica.[16] Ideas of flooding Kosova with Western peace activists were gaining support in Italy, Spain, and elsewhere when NATO bombing was announced. This "hands-off" aerial bombing marks a different type of warfare. War in the late twentieth century has had particular power to focus political, social, and economic forces and to reshape group identities. "War is furthermore an intensely gendering activity. Traditionally, it has constituted a rite of passage that makes men into Men, and it assigns anchoring symbolism to the identification of women with peace, with the hearth and the land or terrain over which war is waged. Perhaps less well understood are the many ways in which twentieth-century war has transformed and redefined gender relations."[17]

In this structural gender transformation, Margaret Higonnet argues that modern warfare has almost entirely eliminated the civilian role and has lessened the distinctions between battlefront and home front and the divisions between men and women as actors and victims.[18] Modern bombing raids constitute attacks not just on the instruments of state, but also on the institutions and modalities of civil society and, as a result, on the structural relationships between women and men. The construction of discourses of female victimhood and maternity shape group identities. The latter identity, mothers, can become instrumental for intervention and dialogue with women protesting conscription of their sons. While not politically coherent, they may establish common ground with those separated by ethnicity or national alignment.[19] For the Kosovar Albanians in their tightly knit parallel social and political structures, the increasing ethnic cleansing under Serb domination ripped apart the fabric of their communities. The NATO bombing, the exodus of citizens as refugees, and their return and subsequent international intervention led to further divisions and confusion in terms of local "ownership" of the reconstruction processes. In 1999, with UN intervention, locals joked that they had suffered an invasion of locusts who all drove white jeeps. The recognition of the significant part Kosovar Albanian women had been playing throughout the decade up to 1999, during ethnic cleansing, during the bombing, in the refugee camps, and in consolidating the peaceful return, was not highlighted in rehabilitation arrangements or facilitation for constructing new socioeconomic and political institutions.[20]

Although it is not easy to chart how the movement from war to postwar developed across Kosovar society, the cessation of violence did prove an opportunity to move beyond regenerating prewar social and political relations and institutions, to actual social transformation. Many women who had been active in the alternative system in Kosova since 1989 were very keen to see change after the NATO bombing. In several discussions in March 2000, when gathering evidence for the GA, women and men in Kosova explained to me their belief that a "new Kosova" could now be built that would bring forward their hopes for a just and democratic future. For many of the women activists, this meant changing minds, not just legislation, as for them attitudinal change in areas concerning women's rights, particularly gender-based sexual violence (GBSV), was vital to securing successful policy implementation.

With around half of the population under twenty-five years old, the potential for extensive social and cultural change, under the UN Interim Administration Mission in Kosova (UNMIK) following Resolution 1244, is broad. Key tasks are to promote substantial autonomy and self-government in Kosova, perform basic civilian administrative functions, facilitate a political process to determine Kosova's future status, support the reconstruction of key infrastructure and humanitarian and disaster relief, maintain civil law and order, promote human rights, and ensure the safe and unimpeded return of all refugees and displaced persons to their homes in Kosova. The UNMIK mandate also entails development of democratic structures to become self-sustaining. In democratization activities, the efforts of women's groups and the lessons learned from the Organization for Security and Cooperation in Europe (OSCE) in Bosnia have proven moderately successful.

. To implement the mandate and increase the participation of Kosovar communities in governance, UNMIK established a Joint Interim Administrative Structure for Kosova. Local women's groups actively protested when no women were appointed to this elite decision-making body. This was later rectified by co-opting a woman. Of the twenty departments developed as central administrative bodies, each with an UNMIK and a Kosovar cohead, only two were coheaded by local women. The departments were allocated to political parties—the Democratic League of Kosova and the Democratic Party of Kosova—to cohead with UNMIK officials. Only the Department of Democratic Governance and Civil Society Support was allocated to an independent, a woman. UNMIK administration was centrally involved in creating new political and economic institutions in response to the requirements of postwar recovery and longer-term development.

In theory, postwar creation (rather than reconstruction) of new institutional and societal formations is an excellent situation from which to address existing gender inequalities and to extend gender awareness in policy making. This requires planning and resources. Resources to support women's involvement in re/construction, in terms of bilateral and multilateral donors, involve such factors as volume of aid, means of distribution, timing, and its intended purpose, plus any attached conditions. Much media attention and international reporting focused on the need to support women in transition from war to peace. Pictures of women and children refugees from Kosova and women's suffering under the Afghan regime were widely displayed in the media. Yet, the 2002 Needs Assessment for Afghanistan, prepared by the World Bank, did not include any specific sector for women or gender issues. Rehn and Sirleaf show that only .07 percent of funds were requested for women's specific projects in the $1.7 billion UN-sponsored Immediate and Transitional Assistance program for 2002. "The World Bank Group Transitional Support Strategy for Kosovo does not mention gender or women at all. Nor did the UNMIK Consolidated

Budget for 2002, except for a gender-training project costing $31,000 or approximately .006 per cent of the total budget of $467 million."[21]

These figures speak volumes about rhetoric and reality in terms of the human interest in supporting women's needs, interests, and active integration. Media interest in "women's problems" is high, yet it is often the smaller feminist donors that actually gave direct support to women's projects within a gender-sensitive frame. In Kosova, the lack of funds, within a gender-aware framework of planning, highlighted the reason why implementation of the $10 million Kosovo Women's Initiative (KWI) needed careful planning to maximize gender equity and support for women and girls over time. The KWI funding followed similar initiatives in Bosnia (BWI $5 million) and Rwanda (RWI $7 million) and expectations among civic groups, particularly women's groups, were high for both the implementation and monitoring of change. Yet, initially there was frustration and disappointment with its administration.[22]

In learning lessons on gender-based approaches, it seems that sections of the UN High Commissioner for Refugees (UNHCR) in Kosova drew on the Bosnian experience very directly. This was particularly apparent in the implementation of KWI funds. Relevant comparisons included the need to mainstream analyses made from women's experience of working on GBSV, but the situation for Kosovar women's groups was markedly different from that of many Bosnian women's groups. Throughout the 1990s, Kosovar Albanian women had been developing their own groups and were actively involved in their own assistance and protection programs. The KWN website gives a chronology of some of these activities.[23] Their experience in Kosovar Albanian human rights groups, NGOs, and working internationally (such as participating in the Helsinki Citizens Assembly or the UN Beijing Conference on Women) meant that, although small in number, some Kosovar Albanian women were very well trained and organized in conducting social programs to intervene and alleviate distress.

In implementing KWI programs, local criticism also centered on funding processes that lacked transparency, with much funding channeled through international umbrella groups. At times, some umbrella groups appeared to operate ad hoc decisions on speedy expenditure, rather than develop strategic longer-term plans within gender-sensitive frameworks. The UNHCR is a service largely based on emergency aid, not on long-term development practice. Without great care being taken, local groups could have developed *only in response* to perceived international needs and thereby become dependent on international short-term funding.

Very early on in the GA process of gender analyses across areas of education, employment, health, human rights, and politics, it became apparent that there had been discrimination against women during the postconflict period. As a result, the potential contributions of women had been marginalized and at times undermined. This has been particularly apparent in the international community's lack of regard for mainstreaming gender issues *within* the political and policy-making processes that they control, such as in the administration of the territory. As few women were appointed to key decision-making positions, the roles of Kosovar women within the emergent politics had not been acknowledged. No account was taken of their work within the parallel system since 1990, their participation in the war (at home and in the refugee camps), and their key involvement in re/construction processes locally and regionally in Kosova since 1999.[24] Many women lost male family members and found themselves heads of households; yet, these women's needs were being ignored. In the initial restructuring of the political scene, some UNMIK decision makers chose to work in a top-down manner, consulting only with those they considered to be the male power brokers. This effectively denied community leaders, local NGOs, and wider sections of the community their voice in the newly established systems. Lack of local "ownership" of the processes led to a lack of trust.

With these points in mind, there remains a need to assess how quickly and how far processes for women's integration have been developed and how far ideas of gender analysis have been mainstreamed in key areas of political, economic, and social reconstruction and rehabilitation. Such areas include participation in education on women's human rights and democratic development, facilitation of organizations to incorporate women into decision-making structures, and the establishment of mechanisms to facilitate women's integration into all areas of social and economic life. Integral is the extent of encouragement given to increasing women's social, economic, educational, and political participation—in both "informal" civic fora and organizations, and at the formal levels of power. In human rights work, some gains from women's activism are becoming apparent. Initially, it had not been recognized that sex- and age-disaggregated statistics are vital for gender analysis. These two processes toward gender equity began to come together in the political arena following lessons learned from the Bosnian elections. In the 2000 municipal elections in Kosova, the OSCE administration proposed a 30 percent quota for women candidates and statistical data became disaggregated. The steady increase in women candidates trained and elected continued in the 2001 parliamentary and 2002 municipal elections.

### Gender Analysis and Women's Human Rights

The term "gender" is used to refer to the culturally, socially, economically, and historically defined roles of women and men and to understand how the unequal power relations between them are shaped and built into social institutions, such as the family, legal systems, religious systems, and beliefs. As gender roles are learned socially, from a variety of sources within a culture, and are not biologically determined, they can and do change. Gender analysis forms the base on which mainstreaming the training and development required to ensure equitable progression for women and men in any re/construction and re/integration processes depend. Working with gender issues means looking at the roles, needs, involvement, and decision making of both women and men in a community. The UN is committed to gender equality in all its policies and programs, defining gender mainstreaming as a strategy for making women's as well as men's concerns and experiences an integral dimension of the design, implementation, monitoring, and evaluation of policies and programs. The ultimate goal is to achieve gender equality. By understanding how a community or group works and ensuring that the views of women, as well as those of men, are heard within that community or society, efforts can be made to include them actively in projects and decision making. Given the unusual situation in Kosova—with the UNMIK officials forming an administration, in coalition with local party politicians and independents—these processes need to be two way and transparent. It could be argued that rather than meeting with emancipation movements, such as those for women's rights, the UNMIK administration initially "smothered" such activities, as it was unable to see their true value in context. Lack of understanding of local cultural norms led to some crude reductions about "Muslim women" in patriarchal society.[25] Central to mainstreaming processes is engendering policy-making implications for different groups and gender mainstreaming throughout administrative and political decision making. I focus briefly on the areas of women's human rights—specifically considering violence against women, justice, and peaceful reconstruction through developing gender balance within the emerging Kosovar political scene.

The July 1999 UN secretary-general's report on the UN mission in Kosovo notes that "UNMIK will embed a culture of human rights in all areas of activity and will adopt human rights policies in respect of its administrative functions."[26] Respect for and promotion of human rights and principles of democratic governance should, therefore, be at the heart of all work of the interim administration. In December 1999, the OSCE released two human rights reports—*Kosovo/Kosova—As Seen, As Told*, Part I, covering October 1998 to June 1999, and *Kosovo/Kosova—As Seen, As Told*, Part II, for the period between June and October 1999. The first concludes that Yugoslav and Serbian forces committed extensive human rights abuses and violated the laws governing armed conflict, with their victims being overwhelmingly Kosovar Albanians. This report also notes that the violence against women "differed notably from the way in which men were targeted. Much of the violence that women suffered seems to have been directed towards their gender in a way that appears also to have been intended to humiliate the whole of Kosovo Albanian society."[27] The second report details human rights violations against minorities. Crimes against women in each report support the evidence in the U.S. State Department December 1999 report "Ethnic Cleansing in Kosovo: An Accounting" and the Human Rights Watch March 2000 report "Kosovo: Rape As a Weapon of Ethnic Cleansing." High levels of interethnic and political violence between Kosovar Serbs and Albanians were reported, yet UNMIK Police reports detail cases of violence against women that show these crimes to be as common as each of the former.[28] The use of women's bodies as battlegrounds in times of war has long been documented by feminist writers.[29] Recognition of the particular abuse and torture faced by women has only been achieved by the work of many local women's groups and international feminist reports. Here is a key interventionist strategy that has been successful, informing significant international reports and calls for change.

The tense and violent circumstances in Kosova in early 2000 made it urgent to implement policy on human rights abuses. Internationally, many feminist groups and campaigns made enormous efforts to expand human rights dialogues to become inclusive of all abuses, recognizing some practical limitations of "universality." Through NGOs—at official tribunals and alternative fora—women have worked to expand the notion of human rights to incorporate fully a gendered perspective. At the Vienna Conference on Human Rights in June 1993, activism and analysis on issues of violence against women initiated acknowledgment of violence against women as a public crime rather than a private misfortune and linked issues of violence against women in local and household contexts to violence across international systems. One common tie for women is in struggles over laws and social changes that give women measures of control over their bodies: access to abortion, resisting enforced pregnancy or sterilization, enjoyment of sexuality, and laws that criminalize rape in marriage.[30]

A successful demand from the Beijing Conference was the establishment of an effective International Criminal Court (ICC)[31] that includes women's concerns and a gender perspective throughout its statute, such as the inclusion of sexual violence, military sexual slavery, and rape in the definitions of crimes against humanity and war crimes. The Security Council created ad hoc tribunals for the former Yugoslavia and Rwanda that established precedents against sexual violence. Resolution 1325 epitomizes a new regime moving toward reducing gendered inequalities. Henry Carey notes that "[e]xisting criminal prohibitions of violence against civilians have not protected women due to sexism, oversight and ignorance of women's needs as heads of households (with insecure land tenure and economic security) and their vulnerabilities to rape during wars."[32] Considerations of violence against women highlight areas of work attempting to achieve gender-based violence reduction/elimination and gender equity in terms of justice.

### Rape in War and Trafficking in Women

How does wartime violence differ from peacetime violence? The term "sexual violence" is often associated with rape, yet the literature shows that both in war and in peace it is a multifaceted phenomenon that can include prostitution, sexual slavery, and genital mutilation. Inger Skjelsbaek argues that war creates a further dimension in which power distinctions become intertwined, "The logic of the aggressors appears to be that the men and women who have become powerless are seen as 'rapable' and those that have been raped become feminized and ultimately more powerless."[33] This helps explain why most rape victims are women, as they represent the most powerless of the powerless. Evidence shows that essentially "rape and other forms of sexual violence were used in Kosovo in 1999 as weapons of war and instruments of systematic 'ethnic cleansing.'"[34] Documents demonstrate that these rapes were not isolated incidents but were used deliberately to terrorize the civilian population, take money from families, and push people to leave their homes. Women were separated from men and kept in places such as armament factories, mosques, and schools, and hundreds of women were taken into woods, telling of their rape only reluctantly when rescued. Rachel Wareham notes, "During the mass expulsions from Prishtina in April 1999, women were taken from the train in Fushe Kosovo (the first station after people had been forced on to the train in Prishtina) and from Hani i Elizit Cement Factory (the last place before the border with Macedonia). There are numerous accounts of rape of many women in various rooms and locations at the Kosovo Polje train station."[35]

Accounts of the brutality give evidence of gang rapes taking place over several days, including some very young women as victims. Many victims bore bites over their breasts and legs, and with few exceptions, the rapes documented by the Human Rights Watch were gang rapes. One recurring aspect of the testimonies from women who were returned was that the majority claimed they were not raped, even before the questions were being raised. The fear and shame of disclosure was such that it took a long time to encourage traumatized women to open up toward any therapeutic or counseling help available to them.

Combined oppression through gender and ethnicity is apparent in wartime. As women are generally considered to be "culture bearers" both in educating young people and as symbols of their communities, they can be abused and tortured as members of those particular groups. Albanian women in Kosova were abused because they were women of a particular ethnic group.[36] Clearly, in tightly knit communities where kinship ties are strengthened by codes of honor for women's chastity and men's role in protection, the raping of women was designed to pull apart families, clans, and communities. For those women returning as widows, traumatized by the brutality of their harsh treatment, their need to be supported as heads of households was apparent. This was why local women actively challenged some of the UNMIK policies in certain areas as discriminating against women.[37] Widows in Kosova are particularly vulnerable given traditional considerations for them not to gain custody of children or property rights. Things are changing in these areas, but in the immediate postwar period humanitarian agencies and the UN administration did not take into account the particular circumstances for widows, as women. Much is required, particularly to give rural women heads of households the support and long-term assistance needed to undertake the difficult tasks of ongoing family support.

Various examples of local women's groups able to exercise good practice in terms of helping women deal with traumas in culturally sensitive ways are noted in the UNIFEM report on violence against women in Kosova.[38] Self-help groups for rape survivors were developed in the Center for Protection of Women and Children in Priština. Motrat Qiriazi, long established in rural group work in eastern Kosova, worked also in Priština and Mitrovica, encouraging women out of their isolation and enabling them to support each other. There was local recognition that much of the international intervention was bypassing women's needs in vital areas. This was as much through inability to gauge women's needs in their own context as through neglect. The Kosovo Center for Rehabilitation of Torture Victims advertises its services through posters outlining some symptoms of trauma it supports, rather than psychiatric care. In this context, local women activists suggested having centers for women that specialist support workers attend when required, rather than having local women visit experts at clinics or medical centers.

Emerging from war, new means of violence are visited on women. Trafficking in human beings is the third largest source of profit for international organized crime after drugs and arms. Trafficked women are particularly vulnerable to physical violence, including rape, unlawful confinement, confiscation of identity papers, and enslavement. Patterns of trafficking in women vary due to changing regional conditions and potential new markets. Some women are actually sold outright; others are so manipulated and exploited by traffickers that only entry into prostitution enables them to survive. As to some reasons for the rise in trafficking, the UN Special Rapporteur on Violence against Women proposes, "The enormous profitability of exploiting women as prostitutes; the feminization of poverty in the victims' home countries; official policies of international development banks and lending organizations encouraging the development of tourist sector services; lack of an effective international regime for collecting data, providing information and penalizing organized international traffic networks."[39]

The risks for traffickers remain low with few successful convictions. In Kosova, there have been no entry visa restrictions since 1999 and over 100,000 "international" men are present—60,000 aid workers, the remainder in uniform. Prostitution in Kosova before the intervention of international agencies in 1999 seems to have been limited, and local evidence shows that Kosovars believe the growth was fueled by the presence of internationals, with money alongside poverty. International human rights standards are binding on the UN, OSCE, and international NGOs. It was a cause for concern for women activists that initially key UNMIK officials did not express unease with regard to uncovering and halting staff involvement in using services of prostitutes trafficked for sex. Without specific codes of conduct in these agencies, it becomes difficult to implement good practice in curtailing such activities.

In 2000, no funded services or programs were taking into account the social welfare of women engaged in prostitution. There were examples of community-based women's activism providing assistance to women in crisis and the UNIFEM reports contributed to the developing knowledge-base on trafficking in Kosova. Established groups such as Motrat Qiriazi[40] had begun work on these problems as refugees in Macedonia. They ran meetings for women and girls and in most, trafficking and prostitution were discussed and presented by means of role-play. Local women's grassroots activism coupled with international feminist studies have intervened to push the international institutions toward a more detailed examination of the facts of gender violence and the ways in which policy in this field could be implemented. As can be seen, with recent meetings in Warsaw (September 2002) and in Tirana (November 2002) on trafficking in women, ending the traffic in women is now a major aspect of international political policy making. In Kosova, the OSCE has been strengthening the capacity of legal aid NGOs. Two organizations with previous experience in dealing with victims of trafficking—the Centre for Protection of Women and Children and the Association for Legal Aid for Women—were selected for specific training on particular legislation, relevant police standard operating procedures, and court proceedings, as well as attention to UNMIK Regulation 2001/4 on the Prohibition of Trafficking in Persons in Kosovo.[41]

Women survivors of sexual abuse need culturally appropriate psychosocial assistance. Some skilled women leaders were aware that survivors were cautious of identifying themselves. Yet, international intervention in this area tried to use such women leaders as service providers, rather than respecting local agendas and including local women in decision making on internationally funded projects. In his report on women, peace, and security, the UN secretary-general notes that prostitution, often combined with trafficking, increases in the context of international interventions. Although codes of conduct establish expected standards of behavior from UN staff, further measures are needed. "All missions have clear instructions to thoroughly investigate any allegations of sexual exploitation or assault by any peacekeeping personnel and to ensure that offenders are duly disciplined."[42] The secretary-general calls on the troop-contributing states to improve their efforts to ensure that such violations do not occur, effectively investigate and prosecute cases of alleged misconduct, and set up adequate accountability mechanisms and disciplinary measures. Rehn and Sirleaf note that "[a]lthough codes of conduct can be useful tools for deterring peacekeeping violations, this code is a skeletal outline of basic human rights principles and trivializes violations against women, referring to 'immoral acts of sexual, physical or psychological abuse' or 'exploitation' of the local population especially women and children."[43]

Many women are unlikely to see justice, with perpetrators punished, or receive reparations for the violations suffered. However, an international legal framework has been constructed by women's rights campaigners to address such grievances. Outcomes are apparent, such as the victims and witness units now being established within the ICC. These will provide protection, counseling, and other security measures and the ICC will create a Trust Fund for Victims. Significant for women will be the effects at the national level with the states setting in motion processes of national law reform. In order to implement such measures successfully, it is recognized that gender representation, if not gender balance of women and men in top policy-making positions, is required. One key means of developing these processes is to encourage greater representation of women in political bodies.

**Participatory Politics**

The absence of women in governance structures is now recognized as an obstacle to democratization processes in several contexts, and lessons have been learned. Including everyone in governing structures has been acknowledged as an essential foundation in democracy building. Although soldiers were becoming elected officials, little concern was being given to many of the women peacemakers and community builders throughout southeastern Europe who were prepared to become candidates. The officials administering the elections from the OSCE learned from Bosnia that bringing new actors into the democratization process was essential to move these processes forward. It was in this context that a 30 percent quota system for women was introduced and applied first at the municipal elections in Kosova in 2000 through an UNMIK resolution.[44]

The relationship between citizens and government was a precarious one as there was no national government. At this time, lack of local trust in the UN processes and latent resentment from the conflict meant that many citizens, especially women, were wary of participating in formal politics. For many women, local community politics had been the main locus of their activism. Yet, the traumatic displacement and upheavals of varying interventions meant that during the re/construction phase the democratization of the political system in Kosova had begun to offer opportunities for women to become more involved in formal political activities than was previously the case. This was especially apparent in women's self-organization through their significant community involvement, but also in electoral participation and education at municipal levels. I have detailed elsewhere[45] the processes that were undertaken to encourage women to enter the first democratic process at the municipal level, including women's conferences, local coalitions to support women candidates, and work through the OSCE for international educational seminars supporting women's participation.

As a "first attempt," there was only a low level of success in this realm, yet women made up more than half of the voters and 1,322 women stood in 30 municipalities. All of these women participated in party selection meetings, discussion of list priorities, and training and educational programs. In the burgeoning circumstances of postwar democratic development, the seventy-six (8 percent) women elected in 2000 as officeholders are earning reputations as constructive political leaders who can work across ethnic and gender divides in developing democracy. The most recent success has been shown in the municipal election of October 2002 with 28.5 percent women candidates elected. Of the two larger parties, the Democratic League of Kosova and the Party of Democratic Kosova elected 128 and 89 women, respectively.[46] As the municipal level is one at which women do believe they can make a difference, the various coalitions of women's groups from grassroots and political parties have paid rich dividends both in terms of joint collaboration and in making a difference politically. This can be seen in terms of widening access—across ethnicities and age groups—and in the way of "doing" politics differently, "in community."[47]

Kosovar women continue to work at various levels to consolidate their collaborative successes from grassroots to government. Those present in Zagreb in June 2002 worked to create the National Action Plan for Gender Equality. As the KWN notes, "Kosovar women have, during history, been involved in the development of Kosova's society. Their movement has been extremely visible during the 1990s and also during the war in Kosova. An increased development has occurred especially in the past three years. Now women act in all regions of Kosova in an organized manner. Aware of their work and the results they achieved, as well as the problems and shortages they faced, based on the work experience, and the actual situation, they decided to work in a common strategy for action."[48]

Accordingly, the plan is under public review by various institutions, organizations, and experts. A higher level of cooperation between formal elected officials and informal grassroots activists is now developing in Kosova in the promotion of women's rights.

## Peace Making or Peace Building?

Feminist interventions in peace and security issues have noted the different ways of "making" peace with women working to "build" peace. Building peace implies something that has to be constructed and that will remain in place for some time. As women often work at grassroots levels doing very practical work, such as providing trauma therapy, counseling, and legal and business advice, this creates and sustains dialogue between groups that are in conflict. Examples of this were apparent at the September 2000 meeting organized by Women Waging Peace,[49] where Kosovar Albanian and Kosovar Serb women worked together on issues of peace and security at a time when some prominent male citizens were still engaging in violence and recrimination.

Women's organizations in Kosova faced various barriers to their ongoing inclusion within the UNMIK agendas—not least the lack of value accorded to their ongoing work at community levels. Conventional peace-building methods do not capture the full range of areas across which women work toward regenerating their communities. In her work on negotiating gender and national identities in conflict, Cynthia Cockburn proposes that one tool used by women's groups to reduce polarization is to organize around political interests shared by women. Another tool is group process, "A democratic polity has to ensure that all its voices are heard, that all are given equal weight and that decision-making is fully shared. At the level of the individual in a face-to-face group, the destructive 'othering' processes to which collectivities (such as ethno-national groups) are prone can be contradicted, and an alternative modelled."[50]

By routinely sharing practical tasks, grassroots groups working together become conscious of the group process and of what is achievable. This is a completely different way of working than hierarchical, top-down initiatives employed by military or governmental structures. The ways that higher levels of trust are gained in women-dominated organizations has relevance for the possibility of groups rebuilding social capital as part of conflict resolution work. This has reaped benefits in postconflict work in Kosova from the early work in Mitrovica by Motrat Qiriazi to the later work in Kosovar women's councils. Caroline Moser and Cathy McIlwaine distinguish the prevalence and importance of different kinds of social capital in community groups, emphasizing the need to adopt a gender analysis of social capital in violent contexts.[51]

Given that peacekeeping has evolved into multiple areas of humanitarian relief—such as human rights monitoring, refugee return, civilian policing, land mine removal, demobilization, elections, and nation building—concern with gender mainstreaming is wholly relevant. Considering the policy frame for future developments, Moser proposes a conceptual rational for a gender framework in an operations context intended to ensure that violence-reduction initiatives incorporate a gender perspective. Moser argues for the incorporation of agency and identity in requiring policy makers and planners to recognize the important components of effective violence reduction. Key aspects of such a framework involve introducing a gendered continuum of conflict and violence, identifying the gendered causal factors, examining the gendered costs and consequences, and developing an integral policy approach. Meeting the practical needs and taking account of underlying strategic interests, this framework is globally applicable while recognizing the importance of context specificity.[52]

## Conclusion

As can be seen from the Kosovar context, the processes of recognizing the gendered needs and contributions of women in peace building have not been linear and much remains to be achieved. The trend of recognition of gender analyses as critical variables in such work is becoming a positive one at all levels. Some examples have been noted in areas where women's activism and analyses have intervened to make strategic inroads into developing "new" policy agendas. The UN General Assembly's traffic in women and girls resolution[53] is being followed, particularly on strengthening national programs. This international work shows the willingness to recognize women's long-term and significant work in these areas and to include feminist knowledge gained through years of joint research and study. While some women successfully organized during and immediately following the conflict in Kosova, many women needed additional support to ensure their continuing active participation in civil society organization and to enter public life. Several women political activists in Kosova stood out for what they believed in, sometimes against official international pressure, in the knowledge that their women's networks had identified useful paths toward strengthening sustainable democratic ties in their communities. These women were demonstrating alternative ways of working "in community" that were initially neither respected nor supported by the peacekeeping authorities. However, the international recognition of the important part women's organizations play in peace building can be seen as a successful intervention.[54]

In terms of translating power politics to global responsibility, women working across differences in small groups and in collaboration at various levels (e.g., elected officials and community activists) often learn from each other's experience in terms of commonalities and differences between them. Some of the most successful outcomes for women's inclusion within Kosovar society since 1999 have been those of the KWN, which initially received very little support from UNMIK organizations. Its active website and newsletters testify to an amazing array of activities, including hit pop records and broad-based, popular community performances of plays highlighting issues of violence and trauma suffered by women. This intervention for peaceful reconstruction in Kosova is immeasurable. Bilateral involvement of international feminist groups who regularly engage in feminist analysis helps form an important bridge linking local groups and UN missions. Certainly, feminist responses recognize issues of difference much more closely than many other analyses of peace and democracy building. As gender-sensitive women are differently positioned, yet look toward common ties, issues of age, class, disability, ethnicity, race, and other factors are always present in their dialogues about peaceful development.

In his concluding observations on women, peace, and security, Kofi Annan states that "[c]hallenges to fully utilizing women's contributions across a wide range of activities relevant to peace and security persist at many levels."[55] The 2001 G8 Statement by Foreign Ministers[56] emphasizes the importance of the systematic involvement of women and their full and equal participation in all phases of conflict prevention, resolution, and peace building. This widespread international recognition of the role of women in conflict prevention, resolution, rehabilitation, and re/construction offers optimism for direct change in the gendered power structures involved in international interventions following war. Feminist studies, using gender analyses as integral, acknowledge how power relations shift and change, recognizing community activism and intervention by women as crucial throughout conflict and re/construction situations, with "social capital" vital in struggles for peace, justice, and reconciliation. In this way, the political power of local women's organization, coupled with international feminist analyses, can help lead to global responsibility for an inclusive, just, and sustainable peace.

## Notes

1. The spelling "Kosova" is used by the majority population in Kosova. It has remained an important symbol of their independence struggle and democratic consolidation.

2. Chris Corrin, *Gender Audit of Reconstruction Programmes in South Eastern Europe* (New York: Urgent Action Fund and Women's Commission for Refugee Women and Children, 2000); see also the International Rescue Committee, available at www.theirc.org (accessed March 27, 2003).

3. UN Security Council, "Resolution on Women and Peace and Security," S/RES/2000/1325, October 31, 2000.

4. UN Security Council, "Report of the Secretary-General on Women, Peace and Security," S/2002/1154, October 16, 2002.

5. Elisabeth Rehn and Ellen Johnson Sirleaf, *Women, War and Peace: The Independent Experts' Assessment on the Impact of Armed Conflict on Women and Women's Role in Peace-Building* (New York: UN Development Fund for Women, 2002).

6. See Valerie Bryson, *Feminist Political Theory* (Basingstoke, UK: Macmillan, 1992); Diana H. Coole, *Women in Political Theory* (Brighton, UK: Wheatsheaf, 1988); Chris Corrin, *Feminist Perspectives on Politics* (London: Pearson, 1999).

7. Julie Mertus, *War's Offensive on Women: The Humanitarian Challenge in Bosnia, Kosovo, and Afghanistan* (West Hartford, Conn.: Kumarian, 2000).

8. See Lepa Mladjenovic and Divna Matijasevic, "SOS Belgrade 1993–95: Dirty Streets," in Chris Corrin, ed., *Women in a Violent World: Feminist Analyses and Resistance across "Europe"* (Edinburgh: Edinburgh University Press, 1996), pp. 119–132.

9. Various articles addressing these topics are to be found in the *Journal of Peace and Conflict Resolution* (1998–1999).

10. Enver Hasani, *The Dissolution of Yugoslavia and the Case of Kosova: Political and Legal Aspects* (Priština: Albanian Institute for International Studies, 2000); Tim Judah, *Kosovo: War and Revenge* (New Haven, Conn.: Yale University Press, 2000); Michael Waller, Kyril Drezov, and Bulent Gokay, eds., *Kosovo: The Politics of Delusion* (London: Frank Cass, 2001).

11. John Sloboda, "So Much Expended for So Little Good," in Waller, Drezov, and Gokay, eds., *Kosovo: The Politics of Delusion* pp. 112, 111–119.

12. Sloboda, "So Much Expended for So Little Good," p. 112

13. See Chris Corrin, "Post-conflict Reconstruction and Gender Analysis in Kosova," *International Journal of Feminist Politics* 3, no. 1 (2001): 78–98.

14. Mertus, *War's Offensive on Women*, p. 46.

15. Rehn and Sirleaf, *Women, War and Peace*, p. 113.

16. See Corrin, "Post-conflict Reconstruction and Gender Analysis in Kosova."

17. Margaret Higonnet, foreword to Svetlana Slapsak, ed., *Essays and Case-Studies from Yugoslavia and Russia* (Ljubljana: TOPOS, 2001), pp. 10, 9–16.

18. Higonnet, foreword, p. 15.

19. Current examples are Russian mothers protesting conscription of their sons into the war in Chechnya and some instances of women in black groups in the former Yugoslavia.

20. See Mertus, *War's Offensive on Women*; Rehn and Sirleaf, *Women, War and Peace*.

21. Rehn and Sirleaf, *Women, War and Peace*, pp. 124–125.

22. Many reasons for the extent of these frustrations are outlined in Corrin, *Gender Audit*; see also Jock M. Baker and Hilde Haug, *Final Report of the Kosovo Women's Initiative*, EPAU/2002/12 (Geneva: UN High Commissioner for Refugees, Evaluation and Policy Analysis Unit, 2002).

23. See www.womensnetwork.org (accessed March 27, 2003).

24. Several recent works provide details on women's work on human rights, refugees, integrated development packages, gender-based violence, trauma counseling, reproductive and children's health, and rehabilitation of former combatants. See Cynthia Cockburn, *The Space between Us: Negotiating Gender and National Identities in Conflict* (London: Zed, 1998); Corrin, *Women in a Violent World*; Mertus, *War's Offensive on Women*; Caroline Moser and Fiona Clark, eds., *Victims or Perpetrators: Gender, Armed Conflict and Politics Violence* (London: Zed, 2001); Rehn and Sirleaf, *Women, War and Peace*.

25. Rachel Wareham, *No Safe Place: An Assessment of Violence against Women in Kosovo* (Priština: UN Development Fund for Women, 2000), p. 28.

26. UN Security Council, "Report of the Secretary-General on the United Nations Interim Administration Mission In Kosovo," S/1999/779, July 12, 1999.

27. Organization for Security and Cooperation in Europe (OSCE), *Kosovo/Kosova— As Seen, As Told, Part I, An Analysis of the Human Rights Findings of the OSCE Kosovo Verification Mission, October 1998 to June 1999* (Warsaw: Organization for Security and Cooperation in Europe, Office for Democratic Institutions and Human Rights, 1999), chapter 16.

28. See the UNMIK Police website for crime statistics, available at www.civpol.org/unmik (accessed March 27, 2003).

29. See Cynthia Enloe, *The Morning After: Sexual Politics at the End of the Cold War* (Los Angeles: University of California Press, 1993); Azza Karam, "Women in War and Peace-Building: The Roads Traversed, the Challenges Ahead," *International Feminist Journal of Politics* 3, no. 1 (2001): 2–35; Sheila Meintjes, Anu Pillay, and Meredeth Turshen, eds., *The Aftermath: Women in Post-conflict Reconstruction* (London: Zed, 2001); Moser and Clark, *Victims or Perpetrators*; Louise Olsson and Torunn L. Tryggestad, eds., *Women and International Peacekeeping* (London: Frank Cass, 2001).

30. See Julie Peters and Andrea Wolpe, *Women's Rights Human Rights: International Feminist Perspectives* (London: Routledge, 1995).

31. In 1988, both the treaty to establish the ICC and the Optional Protocol to the UN Convention on the Elimination of All Forms of Discrimination against Women (Women's Convention) were adopted. Both strengthen women's access to justice.

32. Henry F. Carey, "Women and Peace and Security: The Politics of Implementing Gender Sensitivity Norms in Peacekeeping," in Louise Olsson and Torunn L. Tryggestad, eds., *Women and International Peacekeeping* (London: Frank Cass, 2001), pp. 50, 49–68.

33. Inger Skjelsbaek, "Sexual Violence in Times of War: A New Challenge for Peace Operations?" in Olsson and Tryggestad, eds., *Women and International Peacekeeping*, pp. 71–72.

34. On sexual violence and armed conflict, see www.flora.org/flora.mai-not/17300 (accessed March 27, 2003). On how sex edges guns and drugs in the world's illicit trade, see www.hotcoco.com/news/stories (accessed March 27, 2003). Related sites include (among others) www.web.amnesty.org (accessed March 27, 2003), www.fmreview.org (accessed March 27, 2003), www.unifem.undp.org (accessed March 27, 2003).

35. Wareham, *No Safe Place*, p. 63.

36. See Rada Boric and Mica Mladineo Desnica, "Croatia: Three Years After," in Chris Corrin, ed., *Women in a Violent World*, 1996), pp. 133–152.

37. In undertaking interviews for the GA, I was given the example of tractors—families who before the conflict had owned tractors were to be given tractors in replacement for those lost. However, UNMIK officials decided that women-headed households would be supplied with suitable male drivers to plough their lands. Not only were the women furious at not being consulted, they were indignant at having no choice to train to use heavy equipment. This was rectified later, again after local protest by women's groups. See Corrin, "Post-conflict Reconstruction and Gender Analysis in Kosova."

38. See Rehn and Sirleaf, *Women, War and Peace.*

39. UN Commission on Human Rights, "Report of the Special Rapporteur on Violence against Women, 53rd session of the Commission on Human Rights," EC/CN.4/1997/47, February 12, 1997.

40. Motrat Qiriazi (Sisters Qiriazi) works with rural women and girls to support them in taking control over their lives and making positive changes for themselves and their communities. Having worked with women in isolated rural communities before the conflict in Kosova, Motrat Qiriazi was well placed to include rural women in the ongoing process of re/construction. It is a founding group in the KWN.

41. Carsten Weber, the director of the OSCE Human Rights and Rule of Law Department, notes the two types of legal assistance needed: "First, when alleged victims act as a witness or injured party in criminal proceedings against an alleged trafficker; secondly when they are charged with a criminal offence such as prostitution or illegal entry into Kosovo." See OSCE, "OSCE Project Offers Better Support for Trafficking Victims in Kosovo," Press Release, October 9, 2002, p. 1.

42. UN Security Council, "Report of the Secretary-General on Women, Peace and Security," paragraph 45.

43. Rehn and Sirleaf, *Women, War and Peace*, p. 72.

44. UN Interim Administration Mission in Kosova, "Regulation No. 2000/39—On the Municipal Elections in Kosovo," UNMIK/REG/2000/39, July 8, 2000; in sec-

tion 4.2, it states that "[e]ach candidates' list shall include at least 30% female candidates in the first 15 candidates. Within the first fifteen candidates on each candidates' list, at least one female shall be placed among the first three candidates, and at least one female shall be placed in each full set of three candidates thereafter. This rule shall not apply to those lists comprised of less than three candidates."

45. Chris Corrin, "Developing Democracy in Kosova: From Grassroots to Government," *Parliamentary Affairs* 55, no. 1 (2002): 99–108.

46. For breakdown and detailed statistics, see the OSCE press releases on municipal elections, available at www.osce.org/news/ (accessed March 27, 2003).

47. See Cockburn, *Space between Us*; Rehn and Sirleaf, *Women, War and Peace.*

48. Kosova Women's Network, *KWN Voices—Newsletter of the Kosova Women's Network* 1, no. 4 (October 2002): 6, available at www.womensnetwork.org/english/pdf/kwn_voices_issue4_eng.pdf (accessed March 27, 2003).

49. See Corrin, "Post-conflict Reconstruction and Gender Analysis in Kosova."

50. Cockburn, *Space between Us*, p. 227.

51. Caroline Moser and Cathy McIlwaine "Gender and Social Capital in Contexts of Political Violence," in Moser and Clark, eds., *Victims or Perpetrators*, pp. 178–200.

52. Caroline Moser, "The Gendered Continuum of Violence and Conflict: An Operational Framework," in Moser and Clark, eds., *Victims or Perpetrators*, pp. 30–52.

53 UN General Assembly, "Traffic in Women and Girls," A/RES/53/116, February 1, 1999.

54. Certainly, reports from the UN secretary-general, foreign ministers' G8 Group, and reviews by UNIFEM and the UNHCR show the effort and resources being channeled into making use of women's skills and experience in this field. Also, a collection documenting fifty successful conflict resolution-prevention stories from the NGO community, including women's organizations, is available at www.oxford researchgroup.org.uk/wpwhome.html (accessed March 27, 2003).

55. UN Security Council, "Report of the Secretary-General on Women, Peace and Security," paragraph 67.

56. "Conclusion of the Meeting of the G-8 Foreign Ministers' Meeting, Attachment 2, G-8 Roma Initiatives on Conflict Prevention," Rome, July 18–19, 2001, available at www.g7.utoronto.ca/g7/foreign/fm091901_con_att2.html.

# Index